NORTH DAKOTA INDIANS

An Introduction

Mary Jane Schneider
University of North Dakota

KENDALL/HUNT PUBLISHING COMPANY
4050 Westmark Drive P.O. Box 1840 Dubuque, Iowa 52004-1840

Contents

Preface to the First Edition

The need for an introductory text became apparent to me shortly after I agreed to teach a course called Introduction to Indian Studies in the newly formed Department of Indian Studies at the University of North Dakota. Not only was the Department new, but the recently hired faculty, all academically trained in disciplines tangent to Indian Studies, had no familiarity with Indian Studies as a discipline. We were all agreed on the need for an introductory course and we all had some ideas of the content. A trip to the library furnished me with additional ideas, but it was the students who eventually defined the content and practice that is formalized in this text.

The first class and I spent several frustrating weeks trying to adjust to our differing expectations for the course. A courageous, although not particularly polite student, finally pointed out that the class was not successful; an introductory course should introduce the students to various topics and information relating to North Dakota Indians. This confrontation opened the door to discussions concerning the content and organization of the course. It became my task to recognize the questions, locate the answers and organize the material. This textbook grew out of the research I did for that and subsequent introductory classes. Students and other Indian people who discussed their concerns and presented their views and ideas on different issues were also instrumental in shaping the final product.

The need for a text became greater when the North Dakota legislature approved a requirement for teachers to have a course in Indian Studies in order to be certified to teach in North Dakota. Across the state colleges added an introductory course in North Dakota Indians to their curriculum and many teachers with little knowledge of North Dakota Indian issues suddenly found themselves teaching Indian history and culture.

North Dakota Indians: An Introduction is a text and resource guide for college students and teachers. Because the book is intended for use in North Dakota, the materials generally relate directly to the major contemporary tribal cultures of North Dakota: Arikara, Dakota, Hidatsa, Mandan, Lakota, and Turtle Mountain Chippewa. Information from other areas or concerning Indian people in general is included when necessary. The chapters are organized topically, not by tribe or reservation, and a major concern has been, when possible, to present both Indian and non-Indian viewpoints. The chapters on Indian origins, Indian historical methods and Indian economics are based on original research designed to explicitly present Indian perspectives on these topics.

The book should also serve as a model for Indian Studies courses in other states and regions. Some aspects of North Dakota Indian life are unique to North Dakota tribes, but the general content of the book and its organization may guide other teachers.

Preface to the Second Edition

What's New in This Edition

Many things in Indian country are different from what they were when the original version of *North Dakota Indians: An Introduction* was published. Most remarkable is the shift from bingo to casino gambling. Less noticeable is the increase in Native American population. These and other changes are explored in this revision. In order to accommodate the changes, some chapters have been rewritten, some have been deleted, some new ones have been added. New in this edition are biographies of some North Dakota Indian leaders. These may be found throughout the text at the end of relevant chapters.

Chapter One remains an introduction to concepts and ideas relevant to Indian history and culture. With the exception of the section on ethnocentrism, this chapter is entirely new. It introduces the idea of errors in public knowledge about Native Americans, a theme which appears throughout the book, and introduces the concept of culture.

Chapter Two has a new introduction, but the remainder of the chapter has been retained from the first edition. Topics such as Indian identity, federal identification of Indian tribes, and the nature and significance of reservations are examined.

The original Chapter Three, which covered American Indian origins has been divided into two chapters. Rather than summarizing origin traditions, Chapter Three, American Indian Traditions, now provides examples of origin narratives from the Arikara, Chippewa and other North Dakota tribes. Summaries are given for some tribes. A discussion of oral traditions and various memory devices, mostly retained from chapter four of the earlier edition, and other information relating to oral tradition completes the chapter.

Chapter Four is an overview of the manner in which scientists have studied Native American origins. Among other things it mentions recent genetic theories. The section on linguistics from the previous work is included.

Plains Life Before European Contact, Chapter Five, replaces the discussion of archaeological evidence which originally appeared in chapter four with something less technical. This chapter is now a culture history of the plains, focusing on the way in which the precontact people lived. It incorporates the major theme of the book and forms a base for the study of traditional cultures.

Chapter Six is retained in its entirety from the earlier edition. It covers the seven tribes living in North Dakota at the time of the establishment of the reservations.

Chapter Seven retains most of the earlier material, but adds a new section, New Approaches to Self-Determination, to the end of the chapter.

Chapter Eight has been moved from its position as chapter thirteen because it appears to fit better with Federal Indian policy issues. Except for new paragraphs dealing with new issues of jurisdiction and changes in the tribal court system, the chapter remains the same.

Chapter Nine describes North Dakota reservations. Some figures have been updated, but the chapter has not been drastically changed.

Chapter Ten retains the same information as the earlier chapter nine, but all the population figures have been updated. In many cases, the figures from the 1990 census have been added in such a way as to provide comparative data. Some discussion of North Dakota geography has been eliminated.

The economics of employment, Chapter Eleven, is similar to chapter ten in the previous edition. However, all the statistics have been redone to include information from the 1990 census. Since the 1990 census was not totally comparable to the 1980 census, some tables are different from the earlier book.

Chapter Twelve is new to this volume. Some of the information is similar to that previously found in chapter eleven, but the importance of environmental issues warranted a different focus.

Chapter Thirteen is also new, although it too, has some similarity to the chapter thirteen in the first edition.

The last two chapters on education and Indian health are composed of information retained from the earlier volume and new data. The new information updates and enlarges upon previous work.

The final chapter has been retained from the earlier edition.

Minor changes reflecting the changes in the text have also been made in the bibliography. Some new illustrations have been added to facilitate better understanding of the materials. Also new to this edition are mini-biographies of tribal people. These are intended to add a human dimension to the general historical orientation of the text. The individuals described have been selected to represent different tribes at various times. Many other people could have been included and teachers may want to assign students to research and write additional mini-biographies.

Acknowledgements

Many friends, students, and colleagues from various disciplines asked pertinent questions and made helpful comments on the first edition. Some of their efforts have been incorporated into this revision, but I could not include them all. That does not mean that I do not thank them for their help, I certainly do. I owe especial thanks to Birgit, Ann, and Tom who did heroic duty in dealing with more than 500 pages of manuscript in a very short time. I also thank Audrey and Caren for their work in catching my errors. All of you made this book better than it would have been. You can take credit for the improvements and I, as usual, will accept responsibility for errors and flaws.

I am fortunate in having as partner a very special person whose unquestioning support and ready willingness to discuss various ideas has made this and other books possible. To my husband, Fred Schneider, for his photographs, conversations and cooking, I can only give my deepest "thank you."

Chapter 1

Introduction

From childhood on, most Americans are exposed to a variety of ideas and beliefs concerning American Indians. These ideas are so common that young children can do drawings of "Indians" without ever having seen one. These youthful works usually show a person with feathers in his hair and a bow and arrows in his hand (Clifton 1989:7). This depiction is based, not on the truth, but on erroneous ideas about Indians which have come from many different sources.

Mistaken, misleading descriptions of Indians can be traced back to some of the earliest European visitors and settlers. The first known Europeans to meet native North Americans were Norsemen who visited the coast of Labrador and Newfoundland around 1000 A.D. The records of these visits, the Icelandic or Vinland sagas, are not clear, but archaeological discoveries at L'Anse aux Meadows, New-foundland, provide conclusive evidence of this contact (Fagan 1991:16-17). The sagas mention two different visits, each of which ended in violence between the local inhabitants and the Norsemen. In the first instance, Thorvald, brother of Leif Eriksson, led an expedition along the coast. When the explorers encountered men asleep under skin boats, they killed all but one. Soon after, the Norsemen were attacked and Thorvald was killed, probably in revenge for the earlier attack (McGhee 1984:9-10).

Another story tells of an expedition led by Thorfinn Karlsefni which wintered at the same spot as Leif's expedition. The first meeting with the natives was peaceful and some trading took place. At a later time, trade continued, but one native was killed when he tried to take some Norse weapons (McGhee 1984:10).

In Erik the Red's version of the story, Thorfinn Karlsefni established a settlement called Straumfiord and then moved on to another location. The natives at this new location traded peacefully at first, but three weeks later attacked the little group and the Norsemen decided to return to Straumfiord. During the return, five natives were killed. Unfortunately, the sagas provide no details on the causes of the conflicts and we are left to wonder why they happened.

On another exploring trip, Thorvald Eriksson was killed. The last contact between Norse and natives occurred as the Norse were returning to Greenland. They captured two native boys and took them back to Greenland. The Norsemen called the natives "Skraelings." At this point in time, there is no way of identifying the "Skraelings" with any of the later native peoples known to live in the region. They were probably Indians, although Inuit (Eskimo) people also frequented Labrador and Newfoundland (McGhee 1984:10). The few contacts between Norse and natives provide little information about the aboriginal inhabitants of North America, but they do indicate the difficulties inherent in contact situations. It would not be surprising if each side concluded that the other was unaccountably hostile.

The next stage of contacts between Europeans and native North Americans created more opportunities for misunderstanding. Columbus and the Europeans who followed him generally found the natives they encountered to be friendly, hospitable and helpful people. All too often, the warmth of the Indians was repaid by hostility on the part of the Europeans.

Giovanni Verrazzano explored the coast of North America between what is now South Carolina and Maine in 1524. Everywhere he and his crew were welcomed. In Narragansett Bay, a crowd of Indians paddled out to the ship and boarded it. Verrazzano reported: "They are very generous and give anything they have. We formed great friendship with them" (Sauer 1971:60). The natives brought them food and showed them the best place to anchor their ship. Not until Verrazzano sailed on to a northern coast, probably in what is now Maine, did he meet natives who were hostile. Unlike the Narragansett who were not interested in trade goods, the Maine Indians knew what they wanted and were wary of the Europeans, refusing to get close to them. Some men who went to explore were shot at by the Indians (Sauer 1971:61). The scholarly conclusion is that the Maine Indians had had bad experiences with other Europeans, probably cod fishermen. What was handed down, however, was the idea that Indians were hostile and later European immigrants feared contact with native people.

Many wrong ideas and assumptions about Native Americans have crept into modern thinking. The sources of these errors are numerous and complicated. One kind of mistake involves the twisted logic that makes an Indian victory into a loss, such as occurred with some interpretations of the Battle of the Little Big Horn.

In a column which appeared in the *Grand Forks Herald* and other newspapers, Lakota writer and editor Tim Giago wrote, "History is made by winners, unless the winners are Indians" (Giago 1991). The column dealt with the controversy over changing the name of the Custer Battlefield National Monument to Little Big Horn National Monument, but the implications were much broader. As Giago and others pointed out, naming the battlefield after the defeated General George Armstrong Custer gave the impression that Custer was the winner. This is only one example of the many ways in which Native American perspectives have been ignored or disparaged.

American Indians were not the only people to suffer from a one-sided point of view. Because the British were the winners in the struggle for North America, the contributions of other groups have also been overlooked. The Spanish, French, Dutch, Portuguese and other Europeans were instrumental in colonizing North America, but textbooks often pay little attention to their efforts. James Axtell (1992:200) critically reviewed sixteen current history textbooks and found numerous problems. "Among the subjects most vulnerable are Indians, the Spanish empire, and the French colony in Canada (Louisiana and the Illinois country being virtually unheard of until the Anglo-American 'discovery' of them late in the eighteenth century)." One author reviewed by Axtell (1992:209) characterized French influence outside Canada as "not great," neatly overlooking Louisiana and many other French locations where French influence is still felt. Afro-Americans and Asian-Americans are other under-recognized and misrepresented groups.

Today, scholars are striving to write a new, less one-sided history of America, but this is not an easy task. Not only is it necessary to take a new look at many cherished ideas, but people are attached to a particular idea and it is often difficult to get them to change. For innumerable decades American school children learned that Columbus discovered America. Even though the information on Norse settlement that is presented at the beginning of this chapter is widely known, people find it difficult to give up the idea of Columbus as the first discoverer. This attitude was obvious during the celebrations marking the 500th anniversary of Columbus' landing in the Bahamas. Some Native Americans argued that Columbus should not be celebrated because he was not the "discoverer" of America, the Indians were. Others took the opportunity to point out European landfalls that preceded Columbus.

Adding to the difficulty of reaching new understandings is the presence of two or more perspectives regarding most historical facts. That Custer was defeated at the Little Big Horn in June 1896, is a fact, but Indians and non-Indians regarded, and still view, the defeat differently. For one, the battle was a stunning victory in the midst of many losses. For the other, the battle was a massacre by uncontrollable or "wild" Indians. The difference in perspective is illustrated by the often repeated phrase, "There were no survivors of the Battle of the Little Big Horn." In fact, there were hundreds of Indian survivors. The difficulty is for writers to treat both sides with equal respect when the number of pages available are limited.

People satisfied with their current understanding will ask, "Why is it necessary to consider different perspectives? If history is written by the winners about the winners, then we already know what we need to know."

The difficulty is that a one-sided approach leads to misunderstanding and erroneous assumptions. If we look at the voyage of Verrazzano only from his report, it is difficult to explain why the Indians around Penobscot Bay were so hostile to him. It would be easy to assume that the Maine Indians, and by extension, other Indians, were unreasonably hostile, but if we look at the issue from the point of view of the Indians, research shows that this part of North America had been visited by European fishermen and traders who treated the Indians badly. The works of other early visitors to the Maine coast show that in 1501 Miguel Corte-Real kidnapped more than fifty Indians from the north coast of Maine and sent them to Lisbon (Sauer 1971:13) and in 1508 Jean Ango of Dieppe arrived in Dieppe with seven Indians and their belongings (Sauer 1971:51). Records from the early contacts are scanty, but it is probable that other visitors also took unwilling native peoples to Europe. These kidnappings and other experiences would account for the wariness and unfriendliness of some people toward later European arrivals. The general conclusion is that Native Americans were friendly to Europeans until experience proved that the Europeans could not be trusted (Axtell 1992:84). Without close attention to both sides of the issue it would be easy to assume that the Indians were hostile by nature and that unsuspecting Europeans were victims of Indian capriciousness. Unfortunately, the idea of Native American hostility is deeply engraved on many non-Indian minds and Native Americans sometimes suffer because of this assumption. If members of a jury believe that Indians are naturally hostile and violent, then an Indian defendant may not be judged fairly.

Other erroneous ideas about Indians have equally detrimental results because they make it difficult for people to interact successfully. Some of these faulty ideas are stereotypes, that is, generalizations from one group extended to the whole, while others are misinterpretations of cultural differences. The belief that all tribal people lived, and still live, in tipis is a common stereotype. Some Plains tribes used tipis, but throughout North America there were many different types of houses. Yet people from tribes that did not use the tipi are sometimes asked, "Do you still live in tipis?" Non-Indians also expect that all Indians once wore eagle feather headdresses, but this is another stereotype. This stereotype has become so common that Indians from tribes that never wore such headdresses now use them in situations where they want to impress tourists with their "Indian" identity. This has meant that a tribe has given up its real history for an imaginary one.

Even people who live in states with significant tribal populations are not immune from stereotypes and misinformation. North Dakotans, like other Americans, have erroneous ideas about the people who first inhabited the state. Perhaps one of the most frequently stated mistakes is the idea that Native Americans receive some type of regular payment from the Federal government just because they are Indian. It is difficult to locate the origin of this idea, but it probably goes back to treaties that provided food, clothing and other subsidies to Indians. Another possible source of confusion is the fact that the largest employer on most reservations is the Federal government. Banks, storekeepers and others who cash government payroll checks may not realize that the person has worked for the money (there are other stereotypes regarding Indians as workers) and may assume that the check is some sort of regular Federal payment. The fact is that Indians do not receive regular support from either Federal or state governments. There are times when a tribe may receive a special payment because of money the Federal government owes the tribe, but these payments are extremely rare and, when the money has been paid, there is no more.

This book will focus on some of the common mistakes people make when they think about Indians. The goals are to present information that will enable people to have a better understanding of the sources of some of the misinformation, to present a Native American perspective when possible and to provide new knowledge that may be used to educate others.

Some Basic Concepts

In order for students to approach the subject in a scholarly fashion, there needs to be a basic understanding of some of the terms that will be used throughout the book. Often these terms are sources of misunderstanding and these need to be examined before moving on to other ideas.

Culture is the basic concept employed throughout this book. People often use the word culture to refer to literature or art or music, but this is an incomplete definition. Tribal peoples frequently use the word culture when they refer to the way people lived in the past. When Gary Pigney, a member of the Standing Rock Sioux tribe told reporter Lucile Henderson (Hendrickson 1981:19), "The culture is fading fast," he was using culture in the sense of a past way of life.

Figure 1.1. Modern powwows represent a mix of indian tradition and current technology. F. Schneider Photo

Although people use the term culture in different ways, a basic definition of culture is "learned, shared, patterned behavior" (Taylor 1973:25). Biology and culture form two parts of the human whole. Because culture is learned, it is the opposite of biology, the inherited physical characteristics with which a person is born. Human biology is remarkably similar around the world. In order to distinguish between similar groups, biologists use the idea of the ability of two representative individuals to mate and produce viable offspring that can reproduce themselves. That is, if one animal can mate with another and produce an offspring that can mate with a similar animal and produce a living offspring, then there is not a significant difference between the original mates. For example, a buffalo and a cow can mate and produce offspring, sometimes called beefalo, but these offspring cannot reproduce, so the buffalo and cow, while closely related are two different types of animals, two different species. Unlike animals, all humans can mate and produce children who can produce more children. Thus all humans, even though there may be differences in hair color, eye color, and skin color, are the same species. Because we are human, we share many characteristics. In *Human Universals* Donald E. Brown (1991) enumerates 400 characteristics that he believes are common to all human beings. The ways in which people organize themselves and react to certain events are part of the common experience. When we are very sad, tears fall from our eyes. When we are happy we smile. What makes humans different is not biology, it is culture.

Because culture is defined in its broadest sense as the total way of life which is learned and shared by a group of people, culture includes not just objects and behavior, but the ideas which people use to create, interpret and evaluate objects and behaviors. Values, attitudes, symbols and their meanings are a part of culture even though they are not seen. This aspect of culture is particularly useful in dealing with contemporary groups which may share in modern technologies but retain a sense of themselves as different from others. American Indians watch television, drive cars and speak English but still consider themselves to be Indian.

One way of understanding the concept of culture is to think of culture in the same way we think of language. That is, language is learned. It is shared and it has structure. Culture, like language, is found in a person's head. Not all people speak a language with the same degree of proficiency nor have the same knowledge of their language and not all members of a culture have the same ideas and behaviors. Wahunsonacock, more often called Powhatan and known as the father of Pocahontas, was willing to live in peace with the English colonists who settled in Virginia, but his brother Opechancanough was not. Within very large cultures, there may be significant variations similar to the dialect differences found in languages. Sometimes these major variations are referred to as subcultures. As with language, there are many variations in what a person knows about his or her culture. Some people are not interested in learning a new language or culture, while some people may be. Sometimes people give up one language for another. A person may change cultures. Usually a person adds knowledge of another language to the one he/she already knows and becomes bilingual. A person who knows more than one culture may be said to be bicultural. Languages change over time and so does culture.

People sometimes make the mistake of thinking that culture consists of clothing styles or house types. These may be a part of a cultural system, but even if these traits change, the individuals may still consider themselves to be members of the same culture. The Americans of 1990 are quite different in dress and housing and other artifacts from the Americans of 1890, but we still consider ourselves Americans. By this same measure, the descendants of formerly tribal peoples are very different from their ancestors, but they still consider themselves to be members of the tribe.

Because people do not understand the concept of culture, it is common to hear people say, "Such and such a tribe has lost its culture." Culture may change, but everyone always has a culture. Modern American ideas of appropriate behavior are very different from those held before World War I, but

Americans have not "lost" their culture, only changed it. It is not correct to speak of Indians as having "lost" their culture. Tribal cultures are different from what they were one hundred years ago, but they are living cultures and life means change.

A modern Native American may dress just like other Americans, may drive an average American car, may watch the most popular television programs and may eat pizza, but this person may also speak a language other than English and participate in tribal ceremonies. Modern Indian life is diverse, but non-Indians still think of Indians as separated from contemporary life. Even people who have studied about modern Indian life in the classroom still expect to find tipis or people dressed in hide clothing on a reservation. Perhaps the blame for this difficulty can be attributed to movies that continue to focus on Indians of the past rather than the present-day. *Dances with Wolves*, *Last of the Mohicans* and *Black Robe* may have been good movies, but they contributed nothing to an understanding of contemporary Indian life. Today more than half the Native American population lives off the reservation. American Indians live in every state, although only about half the states have reservations. There are Native Americans who have little connection to their Indian ancestry and there are those who follow tribal traditions exclusively. The variations in Native American culture are as great as they are in non-Indian culture.

It is possible for people to learn to use more than one language, and so it is possible for people to learn more than one culture. Some are more successful in this accomplishment than others. American Indians may be said, in some cases, to be bicultural as well as bilingual. Some non-Indians have learned an Indian culture so well that they are considered Indian by the members of the culture they have learned. An infant begins to learn its culture from the moment of birth, perhaps even before, and continues to learn throughout life.

One aspect of the learning process is an assumption that one's way of life, or one's culture, is superior to all others. In most contexts such a belief in cultural superiority serves to promote group solidarity and acceptance of society's norms and values, but when two cultures meet and each assumes a position of superiority toward the other, problems can arise. Using one's culture as a model against which all others are evaluated is called ethnocentrism. When Europeans described Indians as "uncivilized" they were being ethnocentric because they were applying their values to Indian ways. Indian people were also ethnocentric in their judgment of Europeans as "helpless" because the settlers were unable to survive without Indian assistance. Ethnocentrism and ethnocentric behavior are common to all human beings, but people can learn to recognize their own and others' ethnocentrisms and to comprehend the difficulties which such thinking creates.

In his book, *Dancing with a Ghost*, Rupert Ross (1992:2-3) relates a story illustrating the problem with ethnocentrism. In this story a group of Mohawk decided to host a special event and invite some James Bay Cree. The Mohawk followed their custom of putting out more food than people could possibly eat. The James Bay Cree tradition was to show respect to the providers by eating everything that was set out. There would not have been a problem if each group had been aware of the other's customs, but instead each group interpreted the other's actions according to its own customs. The Mohawk thought the Cree were rude for eating so much and the Cree thought the Mohawk were trying to embarrass them. What is significant is that in interpreting the other's customs according to their own, each group assumed the other was being deliberately insulting. Unsuspecting ethnocentrism often gets people into trouble because it is so easy to misinterpret other people's actions and to misunderstand their attitudes.

While ethnocentrism helps to build and maintain group identity, it often does so by distinguishing between "we" or "us" and all others who are often referred to as "they" or "them". "We" depict ourselves as civilized, humane, generous, clean, intelligent, and brave, while "they" are perceived as savage, brutal, pagan, mean, dirty, unintelligent, lazy and all other negative characteristics. The strongest distinctions between "us" and "them" often develop in situations where one group seeks to dominate or exploit another. When a whole group of people are endowed with characteristics which may be true of only a few individuals, it is called stereotyping. If the stereotype is also accompanied by dislike or hatred and an assumption that all members of the group are characterized by negative attributes, it is described as prejudice, or if these beliefs are directed toward people who have different skin color, racism. Using stereotypes and skin color to keep people in subordinate positions or to prevent their access to jobs, education and justice is discrimination.

The history of European and Indian relations is a progression from ethnocentrism to stereotyping to prejudice and racial discrimination. Despite the fact that European explorers reported that the native people who greeted them were kind, generous and hospitable, the "we" of the Europeans soon became contrasted with "they", who were identified as Indian and endowed with a set of negative characteristics. Many books have been written about the way in which Europeans created an image of Indians that was far removed from reality. These books relate the development of these negative images to the expansion of European colonization and to the subsequent subordination and exploitation of Native Americans. The ethnocentric thinking and the imaginary Indians, complete with feathers, are still very much alive today, shaping relations between tribal peoples and non-tribals.

In order to move away from such myths, it is necessary to accept the premise that each culture must be understood from the point of view of its members. In terms of native history, we must be prepared to accept the fact that each Indian culture or society, and its individual members will have a different perspective concerning events and situations and will react in a different manner. What was important to the Lakota about the discovery of gold in the Black Hills was not the gold but the influx of settlers into an area they held sacred and the subsequent treaty negotiations which the gold fever caused. Time also affects our perceptions. Although the men who entered the Black Hills in search of gold were acting in a manner which many non-Indians would have agreed was right, today we can understand that violating the treaty was wrong. Many of the Indians who have gained the respect of non-Indians or were mentioned in American history books for their military or political prowess were not regarded so favorably by their own tribes. Metacomet (King Phillip), Pontiac, Sitting Bull, Spotted Tail and other Indian leaders were killed by Indians who disapproved of their activities. In some tribes, ancient disagreements over the signing of treaties continue to influence interpersonal relations between tribal members. It is not easy to learn to accept another culture without judging it, and the great variation in tribal cultures and tribal people, past and present, makes the task more difficult, but it must be done if genuine progress toward cross-cultural understanding is to be made.

One aspect of American Indian culture that differs from person to person is the correct term to use in referring to the descendants of the first inhabitants of the Americas. For four hundred years the most common term was Indian. Eskimos were usually thought to be Indian, too, although scholars knew they were not. In the 1970's activists seeking to escape some of the stereotypes and erroneous ideas associated with the word Indian suggested that people use Native American and that caught on with many people. Now, however, Native American includes Indians, Eskimos, Aleuts and Native Hawaiians, while Indian refers to just one of these different groups; so many people prefer to use Indian instead of Native American. Some people are advocating the use of other terms such as Native Peoples, First Nations (now used extensively in Canada), but as long as the Federal government continues to use Indian and many tribal people refer to themselves that way, these other terms will be slow to catch on. In this book, American Indian, Indian, Native American, Tribal Peoples and Native Peoples are used interchangeably. For most Native Americans the important reference point is the tribe. A person identifies as Indian in situations where people may not recognize the tribal name; otherwise a person identifies as a tribal member, such as Hidatsa, Navajo, Cherokee, Lakota.

Tribal names sometimes cause difficulties because some names have been changed over time. Names that tribes use for themselves in their own language are not necessarily the names by which they are called in English. One classic case is that of the "Sioux." The people that we now call Sioux were once members of three different, but related, groups. These were the Dakota, Yankton-Yanktonai, and Lakota. All three recognized that their languages were very similar, but each lived in a different location and had different cultural traditions. Even today, these groups may refer to themselves by these traditional names. This is especially true of the Dakota and Lakota. The word Sioux comes from the term Nadouessiou (there are many different spellings and pronunciations of this word) which was used by the Chippewa and related tribes to refer to the Dakota. Although Nadouessiou's exact meaning is no longer known, it is believed to mean "Lesser Snakes" or enemies (Warren 1885:72). Most of the names we use to refer to contemporary tribes are not the names they call themselves. No one knows where the word Chippewa originated or what it means, but the people called themselves Anishnabe, First People. In Canada, people recognized the self-reference name of Inuit and substituted it for Eskimo. In the United States, Eskimo continues to be the term of reference, although the people call themselves Yupik or Inupik. Some tribes are changing their official tribal names to reflect the traditional ideas. The Sisseton-Wahpeton Sioux tribe recently became the Sisseton-Wahpeton Dakota tribe and the Devils Lake Sioux proposed changing their name to Mini Wakan Oyate, People of the Sacred Lake, to indicate their belief that the lake was sacred instead of the non-Indian idea that the lake was inhabited by evil spirits or the devil.

No matter what name they use to refer to themselves, for Native Americans the most important factor in tribal identity is tribal membership. Generally speaking, a person who is not a member of a tribe is not considered to be Indian. Each tribe has the right, based on aboriginal rights which have been upheld through Supreme Court decisions, to determine its own membership. The Federal government encourages tribes to use the idea of descent to determine membership, but the criteria are based on tribal customs that the tribe believes are significant.

Descent criteria require that a person be able to demonstrate that he or she is related to earlier tribal members. The concept is usually expressed as "blood" or "blood quantum". The idea that inheritance is carried in the blood is outmoded, now we know about genes, but it is still used in reference to Indians. The most common form of descent criteria is known as 1/4 blood quantum. In practical terms this means that one of a person's four grandparents was a tribal member descended from four tribal members. In actual practice, of course, descent is not so simple and calculating correct "blood quantum" is often difficult. To make matters more complicated, some tribes consider any Indian descent while others consider only descent from the tribe in which membership is sought.

Unfortunately, people sometimes equate blood quantum with culture and assume that to be full-blooded makes a person "more Indian" than one who is not. The concept of culture allows us to understand that what a person knows about a culture usually comes from growing up among people who know the culture. It is logical, then, that growing up among people who are tradition oriented, who continue to speak the native language, a person will learn more traditional ways. It is not necessary that this person's relatives all be tribal members, only that this person grow up among those who are most traditional. Thus a person with an Indian mother and non-Indian father may still grow up in a very traditional atmosphere, where he or she learns the language, the history, and many traditional behaviors. The point is that culture may equate with blood quantum, but the two are not necessarily connected.

The results of allowing tribes to set their own tribal membership qualifications are several. First, not everyone who considers herself or himself to be Indian may actually have the legal right, by tribal membership, to be considered Indian. This is becoming a significant issue as organizations move toward the idea that a person who is not a member of a tribe is not Indian. Some people who grow up on reservations and have a strong Indian identity may not be tribal members because they do not meet tribal criteria for membership. Since these criteria vary from tribe to tribe, a person not eligible for membership in one tribe would be a tribal member of another tribe if the circumstances were different. Needless to say, some people feel the membership criteria should be the same in all tribes or should be abolished entirely.

Second, the concept of tribal membership as an identifying marker for Indian identity makes Native Americans the only ethnic group in which people may be included or excluded on the basis of descent. For all other ethnic groups membership is based on self-identification or identification by others, not by a legal definition. This means that a person who would normally be accepted as Native American may be disqualified if she or he lacks tribal membership. In the modern world where affirmative action demands that people pay extra attention to minorities, a person without tribal membership may not be given this extra attention. The first major legislation to legitimize the idea that a person without tribal membership is not Indian was the Indian Arts and Crafts Act of 1990 (Public Law 101-644). Under this law, only those individuals who can demonstrate tribal membership or are certified as an Indian artisan by a tribe may market their art as Indian art. Others are now moving to adopt similar regulations concerning employment, minority eligibility for scholarships, etc. Such legislation is highly controversial, because it excludes some people who consider themselves Indian and places government in the position of using ethnic characteristics to determine eligibility, something we have attempted to move away from through affirmative action programs.

Allowing tribes to establish different criteria for tribal membership recognizes cultural differences between tribes. Many of these differences are based in ancient traditions that are still important to the tribe. Such traditions help to maintain the cultural distinctiveness that is vital to Indian identity. Many ethnic groups in the United States maintain old customs without being considered backward or antiquated, yet we still hear people say that Native Americans should "give up their old ways," and for many years, the educational systems tried to force Indian people to abandon much of their culture. Today, our growing understanding of multiculturalism as a strength rather than a detriment means we can accept cultural differences of many different kinds.

This chapter has introduced the concept of culture and explored some of the ways in which the concept may be used. Because culture is learned, any one person may represent a number of different cultures. As a person lives and learns, his or her culture may also change. All cultures change, but American Indians are often expected to be living in the culture of a century or more ago. Many of the misconceptions and stereotypes about Native Americans derive from poorly understood cultural differences. The differing attitudes towards historical events are really cultural differences and the reason that non-British peoples receive scant attention in history books may be attributed to ethnocentrism. Learning about past and present Native Americans and adopting an attitude of cultural relativism may help to dispel some of the myths and erroneous ideas.

SAKAKAWEA

Until recently, Sakakawea and Pocahontas were the only two Indian women included in American history textbooks. As often happens with such people, much of what has been written about them is more myth than fact. Sakakawea is credited with leading the Lewis and Clark expedition through the wilderness, when, in fact, she simply accompanied her husband, one of several interpreters for the group. While she did not guide the Corps of Discovery through uncharted territory, as so many writers and artists have depicted her doing, she did make important contributions to the success of the expedition.

Another myth is that in later life she lived on the Wind River Shoshone Reservation, dying in 1884. The truth is that the time of her death is only one of the many things that are not known about this woman. So little is known about Sakakawea that even the correct spelling, pronunciation and meaning of her name is a matter for discussion. Neither Meriwether Lewis nor William Clark were linguists and they struggled to find ways to write Indian names. Some people spell the name Sacajawea. Lewis and Clark seemed to suggest a hard "G" sound rather than "J" making the name Sacagawea. North Dakota has adopted the spelling Sakakawea. From a comment made by Meriwether Lewis in his journal for May 20, 1805, the name appears to mean Bird Woman (Ronda 1984:257).

The few facts about Sakakawea's life come mostly from the journals kept by members of the expedition. Her contributions are not singled out, but are mentioned in the same matter-of-fact way as the men's.

Sakakawea, a member of the Lemhi band of the Shoshone tribe, was captured by a Hidatsa war expedition when she was about 12 years old. She eventually ended up as the wife of trader Toussaint Charbonneau. Lewis and Clark hired Charbonneau as an interpreter for the expedition, but Sakakawea also became part of the interpretation process. She knew Shoshone and the expedition leaders hoped she would help them communicate with western Indians.

What makes Sakakawea's story so appealing is her willingness to undertake such a grueling journey soon after giving birth to a son. Jean Baptiste Charbonneau may have been the boy born February 11, 1805. If so, he was about two months old when the expedition left the villages and over a year old when they returned. For most of the journey, his mother carried him on her back. He became a favorite of William Clark, who called him Pomp or Pompey, and, at the end of the expedition, offered to raise him and educate him at St. Louis (Moulton 1987:229n,291n).

James Ronda (1984) organizes Sakakawea's contributions into four categories: knowledge of Shoshone camps, providing geographical information, interpreting, and illustrating the peaceful nature of the expedition. The presence of a woman with a child indicated the group was not a war party. This was probably the most significant in the overall success of the venture, which could easily have failed if the tribes had attacked rather than aided the group.

The Corps of Discovery returned to the Mandan/Hidatsa villages August 1806. On the 17th Clark recorded that he paid Toussaint Charbonneau $500.33 1/3 for his services and the use of his horse and tipi (Moulton 1993:305). Sakakawea received no pay. Charbonneau wanted to continue as interpreter, but none of the Hidatsa leaders could be persuaded to accompany the expedition to Washington, D.C., so he was not needed. When Clark offered to take him to Illinois, he refused saying he had no way to make a living outside the villages. Clark then agreed to provide an education for Jean Baptiste Charbonneau when he was old enough to leave home.

So little is known of Sakakawea's life after 1806 that people disagree about her death. Most scholars believe that she died of a virulent fever December 20, 1812 at Fort Manuel in what is now South Dakota (Ronda 1984:258). Others still cling to the idea that Sakakawea lived into the 1880's, that Jean Baptiste did not die in 1866, but joined her on the reservation, and that her descendants still live among the Shoshone.

The lack of information does not detract from the significance of Sakakawea's life. She was one of the first Native American women to achieve recognition for her contributions and, as such, contradicted the numerous representations of Indians as hostile to whites.

Chapter 2

Definitions of Indian and Reservation

Most people are aware that the word "Indian" was applied by mistake to the inhabitants of the western hemisphere, but few people realize the impact that this mistake has had on Native Peoples. Before contact with Europeans, Native Americans did not regard themselves as Indian or as members of a distinct race (Berkhofer 1978). Rather they thought of themselves as people. Often the name by which a tribe or group referred to itself could be translated as "men" or "people" or "human beings." Other tribes were not always regarded as friendly and so were not necessarily accorded the courtesy of being identified as human beings. Each group or tribe had its own origin tradition and regarded itself as superior in some way to other groups. Individuals knew they were members of a specific tribe and that their tribe was involved in a network of relationships with other tribes and nations. Sometimes the network involved people from the same tribe living in different areas. The people commonly called Sioux referred to themselves as Lakota or Dakota or Koda, meaning friends or allies. This term indicated that these people were part of a group who shared a common identity. The people now called Chippewa called themselves Anishnabe, "First Men" which indicated their feelings of primacy. Arikara called themselves Sahnish, meaning "human beings" or "people."

Indian tribes were divided into distinct settlements or groups called "villages" or "bands" or "families." The concept of tribe came from European travellers who thought the groups were organized in the same way as ancient Europeans. In some instances they were correct, but many times the concept of tribe, although now adopted by everyone, is not really descriptive of the group.

Whether the group was organized into a village or a tribe, they were called by names different from the name we now call the tribe (Table 2.1). The Mandan of western North Dakota lived in two or more autonomous, distinct villages. The different villages were distinguished by name according to their location on the east bank or the west bank of the Missouri: the Nuptadi and the Nuitadi.

The Hidatsa, another North Dakota group, were similarly divided into villages. Three different groups have been united under the term Hidatsa. These three, the Awatixa, the Awaxawi and the Hidatsa proper, used to speak different dialects and have different customs.

The Arikara were originally divided into as many as eighteen different groups although we do not have the names of all of them. Their tribe was divided into groups of four village units. Each village unit was composed of three or four villages. All of these villages operated independently of each other and had different dialects.

Table 2.1. Former Divisions of North Dakota Tribal Groups

Contemporary Name	Major Division	Band or Village	Translation
Sioux	Teton–Lakota speakers	Oglala	They scatter their own
		Sicangu	Burnt Thighs (Brules)
		Mniconju	Planters beside the water
		Hunkpapa	Campers at the horn or end of the camp circle
		Sihasapa	Blackfeet
		Itazipco	Without bows (Sans Arcs)
		Oohenunpa	Two Kettle or two boilings
	Santee–Dakota speakers		Knife bearers
		Mdewakanton	People of the Mystic Lake
		Wahpeton	People of the leaves
		Wahpekute	People who shoot among the leaves
		Sisseton	People of the swamps
	–Nakota speakers	Yankton	Dwellers at the end
		Yanktonais	Little dwellers at the end
		Assiniboine (separated from the Yankton and considered a separated tribe/nation)	
Mandan		Nuitadi	West-side people
		Nuptadi	East-side people
		Awigaxa	
		Istopa	
Hidatsa		Hidatsa	
		Awatixa or Amatiha	
		Awaxawi or Amahamis	
Arikara (called themselves Sanish)		Awáhu	Left Behind
		Hokát	Stake at the shore
		Scириháuh	Coyote fat
		Hukáwirat	East
		Waríhka	Horn-log
		Nakarík	
		Tukátuk	Village at the foot of the hill
		Tšinnina ták	Ash woods
		Witauh	Long-haired people
		Tukstánu	Sod-house village
		Nakanústš	Small cherries
		Nišap[st]	Broken arrow

As noted in Chapter One many of the names we now use to refer to different tribes are not names they call themselves. These names, like the name Indian, came from Euro-American explorers and traders who misunderstood what they were being told. These names came from asking other tribes about the groups in their area. Thus Minnetaree is the Mandan word for Hidatsa. Arikara may be the Pawnee name for the people and refer to the way the Arikara wore their hair. Cheyenne is apparently derived from the Lakota word, "Shiela," meaning people who speak a different language.

When the Europeans began settling the North American continent, there were more than three hundred identifiable groups now called tribes. These "tribes" were sometimes family units; sometimes villages; sometimes united as nations. All were culturally different from each other. What is now North Dakota may have had as many as eight recognizably different groups: Arikara, Cheyenne, Chippewa, Dakota, Hidatsa, Lakota, Mandan, and Yanktonai. Even these groups or tribes were divided into smaller units for most of the year. Because each group had its own name for itself and for people around it and because each group had its own distinctive way of life, the use of "Indian" to describe all the native inhabitants of North America has resulted in generalizations and misunderstandings. One example of a generalization from one tribe to all is found in the attribution of words from one language to all Tribal Peoples. Wigwam, an Algonquian word for a domed, bark covered house, is often used to refer to any Native American house even when the house is a tipi. Papoose is also an Algonquian word and should not be used to refer to infants of other tribes.

Most people have assumed that Indian refers to the native inhabitants of the western hemisphere, but other people who were not Indians were here when the Europeans arrived. These groups, the Eskimo and Aleut, are located in Alaska, Northern Canada and Greenland. They are physically, linguistically and culturally distinct from American Indians. The people of Middle and South America are also American Indians although they, too, are different from North American Indians. Because all these people have been called Indians, we have assumed that there was a common Indian identity and that, somehow, it must be possible to objectively identify Indians. The popular idea of an Indian has characteristics derived from many different nations, although the Plains Indian war bonnet and tipi are important attributes of this stereotype (Ewers 1963/1964).

In addition to stereotypes of Indian culture and physical appearance, the idea of a national Indian identity has created problems in the relations between the Federal government and modern tribal populations. Originally the Federal government treated each tribe as a separate entity and made treaties with each tribe, but as time passed, this position was changed, and later legislation was passed to cover all Native Americans regardless of their situation and their wishes. By treating all Tribal Peoples alike, the Federal government ignored many of the problems which Native Americans have had in adapting to various Federal policies. More recently, the Federal government has sought for objective criteria that could be used to identify people eligible for special Federal programs guaranteed to Tribal Peoples in the numerous treaties and legislations, but has not yet been able to establish criteria that are satisfactory to both Tribal Peoples and Federal agencies. In 1980 the Department of Education conducted a study to determine a definition of Indian that would be used to determine eligibility under the Indian Education Act, but opposition from the tribes, who maintained that developing such a definition ignored tribal sovereignty, prevented any final determination (Costo and Henry 1980).

The right of Indian tribes to determine their own membership has been upheld by the courts, and the Federal government has supported this right, but there are people who claim a tribal identity who are not members of a tribe. Should these people be eligible for Federal services? Rupert Costo, a member of the Cahuilla tribe of southern California and Jeanette Henry, an Eastern Cherokee (1977:154), editors of the *American Indian Historian*, support the idea that a person must be a member of a tribe in order to be considered Indian and believe that tribal membership is sufficient to establish Indian identity. The distinction between individual and tribal identity is significant because the Federal government has reserved the right to determine what is a tribe and has promulgated rules for the definition and identification of a tribe. This right includes establishing procedures for groups to apply for Federal recognition of their tribal status. The procedures are difficult and complex since one necessary element is the ability to prove through documentary sources a continuous recognition of the group as Indian and as a tribe. Most tribes having such information are already recognized, and those groups without the documentation are unlikely to find it. The Federal government, under the policy of Termination, also took tribal status away from tribes.

Indians have been identified on various levels. The Federal government has legal, administrative, political and historical definitions. Agencies within the Federal government, however, apply their own criteria or definitions to determine who is an Indian and who is eligible for services (Costo and Henry 1977:151). Tribal Peoples identify themselves on the basis of values and behavior. Indians are identified by non-Indians on the basis of physical and biological stereotypes. These opposing ideas have served to confuse Indians and non-Indians alike.

Indian Identity

> An Indian is a person who regards him/herself as Indian, is so regarded by other Indians and, on one basis or another, may validly assume the legal status of Indian (Hanson 1962:5 [as cited by Hodge 1981:3]).

The Federal government may define certain legal parameters for Native American identity, such as tribal membership, but most Indians agree that to be Indian is something more than a legal definition. Customs, values, and beliefs are shared by members of a tribe. These attributes are learned as a person grows up in the community. Membership in the Indian community identifies an Indian to other Indians. Membership includes the knowledge necessary to act appropriately, as well as the rights and obligations of being Indian. There are good and bad sides to Indian identity, and membership means a willingness to share both the good and the bad. The sense of community, of shared knowledge, values, and of group belonging, are integral parts of Indian identity. A child who grows up in an urban area, away from the reservation, while claiming membership in the tribe by virtue of descent from one of the tribal members, may not know the customs and values of his or her ancestors. In order to maintain a sense of belonging to a community, children are often sent to visit on reservations and taken to tribal events.

Because each tribe has its own culture, diversity between the tribes in North Dakota and even greater diversities between tribes that live in other areas are apparent. Groups which share a common identity and sense of unity usually speak the same language although the practice of the Federal government of placing different tribes on the same reservation has confused linguistic differences. Language does not necessarily mean a native language but a way of speaking and assigning meanings to words which will be shared by those growing up together or living together for some time.

The Tribal Peoples who now live in North Dakota have varying languages, depending upon the speaker's age and background. Some younger Tribal People do not know their native language and so are learning it in school. Other youngsters can understand the language from hearing their elders speak it, but they are not comfortable speaking it themselves. Some of the older people prefer to speak their native language although all speak English as a second language. In addition to the native languages, Tribal People also use a number of words which have meaning to them, but are rarely used by non-

Indians. Some of these words amount to slang, but they also serve an important function of creating an "in-group" identity. In North Dakota words like "powwow," "Indian time," "Indian taco," "forty-nine," "res" instead of reservation and others are common. *Wasichu*, the Lakota word for White people, is often used in conversations between Indians in North and South Dakota. *Wacipi* (dance) and *wazhapi* (berry pudding) are sometimes used on powwow or fund-raising posters. Names of communities in which Indians live and reservation names are understood by North Dakota Indians to have special meanings that are not necessarily known to non-Indians. To be from Fort Yates has meaning to an Indian while a non-Indian may have no idea where Fort Yates is or that it is the agency town for Standing Rock Reservation. Since many of the Indians who live in Fort Yates work for the Bureau of Indian Affairs or for the tribal government or teach in the schools there, to be from Fort Yates may mean that the person is less tradition-oriented than Indians who live away from the agency.

In addition to sharing a language, customs, values and beliefs are shared by members of an Indian community or tribe. A number of values have been recognized as being important to Indian people, but the two values most often mentioned are a relaxed attitude toward time and a great emphasis on generosity of self and possessions. In tribal society, time was measured by the sun, moon, and the passing seasons. Exact time was not measurable and not considered to be important. This attitude contrasts markedly with today's societal concern for time, where even seconds can be counted. Today traditional Indian events do not always start at a specified time but are held when everyone and everything is ready. Indians refer to this relaxed attitude toward time as "Indian time" in order to distinguish it from "White time," which is more exact. Outdoor powwows on reservations usually run on "Indian time", but the constraints of using parks, gyms and other urban facilities which must be vacated at a specified time mean that most urban and indoor powwows run on "White time". Closely associated with the relaxed attitude toward time is a feeling that things should not be done too quickly. People need time to think, to discuss and to ponder alternatives before any action is taken.

Generosity is part of a much broader value which can be summarized as "people are more important than things." One should give, not only one's possessions to people in need, but also one's time and energy to help others. Sometimes the emphasis on helping others causes a conflict when personal needs for work and savings must be sacrificed to help others. In traditional tribal society, possessions were freely given away rather than accumulated and work was often shared. Today this value is kept alive by networks of relatives who help each other, by the Give-Away ceremony and by helping others who need it. Not all Indian people today are as generous as others. Vance Gillette, a member of the Three Affiliated Tribes, told reporter Greg Turosak (1981:13), "There's nothing wrong with accumulating. But it's not an end in itself. The protestant ethic - work hard and you're favored in the eyes of God, possessions as a yardstick of goodness - I don't see it that way." Some believe that to give away things that one has worked hard to obtain is wrong, but many Indian people do share the tradition of generosity. Participation in community activities and support of community projects through contributions of food, time, money and other necessities are common. Even on college campuses, Indian students are involved in the activities of the Indian community and frequently have benefit meals or dances to raise money for a variety of causes. Despite changes in life style and attitude, these values have persisted and do not show any signs of becoming less important.

Visiting is a popular activity which maintains community cohesiveness. Through visiting, one finds out who is in need, keeps up with the news, and learns of events and activities that are planned. Visiting also makes many occasions into celebrations. While visiting, people will help each other to cut wood, prepare meals, quilt, do farm chores and other tasks. Leisure activities, such as card-playing and television watching, are also part of visiting. In urban areas much visiting takes place during bingo or other similar events. Visiting, however, serves primarily as a means of passing information between families. Individuals who live off the reservation maintain communication through frequent visits and through phone calls and letters when they cannot visit. It is also expected that people who are in contact with reservation residents will pass on the news to those who are not in direct contact so that communication networks can be maintained. The speed with which information moves across the reservation and between reservation and urban community has caused it to be referred to as the "moccasin telegraph." Through these information networks, people who live off the reservation continue to be part of the reservation system and do not feel left out.

In addition to sharing language and values, Indians also share certain attitudes towards non-Indians or Whites. Some Indians believe that their way of life is superior to that of the Whites and find much of White behavior amusing or disgusting or strange. Vine Deloria has discussed, tongue in cheek, some of the ways in which Whites amaze Indians in *We Talk, You Listen*:

> A century ago whites broke the Fort Laramie treaty with the Sioux so they could march into the Black Hills and dig gold out of the ground. Then they took the gold out of the Black Hills, carried it to Fort Knox, Kentucky, and buried it in the ground. Throughout the Midwest, Indians were forced off their land because whites felt that the Indians didn't put the lands to good use. Today most of this land lies idle every year while the owners collect a government check for not planting anything (Deloria 1970:11).

Whites are also viewed as greedy, an understandable attitude for Native Americans to take since Whites took tribal land. Indians also think Whites are greedy because they consume so many material items, always wanting bigger houses, new cars, and more expensive appliances and other goods. Since the life style of many Whites contrasts so noticeably with the traditional Indian value of generosity, Indians regard Whites as less sharing than Indians. Indians who fail to participate in the Give-Away or to contribute to Indian fund-raising or to help in some way, run the risk of being accused of being greedy.

Many Indians distrust Whites and are suspicious of their motives. This attitude is based on poorly recognized cultural differences between Indians and Whites, as well as on a multitude of experiences which have convinced Indians that Whites are not to be trusted. Sometimes these experiences have turned out badly because neither side was able to communicate because of cultural differences and sometimes the Whites have deliberately cheated Indians. The novel *Wind from an Enemy Sky* by D'Arcy McNickle (1978), a Flathead Indian from Montana, used the theme of misunderstanding between Indian and White to show how things can turn out badly despite good intentions on both sides.

Not all Native Americans have negative attitudes towards Whites and Indian-White marriages are fairly common, but an Indian married to a non-Indian may speak negatively about White attitudes and behavior in order to show that she or he is still "Indian." Sometimes Indians who are married to non-Indians and live in less traditional manners, find it useful to express a dislike for White people in order to affirm their basic Indian-ness. Attitudes, then, can serve to maintain Indian identity, either by making clear how Indians differ from Whites and giving this difference a positive emphasis or by using the sharing of negative attitudes as an indication of membership in the Indian community.

Another characteristic which contributes to Indian identity is Indian humor and teasing. Indian humor, like Indian language, stresses the things that Indians find important and is an easy way of uncovering symbolic differences between Indians and non-Indians. Many jokes focus on the relations between Indians and Whites. "The only promise the White man ever kept was, he said he'd take our land and he did." White heroes, such as Custer, are not Indian heroes and this is a source for many jokes. "Custer wore arrow shirts" was popular during the centennial celebration of his defeat at the

Little Big Horn. Needless to say, not all non-Indians found this joke funny. Sharing the common values that make these jokes funny to Indians is part of being Indian (Lincoln 1993). Jokes are also made about affairs which are specifically Indian; such as the Bureau of Indian Affairs, Indian time and activities of the tribal council. Since most non-Indians do not understand the references, these jokes become "insider" jokes, known and appreciated only by Indians. Even more "inside" are teasing comments made about other tribes. Teasing between tribes is common. Dakota and Chippewa, once fierce enemies, tell jokes on each other. This kind of joking serves to maintain tribal identities and to keep people from merging into one general Indian culture, as some social scientists predicted would happen. Joking and teasing, then, are closely related to the maintenance of tribal identity and are an important part of modern Indian life.

No doubt Indian identity is closely associated with the presence of the tribe or some other identifiable group. Criteria used by Indians to determine Indian identity are based on membership in a group. Membership in the group includes participating in group activities, sharing the values of the group and using the language. These characteristics are sometimes referred to as "heart." An Indian has an Indian "heart" if he knows the Indian ways and shares in Indian attitudes and beliefs.

Despite the persistence of Indian identity, a number of groups have not been recognized as Indian by the Federal government, and the members of these groups do not receive the services provided by the Federal government to recognized tribes. Services such as schools and medical care were guaranteed in the treaties made with various tribes, but not all tribes signed treaties, and not all groups have been considered to be separate tribes by the Federal government. This distinction has caused problems for groups who have traditions of being Indian and yet do not have any formal recognition of their identity.

Federal Identification of Indian Tribes

In order to limit services to those legitimately deserving them, the Federal government has searched for many years for some way to distinguish those Tribal Peoples who are eligible for the services guaranteed in the treaties from those who are not. The task is extremely complex, because it involves personal identification and tribal membership rules, in addition to the Federal concerns. Federal definitions generally make reference to membership in a recognized tribe, descent from a member of a recognized tribe to a specified degree of distance, or to residence on a reservation. None of these criteria can override the basic principle recognized by the government and up-held through numerous court decisions that tribes may determine their own membership in any way they want to. Tribes may use criteria which appear to be unjust, but that is a right guaranteed to the tribes.

The Federal government, however, has steadfastly maintained its right to identify or recognize which groups are to be considered tribes. The result of this decision has been that a number of groups which seem to qualify for recognition as Indian tribes are not accepted as such by the Federal government. The commission which investigated Indian-government relations estimated that out of more than four hundred groups claiming Indian identity, only 289 had been recognized by the Bureau of Indian Affairs as eligible for services (American Indian Policy Review Commission 1977:461). Only since the American Indian Policy Review Commission's statement on unrecognized Indians has the Federal government begun to grapple with the problem.

The reasons that tribes do not have Federal recognition are complex and varied. Some scholars have pointed out that the primary criteria for recognition as a tribe seems to be having signed a treaty with the Federal government or in some other way forced the government to become aware of the tribe's existence (Sturtevant and Stanley 1968:15). Tribes on the east coast who peacefully coexisted with European colonists or whose membership was reduced by war and disease to the point where no treaty was considered necessary are some of the groups who now seek to be recognized as tribes. A common example of U.S. policy is that the tribes which fought hardest against domination are the ones that now have Federal recognition. Many of these tribes have large memberships and are able to make themselves heard while the smaller groups are not so fortunate.

Other groups which are not recognized are those whose members moved back and forth across international boundaries. Each national government expects the other to provide for the tribal welfare. Recognition of this movement is particularly important in North Dakota because many Dakota and Lakota fled across the border into Canada during the Plains wars. Some of the descendants of these people have never received assistance from either government. In addition, there is a group of Chippewa-Cree in Montana that has been denied recognition by the U.S. government because they are considered to be Canadian Indians. The Metis are in a similar situation. The Metis, usually called Chippewa in North Dakota, identify themselves as Indian but are not eligible for Federal services to Indians. In North Dakota, the Metis were taken in by the Turtle Mountain Chippewa and given tribal membership, but in other parts of the country this procedure has not been followed.

In some cases, Federal policy has been responsible for removing tribal status. Termination, a policy developed in the 1950's, removed Indian status from a number of tribes on the basis that they no longer needed Federal services. The impact of the Termination policy, which ended reservations and Federal programs, was economically and culturally disastrous for the tribes. Tribal land holdings were allotted to individuals or sold off. The land became subject to taxation. All agencies and services were withdrawn, and the people were left on their own with the same rights and obligations as non-Indians. For people who had been accustomed to having the Bureau of Indian Affairs manage their business affairs, the difficulties were enormous. Those tribes who were not terminated were frightened by the realization that the government regarded Indian status as something that could be taken away, despite the promises of treaties and other agreements.

In 1978 the Bureau of Indian Affairs published rules for recognition of Indian tribes. These rules were designed to make it possible for tribes without Federal recognition to apply for Indian status. As promulgated, these rules were that a group must have "been identified historically and continuously until the present as 'American Indian, Native American or aboriginal'." In addition, recognition would not be given to groups which are "splinter groups, political factions, communities or groups of any character which separated from the main body of a tribe..." Many groups that have applied for Federal recognition, find themselves unable to provide the necessary documentation to prove continuous existence.

Not all tribes agree that other tribes should be permitted to gain recognition. In 1975 the National Congress of American Indians passed a resolution opposing the granting of Federal recognition to the Lumbees of North Carolina. The American Indian Policy Review Commission (1976f:1692-1693) reported, "'Recognized' and 'non-recognized' communities are entrenched in an open battle.... The 'pie' is only so big." Many Tribal People fear that recognition of new groups will mean the further thinning of Federal funds. Other Indians point out that the more people who are recognized as Indian, the more funds there will be to support Indian needs because the larger a minority is, the greater its chances for funds. Despite the two points of view, groups continue to apply, but fewer appear to be successful in gaining recognition.

Further complicating the issue of recognition is the fact that some states have recognized Indian tribes that the Federal government has not. These states have provided reservations and services to the tribal members, but the tribes have not been eligible for all the services accorded to Federally recognized tribes.

Because of recent concerns over the issues of Indian identification, the Federal government has begun to include a definition of "Indian" in the acts relating to Indians. Some acts, like the Indian Education Act of 1972, are all inclusive and include members of terminated tribes and even provide for individuals to ask to be included in the provisions. Other acts, for example, the Self-Determination Act of 1975, are more complicated.

The Self-Determination Act simply defines "Indian" as a person who is a member of an Indian tribe. Subsequent sections define tribe and tribal organizations and other terms. The definition of Indian tribe is interesting because it shows clearly the issue of recognition of Indian tribes by the Federal government.

> 'Indian Tribe' means any Indian tribe, band, nation or other organized group or community ... which is recognized as eligible for the special programs and services provided by the United States to Indians because of their status as Indians.

In other words, an Indian is a member of an Indian tribe, and an Indian tribe is defined on the basis of its members being Indian.

The American Indian Religious Freedom Act (PL95-341) includes Eskimos, Aleuts, and Native Hawaiians under the general term "American Indian." While it is certainly legitimate to recognize the Native Hawaiian's rights to religious freedom and to guarantee access to sacred sites, the Act may not meet either the approval of the American Indians or of the Native Hawaiians. We certainly have a new meaning to the words "American Indian."

Although each tribe has the right to determine its own membership, the Federal government has insisted that each tribe define those people who are eligible for membership. These criteria are included in the tribal constitutions or charters and may differ significantly from the Federal criteria, although the government has attempted to get each tribe to adopt essentially similar criteria. Some tribes choose to define membership on the basis of descent, while others emphasize residence.

Even descent distinctions vary. Some tribes recognize children of any tribal member while others recognize only those children descended from male or female tribal members. Thus a child may not be considered a member of the tribe if the child's mother marries an Indian from another tribe or a non-Indian, or a child may not be considered a member of the tribe if the child's father marries outside the tribe. These rules are based on ancient kinship systems which usually require that a member of the tribe belong to the clan. Clan membership is acquired at birth, and the child descended from a person who is not a clan member can never become one and so cannot be a member of the tribe. Among the Seminole of Florida, for example, clan membership and descent are reckoned on the basis of the mother so that a Seminole man who marries a non-Seminole woman, may have children who are half Indian and yet not be members of the tribe. In some cases these children will not be eligible for Federal services, and in some cases they will, depending upon the situation and their ages and residence.

Blood descent is used in some form by most tribes to determine membership. Out of 164 tribes investigated by C. Matthew Snipp (1989:362-365), 18 required 1/2 blood quantum, 1 required 3/8, 113 required 1/4, 20 required 1/8 and 11 required 1/16. The remainder used other criteria. The idea of blood descent is that a person must be a descendant of a tribal member and be able to prove this relationship by naming the ancestor. The concept of blood descent has nothing to do with the physical aspects of inheritance. In some cases people are identified as full-blooded because they live in a traditional manner, even though it is known that they have non-Indian ancestors. In the same way, most Indians do not consider a person Indian simply because he or she has an Indian ancestor. Most tribes limit how far back a person can go in naming an ancestor. Usually the ancestor must be a grandparent. A person who has a full-blooded Indian grandparent (that is, one descended from two Indian parents) but no other Indian relative, will be considered one-quarter Indian. Figuring blood quantum is a complex process, since many people are not neatly descended from a single grandparent, and a person's descent can be increased or decreased by fractions depending on the ancestry of one's parents, grandparents and other ancestors. For this reason, most tribes require that a child apply for membership in the tribe and provide for a committee to examine applications. Some tribes issue membership cards to their members.

Membership requirements of tribes that reside in North Dakota are found in their constitutions. Currently, all the tribes require that the members show 1/4 blood quantum and be descended from a tribal member. In most cases, people who are descended from members of other tribes are not eligible for membership in any North Dakota tribe, but the Three Affiliated Tribes have broadened their criteria to allow some acceptance for descendants of other tribes. To be eligible for membership, the tribes now found in North Dakota do not require that children be born on the reservation. Because two North Dakota reservations do not have hospitals and many Indian people live in the cities, such a requirement would be prohibitive. Requirements for membership may be changed by the tribes in order to meet new needs of the tribes. As applications increase, some tribes are becoming more restrictive, while others are becoming less strict in their requirements. Some tribal members are beginning to question the concept of blood descent because it seems to place Tribal People in the same class as animals. All the North Dakota tribes have enrollment officials who review the applications for membership. The Turtle Mountain Chippewa recently engaged in developing tribal rolls (lists of all tribal members past and present) to be used in distributing funds from treaty claims cases. Since many Turtle Mountain Chippewa descendants live off the reservation and have had little contact with the tribe and others were denied membership for a variety of reasons, the task of creating these rolls was immense, but no payments could be made until the rolls were finished and approved. This task was completed in 1993 and payments were made in January 1994 (Bailey 1993).

Despite the complications of tribal membership and Federal status, most Indian people are secure in their identity. Even those people who do not have tribal membership have identity as Indian and are accepted as such by others. After all is said, "heart" is the most important Indian factor, and no government can change it.

Reservations

The definition of an Indian reservation, like the definition of Indian, is complicated by social, historical, political and legal factors. We have state and Federal, open and closed reservations, different ideas about what constitutes a reservation and different political and legal issues relating to reservation policy. To most people, a reservation is land set aside for use by Indians. While basically accurate, this conception overlooks the complications of origin, judico-legal Federal attacks on the reservation land base, White residence on reservations, and the question of legal control over reservation residents and property.

In the history of Indian-White relations, treaty-making and reservations are closely intertwined. Reservations were originally established by treaty between colonial governments and sovereign native nations. Both parties agreed that the Indians had aboriginal rights to the land and that these rights must be abrogated; that is, legally abolished, through purchase or treaty. Since Tribal Peoples were in the majority, they held sufficient power in those early days to make sure that they did not relinquish all their lands but reserved some land for their own use. The Federal government continued the policy of making treaties with native nations and included lands reserved for Indian use in these treaties. Most of the lands were in the eastern section of the country and when the pressure for Indian land grew too great, the Indian nations were coerced into exchanging their reserved homelands for land in Indian territory which was to be a vast reservation west of the Mississippi where all Tribal Peoples would reside. Between 1812 and 1840 many of the eastern tribes exchanged their land as they had little choice but to move under White pressure, but the larger nations in the southeast fought their removal to Indian territory until Federal troops forced them to move. Many tribes were divided by these moves and some segments lost their Federal recognition when the government argued that, since the majority of the tribe had moved, those who remained in the original homelands had forfeited their tribal membership. The reservations established during this early period can be considered land set aside or reserved by Indians for their own use because these reservations were made under agreements which treated the tribes as sovereign nations with aboriginal land rights.

Westward expansion, however, changed the treaty-making process. The original intention of establishing the great plains as a home for all Tribal Peoples did not last long. By 1850, demands were being made for opening the area to White settlement. Other requests were made for migrants to pass through the area on their way to California and Oregon. In 1854 Kansas and Nebraska were created out of the middle of Indian territory. Tribes settled in Kansas and Nebraska were either moved to other areas or provided with enough land for each family to have a small farm. Thus began the process which culminated in the Plains wars.

Treaty-making with the numerous Plains tribes was an arduous process, and Congress eventually balked at the necessity to review so many treaties. Between 1852 and 1856 some fifty-two treaties were negotiated. In 1867, however, President Grant formed a Peace Commission whose task was to "insure civilization for the Indians and peace and safety for the whites." To accomplish this peace, the Commission was to establish boundaries for each of the Plains tribes (Prucha 1975:105). The Treaty of Ft. Laramie of 1868 defined the boundaries of the Great Sioux Nation and stated that White people would not settle on the reservation. In return, the Lakota would not injure White people who passed through their reservation. The discovery of gold in the Black Hills, however, brought Whites onto the reservation in numbers sufficient to irritate the Lakota. The government made no attempt to remove the settlers, and when the Lakota attempted to drive the invaders out, the Army was sent in to quell the tribe. Because of the eventual success of the Army, in the later years of western development, Indian nations were regarded as conquered nations and the land was considered to have been obtained by conquest rather than through purchase or treaty negotiations. Indian nations were forced to negotiate and were required to accept what was offered them, sometimes land of poor quality. Some non-Indians had humanitarian concerns for the "conquered" people while others believed that the establishment of reservations would provide an opportunity for Indians to learn White ways. As a result, the treaties made during this time period contain not only provisions for the reservation itself but also provisions for agents, education, tools, health benefits, clothing, food and other necessities. The reservations that were established during this later treaty-making period, then, are lands reserved by the Federal government for use by Indians.

All treaty-making between the Indians and the U.S. government stopped in 1871 when Congress passed a law prohibiting further treaties. Subsequent reservations were established by executive order or by congressional statute. The lands which were used for these reservations were considered by the Federal government to be public domain lands acquired by conquest, and this judgment has always left open the issue of the eventual disposition of these lands. The other effect of these agreements was that they were generally unilateral; in fact, the tribes had little or no opportunity to negotiate. The decisions were made by the Federal government and applied to the tribes. Reservations that were formed out of public domain lands were little centers of Indian concentration in the midst of encircling White settlements. This decision, too, had an effect on Indian land tenure because it submitted these lands to constant pressure from Whites who wanted to increase their own holdings. The Federal government still creates reservations by this process. In 1979 the government provided a reservation for the Cayugas in New York state by turning a state park over to the tribe in payment for lands lost by illegal White encroachment under the Trade and Intercourse Act of 1790.

Despite the wording of treaties which states that the treaties shall be in effect for perpetuity or "as long as the grass shall grow", it is unlikely that most non-Indians expected the reservations to be permanent. The events of history suggest that the provision of land for reservations was considered to be a temporary measure, mainly to help the Indians adjust to White culture. Ever since the first reservation was established, there has been constant pressure on the land. White people paid little attention to the setting aside of lands for Indian use or to the laws prohibiting settlement on Indian land. Most often non-Indian encroachment resulted in the opening of that land to White settlement while the tribes for whom it had been reserved were moved to new lands or paid for the stolen land. Such practices have resulted in a series of claims which Indian tribes filed against the Federal government for not protecting the treaty rights of the tribes.

In 1887 Congress passed the Dawes or General Allotment Act which parcelled out reservation lands to individual Indians and sold the rest to non-Indians. If there had been a consistent belief on the part of the non-Indians that the reservation land belonged to the tribes, there would not have been these Federal policies which opened the land and reduced the land base. Colson (1971) has argued that most non-Indians regard Indian reservation lands in the same way they regard other public domain lands, like military bases and national parks, as land set aside for a particular use until something better comes along. Colson points out that under this system the land is administered by the Federal government, not the people who are using it. The Federal government or the state retains control over the land and can determine its final disposition. Since the Federal government retains control over the land, the people have the right to pressure the government to change the policies about the land in question. Thus there are citizen groups which constantly attempt to have Indian reservations terminated. Such pressures have been successful twice. One produced the Allotment Act, and the other resulted in termination.

The Allotment Act had a continuing impact on reservation lands. The lands which remained after allotting the reservations to individual Indians were sold to Whites who settled on the reservations. Most reservations are more White-owned than tribal-owned. Today most reservations are composed of allotted lands, tribal lands and trust lands.

Allotted lands are individually owned by Indians or non-Indians. All the reservations in North Dakota are allotted, and all have some non-Indian residents on them. Tribal lands are those owned by the tribe. Some of these are lands bought through land consolidation programs aimed at restoring the land base. Trust lands are lands still held by the Federal government. Some of these are used for government offices, post offices, and other purposes, while other trust lands are simply those lands which were never sold off during allotment.

The discussion should have made clear several characteristics of reservations. First, with the exception of land which has been purchased by the tribe, reservations are not owned by tribes but are considered to be owned by the Federal or state government or by individuals. Through allotment, most reservations are open to settlement by non-Indians. Closed reservations are those few which were not allotted and on which only members of the tribe can own land. Second, reservations are paper or legal entities whose boundaries can be shifted by the will of Federal bureaucrats. In 1910, Fort Berthold was opened for settlement by non-Indians and one part of the reservation was removed from reservation boundaries. In 1970 the court ruled that opening the land to White settlement did not remove land from the reservation, and so the land was restored. Some of the terminated tribes have had their reservations restored, demonstrating again, that the reservations are not physical, but legal entities over which tribes have little control. Third, reservations are places where both Indians and non-Indians live. Indian people do not all live on reservations, and not all the Tribal Peoples on a reservation are members of that tribe. Because many reservations were established for the use of several different tribes, reservation and tribe are not the same unit. A legal definition of reservation, then, includes the idea that reservations are lands set aside for use by Indians but held in trust and administered by the Federal government as directed in treaties, executive orders or Federal statutes.

Indian Definitions of Reservation

Indian definitions of reservation are very different from the historical/legal definitions employed by the Federal government and legal concerns. Indian definitions include concepts and values relating to the land and the people, as well as beliefs in the permanence of the reservation and of Indian control of the reservation. Growing out of twenty to fifty thousand years of residence on this continent, the Indian attitude toward the land is one of reverence for the beauty and bounty of the earth, as well as a feeling of kinship with the creatures of the earth. Human beings are regarded as part of the circle of life which begins and ends with the earth. While many of these feelings have been eroded by White impact, a strong sense of relationship to the land remains. Non-Indians find this idea awkward to comprehend. This feeling is well represented in the current debate over the Black Hills of South Dakota.

The Black Hills, known as Paha Sapa to the Lakota, is the sacred place of the Lakota and other tribes. Among other things, many Lakota believe this to be where the tribe originated. Originally guaranteed to the Lakota people in the Treaty of Fort Laramie of 1868, the Black Hills were considered to have been forfeited by the Lakota when the later treaties reduced the land base. Ever since, the Lakota have sought to have the Black Hills returned to them. The Indian Claims Commission reviewed the case and agreed that the Black Hills had been taken away without just compensation and agreed to pay for the Black Hills and other lands. Traditional Indian leaders, however, still refuse to accept the money and argue that the Black Hills are sacred land which cannot be sold. To accept the money offered by the Federal government would be equivalent to selling the land since it would remove all claims to the region by the Lakota. The return of the sacred Blue Lake to Taos and the new American Indian Religious Freedom Act have given hope for the return of the Black Hills to the Lakota. Some Lakota have already signed the agreement to accept payment for the land, but so far, there has been continued hope for the return of the sacred land.

Even for those Indians who have lost some of the feeling for the land itself, the reservation has meaning. Reservation land is the link to the past when all lands were Indian-owned. The reservation symbolizes Indian primacy and original claims to the land. So long as these lands remain in Indian hands, these claims will stand to serve as reminders to non-Indians that they are not the original owners of the continent. For many tribes, the reservation is not only the original homeland but also the sacred land: which combines into a single symbol the strength of the past.

The reservation also symbolizes the Federal government's historic recognition of tribal sovereignty and the right of Indians to retain their separate status. By continuing to honor the agreements made in treaties, the government unwittingly provides continued support for Indian identity. Thus the idea of termination, to Indians, means not only the termination of the reservation but the end of Indian culture.

Reservations have concentrated the members of a tribe in a location and by doing so have made it possible for language to be maintained, for traditions and customs to be shared and attitudes to be reinforced. Consequently, the reservation has made it possible for Indians to maintain their cultural identity and to pass this identity on to their children. Today the reservations serve as reservoirs of traditional culture and knowledge. Indians and non-Indians come to the reservation seeking information about other ways of living and other values. Thus the reservation supports Indian identity in the face of the dominant society and acts as a reservoir of culture.

For many Indians the reservation is simply home. Home is where people care about you and accept you and are glad to see you. Home is where a person feels comfortable. Home is where kinship relations and other ties bind you to people who are supportive of your needs and will help you toward your goals. The reservation is a place to regain one's values and to feel a strengthening of Indian identity.

The reservation also offers strong psychological support. Off the reservation, the Indian is a minority. Being a minority in America, where prejudice against minorities and ignorance of other cultures is common, can be uncomfortable and even psychologically devastating. On the reservation, an Indian is a majority, and there is a special security and comfort in being part of a majority.

Not all Indians believe in reservations. Oklahoma has more tribes than any other state, but has no reservations. It is not surprising to find a member of an Oklahoma tribe speaking out against the reservation system. Ed Pecore (1987), former chairman of the Potawatomi in Oklahoma said, "I think the reservation system is something that has gone by, that should die in history... I think Indian people ought to be given a shot at the American way of life like anybody else." Others believe that reservations have created a dependent people who are unable to adjust to a world dominated by a different culture. A few Indians have joined the White backlash groups which are trying to terminate the special status of Indians, but these people do not represent the feelings of most Indians (Costo and Henry 1977:67). Even Indians who are highly critical of reservations and outspoken about the problems that occur on reservations, would fight alongside their brothers and sisters to protect the reservation system from termination.

When people say a reservation is like a prison or a zoo, they are speaking in a symbolic manner because reservations are not surrounded by fences or walls as prisons are nor are the conditions similar to those found in zoos. Many non-Indians, hearing the reservations called "prisons," have thought that reservations were fenced and had gates through which people were checked. Once, Indian people had to have permission from the agent to leave the reservation, but this is no longer true. Even in the old days, the reservations were not fenced. In North Dakota, the only way to know when you are entering a reservation is to note the sign marking the boundary. There is a danger that if too many people believe the reservations are actually like prisons, they will seek to have them terminated, believing that this termination will help Indian people. Indian people, however, will fight to keep the lands they have reserved because the lands are an important attribute of Indian identity and exemplify the Federal government's obligation to Indian people.

This chapter has reviewed some basic information relating to Native American identity. Tribal identity is culturally determined by growing up among other Tribal Peoples. A strong part of this identity consists of attitudes and values that tend to differentiate Tribal Peoples from non-Indians. Among these values are generosity and the idea of Indian time, and acceptance of the reservation as home.

Chapter 3

Native Oral Traditions

Questions concerning the origin of human beings in general and of Native Americans in particular have puzzled people for many generations. Some of the earliest European visitors to what is now called North America wondered how the Native Peoples had come to populate the continent (Huddleston 1967). Although no one has recorded whether ancient Native Peoples asked about European origins, it is probable they did.

Not only do people wonder about the origins of others, they also ask questions about the origin of the world and their place in it. They wonder how certain customs and traditions developed and why people look and act differently. Most societies have provided elaborate answers to such questions. For most of human time, the answers have been found in religious beliefs rather than in science. All over the globe, people have found answers in the Bible, the Koran, and for American Indians, in the Great Spirit or Creator.

When Europeans first came in contact with Native Peoples and wondered where they had come from and how they had arrived in what is now North and South America, they sought answers in the Bible (Huddleston 1967). The earliest explanation was that American Indians were the descendants of the sons of Noah. Later, other theorists advanced the idea that Indians were remnants of one of the Lost Tribes of Israel. Not until 1729 did anyone offer an explanation of Native origins that was not based on some element of information in the Bible (Huddleston 1967:11). Many people still prefer a biblical or theological answer to the question of human origins.

Because Europeans and their descendants believed the Bible contained the most accurate answers to the questions of origins, they tended to disregard the Native American origin traditions or to categorize them as stories or legends. Today we recognize that the extensive tribal narratives are equivalent to the Bible and that they serve a similar purpose.

Tribal People, too, asked questions about their origins and found the answers in their religious beliefs. For Native Americans, however, each local unit often had a different origin narrative. The people we now call Hidatsa had at least three different origin traditions. The Awaxawi believed that they had once lived elsewhere, while the Hidatsa-proper believed that they had originated under a lake to the east and migrated to the Missouri. The Awatixa, however, placed their creation on the Missouri River, where Charred Body had established an earth lodge village peopled with supernatural beings. Despite the uniqueness of each origin tradition, we find general similarities in origin explanations across North America.

One of the more common beliefs is the earthdiver version in which the earth was covered with water and a bird or animal was sent down to bring up mud to make land. Sometimes the bird is a duck; other times the animal is a muskrat or a beaver. Once land has been created, the Great Spirit makes humans to live upon it. Another common tradition is that the universe is composed of different levels of living. People were created on a lower level but, when they became decadent and disobeyed the spiritual laws, they were destroyed. A few good people were saved by climbing to another level. Other tribes believe that people were created elsewhere, perhaps under the present earth, and migrated to their present location. The Arikara say that the earth was once filled with giant people who stopped following Nesaru, the Creator. Nesaru became angry and vowed to destroy the bad people. He changed the good people into kernels of corn and sent them down under the earth to live until he released them (Dorsey 1904:12).

The Bible and Native traditions are alike in their accomplishments, but they are very different in their specific orientations. Biblical and tribal origin stories provide explanations for the order of things. Unlike scientific explanations which often raise more questions than they answer, theological explanations answer all or most questions. Obviously these explanations provide detailed answers to such questions as "How did the earth come to be?" "How did we get here?" "Why are there other people who do not speak or act in the same way we do?" In addition, the customs, practices and ceremonies are explained and often described. If someone wants to know why there is Easter or why people celebrate Christmas, the answer will be found in Christian sacred traditions, the Bible. Likewise, the reasons for Native People's ceremonies are found in their sacred traditions. Reasons for certain kinds of behavior are included in the traditions. The religious answers identify good and bad behavior and tell what will happen if the moral laws are not obeyed. One of the Mandan stories explains that the punishment for murder is the destruction of the entire village by supernatural forces. Many religious explanations also forecast the end of the world or the destruction of the present world level. Destruction will come to those who forget the traditional ways. These narratives are a strong force for maintaining group identity.

The Bible and American Indian sacred stories are very different in content and these differences correlate with major differences in attitudes and values. In Genesis, God gives man dominion over the plants and animals, but in many Native traditions, humans and animals or humans and plants can take each other's form, as in the Arikara story of Nesharu changing people into corn and storing them underground. Obviously, a person will have a different attitude towards plants and animals if they are believed to be interchangeable with humans than he or she might have if they are believed to be inferior.

For many Tribal People, the traditional origin narratives provide all the necessary answers so that scientific explanations are not needed. People who believe they were created on this continent see no reason to accept geological/archaeological theories that suggest an origin elsewhere. Some Native People feel that Euro-Americans would like to think of Indians as migrants because the Europeans immigrated to North America, but others think it is just another indication of how Euro-Americans have disregarded Indian history.

Origin Narratives

In the next few pages, the origin and historical narratives of some of the North Dakota tribes are presented. These shortened versions do not provide much indication of the complexity of the traditions. Like the books of the Bible, tribal narratives deal with many different events and beings, all of which are significant in determining the culture of the tribe. One example of this comes from the lengthy traditions concerning the exploits of Spring Boy and Lodge Boy, two sacred beings who try to rid the world of monsters. When Spring Boy is captured and taken above and tortured by the evil beings he is trying to overcome, he survives, slays the beings and instructs the Hidatsa to perform the Naxpike ceremony to commemorate the event.

Because these stories are so lengthy, only brief excerpts can be given here. This is like presenting Genesis or a summary of one of the biblical books without indicating how much more there is to know. People should consult the references in order to gain a real sense of the complexity of these traditions.

Arikara

The Arikara origin story was first collected in 1903 by James Murie, a Skidi Pawnee, who had learned to speak Arikara as a boy at school. Mr. Murie spoke Pawnee and he found the Arikara language to be similar enough that he was able to adjust what he had learned at school with that spoken by the elders at Fort Berthold. The stories were prepared for publication by George Dorsey (1904). Later Melvin Gilmore (1930a) collected another version of the origin story. The Arikara elder, Hand, told this story to Murie.

> Nesaru in the heavens planted corn in the heavens, to remind him that his people were put under ground. As soon as the corn in the heavens had matured, Nesaru took from the field an ear of corn. This corn he turned into a woman and Nesaru said, "You must go down to the earth and bring my people from the earth." She went down to the earth and she roamed over the land for many, many years, not knowing where to find the people. At last the thunders sounded in the east. She followed the sound, and she found the people underground in the east. By the power of Nesaru himself this woman was taken under ground, and when the people and the animals saw her they rejoiced. They knew her, for she was the Mother-Corn. The people and the animals also knew that she had the consent of all the gods to take them out.

> Mother-Corn then called upon the gods to assist her to lead her people out of the earth. There was none who could assist her. She turned around to the people, and said: "We must leave this place, this darkness; there is light above the earth. Who will come to help me take my people out of the earth?" The Badger came forth, and said, "Mother, I will help." A Mole also stood.up, and said, "I will assist the Badger to dig through the ground, that we may see the light." The long-nosed Mouse came, and said, "I will assist these other two to dig through."

> The Badger began to dig upwards. He became tired, and said, "Mother, I am tired." Then the Mole began to dig. The Mole became tired. Then the long-nosed Mouse came and dug until it became tired. It came back. The long-nosed Mouse said, "Mother, I am tired." The Badger began to dig upward. When he became tired the Mole went up. The Mole said, "I was just about to go through when I became tired." The long-nosed Mouse then ran up, and said, "I will try."

> The long-nosed Mouse stuck its nose through the earth until it reached up to its ears, and it could see just a little light. It went back, and said, "Mother, I ran my nose through the earth, and it has made my nose small; all the people that I shall belong to shall have these long noses, just like mine, so that all the animals will know that it was I who dug through the earth first, making my nose small and pointed."

> The Mole was so glad that it tried again. It went up to the hole, dug through the hole and went through. The sun had come up from the east. It was so bright that it blinded the Mole. The Mole ran back, and said, "Mother, I have been blinded by the brightness of that sun. I can not live upon the earth any more. I must make my home under the earth. All the people who wish to be with me will be blind, so that they can not

see in the daytime, but they can see in the night. They shall stay under the ground in the daytime." The Mother-Corn said, "Very well."

The Badger then dug through, making the hole larger, and, as it went out, the Badger closed its eyes, but, as he stuck his feet out, the rays of the sun struck him upon the face so that he got a streak of black upon it, and he got black legs. The Badger went back into the hole, and said, "Mother, I have received these black marks upon me, and I wish that I might remain this way, so that people will remember that I was one of those who helped to get your people out." The Mother-Corn said, "Very well, let it be as you say."

The Mother-Corn then led the way and the Mole followed, going out of the hole; but, as they were about to go out from the hole, there was a noise from the east, and thunder, which shook the earth, so that the earth opened. The people were put upon the top of the earth. There was wailing and crying, and, at the same time, the people were rejoicing that they were now out upon the open land. As the people stood upon the earth, the Mother-Corn said, "My people will now journey west. Before we start, any who wish to remain here, as Badger, long-nosed Mice, or Moles, may remain." This was then done. Some of the people turned back to the holes of the earth and turned into animals, whichever kind they wanted to be.

Once on the surface of the earth, the People began to wander, looking for a home. As they moved toward the west, obstacles were put in their way. One barrier was a great water. A bird made a path through the water, but before everyone had made his way through, the water closed over them. These People in the water became the fish and other water dwellers. Another obstacle was a tall cliff. Again a bird made passage for them. Those People who did not proceed through the cliff became birds and other creatures of the air. A great, dense forest was the third barrier. An owl found a way through and led some of the People through but again not all passed through safely. Those People who stayed in the forest became the deer, moose, bears, and other animal people. Finally, the Arikara came to a beautiful land where all the necessities of life could be found. A beautiful woman came to them, and the Arikara recognized her as Mother-Corn. Mother-Corn lived with them and taught them how to live and work on the earth and how to pray to Nesaru, the Man Above. When Mother-Corn died she left the corn plant to the people as a reminder that she was always with them, guiding and caring for them. The Arikara say that the beautiful place where they learned to live was the valley of the Loup River in what is now Kansas. Many years later, the Arikara moved from the Loup to the Missouri and eventually moved up the Missouri to present-day North Dakota.

Chippewa (Ojibwa)

The origin tradition of the Chippewa is closely associated with the Grand Medicine Society (Midewiwin) religion. The story as related by William Warren (1885:79), a Chippewa who became a historian of his people, clearly indicates the association between the Midewiwin and the migration of the Chippewa.

> Our forefathers, many strings of lives ago, lived on the shores of the Great Salt Water in the east. Here it was, that while congregated in a great town, and while they were suffering the ravages of sickness and death, the Great Spirit, at the intercession of Man-ab-o-sho, the great common uncle of the An-ish-in-aub-ag, granted them this rite wherewith life is restored and prolonged. Our forefathers moved from the shores of the great water, and proceeded westward. The Me-da-we lodge was pulled down

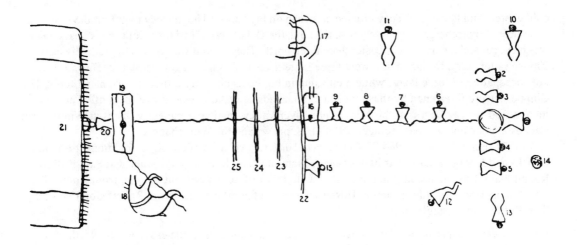

Figure 3.1. Sikassige, a Chippewa man from White Earth, Minnesota, drew this illustration of the Chippewa origin for W. J. Hoffman. The Great Spirit is the large figure at the right, sitting on the world. The figures on either side of the world are the two men and two women the Great Spirit created. The rest of the figures are spiritual beings who helped in the creation. Line 22 marks the earth and the beginning of the Midewiwin ceremony. People who pass through the four stages of the ceremony live on earth in a sacred manner, as shown in 21.

and it was not again erected, till our forefathers again took a stand on the shores of the great river where Mo-ne-aung (Montreal) now stands.

In the course of time this town was again deserted, and our forefathers still proceeding westward, lit not their fires til they reached the shores of Lake Huron, where again the rites of the Me-da-we were practised.

Again these rites were forgotten, and the Me-da-we lodge was not built till the Ojibways found themselves congregated at Bow-e-ting (outlet of Lake Superior), where remained for many winters. Still the Ojibways moved westward, and for the last time the Me-da-we lodge was erected on the Island of La Pointe, and here, long before the pale face appeared among them, it was practised in its purest and most original form.

Warren also discusses the separation of the Chippewa, Pottawatomi and Ottawa into three distinct tribes. The Chippewa then divided into a northern and southern division which were further subdivided into groups named according to their location or some specific tribal characteristic. Skirmishes with the Dakota and relations with fur traders comprise much of the later history of the Chippewa.

Dakota

The Dakota origin tradition is not only very different from that given by other Siouan-speaking groups, but different Dakota divisions apparently had different traditions. In a version collected by Ruth Landes (1968a:22) from the Mdewakanton Dakota in Minnesota, the People came from a land of cold winters and lots of ice. They crossed an ocean on big "arks." The journey took four days and was complicated by icebergs. When they reached land, the Dakota remained there four to six years. Game was plentiful and the living was easier than in the north. They moved westward and gradually came to Chippewa territory. In this region were three large lakes which the Dakota explored. During the Dakota occupation of these lakes, white men came in big boats and taught them to use metal tools. The Chippewa were threatened by these tools and attacked the Dakota, who drove them off. The Dakota then moved further west into the Mississippi River Valley, made permanent villages at Winona and LaCrosse and came in closer contact with the Chippewa and the Winnebago.

In 1972, James Howard (1984:37-41) collected different versions of the origin traditions from Simon Hanska and George Bear of Birdtail Reserve, Manitoba, and Robert Good Voice and Sam Buffalo of Round Plain, Saskatchewan. Each man told a slightly different story, but the one from Round Plain differs most from the Mdewakanton. Howard combined the information from Robert Good Voice and Sam Buffalo into a single story.

> Many years ago the Dakota people landed on a peninsula on the east coast of North America. They were surrounded by waters and could go no further, so they prayed. Finally, in response to their prayers, they heard a great voice, and above the surface of the ocean, in the direction of the sunrise, they saw the heads of two spirits. These were the Unktehi [Underwater Panthers]...

> These spirits told the people to travel west, following the c'anku duta, the 'red road'... The people looked toward the west and saw that their path seemed to lead into the sea. They feared that they would be drowned, but they had faith and followed the red road.

> When they came to the water, one man stepped on it, and it parted, revealing a dry path. The rest followed. The red road led the Dakota west to the Minnesota country...

Hidatsa

The Hidatsa were originally divided into three distinct and separate sub-tribes or villages: the Awatixa, the Awaxawi and the Hidatsa-proper. These villages recognized a common alliance for protection but operated as culturally and linguistically autonomous units. Each of these villages or sub-tribes (they probably occupied more than one village each) had its own origin story. One of the earliest references to the Hidatsa origin tradition comes from David Thompson, an employee of the Northwest Fur Company who visited the Mandan and Hidatsa in 1797 (Thompson 1962). The most complete versions are found in Alfred Bowers' book (1965). He relates the three different stories and points out (1965:302) that they are essentially unchanged from the time Lewis and Clark collected similar stories from two Hidatsa villages.

The Awatixa had no tradition of living anywhere other than on the Missouri where they had been created by Charred Body. The Awaxawi claimed that they had lived along the streams to the east as agriculturalists, and when they moved to the Missouri, they retained their agricultural way of life. The Hidatsa-proper origin tradition places them under the earth near a great lake to the east which people have interpreted to mean Devils Lake. According to tradition, the Hidatsa-proper came up from below by a vine, but a pregnant woman remained stuck in the exit hole and so there are still Hidatsa in the under world. The Hidatsa-proper moved around the plains, living as well as they could until they came to a great river. On the river they met the Mandan who invited them to cross over to the other side to settle. The Mandan gave the name "Minitaree" or "Cross-the-Water" to the Hidatsa-proper, in reference to this ancient meeting. The Hidatsa-proper had no knowledge of corn growing and had to be taught the techniques by the people living on the Missouri River.

Wood's recent research into Hidatsa origins unites the Awaxawi and Hidatsa-proper into a single tradition of an origin under the earth (Wood 1986:30). After climbing to the surface, the group wandered around until the Awaxawi separated from the others and settled near Devils Lake, where they lived as agriculturalists. The Hidatsa-proper continued their migrations and traveled so far to the north that they forgot how to grow corn. Eventually they, too, arrived at the Missouri (Wood 1986:36).

Lakota

The origin narrative of the Lakota, specifically that of the Oglala, was originally collected by James Walker, a physician stationed at Pine Ridge from 1896 to 1914 (Walker 1983). A group of holy men became convinced that Dr. Walker should be taught the traditions of the Oglala and they adopted him into the Buffalo Society. Several members of the society, among them, Long Knife (George Sword) and Gray Goose (Thomas Tyon) acted as teachers, interpreting the language of the holy men into the Lakota that Walker understood (Walker 1983:43). Sword became interested in the project and agreed to write stories and histories for Walker.

Walker believed the Lakota origin tradition was comparable to the stories of the ancient Greeks, Romans and Norse and he edited them to form a chronological account, from the creation of the world to the creation of humans (Walker 1983). As a result, these stories seem very similar to those known to Europeans.

The Lakota begin with the creation of the earth and universe. In the beginning, the only thing in existence was Inyan, the Rock. Because Rock always existed he is the first of the superior gods. Inyan had many powers, but he had no way to exert them because nothing else existed. Inyan decided to create something and he took his blood and made a disk which he named Maka, Earth. Inyan's blood became blue waters and the blue sky dome. Inyan used so much of his blood that he became hard and dried up. "Thus in the beginning there were Inyan, Maka, and the waters, all of which are the world; and Nagi Tanka, named Skan, the blue dome which is the sky above the world. The world is matter and has no powers except those bestowed by Nagi Tanka" (Walker 1983:207).

Sun, daytime, nighttime and other beings were created and they began to fight among themselves. Because of this struggle, the secondary gods were made: the Moon, Passion, Wind, and the Thunderstorm. More and more beings were created, including animals, birds and insects, and the rivalries and jealousies increased and all of those led to more creation. Finally, Skan declared that the Creation was complete and nothing else would be made.

The Gods lived under the ground where they enjoyed great feasts, but jealousies continued and the beautiful Iya tried to seduce Wind away from his wife, Moon. As a result, Iya and others were banished to the surface of the earth. Wind begged to be allowed to accompany them and Skan agreed.

At first, the only people on earth were Waziya, the Wizard; Wakanka, the Witch, his wife; their daughter Anog-Ite, Double-Faced Woman; and the Trickster, Iktomi. Iktomi decided to play a trick on Anog-Ite. He got her to tell him how to lure the people out of the underworld where they were living. As a result of Iktomi's enticement, six men and their wives and children led by a young man, "Tokahe, the First One", left the underworld and ventured through a cave to the earth's surface. (The Lakota say that this cave was in the Black Hills, perhaps Wind Cave.) Previously Iktomi had made Tokahe think that the world was full of wonderful food, clothes and beautiful women who lived forever. When the group emerged however, they found that they had been fooled by Iktomi and that there was nothing for them in the world. Waziya, and Wakanka took pity upon the Oglala and brought them food and water.

Then Waziya and Wakanka led them to the land of the pines where they showed these newcomers how to hunt and to live as men do. That is how the first people came to earth. Their children are the Lakota.

Later, a great flood destroyed all but one of the People. One beautiful woman was saved by an eagle who allowed her to grab onto his feet, and she was carried away to a tree on a cliff. The woman gave birth to twins, whose father was the eagle. From these came a new tribe of Sioux. The blood of all the people who drowned became pipestone, sacred to the Sioux, and the eagle feather became the sacred symbol of the warrior.

Due to the collaboration of the holy men, the traditions collected by Dr. Walker are among the most complete for any Plains tribe. Even though the men who taught the stories to Dr. Walker were the last of those who grew up before the reservation era, elements of the traditions have been handed down to later generations.

Mandan

In 1833, Prince Maximilian spent the winter among the Mandan and Hidatsa. He became friends with Dipauch, a Mandan living at Fort Clark, who related a Mandan origin tradition (Wied-Neuwied 1906:315).

> Before the existence of the earth, the lord of life created the first man, Numank-Machana, who moved on the waters, and met with a diver or duck, which was alternately diving and rising again. The man said to the bird, 'You dive so well, now dive deep and bring up some earth.' The bird obeyed, and soon brought up some earth, which the first man scattered upon the face of the waters, using some incantations, commanding the earth to appear, and it appeared. The land was naked; not a blade of grass was growing on it; he wandered about and thought that he was alone, when he suddenly met with a toad. 'I thought I was here alone,' said he, 'but you are here, and who are you?' It did not answer. 'I do not know you, but I must give you a name, You are older than I am, for your skin is rough and scaly; I must call you my grandmother, for you are so very old.' He went further and found a piece of an earthen pot. 'I thought I was here alone, but men must have lived here before me, I must, likewise call you my grandmother.' On going further he met with a mouse: 'It is clear,' said he to himself, 'that I am not the first being; I call you also my grandmother.' A little further on he and the lord of life met. 'Oh, here is a man like myself,' exclaimed he, and went up to him. 'How do you do, my son?' said the man to Omahank-Numakshi; but he answered, 'I am not your son, but you are mine.' The first man answered, 'I dispute this.' But the lord of life answered, 'You are my son and I will prove it; if you do not believe me, we will sit down and plant our medicine sticks which we have in our hands in the ground; he who first rises is the youngest and son of the other.' They sat down and looked at each other for a long time, till, at length, the lord of life became pale, his flesh dropped from his bones, on which the first man exclaimed, 'Now you are surely dead.' Thus they looked at each other for ten years, at the end of which time, when the bare bones of the lord of life were in a decomposed state, the first man rose, exclaiming, 'Now he is surely dead.' He seized Omahank-Numakshi's stick, and pulled it out of the ground; but at the same moment the lord of life stood up, saying, 'See here, I am your father, and you are my son,' and the first man called him father. As they were going on together, the lord of life said, 'This land is not well formed, we will make it better.' At that time the buffalo was already on earth. The lord of life called to the weasel, and ordered him to dive and bring up grass, which was done. He then sent him again to fetch wood, which he brought in like manner. He

divided the grass and wood, giving one half to the first man. This took place at the mouth of the Heart River. The lord of life then desired the first man to make the north bank of the Missouri, while he himself made the south-west bank, which is beautifully diversifed with hills, valleys, forest, and thickets. The man, on the contrary, made the whole country flat, with a good deal of wood in the distance. They then met again, and, when the lord of life had seen the work of the first man, he shook his head and said, 'You have not done this well: all is level, so that it will be impossible to surprise buffaloes or deer, and approach them unperceived. Men will not be able to live there. They will see each other in the plain at too great a distance, and will be unable to avoid each other, consequently they will destroy each other.

The Mandan origin story goes on to describe how the two men made other animals, medicine pipes, tobacco, and humans. This creation took place along the Missouri River. Lone Man created more humans who grew and flourished. The first people he created were Mandan, and Lone Man eventually came to be one of them and helped them. Some of the happenings of this ancient time account for various customs and ceremonies of the Mandan.

A different origin tradition was known to other Mandan. As Wolf Chief, a Mandan/Hidatsa elder, told the story to Alfred Bowers (1950:156-163):

A long time ago the Missouri River flowed into the Mississippi River and thence into the ocean. On the right bank there was a high point on the ocean shore that the Mandan came from. They were said to have come from under the ground at that place and brought corn up. Their chief was named Good Furred Robe. He had one brother named Corn husk Earrings and another younger brother called No Hair on Him or Head for Rattle after the gourds. They had a sister named Cornstalk.

In this early time when they came out of the ground, Good Furred Robe was Corn Medicine, and he had the right to teach the other people how to raise corn. The people of Awigaxa asked him to teach them his songs so as to keep the corn and be successful in growing their corn. Good Furred Robe also had a robe, which, if sprinkled with water, would cause rain to come.

The People moved up the Mississippi, building villages and planting gardens along the way. During these years of traveling, the Mandan developed the bow and arrow, pottery and pipestone pipes. Eventually they changed the direction of their wandering and returned to the Missouri. The Awigaxa moved up the Missouri where they found the other Mandan created by Lone Man and First Creator.

Lone Man had been reborn as a Mandan and lived with the people for many years. He made four turtle drums out of buffalo hide and taught the Mandan to dance in order to free the animals which the evil spirit, Hoita, had imprisoned. Another enemy of the Mandan tried to drown these people by creating a flood, but Lone Man built a wall to protect them. Today this wall is commemorated by the wooden structure called the sacred ark.

After many years, Lone Man decided to return to his home, the south wind, but he promised the Mandan they would always have his help and that some day he would return. Each spring he sends the warm south wind so that the people will know that he still cares for them. Before Lone Man returns to the Mandan, he will send a sign. The Missouri River will change its course and flow in the opposite direction. The big trees will grow with roots sticking up at the top and the antelope will have no flesh on the lower part of their chests. Some Mandan believe that the building of Garrison Dam and the subsequent change in the course of the river are Lone Man's signs warning of the end of the world.

Remembering and Recording Traditions

For most of human history, all knowledge was handed down verbally from generation to generation. Stories were told by the elders to demonstrate how wisdom was acquired and to explain the natural phenomena and important events of the tribe. Oral narratives included both origin traditions, historical traditions and stories told for teaching or entertainment purposes. Most of the northern plains people distinguished between stories which are historical in purpose and stories which are told to amuse. The Lakota distinguish three kinds of oral narratives (Theisz 1975:6): *Ehanni woyake* deal with the beginning of the world, the creation, the sacred beliefs and deities of the Lakota. *Ehanni wicooyake* are historical accounts of recent events usually related to specific bands and include heroic deeds, migrations and other events, and the *ohunkanka woyake* are stories designed to teach a moral or to amuse.

Among the Hidatsa, narratives are of two kinds *mashi*, a story, and *mashi-aruhopa*, a holy story (Beckwith 1938:xvi). The Mandan distinguish between *hoge* and *hohohopini'i*. *Hopini* is the Mandan word for mysterious power. Sacred stories concern the origin of the land and the people, as well as the origin of sacred ceremonies and the sacred bundles. Such stories should be told only during the winter and are often withheld from unbelievers. In order to avoid telling sacred stories, a different story or an origin story from another tribe might be substituted (Warren 1885:57). Bowers (1965:203) notes, however, that the origin stories which were told to him by the Mandan and Hidatsa were similar to those collected by Thompson in 1797 and by Lewis and Clark in 1804, suggesting that the traditions were accurately told to outsiders. True stories or histories could be told at any time, but researchers have been less interested in recording such stories, so it is easier today to find books of sacred stories than it is to find historical traditions. Many tribes retain strong oral histories however, and some are beginning to collect them so that future generations will have access to them.

Non-Indians often question the validity of information stored in the mind rather than on paper. Evidence has shown that people who are trained in oral history can remember large amounts of data and that an orientation toward oral presentation and recall develops its own methods. Bea Medicine, Standing Rock Sioux, described how she was taught the traditions and histories of her people.

> As a child growing up, whenever the old people got together, they talked about the history that had gone before us. This is very typical of societies that do not have a written language, the bringing into the consciousness of children and adults the oral traditions that are of importance to us. As a child I was taught not only the oral history but stories in our language we would have to remember precisely when we were asked them (Ortiz 1978:112).

The tribal historians were recognized for their ability to remember stories and repeat stories exactly every time. In his testimony at the Wounded Knee Trial in 1974, Father Peter Powell said, "I have been told by old people that the tribal historian was second in importance only to the great holy men of the people" (Ortiz 1977:65). Tribal historians had a great responsibility to their people, to remember accurately the events, the stories and philosophy which formed the sacred identity of the People. In a description written in 1889, Dr. Josiah Janney Best described one of the leaders of the Hidatsa, whom he called Gros Ventres:

> One of the best speakers in the councils here is Good Bear, second chief of the Gros Ventres... He is forty-two years old and is spokesman for the Gros Ventres. He is a fluent speaker and in a few minutes warms up, his black eyes sparkling like diamonds and words falling from his lips thick and fast, and his logic is good. He is

courteous in his manners and is always polite in answering a question. Endowed with a good memory, which is the basis for his logic, he can recall any promises the whites ever made them, even quoting their own language (Brown 1976:20).

Contemporary Navajo healers learn thousands of verses to songs used in healing ceremonies, further evidence of their ability to recall large amounts of information. Despite Anglo-American emphasis on the written word, these examples should suffice to indicate that oral traditions can survive for long periods of time without being written down.

Songs were also important in passing down traditions. Contemporary Hunkpapa linguist and singer, Earlwin Bullhead, is collecting and translating songs from earlier times and finding that they provide many insights into Lakota history and culture.

In addition to the emphasis placed upon remembering the narratives, memory aids helped people to recall historical events and other kinds of information. Some of these aids, like the winter counts, are quite elaborate, and some are very simple. Throughout North and South America a variety of devices were used to help recall and maintain tribal histories. Some of these are permanent, for example the carvings on rock walls, but some , like names given to commemorate an event and paintings on tipis or hides, are not. Memory aids are similar in that they are symbolic. Some thing, a sign, a name, or a word represents information which may be an event, a place, or a time, and when the symbolic meaning is forgotten, the information is lost. The figures or marks painted on the hides used as winter counts are sometimes identifiable, but unless we know what the mark stood for and have an explanation of the event, we cannot tell what the symbol means. A tipi-like structure is often used to represent a Sun Dance, but the symbol does not tell why this particular Sun Dance was memorable. Only if the interpretation has been handed down or recorded in some way is it possible to know that the symbol indicates a Sun Dance during which the center pole grew leaves, a very unusual and sacred occurrence. One of the frustrations of working with memory devices is that, unless the meaning of the symbol is handed down, we have no way to find out what the symbol represents. Much information has been lost because the meaning of paintings on robes or tipi covers has been forgotten.

Another difficulty in working with symbols is that they are often personal or individualized. Not only did each tribe have different symbolic systems, but each tribal historian employed his own set of symbols and explanations, and so we have practically no way to use the memory devices of one group to help us interpret another's.

There are numerous examples of memory devices used by northern Plains tribes. Paintings on hides served a number of different purposes. Some paintings recorded personal experiences or records, particularly military actions. Some paintings were vision experiences or protective devices, while other paintings, usually more complex and more detailed than the other kinds, were winter-counts or records of events marking the years.

One of the most famous hide paintings is the battle scene painted by the Mandan Chief, Four Bears (Mato-Topa) on a buffalo hide robe. He was so proud of his war record that he made a copy of the robe for Prince Maximilian and another for George Catlin. Both men recorded Four Bears' account of his war exploits. One scene depicts a fight between Four Bears and a Cheyenne. The story goes that the Mandan were on a military expedition when they met four Cheyennes with horses. The Cheyenne leader, noting that the Mandan were on foot, dismounted to make the fight more equal, and the two parties began to fight. The chiefs, after firing their guns at each other, seized their weapons for hand-to-hand combat. The Cheyenne had a knife, and Four Bears had an axe. Although Four Bears was wounded, he managed to get the knife away from the Cheyenne and stabbed him. The Cheyenne ran away, and Four Bears made a wooden model of the knife to wear in his hair and painted the exploit on

Figure 3.2. The fight between Four Bears and a Cheyenne was recorded on a robe. This illustration is based on a sketch by George Catlin.

his robe (Thomas and Ronnefeldt 1976:203). The scene (Fig. 3.2) painted on the robe shows Four Bears grabbing the knife of the Cheyenne and bleeding from the cut he received. In Four Bears' hand is his tomahawk and he is aiming it at the Cheyenne's head.

Winter counts, a translation of the Dakota *waniyetu wowapi* "winter record" or *waniyetu yawapi* "winter count," combined calendars with historical record-keeping. Each year or "winter" a memorable event would be selected and recorded on a hide kept specifically for the purpose (Fig.3.3). The record was in the form of a pictograph or symbol which helped to recall the event. The keeper of the count would compose a brief description of the event. For example, in 1833 there was a remarkable meteor shower over the plains, and many tribes chose this as the memorable event of the year. Often referred to as "the year the stars fell," the meteors are indicated by stars, by dots, or by other means. No date is given for the year, but astronomical records supply the date, 1833. Because the event was so unusual and affected so many different tribal groups, historians have been able to use it to date accounts that would otherwise remain undecipherable. Most years, however, had no immediately identifiable memorable events and so different methods were used to select the marker for the year. Sometimes the event was selected by the council of elders, and sometimes the choice was left to the discretion of the record keeper. One man would be in charge of the winter count. As the man got older some younger person would be taught the events that were symbolized on the hide and the information would be passed on.

Deloria (1974b:12) has suggested that the events recorded in the winter counts were significant only to the band or family keeping the count, but historians may also argue that these are equal to the journals or diaries kept by immigrants to the northern plains and are filled with the small details that made life interesting. Howard (1976:2) has demonstrated that close examination of a winter count can

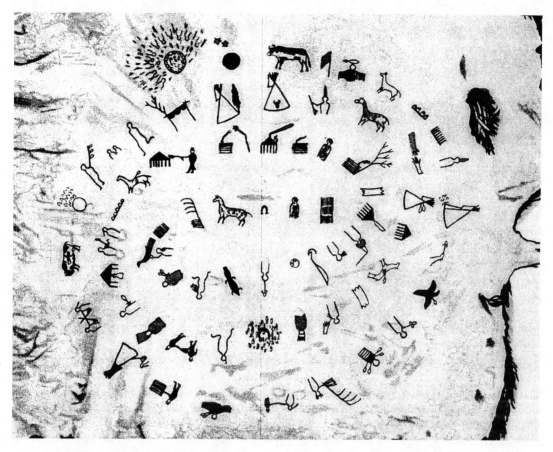

Figure 3.3. Lone Dog's Winter Count was copied onto hide for Scholarly study.

provide a great deal of information relevant to tribal history. Despite the variations in the counts, from keeper to keeper and from tribe to tribe, these counts are true sources of plains Indian history. They include those events which were considered important to the tribes, not to White people. The counts contain a wide variety of information and provide insights into traditional culture. The Battiste Good winter count (Mallery 1893:293-328) contains much information about horses and conflicts between people of different tribes, but the account also mentions *heyoka*, or contrary soldiers, and *winkte*, a man who dressed and acted like a woman. Death by starvation was common in many years. Later the presence of white military and the distribution of blankets and other goods are mentioned in Good's account. Most historians, however, have ignored these accounts or included them as interesting items but irrelevant to the writing of Indian history.

The winter counts contain information of interest to non-Natives, too, because they mention natural phenomena, such as the giant meteor shower, heavy snows, diseases, like the smallpox and cramping diseases which struck the Lakota, and geographical information. The winter counts report on the introduction of the horse and gun into various Plains tribes and describe the establishment of trading posts among some of the tribes. The presence of missionaries and white women are also noted in some counts.

The Chippewa used birch bark rather than hide as a recording medium and made much more use of rock art than did the Plains tribes. Probably the most important records of the Chippewa are the birch bark scrolls used in the Midewiwin or Medicine Lodge Ceremony. These scrolls indicated the various steps a person passed through in order to become a fully initiated member of the lodge. Selwin Dewdney, (1975) who made a study of the scrolls, has suggested that the scrolls not only refer to the Midewiwin and carry symbols and information about the ceremony but that they are also maps of the migration of the Chippewa. The relationship between the Midewiwin and the migration of the Chippewa from the Atlantic to Minnesota has been shown in the origin tradition. Dewdney's suggestion that these scrolls are maps and that the Midewiwin has historic, as well as religious significance, is intriguing. Utilizing the scrolls as maps, Dewdney has traced the route of the Chippewa along the Great Lakes to Leech Lake.

For the Chippewa and other tribes north of the Great Lakes, rock art was an important means of recording information. The Chippewa distinguished between signs that were generally known, such as direction signs, and those whose meanings were known only to the initiated. The former was termed *kekeewin* and the latter *kekeenowin* (Mallery 1893:35). Some of the signs painted or carved on the rock walls undoubtedly had historical significance; unfortunately, they are difficult to decipher today. Dewdney (1975:172) has suggested that large numbers of rock paintings appear to match the locations where the Chippewa are said to have rested during their migrations. Using the sacred scrolls as maps, Dewdney has attempted to match the rock art with the resting places indicated on the scrolls. The results are inconclusive but thought-provoking. Some of the rock paintings are like the symbols used on the scrolls, but we have no way to demonstrate that the two are related.

Rock art is also common along the western periphery of the plains where rock walls and boulders provide suitable surfaces. Like the paintings done on hide, rock art is symbolic and often difficult to interpret, but evidence from recent times establishes that the artists were recording significant events. In Montana, the Explorer's Petroglyph (24ML402) shows two White men in a boat. Cramer (1974) has attempted to demonstrate that this is an Indian depiction of William Clark's boat trip down the Yellowstone in 1806. The Joliet Petroglyphs (24CB402) also appear to date from historic times, but they depict battle scenes, dances and warriors. The details on these petroglyphs are so exact that the artist must have been recording an actual event. Some of the rock art in Wyoming and Montana has been tied to specific tribes, but most remains a fascinating puzzle.

One of the common myths about tribal naming practices is that a child was named for the first thing a mother saw after the child was born. In fact names were considered to be very important and were given only after much thought and prayer. The right name could make a child healthy, while the wrong one might make it sick. Names were also used as an aid in recalling events, particularly those of importance to an individual or a family. Tribal names were not permanent but could be changed for many different reasons. Some names were earned or awarded on the basis of performance. Wolf Chief's boyhood name was Coming Thunder, given to him by his grandfather in commemoration of the sacred Waterbuster bundle which was associated with thunder. Among the Lakota, the children's first names were based on their position in the family: first son, second son, first daughter, second daughter, and others in the line of birth. These names were used to refer to the individual until a new name was given. In receiving a different name, the child might be given one that referred to some particular character-istic of that child or that reflected the good wishes of the family for the child's future. If the child did not seem strong, a new name might be given in the hope that the new name would better suit the child. Buffalo Bird Woman was first given the name Good Way, but her father renamed her Buffalo Bird Woman because she was a sickly child, and it was thought the new name might give her more strength (Wilson 1921:8). As a boy got older, he might be given a name formerly used by an old man. Such a name could be a symbol or reminder of an honor or event in the life of the elderly person. As the person aged, he might choose to give away his name rather than have it die with him. Thus these names, handed down to others, came to be reminders of significant events in the history of the tribe or band. A grandparent would often pass a name on to a grandchild in order to keep the name in the family. Although Lame Deer received his great-grandfather's name in a vision, he was reminded of an event in the life of his namesake.

> I saw that this was my great-grandfather, Tahca Ushte, Lame Deer, old man chief of the Minneconju. I could see the blood dripping from my great grandfather's chest where a white soldier had shot him. I understood that my great-grandfather wished me to take his name (Lame Deer 1972:16).

The re-use of names, particularly the giving of a name to a non-related person, has been confusing to non-Indian historians and has often made it difficult to know which individual is being discussed. Wolf Chief was originally the name of a Hidatsa warrior who was known to Maximilian and may have been the uncle of Coming Thunder, who took the name Wolf Chief when he became a successful warrior. In this instance, the passage of time between the use of the names helps to keep the individuals separated. On the other hand, for traditional Tribal Peoples the event is more important than the individual and using names in this way fits into tribal historical concepts. In addition, the re-use of names also confirms the cyclical nature of tribal history.

Names of villages or bands were also related to origin stories or had historical significance. Among the Arikara one of the villages was called Awahu "Left Behind" because it was located at the end of a string of twelve villages (Gilmore 1927a:347). Another village was known as "Coyote Fat" because of some particular event in its history. The divisions of the Dakota were named according to their habitat or some particular characteristic. The Mdewakantonwan band lived near Spirit Lake in Minnesota. The Wahpekute lived and hunted among the leaves, or deciduous trees, as did the Wahpeton. The Teton lived on the prairies. The names of the divisions of these groups also reflect historical events. Thus Sicanju referred to a time when members of the division were burned and Itazipcho referred to a situation in which members were caught without their bows when they needed them (Sneve 1973:2-3).

The different methods of recording information reflect different concepts and methods employed by Indian historians. The availability of Indian history will vary from tribe to tribe and division to division; it is important to approach it with an awareness of the variation and an appreciation of the differences rather than rejecting oral histories, winter counts and other materials because they are different from non-Indian documents. Such materials are documents, too, and have a vital purpose in maintaining tribal history.

One of the difficulties faced by non-Indians who want to use Native American histories is the difference between Indian and non-Indian ideas about history. Tribal oral traditions differ from non-Indian in not distinguishing between humans and other creatures of the earth and supernatural phenomena. In this respect, Native traditions are comparable to the Bible and other religious works. Indian oral traditions account for the origin of people and animals and for the origin of sacred ceremonies. Animals and humans influenced each other and shared many events. Coyote often appears as an initiator of action. He is able to assume human form, just as some humans are able to assume other forms. This connection between the animal and the human world was part of tribal beliefs in the commonality of all creatures and explains why Indians regarded themselves kin to the animals. However, this concept makes it difficult for Euro-Americans to deal with tribal historical traditions. Since Euro-Americans have been taught to reject anything which does not appear to have objective reality, most historians ignore the oral traditions or classify them as folklore rather than history.

Another characteristic which differentiates tribal historical concepts from Euro-American concepts is a lack of concern with the details of events. To Native historians, the results were much more important than the event. Deloria (1974b:113) has pointed out that each tribe has cultural heroes, individuals who greatly changed the course of events of the tribe. These culture heroes often have superhuman traits, but unlike Euro-American culture heroes, Indians have little concern for these people as individuals. Whereas the disciplines of biography and of historical analysis center around the backgrounds, personalities and lives of important people, American Indians do not consider this information to be significant. White Buffalo Calf Woman, one of the most important individuals in Lakota history, brought the pipe and its ceremonies to the Lakota. Nothing is known about White Buffalo Calf Woman as an individual other than her beauty which served to demonstrate her supernatural powers. Nor is there a concern about such details. White Buffalo Calf Woman's gifts are important. People know how the pipe came to the Lakota, how the ceremonies are conducted and the sacred meaning of the pipe and ceremonies, but no one ever seeks to know more about White Buffalo Calf Woman as a personality. There are no debates over her exact looks or attempts to reconstruct her life story. The concern is with the event, and how it affected the Lakota. By emphasizing the event and not the details, people find history easier to recall. Since these histories were oral, eliminating details made them easier to teach to children and others.

Euro-Americans, however, expect historical details to be exact and often rely on details to help them determine the accuracy of a document or account. From the non-Indian perspective, then, tribal narratives are not considered to be historical documents because the details may vary from narrator to narrator. The event and the effect of the event will remain the same, but details may vary.

Places assume a great significance in tribal history. This influence may be related to the traditional attitude of concern for the land. Many locations were sacred because of the events that occurred there or because the supernatural seemed to be very close at that site. Warm springs or unusual rock formations were obviously areas of special power which figured prominently in Indian histories. Traveling from place to place, the people were concerned with the events that occurred at certain locations, with knowing where specific locations were and with relating places to people. Often survival depended upon knowing where game animals could always be found or where fresh water would be available during the driest summers. Place, then, assumed great importance in Indian history. Bowers reports that the Hidatsa told him that

> ...It was the custom of many families to return to living sites and to point out to the younger people the depressions of lodges where certain relatives had lived, their graves, or earth rings on the prairies where various ceremonies such as the Naxpike or Wolf ceremonies were held (Bowers 1965:2).

Such customs suggest the importance of place in the history of the tribe. A similar attitude toward place is also evident in the placement of the Nueta Congregational Church in the center of the former Sun Dance lodge circle (Case 1977:115).

The histories developed using these concepts are oral histories that account for the origins of the earth, of humans and animals, of sacred ceremonies as well as migrations, wars and events which are more often considered by Anglo-European historians to be the real stuff of history.

Every people's sacred stories provide many answers to the numerous questions that people naturally ask. Each group answers the questions differently because the answers reflect the location and culture of a particular group. The belief in these traditions provides the security of faith and gives people strength to face the unknown.

BUFFALO BIRD WOMAN (MAXIDIWIAC)

Buffalo Bird Woman, Hidatsa, was born around 1840 in a Hidatsa village on the Missouri River. Her grandfather, Missouri River, was keeper of one of the important sacred bundles and when she was about four years old, he was chosen to lead the search for a new location for the village (Wilson 1934:351-353). Missouri River laid the village out in a sacred manner and for forty years Like-a-Fishhook Village was a commercial and administrative center for Hidatsa and Mandan people and, later, for the Arikara.

Buffalo Bird Woman's other grandfather, Big Cloud, was a good hunter and religious man, who had Otter and Turtle for wives. Buffalo Bird Woman was closest to her grandmother, Turtle. Turtle had four daughters, Wiati, Corn Stalk, Strikes Many Women and Red Blossom. These four daughters married Small Ankles, Buffalo Bird Woman's father. The family was large by modern standards, although not unusually so by Indian standards. Buffalo Bird Woman had six brothers and one sister (Gilman and Schneider 1987:21).

When she was 16, Buffalo Bird Woman married Magpie. She described to Gilbert Wilson (Gilman and Schneider 1987:108-110) how Magpie's family arranged the wedding. Magpie's father, Hanging Stone, first approached Small Ankles and his two wives, saying, "I wish my boy to live in your good family." In the evening, Hanging Stone and his wives brought four outfitted horses and three guns to Buffalo Bird Woman's earth lodge. This first offer was rejected, but a later offer with better horses was accepted. Small Ankles knew Magpie and thought that he would make a good husband. Buffalo Bird Woman agreed and her family set to work preparing a feast, a feather bonnet, and other gifts to give to Magpie's family. When all was ready, Buffalo Bird Woman, her sister Cold Medicine, and other members of her family went to Hanging Stone's lodge, carrying all the gifts. The groom's family sent word to all the relatives to come to the feast. The relatives brought gifts, too. In the evening the gifts were sent by the groom's family to the bride's family and they were distributed to the relatives that had helped prepare the feast. A few days later Buffalo Bird Woman and Cold Medicine went to bring Magpie to their lodge where they had prepared a bed and Small Ankles had provided a horse. Girls who were married by gift exchange "were those who had parents to look after them," said Buffalo Bird Woman. The other way for a couple to marry was for them to go off together. Men preferred the second way because they did not have to give gifts.

After thirteen years of marriage, Magpie died of tuberculosis. Even though she knew that Son of a Star was interested in her, Buffalo Bird Woman waited to marry again. When her mourning period was finished, Son of a Star offered four horses and her parents agreed. This marriage lasted until Son of a Star's death at an advanced age.

Buffalo Bird Woman had one son, Goodbird. Goodbird grew up in a time when government agencies and missionaries were beginning to affect Hidatsa culture. Goodbird attended school and later became a Congregational minister at Independence. When Goodbird was 16 years old, the family, along with the other residents of Like-a-Fishhook Village, left the village and moved across the Missouri River to set up farms (Wilson 1914:55). The families of Buffalo Bird Woman, her brother, Wolf Chief, and other relatives settled in an area they called Independence. Here, Goodbird became a farmer and was hired by the agent as an assistant farmer (Wilson 1914:59-60) before receiving his calling as a minister.

Unlike Goodbird, Buffalo Bird Woman paid little attention to the presence of non-Indians and their ways. She never spoke English and never gave up her hold on traditional ways. Toward the end of her life she was approached by Reverend Gilbert Wilson who asked if she would teach him about pre-reservation Hidatsa culture. Goodbird was enlisted as interpreter and, for twelve summers, Buffalo Bird Woman and Wolf Chief described how objects were made and used, showed how gardens were planted, told stories and provided details on pre-reservation Hidatsa culture that are not available anywhere else. Wilson (1924:130) wrote: "Her patience and loyal interest in these studies have been invaluable. On a sweltering August day she has dictated for nine hours, never flagging, though often lying prone on the cabin floor when too weary to sit longer in a chair."

Buffalo Bird Woman died in the 1920's without knowing that her tremendous effort to record information for later generations would become so significant. She was aware that times were changing, but little did she think that her words would be used by Hidatsa and others as a source of personal and cultural history that have been essential in reviving traditional customs.

Chapter 4

Scientific Studies of Aboriginal Origins

Scientists and geologists also ask the question "Where did Indians come from?", but they look for the answer in physical evidence. For more than a century the search has focused on stone and bone tools, pottery, and other long-lasting materials. Much of the archaeological research still relies on the usual materials, but genetic studies and others are also providing new information concerning the origin of Tribal Peoples.

On the basis of currently available information, scientists have placed the origin of human beings in Africa approximately four million years ago (Leakey and Levin 1977:88). From their point of origin, these early humans spread into Europe and Asia, where adaptations to different environments resulted in the many different cultures and languages now known throughout the world. Sometime before 25,000 years ago, some of the people living in northeastern Siberia crossed from Asia into what is now Alaska. These people adapted to the new environments of North and South America and became the original inhabitants of the continents.

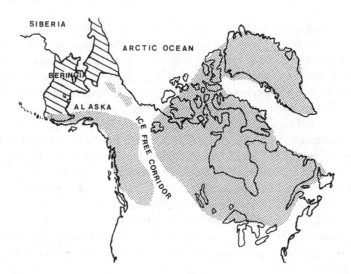

Figure 4.1. Scientists believe that thousands of years ago, glaciers covered the northern half of North America and lowered the ocean levels so much that Alaska and Siberia were connected. This land bridge, called Beringia, would have allowed men and animals to move from Asia into North America and vice versa, but most of the time the way into the interior was blocked by glaciers. Twice, between 32,000 to 36,000 and 20,000 to 28,000 years ago, the glaciers melted enough to leave a corridor enabling the first humans to reach North America.

The distance between Asia and Alaska is as short as 55 miles, and scientists have suggested several ways in which people could have traversed this passage. Even today, polar bears and other arctic animals move between the continents by crossing the polar ice cap in winter. It is possible that the people who became Native Americans crossed the Bering Strait in boats or walked across the ice, but the woolly mammoth, giant moose, and other large game animals must have moved from Asia into America by foot. Geologists have hypothesized that Asia and Alaska were once connected by a wide, grassy, tundra-like plain, which they call Beringia, formed when the glaciers that covered Europe, Asia, and North America lowered the water level of the oceans. The animals seeking food and water in this area would have crossed into North America without knowing it. Following the herds, small groups of hunters also crossed into America. The population grew quickly and soon people reached all the way to the tip of South America.

The geological evidence for the glaciers and the lowering of the sea level is well accepted, but the archaeological evidence for human beings entering the New World is the source of much disagreement because single artifacts or human remains have not provided dates that can be accepted unquestionably. Some scientists believe that there was a single migration. Others think that there were several migrations. Most agree that the Eskimo were a much later arrival, but whether they were the second or the last of many small groups to arrive is often debated.

Some researchers have been looking at other sources of information to provide answers to the origin question. People first recognized physical similarities between Native American and Asian populations. Straight, dark hair, high cheek bones, a broad face, brown eyes and the presence of a sacral spot in newborns were common to both groups. As research progressed and scientists were able to conduct more detailed studies, studies of blood types and, more recently, genes provided more information. Not all of the information fits together and not all of it is accepted by all researchers, but it is worth reporting.

We have known about different blood types for many years. In these studies, some populations have greater frequencies of A, B, or O blood types. Northeast Asians, those most likely to have moved into North America, often have B blood type, but it is rare among Native Americans (Turner 1989:88). More recent studies, however, show similarities between Asians and Native Americans.

One new source of information is genetic comparisons. If Native Americans are descended from ancient Asian populations there ought to be some genetic similarities between the two groups. Luigi Luca Cavalli-Sforza (1991) and his colleagues have studied the worldwide distribution of more than 100 inherited characteristics and have organized them into family trees that they believe reflect the spread of humans throughout the world. One of the oldest and most completely known genetic differences is the blood antigen known as the Rh factor. This factor is either positive, Rh+, or negative, Rh-. The Rh factor is a significant health issue, because an Rh-negative mother who is carrying an Rh-positive fetus will have difficulty delivering a healthy child, unless corrective steps are taken. The frequency of Rh-negative genes is much greater in Europe than it is in other parts of the world. It is almost absent in Asian and Native American populations. By subtracting the percentage of Rh-negative individuals from different populations, scientists calculate which populations have been separated longest from each other.

Much more refined studies of genetic distance use mitochondrial DNA, other genes, serum proteins, immunoglobulins and many other physical characteristics of humans. As our analytical techniques improve, other studies will undoubtedly provide more information on physical similarities and differences between Asian and American Indian populations.

Another source of information attracting much attention is dental patterns. Christy G. Turner (Turner 1989; Greenberg, Turner, Zegura 1986:480) has defined 28 patterns of tooth root and shape which he believes vary across time and space. He found that in some populations, the front teeth are curved rather than straight, a characteristic known as shovel-shaped incisors. Turner calls groups that have this trait Sinodonts and groups without the trait are called Sundadonts. American Indians fall into the Sinodont group (Turner 1989:90). Turner (Greenberg, Turner, Zegura 1986:480) draws four major conclusions from his analysis.

1. All New World populations resemble each other more than they do most Old World populations.

2. Dental variation is greater in the north than it is in the south.

3. New World groups are more like Asians than like Europeans.

4. Aleut-Eskimos, greater Northwest Coast Indians (Na-Dene) and all other Indians (Macro-Indian) form three New World dental clusters.

From this information Turner postulates that there were three separate migrations into North America, but all were of the same basic stock of people since all have the Sinodont dental pattern (Greenberg, Turner, Zegura 1986:480). A second migration brought in Northwest Coast and interior Athabaskan speakers, now called Na-Dene. The third wave was the Eskimo. All of these entries occurred in ancient times and each group developed distinctive ecological adaptations and cultures.

Scholars using these innovative approaches to American Indian origins often look to linguistic evidence to contradict or confirm their findings (Cavalli-Sforza 1991:104). Language relationships are thought to operate on the same principles of changing over time and space as the physical characteristics, but they serve as an independent check on the findings from the other data. Some scholars believe that the linguistic data confirms the other studies, but many scholars do not agree.

Linguistics

The study of similarities and differences between languages can provide information relevant to human prehistory. Linguists who specialize in historical linguistics analyze the similarities and differences between languages and identify ancient relationships and reconstruct ancient languages. This work is complex and difficult and often speculative, but the results can be fascinating. The assumptions underlying the work of these linguists are that languages change over time and that these changes are patterned and can be identified through comparisons between languages. Much historical linguistics has centered on European languages and in determining the relationships between them, but sufficient work has been done with North American Indian languages to provide information that can be related to the archaeological and oral traditions.

The first requirement in the study of language relationships is either a living speaker of the language or a word list, dictionary or lexicon for the language to be studied. North American Indian languages were not written languages, and much attention has been focused upon writing dictionaries and grammars for these languages. This work is done by descriptive linguists. Descriptive linguists work with people who speak the language fluently. Using the phonetic alphabet, a system of symbols used to represent sounds, linguists can reproduce on paper the sounds of a spoken language. By this method a spoken language becomes a written language. Not all American Indian languages have been written and for many languages the last native speaker has died, and so the language will never be fully known. Early missionaries and interested people often collected examples of words, and sometimes these are all that remain of a native language. Since these early people were not trained linguists, their symbols are not always accurate and this inaccuracy often creates difficulty in understanding how the word or phrase was actually spoken. Other North American Indian languages are well known and have word lists, dictionaries, grammars and living speakers who can provide information about the language. Most North American Indian languages fall between these two extremes which makes the work of the historical linguist perplexing. Often the historical linguist must first compile the materials needed to make the analysis.

Establishing Relationships Between Languages

The historical analysis of language proceeds through a series of steps which are designed to prove relationships between languages and to enable the reconstruction of former languages. The first recognition of language similarities is usually similarities between words. For example, the Lakota word for woman, *winyan* or *wea* is similar enough to the Hidatsa word for woman, *wia* or *mia* to suggest some kind of a relationship between the two languages. Finding additional similarities, like the word for water , Lakota = *mni* or *mini*, Hidatsa = *midi*, and the word for dog, Lakota = *sunka*, Hidatsa = *masuka*, strengthens the idea of a connection. The Lakota word *tipi* and the Mandan word *ti* both meaning "house" or "dwelling", imply another set of related languages. In order to determine how closely related two languages may be, linguists have devised a list of two hundred words for common items: sun, stone, tree, parts of the body such as hand, head, eye, common activities such as breathe, die, dig, drink, eat, and descriptive words such as big, dirty, dry, long, straight, green, white and black which are likely to be found in all languages. To compare two languages, the researcher lists the words for these items in each of the languages to be compared. Table 4.1 shows how three related European, Romance, languages compare. Table 4.2 compares three Algonquian languages. Rules for determining whether the words represent true similarities, follow a relatively simple procedure. After the lists have been made, the number of words which are the same in both languages can be counted.

Since similarities cannot be accidental, there must have been some historical connection between the languages. The possibilities for connections are limited. The languages were either a single language at one time, were near enough to have influenced each other through borrowing or were similarly influenced by another language (Chafe 1968). Usually, distinguishing between these possibilities involves considerable work on the part of the linguist, but some tribes have oral histories which tell of the relationship between two tribes and their languages.

The Pawnee and the Arikara tribes each recognize that they were once a single tribe and that their languages are still very similar to each other (Parks 1979:202). Hidatsa and Crow people also recognize that they were once one tribe (Lowie 1956:134) and have traditions regarding their separation. When oral histories confirm language relationships, the work of the linguist is made a little easier, although many questions always remain to be answered through further research. When historical knowledge about tribal relationships is lacking, there are ways to determine the nature of the relationship. One way of substantiating language relationships is by demonstrating that not only are some of the words similar, but the way in which sentences are formed is also similar. Not only should single words match, but similarities in the way words are formed, in the use of suffixes and prefixes, case endings, verb formation and the overall patterns of the languages themselves should be found. While it is possible for single words to be borrowed from one language to another, probably whole grammatical structures will not be borrowed, and so studies of grammars can demonstrate suspected language relationships. Both Lakota and Hidatsa languages show some similarities in their grammatical structures and this supports the idea that the languages were once related. In both languages the adjectives follow the nouns and pronouns, for example Mato topa, Four Bears, while the adverbs usually precede the words they modify. If all the words and all the grammatical rules were the same for both languages we could conclude that we were dealing with dialects of the same language, but, in fact, the differences between Lakota and Hidatsa are much greater than the similarities, which leads to the conclusion that the languages may have descended from the same language but that they have been separated for hundreds of years. On the other hand, the similarities between Dakota and Lakota are so close that speakers of the two languages are able to understand each other by making allowances for differences in pronunciation, so these may be considered dialects.

Table 4.1. Examples of Related Words in Romance languages (Yuen Ren Chao 1968:86).

French	Spanish	Portuguese	Meaning
main	mano	mao	hand
deux	dos	dois	two
homme	hombre	homen	man
dent	diente	dente	tooth
blanc	blanco	branco	white

Table 4.2. Examples of Related Words in Algonquian languages (Bloomfield 1933:359,381-381).

Fox	Menomini	Ojibwa	Meaning
askutE:wi	esko:tE:w	iskudE:	Fire
mahkesE:hi	mahkE:sen	mahkizin	Moccasin
neniwa	enE:niw	inini	Man
ehkwa	ehkuah	ihkwa	Louse

Very detailed comparisons, including sounds as well as grammatical differences, have been carried out by Joel Sherzer (1976). For sounds, Sherzer notes that the use of nasalized vowels is a family trait of Siouan languages (Sherzer 1976:170) and for grammar, Sherzer notes that no languages in the plains distinguish between masculine and feminine gender (as most European languages do) and that Algonquian languages distinguish between animate and inanimate gender (Sherzer 1976:178). Such comparisons can help to confirm historical relationships between languages.

Using the kinds of information available from these detailed analyses, languages can be grouped into families of related languages. A language family can be likened to a family tree, with some languages more closely related than others. The fact that a language is included in a group of related languages does not mean that the two languages are mutually intelligible, only that they were apparently related at some time in the past or that they are descended from a common ancestral language. The family tree diagrams for Siouan and Algonquian languages (Fig. 4.2, Fig. 4.3) indicate the more closely related languages by the shortness of the lines while the more distantly related languages are separated by longer lines. Because Dakota, Nakota and Lakota are so closely related they are mutually intelligible, they are found on the same line. Mandan and Dakota are very distantly related. One other point of confusion about language families is that the families are often named from some known group. Thus the Siouan language family is sometimes confused with the ethnic group Sioux, and people take the idea of speaking a Siouan language to mean that all the tribes in the family speak the same language. A person who speaks Hidatsa does not speak Sioux, but the Hidatsa language is a member of the Siouan language family.

Table 4.3. North Dakota Language Families

SIOUAN LANGUAGE FAMILY

Dakota

Lakota

Yankton - Yanktonai

Mandan

Hidatsa

CADDOAN LANGUAGE FAMILY

Arikara

ALGONQUIAN LANGUAGE FAMILY

Chippewa

The languages found in North Dakota today (Table 4.3) represent several different language families. The family tree diagrams also show that all of the languages spoken in North Dakota are related to languages found in other parts of North America. Speakers of Siouan languages are also found in the southern plains and in the southeastern United States. Algonquian speakers are a very large group, ranging from the Rockies to the Atlantic Coast. Caddoan speakers are also found on the southern plains. Finding related languages in other parts of the country suggests that groups of people moved from one part of the country to another. Some of the Siouan-speakers have a migration story that they came from the east, and the presence of Siouan languages on the east coast tends to support this claim. The Mandan tradition that they originated near the mouth of the Mississippi is partially supported by the fact that the Ofo and Biloxi languages once spoken by people along the Mississippi gulf coast are distantly related to the Mandan language. Language relationships, then, can be helpful in gaining some idea of where different groups might have originated.

Linguists are interested in more than establishing language relationships. They want to know how long these relationships have existed and what the original language was like.

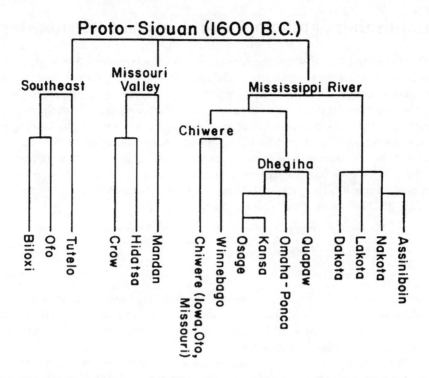

Figure 4.2. Family tree of Siouan language family showing descent from original or Proto-language. After Grimm (1985).

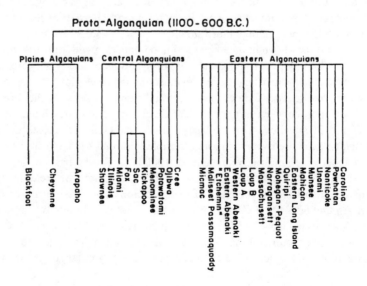

Figure 4.3. Family tree of Algonquian language family showing descent from original or Proto-language. After Goddard (1978a, 1978b).

Establishing Chronologies for Language Relationships

The study of time and language relationships is called glottochronology. The study of the original language is called comparative reconstruction. Glottochronology uses a formula and the comparative word list mentioned earlier to determine how long two languages have been separated. The formula is based upon the assumption that language change proceeds at a fixed rate and that the degree of difference between two languages can indicate the length of separation between the languages. At first, changes are in the nature of dialect differences, but later these dialect differences may become so pronounced that the languages will be mutually unintelligible. Imagine that the differences between New York and New Orleans English become so great that, after many generations, people no longer understand each other at all. The question is, how many generations would it take?

The formula that has been worked out is (Gudschinsky 1956):

$$T = \log C / (2 \log r)$$

C = percent of cognates

r = constant of .805

The cognates, words which are similar in the two languages, are counted, and the percent of similarity is then calculated. The word list is usually two hundred words, but some have used a word list of one hundred words. The two hundred word list produces more accurate results and is preferred, but data limitations often make adjustments necessary.

The formula will give a general idea of how long the languages have been separated. In slightly easier terms, it appears that even after 1000 years a language will still have 80% of the words it started with. Twenty percent of the words will be different from the original (Price 1978:31). Linguists have tried different ways of calculating the percent of cognates and have tried to make the process more accurate, but the basic problem lies in the assumption that all languages change at the same rate. We find it difficult to support this claim because we know from modern experiences that some languages change very rapidly while others change more slowly.

The procedure is most useful when it can be used in conjunction with oral traditions and archaeological evidence. Sometimes glottochronological dates have correlated nicely with archaeological dates, but more often the two dates do not coincide. When most linguists give glottochronological dates, they either give a range or provide several dates in order to indicate their sense of the differences.

The length of separation between Pawnee and Arikara ranges from three hundred to five hundred years. Parks (1979:205-307) believes, on the basis of historical evidence, that three hundred years is not enough and that five hundred years is more plausible. Grimm (1985:14) suggests that Crow and Hidatsa separated about nine hundred years ago, or 1000 A.D. On the basis of his analysis, Grimm (1985:16) thinks that the original Siouan speakers separated into three different groups around 1600 B.C. These groups are identified on the basis of their location as Mississippi River, Missouri Valley and Southeastern. Around 600-400 B.C. each of these three groups split into two or more new groups. The Missouri Valley separated into the Mandan and Hidatsa and the Mississippi River separated into the Dakota-Lakota-Nakota group and the Dhegiha, Chiwere and Winnebago groups. The next divisions came around 1000 A.D. when these groups separated into the languages we now know from living speakers.

Dating the separation of languages into different languages and dialects is still very speculative, but the information derived, particularly when used in conjunction with other data, can be useful. In addition to knowing when languages differentiated, linguists also want to know what the original language looked like. They use a process called comparative reconstruction to recreate the original language.

Comparative Reconstruction

Comparative reconstruction involves studying the internal changes which have occurred in languages in order to determine what the original or proto-language might have been like. The proto-language is the language from which other related languages would have derived. The basic concept of internal reconstruction is that languages do not change randomly. Changes occur in patterned ways and a change in one aspect of a language will be accompanied by changes in another. Because this is particularly true of sound changes, reconstruction linguists work particularly with sound changes.

Chafe (1968:70-71) has worked on the reconstruction of proto-Siouan. He compared the same words in Dakota, Hidatsa, Mandan, Biloxi and Ofo in order to find out the similarities and differences. For example, the word for "heart" in Dakota is *chata*, in Hidatsa *rata*, in Mandan *natka*, Biloxi *yati* and Ofo *cati*. His analysis showed that, in general, all the languages retained the "a" sound in the same place and on this basis he was able to assume that the original language also used "a". The "t" following the "a" is the same in all five languages and so it is pretty certain that the "t" was also found in the original language. On the other hand, the words are all different in their initial consonants and so Chafe has to guess what the original sound might have been. On the basis of other words in the study he assigns the sound "y" to the first consonant of the proto or reconstructed form for "heart". The final sound also varies, but Chafe assigns it the sound of "e". The resulting word is *yatke, which Chafe suggests is the word from which the other words for "heart" eventually derived. This is a highly simplified description of an extremely complex and lengthy process, but it should help to explain how reconstructing a long ago language can be done.

One reason for doing these reconstructions is that they can provide some clues about the original life style of the speakers of the language and shed further light on the origins of some of the tribes. The assumption behind such studies is that the language will reflect the environment, technology, social organization and religious beliefs of the speakers. Using this idea, studies of proto-Indo-European have provided considerable information about the cultures of the ancient people who eventually became speakers of English, German and other related languages. If the words relating to the environment, kinship, technology and beliefs can be reconstructed, we should learn something about the users of the language. Using this idea, Frank Siebert, Jr. (1967) looked for linguistic evidence of the origin of the Algonquian-speaking people. Siebert listed the words for kinds of animals, birds, fish and trees that were used by the Proto-Algonquian speakers and plotted the distribution of the species identified by these terms. For example, Proto-Algonquian speakers identified both the woods bison and the caribou. The only area in North America where these two species overlap is the area just north and east of the Great Lakes. Using glottochronological evidence Siebert suggests that the Proto-Algonquian-speaking people originated in this area about 1200 B.C. and spread out from there in different directions. Some went south and became the Central Algonquian speakers. Others moved west and are today known as Cheyenne and Blackfeet and Arapaho and Atsina. Others became the Ojibwa or Chippewa. The location identified by Siebert corresponds quite well with the origin traditions of the Chippewa, although the archaeological evidence is not sufficient to corroborate or disprove the idea.

The study of Native American languages can provide information about the history of Native North Americans. So far no demonstrated relationship has been noted between any American Indian language and any Asian, European or African language (Spencer, Jennings, et al. 1977:44), but Joseph H.

Greenberg (Greenberg, Turner, Zegura 1986) thinks he can see some connections between Asian and American Indian languages. From time to time, people who are not linguists make claims about similarities between American Indian words and Japanese, Chinese or Egyptian words, but without more detailed evidence of linguistic similarities, a single word is not sufficient, particularly when the two languages being compared are widely separated in time and space. The great linguistic diversity in North and South America can be attributed to different waves of people reaching the Western hemisphere at different times or to sufficient time for the languages to diversify and become distinct. The archaeological evidence for the antiquity of humans in North and South America tends to support the second reason.

A modern example of language change is occurring in North Dakota (Crawford 1976). Many Algonquian-speaking women, Chippewa or Cree, married French fur traders. In order for these people to communicate, the women either had to learn French or the men had to learn Cree or Chippewa. What developed was a language composed of both Cree/Chippewa and French. This language is called Michif, an Algonquian pronunciation of the French word, Metis, meaning Mixed. Today this language is spoken by many of the residents of Turtle Mountain Reservation, although it is losing in popularity as most school children learn English rather than their native language.

In Michif, the nouns and noun phrases are taken from the French and the verbs are Cree/Ojibwa (Crawford 1976:6). English words have also been incorporated into the language, indicating the ability of the language to change. Until recently, Michif was a spoken language only. Today several programs have been written to produce a Michif dictionary, grammar and other written materials for teaching the language.

The study of languages is very complex and specialized, but the information provided by linguists can be useful evidence for Indian history and prehistory. When used in conjunction with archaeological and other data, linguistics can provide information on the origins, population movements, contacts and culture change of peoples.

Scientists use different methods and materials to answer the question of American Indian origins and pre-history, but the scientific explanations are not as detailed or as complete as the origin traditions, and so many Indian people prefer the traditional answer. Such attitudes also reflect American Indian beliefs about their rightful claim to ownership of the American continent and indicate some of the ways in which tribes have managed to maintain their identities despite three hundred years of contact with non-Indians.

Chapter 5

Plains Life Before European Contact

The first non-Indians to explore the Plains were Spaniards led by Francisco Vazquez de Coronado who entered the southern plains from New Mexico in 1541. The travellers described the region as a "sea of grass" and compared it favorably to Spain. They found it a hospitable environment inhabited by numerous groups of Native Peoples representing two basic lifestyles. Some tribes were exclusively hunters and gatherers, while others also grew some vegetables. Those who planted lived in villages part of the year, while the others lived in tipis year round. The Spaniards noted that those who lived in villages had more possessions than those who were nomadic. None of the people had horses (Hodge 1907).

Later non-Indians exploring the Plains did not find it so welcoming and referred to the area as the Great American Desert. In the mid-1800s scholars came to believe that, despite the evidence from Coronado's expedition and other explorers, the plains could not sustain human life (Wedel 1981:18-19). Historians, anthropologists and other scholars declared that Tribal Peoples had not occupied the plains until the horse became available to them. Clark Wissler, Curator of Anthropology at the American Museum of Natural History and author of many works describing Indian cultures concluded (1914:11) that Plains Indian culture was "of recent origin and developed chiefly by contact with Europeans." He went on to say, "The peopling of the Plains proper was a recent phenomenon due in part to the introduction of the horse." Although this idea of Plains Indian culture as a recent development was introduced over 100 years ago and much evidence contradicting the idea has been uncovered, scholars still include it in their work and use it to interpret Plains Indian culture. Carl Waldman, the author of the very popular *Encyclopedia of Native American Tribes*, (Waldman 1988:189) writes, "The Great Plains Culture Area is different from other Native American culture areas in that the typical Indian way of life evolved only after the arrival of whites. What made the nomadic buffalo-hunting life possible was the horse...." Such statements deprive Plains Indians of their history and support those non-Indians who argue that Plains Indians have no claims to land "because they are newcomers, too."

The truth is that Coronado and his men were observing ways of life that had existed for thousands of years before the horse and gun were introduced. In both North Dakota and the Great Plains archaeologists have uncovered evidence of human occupation dating back to 12,000 years ago. Even more significant, these investigations show that many of the cultural characteristics of Plains Indian life developed long ago and continued into modern times. This chapter will provide a brief history of the development of Plains Indian culture as it existed at the time of the first encounters with Europeans. The emphasis will be on the antiquity of certain customs and traditions, but another goal is to dispel some of the erroneous ideas people have concerning ancient tribal life.

The first requirement for understanding the history of Plains Indian cultural development is a general overview of time depth and cultural development. Archaeologists distinguish different periods and name them according to some distinctive element of the time. The first of these periods is called Paleo-Indian and refers to a way of life that existed during a time when the climate and animals were very different from what we know today. There were mammoths, mastodons, giant sloths, camels, tiny horses and giant bison. The people, however, were neither giants nor cavemen; they were American Indians and their distinctive projectile points are found throughout the Americas. The Paleo-Indian period dates from 12,000 to 8,000 years ago.

Following a change in climate, which saw the large animals of Paleo times disappear or decrease in size, came a time which archaeologists refer to as the Archaic period. During the Archaic people adapted to regional resources and it is easier to distinguish between different groups. There are Plains Archaic People, Desert Archaic People and obvious groupings within these regional groups. The Archaic in the northern plains dates from 8,000 years ago to almost modern times. During this time many changes occurred, but the basic pattern of hunting bison and gathering plant foods remained unchanged.

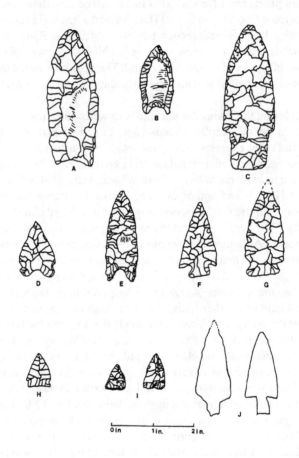

Figure 5.1. Projectile points from North Dakota and nearby areas. A. Clovis (Schneider 1975); B. Folsom (Schneider 1975); C. Alberta (Pettipas 1969); D. Oxbow (Joyes and Jerde 1970); E. McKean (Frison 1978); F. Pelican Lake (Joyes and Jerde 1970); G. Besant (Joyes and Jerde 1970); H. Avonlea (Joyes and Jerde 1970); L. Lake Tewaukon (Haberman 1978); J. Metal points from Deapolis Site (Lehmer 1971).

Some archaeologists feel the Archaic did not end until Indians adopted the gun and the horse. Others feel the Archaic continued until the bison were no longer available in sufficient numbers to sustain tribal peoples.

Around 1 A.D., in some parts of the plains, Archaic peoples adopted new technologies and made other changes in their way of life. This new way of life is called the Woodland culture. Archaeologists do not know whether the changes came about because Archaic people met Woodland people and learned new ideas from them or whether people living this way of life moved into the plains. The new way of life included the bow and arrow, pottery-making, permanent houses, burial in mounds, and extensive trade. Later, limited growing of corn, squash, beans, and sunflowers was adopted. This way of life changed into the Plains Village tradition and continued into historic times, ending either with European trade goods or the reservation way of life.

The Plains Village way of life which appeared around 1000 A.D. was marked by villages along the Missouri River and its tributaries. At first, these villages were composed of long rectangular houses arranged side by side. Some towns had only a dozen houses while others had as many as 30 (Lehmer 1971:69). Some villages were surrounded by sturdy palisades, but others were not. All of these villages show signs of extensive gardening as well as buffalo hunting.

The reason that archaeologists believe that the Archaic and Woodland ways of life continued into recent times is that the basic means by which people earned a living did not change for many centuries. The addition of horses and guns did not change the dependence on the buffalo or stop people from planting their gardens. Only the disappearance of the buffalo and the reservation emphasis on cash crops changed the subsistence pattern.

It is important to note that while the basic way of life remained constant, changes did occur. Some of the changes were stylistic, for example the shift from square houses to round houses and the abandonment of burial mounds for scaffold burials, while others were technological, like pottery and the bow and arrow. Archaic people added the bow and arrow to their technological inventory and continued to use it even after obtaining guns. Euro-Americans sometimes think that their technology was so superior that Tribal Peoples immediately substituted the new for the old, but this was not necessarily the case. The old, flint-lock, muzzle-loading guns were slow to load and could explode, so Indians continued to use bows and arrows and spears, even after guns were available. Buffalo Bird Woman, a Hidatsa elder, recalled that her grandmother, Turtle, refused to give up her buffalo bone hoe even after the other women switched to iron hoes (Wilson 1921:19).

One source of disappointment in studying ancient tribal history is the inability to link sites and other information with known tribal groups. Most people want to know where the Lakota originated or where the Mandan lived. In general, archaeologists do not connect modern tribes with ancient sites, because there is no way to be certain which tribe actually occupied a site. Even though a known tribe may inhabit the region today, other tribes may have been in the area at other times. The Euro-American traders and explorers tried to identify the tribes with whom they interacted and, while they had difficulties with names, we can sometimes link tribes to locations. Meriwether Lewis and William Clark asked the tribes they met on their journey up the Missouri to point out former village sites. From this information, it appears that the North Dakota Historic Site known as On-a-Slant-Village was once occupied by the Mandan. We cannot, however, identify the occupants of the Menoken Site, another North Dakota State Historic Site near Bismarck. Rather than link sites with known tribes, archaeologists identify sites and cultures by names based on some aspect of the site or the evidence and not on tribal names.

Euro-Americans may have wondered how people could live by hunting if they did not have horses or guns, but Native Peoples developed many different ways of taking game. Some of these techniques have a long history. In Paleo-Indian days the people hunted large, elephant-like animals called mammoths. By careful analysis of sites where these animals were trapped, killed and butchered, archaeologists have learned a great deal about ancient hunting techniques. At the Colby site in Wyoming (Frison 1978:109) the bones of six butchered mammoths were stacked in two piles with a mammoth skull on top of one of the piles. There is no evidence indicating how the animals were killed or butchered, nor is it known why the bone piles were made, but it is clear that Paleo-Indians were skillful hunters who successfully stalked, killed and butchered large animals.

Bison hunting also has a great antiquity on the plains. About 11,000 years ago, bison were larger than they are today. There were slight differences between the ancient bison of the northern plains (B. bison occidentalis) and the southern plains (B.bison antiquus), but both eventually merged into the modern, smaller bison (B.bison bison) (Frison 1978:281). As with the hunting of mammoths, size did not deter the Plains Indian hunters. Instead they developed techniques which enabled them to procure large numbers of bison. These techniques continued into modern times.

At the Agate Basin site bison were directed into an arroyo and forced to move through it so hunters perched on the banks could kill them. They may have used spears or long-shafted darts thrown using an atlatl (Frison 1978:150,153). Butchering the dead animals took place further up the arroyo. The separation of kill site, butchering site and living site was characteristic of later Plains Indians. In general, people did not live at the places where they killed the animals, but did gross butchering and then moved the large pieces to another place for processing. The prepared pieces were then taken back to the home site. This not only served to keep the living place clean, but also kept predators away from the main camp.

Driving bison over cliffs and trapping them in corrals probably developed very early, too. By the middle of the Archaic, bison jumps were in use in many parts of the plains. Some of these continued to be used until the reservation period. One such site is the Kobold Site in eastern Montana (Frison 1978:208).

Driving bison requires the cooperation of a significant number of people. The basic technique is for some hunters to go to the rear of the herd and stampede them toward a cliff. The herd is directed to the falling off place by other people hidden behind piles of stones. Still more hunters wait at the bottom of the cliff to kill the bison that are wounded in the fall from the cliff. It is not possible to date the drive lines at the Kobold site, but George Frison believes they are more recent than the earliest bison kills at the site. If he is correct, then people drove the bison toward the cliff without the protection of stones. They may have waved hides or stacked up piles of brush. All this cooperation was necessary because bison are very smart and quick and without a great deal of pressure would escape rather than fall over the cliff.

The advantage of driving bison over a cliff was that large numbers could be killed in relative safety. At a late prehistoric jump site, possibly used by Crow Indians, 200 animals were killed (Frison 1978:238). Most of these animals were butchered, but this was not always the case. When the drop-off was very steep animals at the bottom might be so covered by other bison that they were left without processing. There is evidence from other sites of the hunters taking only tongues, steaks, and other selected cuts. Why eat gristle when you have plenty of steaks?

One other method of killing bison was known to ancient Native Americans, the corral or pound. As indicated by evidence from the Scoggin site, by 4500 years ago, tribal people drove bison down a steep slope into a corral. Archaeologists found the marks of the posts, shored up with stones and bison leg bones, that formed the fence (Frison 1978:211). In later times, the corralling of bison was directed by a sacred man who had the ability to call the bison into the trap (Mandelbaum 1940:190-191). At the Ruby site, which dates around 150 A.D., archaeologists found evidence for a structure next to the corral. Bison skulls were placed around one end of the structure and other bones were found inside. There was no sign of fire or other indication that this had been a house. This structure is interpreted to be a ceremonial center for the sacred leader of the hunt (Frison 1978:220-221).

George Frison (1978) has studied the archaeological evidence for bison hunting and has also carefully observed bison behavior. In his book, *Prehistoric Hunters of the High Plains*, Frison points out that these hunters knew and understood bison very well and that this knowledge informed their hunting techniques. Small groups of hunters could force bison into a trap or a corral, but it took more people and more bison to force a herd over a cliff. The kind of weapon used, a spear, a dart, or the bow and arrow, was also influenced by the hunter's knowledge. Thus, not only did people live on the plains without horses or guns, but over many generations, they became sophisticated and intelligent hunters well able to provide for their families.

The bison were certainly the most important source of meat for ancient hunters, but other animals were utilized too. Prehistoric living sites throughout the plains show a wide variety of animal remains. Sites which date from the late Paleo-Indian times contain bones from camel, deer, wolf, rabbit, moun-

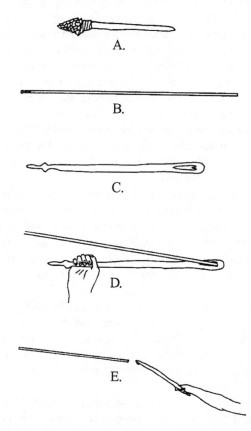

Figure 5.2. The three parts to a dart-throwing system. A. The dart fits into the bound end of the shaft. B. The shaft with bound end to take dart and open end to take atlatl hook. C. The atlatl. D. The shaft fits into the hook on the end of the atlatl. E. The atlatl acts as an extension of the hunter's arm and increases speed and force.

tain sheep, cottontail rabbit, antelope, coyote, swift fox, porcupine, jackrabbit, mule deer, elk and other animals (Gregg 1985:89,91,93). Bones from large birds first appear in early Archaic sites (Gregg 1985:105), but small birds may have also been used. Their bones would be less likely to be preserved.

Ancient Tribal Peoples undoubtedly ate wild plant foods along with their meat, but evidence for this is more difficult to find because floral remains disintegrate quicker than bone or stone. Hackberry seeds found in early Paleo-Indian sites (Gregg 1985:85) imply that these berries were eaten. Grinding stones from these sites suggest that seeds and nuts were being processed into some kind of food. Later sites provide a much more extensive inventory of plant materials, including wild onion, chokecherry and buffalo berry (Gregg 1985:109). Corn, squash and beans do not appear until Woodland or later times, but people certainly had plenty of plant materials to sustain them. Plains Indians well knew the necessity of a balanced diet and a wide variety of plant foods supplemented the meat.

One example of the sophistication of these ancient hunters is found in their hunting technology. Only recently have scientists studied ancient hunting technologies in sufficient depth to become aware of the great developments in that subject. They now distinguish between three major kinds of weapons—the spear, the dart, and the bow and arrow. The basic distinction is made on the basis of projectile points. Large, heavy stone points were probably made for tipping spears. These spears could be thrown although they were equally useful as jabbing or thrusting weapons. A bison might be killed with a thrown spear, but pushing the spear into a vital organ would be much more deadly. Perhaps the cleverest hunting tool was the dart and its associated atlatl or dart thrower. The dart was made of a fine stone or bone point attached to a short pointed shaft. This shaft was inserted into another longer, but lighter, shaft. This shaft often had feathers at the end, like an arrow, to help it fly straight. At the end of this shaft was a hook or hollow that allowed the shaft, with its removable point, to be thrown using an atlatl. Atlatl is an Aztec word for the device that was common throughout North America in the earliest times. The atlatl is a board or leather device that serves to extend the throwing arm and this propels the dart faster and with greater strength than a man could do without it. The replaceable dart meant that a man could reload and fire again. For the Plains Indians, the bow and arrow replaced the dart and atlatl, but it continued to be used in other regions.

People usually think of bows and arrows when they think about Indians, but the bow and arrow was a relatively late development, not coming into the northern plains until after 500 A.D. (Gregg 1985:127). The bow and arrow quickly replaced the atlatl and dart because it was a more efficient weapon (Frison 1978:224). Instead of having to retrieve the shaft in order to reload the dart, the hunter could carry a number of arrows and fire them continuously. In his studies of projectile points embedded in bison bones at kill sites, Frison (1978:223) concluded that the dart and the arrow were equally deadly weapons.

Many of the stone and bone tools known to have been used by post-contact Natives were developed in ancient times. Stone knives, scrapers of various sizes and shapes, chisels, shaft sanders, stone hammers, bone awls, bone scrapers, bone hoes and bone scrapers are only a few of the dozens of tools utilized by the early inhabitants of the plains. These stone and bone tools found in tipi camps and village sites indicate that people worked hides, wood, stone and bone, and generally were creating the same kinds of items as historic tribespeople.

Another technological development was making pottery vessels. Most evidence suggests that this technology entered the plains about the same time as the bow and arrow, but the Naze Site in southeastern North Dakota has pottery dating between 550 and 410 B.C., long before it is found at other sites. In general, pottery making seems to be related to changes in the subsistence pattern. People who lived in tipis and moved a great deal did not always want pottery because it was fragile, but those who lived in villages part of the year could afford the time it took to make the pottery and could manage the care required to keep it from breaking. Animal stomachs and rawhide served as non-breakable containers when people traveled. Archaeologists like to find pottery because its manufacture and decoration are often distinctive and comparisons of the pottery decorations found in different villages can provide information about connections between groups.

Food may be the most necessary requirement for survival, but shelter, especially in regions where temperatures dip well below zero, is also vital. While little is known about the shelters used by the earliest Americans, it is clear that tipis and other houses have a long ancestry on the plains. At the Hanson site (Frison 1978:118-119) investigators uncovered something they think may be floors for some type of shelter. In an area of hard-packed ground, archaeologists found roughly circular, sand covered spots that appear to be places where someone brought in sand to cover the dirt. There are no signs of posts around the edges of the circles and no signs of fireplaces inside them, so it is difficult to positively identify these as floors. If they are floors, then the people may have used brush or some kind of frame that was not anchored in the ground. The Hanson site, dating to around 10,000 years ago (Frison 1978:119), represents one of the earliest examples of how people may have shielded themselves from the weather.

Indications of the use of tipis are first found in the Archaic but, by this time, there is evidence for other structures as well (Gregg 1985:102,109). Scholars believe that the numerous stone circles found throughout the northern plains mark the places where tipi camps once stood. Some historic tribes used

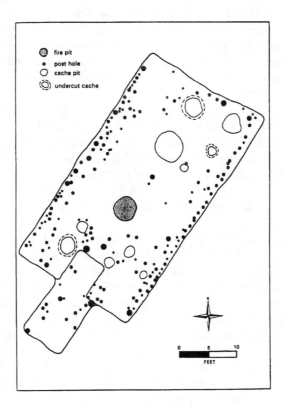

Figure 5.3. A diagram showing the marks of supporting posts, fireplaces, and storage pits that indicate the remains of an ancient rectangular earthlodge. From Lehmer (1971).

stones to hold down the tipi covers when the ground was too hard to drive in pegs (Grinnell 1923:51). These stone circles, usually called tipi rings, are found in small and large groups, often scattered along a ridge near a stream or river. Some of the circles have fireplaces, but many do not. Very little bone or stone refuse or tools occur with these sites so their use is still questioned by some. The rings vary in size and shape and some people believe that not all of them were associated with tipis; some may have been used as ceremonial locations.

Villages do not appear until Woodland times, but there is evidence that some Archaic people may have built houses. At the Red Fox site in western North Dakota investigators found a depression 10 feet square and 6 inches deep. Inside the depression were two fire hearths and a storage pit dug into the ground. This finding has been interpreted as the floor of a house (Syms 1970:134). There are no signs of walls or support posts so the nature of the structure is still unknown.

True houses appear during the transition period between the Archaic and the Woodland, between 100 B.C. to 750 A.D., but it is not until true Woodland times that houses are organized into villages. By 1000 A.D. villages of long rectangular houses appear along the Missouri River. These houses have the floors dug 3 or 4 feet into the ground. Sometimes there are benches around the walls or around the fire hearth. The walls were made of heavy timbers covered with sod. Unlike the later earthlodges, these houses had a ridge-pole. The entrance to the house was a long, covered tunnel (Lehmer 1971:66). A village would consist of 20 to 30 houses, usually arranged side by side. Sometimes a log wall surrounded all the houses in the village (Lehmer 1971:69). These houses eventually evolved into the round lodges known from the Arikara, Mandan, Hidatsa and central plains tribes.

A house that may be transitional between the long and the round was found in western North Dakota near Washburn, at a place where Awatixa Hidatsa believe that Charred Body came down from the sky and created the ancestors of the Awatixa Hidatsa. This house is a rounded square. Like the long houses, the floor of this was also below ground level, but instead of the long tunnel entrance, this house had a ramp leading downward. The supports for the roof were not in the center as in the later round lodges, but there were multiple supports down the center. The roof was probably not ridged, but may have been bridged in a manner similar to the construction of the round lodge. This lodge, dating from 1100 A.D., is the earliest such structure known in North Dakota (Ahler, Thiessen, Trimble 1991:30).

By the time the Europeans entered the northern plains, round earth covered lodges filled villages surrounded by high log walls. Such houses and villages were described by David Thompson for the Mandan (Thompson 1962:172) and by Pierre-Antoine Tabeau (Abel 1939:146) for the Arikara. As late as 1909 there were still a few earthlodges at Fort Berthold Reservation, the final home of the Mandan, Hidatsa, and Arikara.

Like shelter, clothing is a necessary protection from the elements. Unlike shelter, however, clothing does not leave lasting marks or preserve well and so there is no evidence of how ancient Plains peoples dressed. A few clues are provided by materials found in dry caves in Montana and Wyoming. One place, Spring Creek Cave (200-500 A.D.) had scraps of tanned hide and lengths of sinew thread that might have been left from clothing manufacture (Frison 1965:92). Daugherty Cave, a site closely related in location and age to Spring Creek Cave, also preserved hide, both rawhide and tanned, sinew and a strip of porcupine quillwork. A fragment of moccasin appears to have been repaired several times (Frison 1968:283-284). Frison (1978:360) has concluded that by 2000 B.C. people knew how to manufacture adequate, if not sophisticated, clothing. There is no evidence for the ancient development of moccasins or other footgear, but the same need for protection against cold or rough terrain would mandate the development of sturdy footwear.

The presence of well-established villages suggests a large, successful population with a complex organization of people. One of the great difficulties is determining social organization and religious beliefs from the archaeological evidence. Based on his study of bison behavior, George Frison (1978) concluded that bison drives required excellent coordination of a relatively large group of hunters. The bison are too smart and too quick to allow themselves to be driven over a cliff by only a few men. Even men on horseback could not out-maneuver a bison fighting to survive. The size of some tipi ring sites also suggests that, at least some times, large groups camped together. How these groups organized themselves, however, is not known.

Villages changed in size and structure over time. Even when the number of houses in a village are known, it is still difficult to determine the size of the population. How many people lived in a long, rectangular house? How many people lived in an earthlodge? Ricky Roberts (1977) studied population estimates of historic Arikara, Hidatsa and Mandan villages and arrived at an average of 16.62 people per lodge for the Arikara, 14.88 people per lodge for the Hidatsa, and 12.78 for the Mandan. How these figures relate to villages whose tribal affiliations are not known is still a matter for debate. It is clear, however, that by 1000 A.D. there were significant population concentrations in the plains.

The indications of extensive trade networks also imply that elements of a complex social organization existed very early. The 10,000 year old Agate Basin site had projectile points made of different kinds of flint. Some of these were Knife River Flint, mined in western North Dakota, and others were from the Black Hills area. Either the people who hunted the bison at Agate Basin traveled extensively, mining flint wherever they found it or they received the flint or the points in trade. Another site of about the same age as Agate Basin yielded stone from so many different places that researchers concluded the people either traveled or traded in a region of 120,000 square miles (Gregg 1985:93). It is possible that some access to stone resources occurred as groups moved from place to place, but some of the more distant resources were more likely to have been obtained by trade. Later, obsidian stone from Montana and pipestone from Minnesota were highly traded materials. More distinct evidence of trade comes from shell beads found in burial mounds in South Dakota. These mounds date to several centuries after the birth of Christ. Some of the shells are dentalium shells, found only in the Pacific Ocean, while others are conch and other shells from the Gulf Coast (Neuman 1975). Since these are great distances for people to travel, it is most likely that the shells were received through extensive trade networks. Their placement in graves indicates that they were valued objects.

Euro-Americans often have a romantic idea of ancient Indian life. This comes from the work of French philosophers who argued that before tribal people were corrupted by civilization they lived in a utopian manner. According to this belief, there were no murders, no wars, no child abuse, none of the problems of civilized societies. While some tribes may have lived in a happy, peaceful manner, not everyone did. There are numerous indications that ancient Plains Natives suffered from hostile actions of various types.

The heavy wood fences or stockades that surrounded many villages are a strong indication that unfriendly relations existed between groups. The work of putting up these palisades and digging the ditches that accompanied them would not have been done unless there was great need. Not all of the earliest villages were fortified, but within 200 or 300 hundred years all the villages in South Dakota were. At least one of the early villages, Fay Tolton, dating around 1000 A.D. (Wood 1976:42), was attacked and burned. Some of the villagers were killed and their bodies mutilated (Butler 1976:27). The reason for such attacks is not known.

There are strong indications that sometime before 1300 A.D. people from the central plains left their homeland and moved to the Missouri River area in what is now central South Dakota (Blakeslee 1993:199). These newcomers may have felt insecure moving into territory already occupied by others because they also built fortified villages. The population grew until there were at least ten of these villages along the Missouri River. At one of these villages, now called Crow Creek after the Indian reservation on which it was located, a massacre of unimaginable horror occurred two hundred years before Columbus (Willey and Emerson 1993:227-269). Almost 500 men, women, and children were killed and their bodies mutilated. Crow Creek was a village of 50 or more houses. Most of the houses were burned during the attack. Scholars believe that some of the residents fled to safety, but probably half were killed (Willey and Emerson 1993:249). Analysis of the age of the victims indicates that few children and young women were among the dead, suggesting that they were kidnapped by the attackers. Dead victims were scalped, decapitated, and their hands and feet were cut off. Sometimes the leg and arm bones were smashed. The ones who were killed were apparently left scattered around the village, because there are signs that scavengers gnawed at the bones. Later villagers buried the dead in a mass grave at the edge of the village.

Although much is known about the results of the attack, who committed the deed and why is not known. The death of so many and the harsh treatment of the victims is, as far as we know, unique in Plains tribal history. Investigators (Zimmerman and Bradley 1993:215-226) believe that another nearby village attacked the Crow Creek one in order to acquire the resources, either land or stored food, of the village. The people of Crow Creek had suffered from malnutrition and hunger long enough for their bones to be affected and the attackers may have been equally hungry. From later times, we know that fortified villages were nearly impregnable, so scholars believe that the village must have been taken by surprise and this is why they think that people of the same group must have been responsible. Strangers would not have been admitted to the village. Whatever the reason, the Crow Creek massacre stands as a reminder that, long before Euro-Americans entered the scene, relationships among early Plains Tribal Peoples were not always friendly.

Religious beliefs are almost impossible to discern from the archaeological evidence, but cemeteries and other burials provide some intriguing clues about ancient beliefs. There are few burials dating from Paleo-Indian times, but one found near Gordon Creek, Colorado shows that early Plains Indians felt strongly about their deceased. Accompanying the body were stone tools, worked animal ribs and a perforated elk tooth. Red ocher, a naturally occurring mineral often used for paint, colored the bones (Frison 1978:422-423). Later Indians also used red ocher to paint the bodies of the dead before burial, so this custom may have a long ancestry on the plains.

The use of burial mounds as cemeteries is one of the more notable types of burials in North Dakota and other parts of the plains. Large numbers of these mounds, many in groups, are found on ridges overlooking streams or rivers. (Because of their location, a great many mounds have been destroyed by farming and construction activities. Others were damaged by artifact hunters. Today these mounds are protected by state laws regarding cemeteries and by tribal groups who monitor Native burials.) One group of these mounds on the Missouri River dates from 1 - 600 A.D. In a pit inside the mound were jumbled bones from individuals of all ages and sexes. What is interesting about these burials is that they indicate that the bodies were exposed to the elements, then the bones were collected and buried. A few complete bodies were also found, so scientists think that the grave may have been opened at a certain time and the collected bones and the bodies of any recently deceased person placed in the tomb. The custom of exposing the body on a scaffold or placing the bones in a tree was common among later Plains Indians. After the bodies had disintegrated, the bones were collected and buried or placed in a sacred spot. The Mandan sometimes placed the skulls of their deceased in a circle around a buffalo skull and this became a place for visiting the dead or meditation. The burial mounds may have served a similar purpose in earlier times.

Along with the bones, the burial mounds contain stone, bone, and shell beads, stone and bone tools, stone projectile points, stone hammers, and many bison bones. These objects were obviously placed with the deceased and may indicate a belief that the spirits of the dead would enjoy these gifts in the afterlife. The bison bones are especially intriguing because some of them are large segments of the animal, as if whole sections of bison had been placed around the outside of the burial pit (Neuman 1975). These may have been intended to provide food for the deceased in the afterlife or they may have been the results of ceremonies designed to keep the buffalo spirits providing food for the living.

There are other clues to ancient religious beliefs. Throughout the northern plains, ancient people dug into the earth or made large rock outlines of humans and animals. At least one, a turtle figure dug into the ground near the Missouri River in western North Dakota, is thought to be more than a thousand years old (Gregg 1985:119). The use of these figures is not known, but they undoubtedly have a religious significance.

The use of the pipe, another important element in later Plains Indian religious life, also began in early times, even though the manufacture of pipe bowls from pipestone developed relatively late. A stone tube from the Paleo-Indian period Jurgens site (Wheat 1978:89) may have been a pipe. Such pipes, usually made of bone rather than stone, were reported in post-contact times from many plains tribes (Ewers 1986:50). A stone pipe was found at the Cactus Flower site in Alberta which dates around 2180 B.C. A clay pipe bowl dating from around 300 A.D. was found in a burial mound in South Dakota. The bowl is slightly conical, a shape not commonly known. A hole, perhaps for a stem, goes through the base. The upper part of the bowl is decorated with incised lines and dots (Neuman 1975:56). The association of pipe bowls with graves suggests that these were either objects of such extreme personal significance that they were buried with their owner or that these represented a very special gift to the deceased. At best, it is clear that pipes have a long history on the plains.

The archaeological record and early written documents dispel the old idea that people could not have lived in the plains without horses and guns. The evidence shows that people not only lived in the region, but they developed numerous technologies and traditions that continued into recent times. The use of these ancient traditions by historic peoples suggests that later peoples were the descendants of ancient inhabitants, not newcomers to the region. Even the people who are known to have moved into the plains from other places found it useful to adopt the techniques of hunting, the tipi and other ancient customs because these were successful adaptations to the plains environment.

WANATAN (THE CHARGER)

Wanatan, leader of the Yanktonai, is one of the better known traditional Native leaders. He fought for the British in the War of 1812 and visited Washington, D.C. He was known to several non-Indians, many of whom wrote about him, and he signed several treaties. During his lifetime he helped his people adapt to the presence of Euro-Americans, although he died before non-Indian encroachments resulted in the disappearance of the buffalo and the establishment of reservations.

Wanata came from a highly respected Yanktonai family. His father, Red Thunder, had met Zebulon Pike at Prairie du Chien in 1806. Red Thunder's sister married Robert Dickson, a fur trader who organized northwestern Indian tribes to join the British side in the War of 1812 (Robinson 1904:85,87). Loyalty to Dickson and the promises made to increase trade among the Tribal Peoples brought many Indians to the British side in 1813. Among these men was Red Thunder and his 18 year old son. The young man showed such bravery, killing seven and being severely wounded, that he was given the name Waneta, or man that charges the enemy, in recognition (Robinson 1904:101).

Following the American success in the war of 1812, Waneta returned to the area around Lake Traverse and the Red River, where he maintained his hostility to the Americans for several years (Robinson 1904:103). By 1823 when William Keating accompanied an exploring party up the Red River, Waneta was no longer hostile and welcomed the expedition graciously (Keating 1824:6).

Before 1812, the Yanktonai lived in what is now southeastern Minnesota, but by 1823 they had moved west and north into the plains, ranging from Red River to the Missouri (Keating 1823:404). The expedition of 1823 found the Yanktonai near Lake Traverse. Slightly more than a decade later, Joseph N. Nicollet found the Yanktonai and other tribes hunting buffalo near the Cheyenne River (Bray and Bray 1976:177-178). Another decade later, the fur trader Edwin Denig (Ewers 1961:32-33) complained of Wanatan and his followers harassing traders on the Missouri.

All who met Wanatan were struck by his height, over six feet, his good looks and his dignified manner (Keating 1824:448). He sometimes dressed in a colorful combination of Indian and European clothing. "He wore moccasins and leggings of scarlet cloth, a blue breech-cloth, a fine shirt of printed muslin, over this a frock-coat of fine blue cloth with scarlet facings... Upon his head he wore a blue cloth cap" (Keating 1824:450-451).

In traditional tribal custom, Wanatan showed great helpfulness and hospitality to visitors. Nicollet was entering the plains during buffalo hunting season and Wanatan agreed to serve as guide and go-between to prevent the expedition from angering the hunters by unintentionally interfering with the hunt (Bray and Bray 1976:100). For the party described by Keating, Wanatan provided several feasts. Preparations for the feast had begun as soon as word had reached the Yanktonais that the party was on its way. Wanatan's wives put several tipis together to make a double-sized lodge. The ground in the lodge was covered with buffalo robes and burning sweet grass scented the air. While the hosts and guests were smoking, the food was served in wooden bowls. There was buffalo stew with prairie turnips, boiled prairie turnips in buffalo grease without meat, and dog meat (Keating 1824:451). There was more than enough food for all.

The next day Wanatan, dressed in Indian fashion, supervised a dance which had been requested by the visitors. One of the dancers was the young son of Wanatan, who wore traditional men's dress for the first time (Keating 1824:456-457). Although Wanatan apologized for the dance, saying that the best dancers were away, the visitors were impressed.

Keating also recorded how Wanatan made a vow and the manner in which he kept it. Wanatan, planning to make a trip through Chippewa country, made a vow to the Sun that if he returned safely, he would fast for four days and give away all his goods. On his safe return he performed a sun dance, attaching himself to a pole by means of ropes passed through the skin on his arms and breast. He danced for four days before breaking free. At the end of the ceremony, he gave away five horses and all his other property. He and his wives even abandoned their lodge (Keating 1823:449-450). Wanatan's wisdom and religious strength attracted others to his band and he eventually led all the Yanktonais (Ewers 1961:30).

Denig (Ewers 1961:32-33) reports that Wanatan required a trader to pay a large amount of goods in order to winter in Wanatan's camp and, in exchange, Wanatan protected the trader and helped him make a profit. Wanatan would even repay the trader for any goods lost because of Yanktonai depredations. When six horses were stolen from a trader in the spring of 1836, Wanatan waited until fall to force a repayment. When everyone met at Fort Pierre, Wanatan asked the trader to make out a bill for the cost of the horses; he then calculated the number of buffalo robes it would take and took them from a pile he had had his people make. Everyone paid for the transgressions of a few.

The later years of Wanatan's life were unhappy. He suffered from cataracts which eventually made him blind. When Nicollet met him in 1839, Wanatan already recognized the difficulty his eyes caused him (Bray and Bray 1976:178). To the Indians, the loss of the ability to hunt and go to war indicated a loss of spiritual power and Wanatan's followers left him for Red Leaf, a younger man. According to Denig (Ewers 1961:34) Wanatan was shot and killed by one of his own people. His death is variously reported as 1840 and 1848 (Jacobson 1980:7). He left a legacy of dignity and honor to be carried on by his descendants. In 1870 when the Cut Head Band of Yanktonai settled at Fort Totten Reservation, they were led by a descendant of the first Wanatan, also called Wanatan in honor of his distinguished ancestor (Meyers 1967:223).

Chapter 6

Traditional Tribal Cultures of North Dakota

At least seven different Tribal Peoples are known to have lived in this region at various times. Many other Native groups passed through the state on their way to more permanent living places. The Assiniboin, Chippewa, Mandan, Hidatsa, Arikara, Cheyenne and Yanktonai have claims to being the original inhabitants of this area while the Cree, Dakota and Lakota undoubtedly spent time in the area, either hunting, raiding or trading. Each of these groups occupied different parts of the state and usually at different times so that there were not seven different tribal groups in North Dakota at the same time. The Assiniboin and Mandan preceded the Chippewa and Arikara in their respective areas and the Dakota and Lakota are relative latecomers to the northern Plains.

The presence of so many different tribes may complicate learning and teaching about traditional cultures, but the variety also makes the study much more interesting. The cultural diversity in North Dakota was so great that three of the six Plains Indian language families and the two basic ways life, the semisedentary and the nomadic, were represented. In addition, none of the groups we call tribes were homogeneous. Each tribe was divided into family units, bands, clans or villages. Each of these had a separate existence sometimes with distinctive customs and traditions. These distinctive differences are important to scholars because comparisons can help to answer questions about culture change and adaptation to different environments, but it is not possible to deal with these differences in any detail in a single volume. Fortunately, for students the different tribes shared enough similarities to make the study easier.

One of the earliest attempts to list the similarities between Plains tribes was made by anthropologist Clark Wissler (1938). Although he was concerned only with tribes who used the tipi year-round, many of the traits he listed applied equally to all the Plains tribes.

> The chief traits of this culture are the dependence upon the buffalo or bison, and the very limited use of roots and berries; absence of fishing; lack of agriculture; the tipi as a movable dwelling; transportation by land only, with the dog and travois (in historic times with the horse); want of basketry and pottery; no true weaving; clothing of buffalo and deerskins; a special bead technique; high development of work in skins; special rawhide work (parfleche, cylindrical bag, etc.); use of a circular shield; weak development of work in wood, stone, and bone. Their art is strongly geometric, but as a whole, not symbolic; social organization tends to the simple band; a camp circle organization; a series of societies for men; sun dance ceremony; sweat house observances, scalp dances, etc. (Wissler 1938:220).

The earth lodge users differed in the use of gardens, pottery, basketry, fishing, bull boats and having a clan system of family organization. We also now know that all Plains Indian tribes made considerable use of wild plant foods. In *Indians of the Plains*, Robert Lowie (1954:5-7) stresses the importance of the buffalo and the use of the tipi as two traits shared by all the Plains tribes, even those who gardened and lived part of the year in earth lodges.

Despite the aforementioned similarities between the tribes, it is convenient to think in terms of two major distinctions: semisedentary and nomadic because these represent important cultural differences. The availability of garden products opened the possibility of trade, necessitated hoes, rakes and garden ceremonies, and made life a little more secure for the tribes. The earth lodge was large enough to accommodate extra tools, clothing, and people and so the material inventory and social organization became more complex. Pottery and basketry vessels that were too fragile to withstand frequent moves could be used by those who lived in permanent villages and there was more time for elaborate ceremonials.

The Gardening Tribes—Arikara, Hidatsa and Mandan

Even though the Arikara, Hidatsa and Mandan spoke completely different languages and lived in villages many miles apart, the similarities in their architecture, agriculture and technology have caused them to be treated as if they were a single unit. Additional reasons for this treatment are found in the tribes sharing Like-a-Fishhook village and in their modern identity as the Three Affiliated Tribes. Before smallpox epidemics and Plains wars, however, the tribes occupied many separate villages, each with its own government, language and customs. The situation was probably comparable to the one that exists today between major cities in this country. The history, culture and language of New Orleans contrasts strongly with that of New York, even though each city is part of a common cultural tradition and recognizes itself as part of a larger unit. In the case of the Arikara, Hidatsa and Mandan, these larger units are called "tribes," and the differences between them are as great as those between the United States, Mexico and Russia. Similarities in economy and architecture do not make similar cultures and the governments, the social customs, the religious beliefs and practices and the foreign policies of the three tribes were entirely separate and distinct from each other.

Arikara

Closely related to the Pawnee, the Arikara lived along the Missouri River in what is now South Dakota until the 1800s when they moved north to settle near the Mandan and Hidatsa (Smith 1972:9). Originally, there had been as many as eighteen villages (Abel 1939:123), but smallpox epidemics reduced the number.

The villages, like those of the Mandan and Hidatsa, were composed of earthlodges. Numerous Euro-American visitors to the Arikara villages have described the earthlodges (Abel 1939:146, Brackenridge 1906:115) so we have a good idea of their structure and furnishings.

The lodges are constructed in the following manner:

Four large forks of about fifteen feet in height, are placed in the ground, usually about twenty feet from each other, with hewn logs or beams across; from these beams other pieces are placed above, leaving an aperture at the top to admit the light, and to give vent to the smoke. These upright pieces are interwoven with osiers, after which the whole is covered with earth, though not sodded. An opening is left at one side for a door, which is secured by a kind of projection of ten or twelve feet, enclosed on all sides, and forming a narrow entrance, which might be easily defended. A buffalo robe suspended at the entrance, answers as a door (Brackenridge 1906:115).

The interior of the house was furnished with beds against the outer walls. These beds were covered with skins and skins hanging from the ceiling served to partition the beds and aid privacy. The rafters and joists were used storing objects out of the way of children and dogs. At the far end of the lodge, opposite the door, was a sacred place with an altar and shrine for sacred bundles, shields and other powerful objects.

The village that Brackenridge visited had no plan for the arrangement of the lodges and, since most of the lodges were similar in appearance, he had trouble finding his way. The village was surrounded by a palisade.

Outside the palisade were small garden plots and farther from the village were large ones. The basic subsistence of the Arikara was corn, squash, sunflower and bean horticulture which supplemented the diet of bison and wild vegetable foods. Brackenridge (1906:116) described the meal he was offered as consisting of a dish of buffalo meat followed by a stew of corn mixed with beans and cooked with buffalo marrow. Gardening was the work of the women of the tribe. They were also responsible for building lodges, carrying wood, making pottery and baskets, tanning hides and caring for the children (Abel 1939:148-149).

Each summer the villages moved out onto the plains to hunt buffalo (Hurt 1969). During these hunts the families lived in tipis. The men were responsible for locating and killing the buffalo. Everyone worked to butcher and preserve the buffalo meat for winter use. In addition to hunting buffalo, the men were also responsible for protecting the village in both the physical and spiritual senses.

Marriage was arranged by the families of the young man and woman, but the woman always had to give her consent (Curtis 1909:62). The man's relatives went to the woman's family and indicated their interest in the marriage. Gifts were presented to the woman's family. If the marriage was approved, the man moved into his wife's lodge (Curtis 1909:62). An Arikara man could have more than one wife, if he could support them adequately (Brackenridge 1906:121; Abel 1939:182).

The basis for social interaction was found in the kinship system. Kinship was extended to most of the people in the village, and so only a few terms were needed to indicate how a person was to be treated. A woman and her sisters were called mother by all their children (Morgan 1871:293-382). A man would call his father's sisters and their daughters by the same term he called his mother, thereby indicating that he regarded these women with the same respect he felt for his own mother and they, in turn, would care for him as if he were their own son. On the other hand, it was clear from the use of these terms that these individuals were not eligible for him to marry. By extension of terms, it was possible for a man to call someone younger than he, mother or father, or grandfather. Men were also expected to join military or religious societies and they would also refer to their sponsors in these societies as "father" (Lowie 1915).

Government was separate for each village with leadership vested in the hands of men who had achieved military success and demonstrated wisdom, generosity and outstanding moral behavior (Gilmore 1927a:333; 1928b:411). Tabeau (Abel 1939:124) and Gilmore (1928b:411) state that there were four levels of leadership. The highest level consisted of the chiefs of the villages and their assistants. The second rank consisted of men and women who had been initiated into the honorary society of Piraskani because of their outstanding good character. The third group was composed of men who had war honors, but no leadership experiences. All the warriors not in the other classes were in the fourth rank.

Arikara religious beliefs and practices were very complex and highly organized, centering around a belief in a principal creator, called Nesaru. In addition to the Creator, there were many other spiritual figures, including Mother-Corn who was the earthly representative of Nesaru and taught the Arikara how to live on this earth and served as an intermediary between the Arikara and other spirits (Gilmore 1930a). Each of the four directions had a guardian spirit and was associated with an earthly manifestation such as a plant, animal, natural phenomena or planet. In addition to the directions, all things in the world, animate and inanimate, were believed to have been endowed with a spirit which could reveal itself and become a protector for a person who asked for such help in a vision quest (Curtis 1909:151). Symbols were also associated with each spirit and could be included in a sacred bundle, along with songs and prayers which were part of the relationship between the sacred and the earthly people. In addition to the personal bundles, each Arikara village had a bundle that represented Mother-Corn and her teachings. The ceremonies celebrated by the Arikara were held to insure successful crops and buffalo hunts (Abel 1939:216). In the fall a harvest ceremony marked the end of summer and the time for the Medicine Lodge Ceremony, the most sacred of all ceremonies, which lasted fifteen to twenty days (Abel 1939:187-189; Curtis 1909:70-76). During the Medicine Lodge ceremonial time, people feasted, were cured, the societies performed their sacred dances and demonstrations of magic powers were given (Will 1934:16-19).

The major religious ceremonies were associated with successful gardening and bison hunting, but throughout an Arikara's life there were many less important, but highly significant ceremonies. Naming ceremonies, ear piercing ceremonies, blessing ceremonies, and vision seeking, all involved the Arikara in the daily practice of their religion.

Hidatsa

Like the Arikara, the Hidatsa lived in earthlodge villages along the Missouri River and its tributaries. The Hidatsa were originally divided into three separate groups: the Awatixa, the Awaxawi and the Hidatsa-proper, and also like the Arikara's, these villages were devastated by smallpox.

We know a great deal about the traditional culture of the Hidatsa because they were visited by so many traders, explorers, scientists, artists and ethnographers. The records left by Buffalo Bird Woman are of particular interest because they provide details about Hidatsa culture that are not available from any other source.

The Hidatsa earthlodges were similar to those built by the Arikara and Mandan. According to Buffalo Bird Woman, there were two basic styles of earthlodges: one with a flat roof and one with a domed roof. The flat roof was slightly more difficult to build, but was preferred (Wilson 1934:364) because people could sit on the flat roofs to sun themselves or to watch ceremonies. The young men used to go up on the roof to watch for their girl friends.

The interior of the lodge was spacious enough for a large family, storage of food and hides, and a corral for the favorite horses. The beds were placed around the outer wall. The fireplace in the center of the lodge had mats for sitting by it. Behind the fireplace, toward the wall opposite the doorway, was a sacred place. No one was allowed to walk through or play in that area (Wilson 1934:383-394).

The Hidatsa also used other kinds of dwellings. During the buffalo hunts they used tipis (Wilson 1921, 1924). In the winter the Hidatsa constructed smaller lodges in the wooded areas along the river bottoms where there was some protection from the cold and a good supply of timber (Boller 1868). All the living quarters were owned by the women, and it was possible for a man to move in with his wife's family.

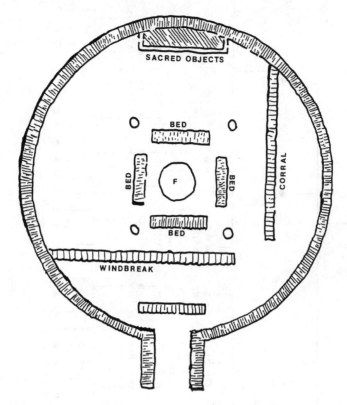

Figure 6.1. Earthlodge interior from a sketch by Karl Bodmer. F. is fireplace.

Gardening was the work of the women. Buffalo Bird Woman described how the fields were cleared, the corn, squash, beans and sunflowers were planted, tended, harvested and cooked (Wilson 1917). Using antler or wood rakes, bison shoulder bone hoes and wood digging sticks, the Hidatsa women were excellent gardeners, growing nine varieties of corn and five varieties of beans. All the vegetables were dried and stored in caches for winter use.

Bison hunting provided a significant part of the Hidatsa diet. During the summer, most of the village moved one to two hundred miles away to hunt buffalo (Bowers 1965:50; Wilson 1924). The hunt was directed by a man selected by the council. This man was chosen for his ability to keep the people working together harmoniously (Wilson 1924:263). Men with buffalo bundles were expected to pray that the buffalo would permit themselves to be killed and prayers were said to the buffalo (Bowers 1965:54). The hunt was usually done by the men all riding into the herd at a signal from the leader (Wilson 1914:51).

Kinship was very important to the Hidatsa and structured all daily relationships between individuals. A person was born into a family and into a clan, or an extended family group, which provided almost complete care for the person from birth to death (Bowers 1965:71-78). Hidatsa clan membership (Fig. 6.2) was handed down from mother to child and a child became a member of his/her mother's clan at birth. Under Hidatsa rules, members of the same clan could not marry, so fathers were always from a different clan than their children. But the father's clan was important to a child, too. Clans gave

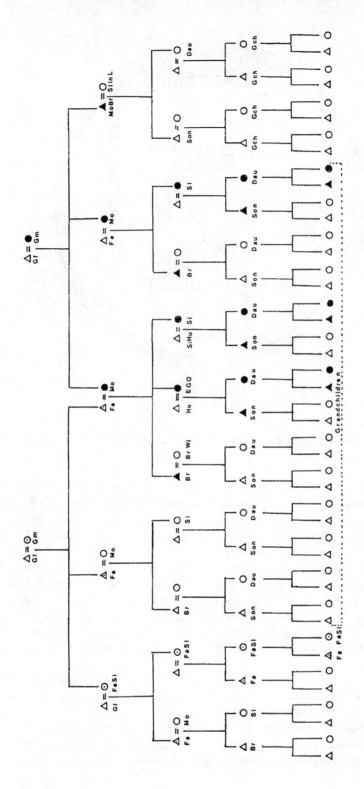

Figure 6.2. Diagram of Mandan kinship system when the speaker is a woman. The △ represents a male and the O a female. The solid figures are the woman's own clan and the dots indicate the members of her father's clan.

names and provided assistance in acquiring sacred bundles, and relatives helped each other to sponsor ceremonies that would bring prestige to the family.

In or out of the earthlodge no one was really alone and no one had to worry about how others would react because the kinship relation specified behavior. A person called "mother" was treated with respect. A person called "cousin" could be joked with. A person called "brother" had to be treated with respect and given care and support. Grandparents provided love, warmth and education for the Hidatsa child.

Buffalo Bird Woman explained to Gilbert Wilson (Weitzner 1979:278-284) that there were three ways for a couple to get married. The preferred way was for the groom's family to offer presents to the bride's family. If the bride's family approved of the marriage, they would accept the offer. If not, they would make an excuse to the groom's family that the girl was too young. If the groom's family was really sincere, they might offer more gifts and the bride's family might accept after all. A well brought-up young woman who was known to be a hard worker would be worth many gifts. The most valuable gifts were horses and the number of horses offered indicated the regard the groom's family had for the woman. This marriage agreement was followed by a ceremonial exchange of gifts and food between the two families. This form of marriage was a source of pride to a woman because it meant she was a desirable bride.

The second and probably more frequent way of arranging a marriage was for the young man and woman to agree to marry. One of the couple would move into the lodge of the other's family and this move would constitute a legal marriage. Some of these marriages were very short because the couple did not know each other well and, since there had been no gift-exchange between families, divorce caused no particular problems. Children of a divorced couple could go with either parent depending upon the situation, although they retained the clan of their biological mother.

The third style of marriage was for a woman's parents to select a husband and insist that the girl marry him. Such a marriage would take place if the parents thought their daughter was becoming promiscuous. An older man who was a good hunter would be chosen. Buffalo Bird Woman did not mention the possibility of eloping, but among other Plains tribes, eloping was another way for a couple to marry. If the families did not approve, or if one of the couple were married to someone else, they might slip out of camp and stay away until everyone had adjusted to the change. After that the couple would be accepted as husband and wife.

In addition to membership in a clan, people were also expected to belong to societies which banded together to help members purchase sacred bundles and sponsor ceremonies (Lowie 1913, 1917; Bowers 1965). The ceremonies sponsored by the societies were important to the functioning of the tribe. Some of the political organization was intimately connected with sacred bundle ownership, as well as the demonstrated ability of the person to lead. Peacetime leadership was held by men who were wise and generous. War leaders were men with a successful record of military and hunting expeditions.

Kinship organized the social behavior of people and religion regulated the interactions between the Hidatsa and their environment. Through the sacred bundles, which were associated with the origin of the Hidatsa as a people, the Hidatsa controlled the forces that threatened their existence. The sacred bundles were objects symbolical of the origin stories and of the powers of the bundles, songs and ceremonies. The foundation of Hidatsa religion was belief in "power" or "sacred energy" that could be obtained through fasting, self-sacrifice, visions, participation in sacred ceremonies and through the purchase of sacred bundles. A man had to have power in order to survive to a respectful and secure old age.

The year was organized around ceremonies which celebrated the planting, growing and harvesting of crops. These spring and summer ceremonies were followed by ceremonies for warriors and for buffalo hunting. Each ceremony involved most of the tribe, although bundle owners and members of the sponsoring societies had the most important duties. During the winter buffalo calling ceremony the whole village had to be silent so that the buffalo would not be frightened away. The Hidatsa Naxpike was very similar to the Mandan Okipa and may be considered to be the Hidatsa sun dance (Lowie 1919). The Naxpike was only one of many important Hidatsa ceremonies, whereas to the Lakota the Sun Dance was the most significant ceremony.

First Creator, with the help of Lone Man, made the earth and all its features and people. Other major figures were Old Woman Who Never Dies, who was concerned with gardening and water fowl; the wife of First Creator, who was concerned with fertility and childbearing; East Wind; South Wind; Grandson; and Spring Boy. The many ceremonies were complex and varied. Each one reflected the origin narrative of the Hidatsa, the social system, the individual powers and the strong desire for the Hidatsa to keep the world in harmony through the practice of their religion.

Figure 6.3. Mandan village painted by George Catlin in 1832. (Courtesy of National Museum of American Art, Smithsonian Institution).

Mandan

Numangkaki, People of the First Man, was the name the Mandan used for themselves (Thomas and Ronnefeldt 1976). Although they recognized a common relationship, the villages that composed the Mandan nation had dialect and cultural differences which gradually disappeared under the pressure of smallpox epidemics and European settlement in the area. Lewis and Clark were told that there had been nine villages which later became two, one on each side of the Missouri (Bowers 1950:11).

Like the Arikara and Hidatsa, the Mandan also used earthlodges for the major part of the year. In the Mandan villages, however, the lodges were arranged (Fig.6.3) with an open space in the center (Bowers 1950:112). In the center of the open space was a log structure representing the willows used by Lone Man to protect the Mandan from a flood. From descriptions by European visitors we know how the earthlodges were furnished (Fig.6.1). The Mandan provide the only known depiction of an earthlodge interior. Karl Bodmer, a Swiss artist, painted the interior of an earthlodge belonging to a Mandan named Dipauch (Hunt and Gallagher 1984:291). The earthlodges, gardens, and all the domestic goods were owned by the women. Men owned horses, pipes, weapons and hunting tools. The sacred bundles were owned jointly by a man and his wives.

The life of the people was organized according to the seasons and to kinship. The seasons established the basic round of activities and ceremonies while kinship organized the groups which performed the economic and religious functions. Small children were taught to treat members of the village on the basis of kinship. Many terms were extended to relatives so that the person behaved toward these relatives as he would to others who had the same kinship relationship. Anyone a child called "father" received the respect and love given to a father. Grandparents were loving teachers and cousins of the same age were close playmates (Bowers 1950:37-58).

In addition to direct family relationships which were extremely close, the Mandan were organized into clans. A child was born into its mother's clan and kept that clan membership throughout his/her life. Each of the clans had important duties within the tribe. Since there were members of each clan in each village, a person had relatives in each village. Some of the responsibilities of the clan were to care for its members, especially the elderly and orphans, to discipline the children and to assist its members in obtaining membership in religious societies and in purchasing the rights to perform certain ceremonies. People were also helped to acquire membership in military, social and religious societies (Bowers 1950:29-33).

Religion was very important to the Mandan. Each person had private prayers and rituals, as well as public ceremonies. Religious beliefs and practices were based on the origin traditions which explained how the gods helped the people to survive by teaching them the sacred ceremonies. The earthly manifestations of the religious traditions were the sacred bundles which contained objects representing the characters and incidents of the origin traditions. Associated with each bundle were songs and rites which explained and dramatized the sacred stories and the right to sponsor or direct a specific ceremony with a specific function. A person or group of people might own a sacred bundle, and some ceremonies were so complex that different people owned sacred bundles which had only a part of the ceremony. Thus people had to cooperate to conduct the sacred ceremonies.

The ceremonies were organized according to the seasons (Bowers 1950:107). Spring ceremonies welcomed the birds and garden spirits. Summer ceremonies brought rain, drove away insects and helped the crops grow well. Late summer celebrations prepared men for war and hunting expeditions. Winter rituals brought the buffalo near the village and provided reassurance that the people would survive.

The major rite of the Mandan was the Okipa, which dramatized the creation of the world by Lone Man and the gift of the animals, particularly the buffalo. The ceremony was held in a special lodge which faced the open area in the center of the village. The ceremony had several parts and took four days to complete. One part of the ceremony was a dance of all the birds, animals and other creatures important to humans. Most important were the buffalo bull dancers. Several times during the ceremony young men would suspend themselves by ropes attached to skewers in their chests or drag buffalo skulls by ropes attached to skewers in their back. The young men who tortured themselves might gain a strong spiritual protector during this experience and so they were willing to sacrifice themselves. Their sacrifice was also believed to bring the buffalo closer to the village. Such a major ceremony renewed the people's sacred beliefs, put the universe in balance, continued the fertility of the bison and other animals and insured the continued interest of the gods for their people.

Seven Council Fires—Dakota, Lakota and Yanktonai

Prehistorically, the great Dakota nation was divided into three dialects and seven major bands or council fires (Fig.6.4). Together these bands made up the *Oceti Sakowin* or Seven Council Fires. These people recognized their relationship by referring to themselves as "kota" or allies. Each of the major bands was further divided into villages or camping units, and these were broken into groups of relatives or large family units (Table 2.1, Table 6.1, Table 6.2, Table 6.3). The three dialect divisions of Dakota, Lakota, and Nakota (more properly Yankton-Yanktonai) also correspond to the geographical positions of these groups in the mid-1700's or later.

The easternmost division was the Dakota, sometimes also called the Santee, although this is actually the name of one of the bands. The four main groups of the Dakota were the Mdewakanton (Spirit Lake People) who occupied seven villages along the Mississippi; the Wahpekute (Shooters among the Leaves) who had a single village on the Minnesota; the Wahpeton (People Dwelling Among the Leaves) living in seven villages; and the Sisseton (People of the Ridged Fish Scales) who were organized into twelve villages. The Lakota were the westernmost division. There were seven bands of the Lakota: the Hunkpapa (Campers at the Horn), the Mnikonju or Minneconjou (Planters beside the water), Sihasapa (Blackfoot), Oohenonpa (Two Kettles), Itazipcho (Those without Bows), Sicangu (Brules or Burnt Thighs) and Oglala (They Scatter their Own) (Dorsey 1894). Each of these Lakota bands was divided into smaller groups who spent most of the year hunting and camping as separate autonomous units. The Yankton and Yanktonai, often called the *Wiciyena* or Those Who Speak Like Men, lived between the Dakota and Lakota and are sometimes referred to as the "Middle Sioux." Some linguists have called the Yankton-Yanktonai dialect "Nakota" because these tribes sometimes used an "n" sound instead of the "d" or "l" used by the other two, but Nakota was never used by the Yankton-Yanktonai to describe their language or themselves (DeMallie 1982:xi).

One of the great mistakes in Indian history was lumping the three major divisions of the Seven Council Fires into a single group called "Sioux." Each of these groups was adapted to different environments and had customs and traditions that were very different from each other. The Lakota became the classic Plains tribe. The Yankton-Yanktonai occupied a marginal position on the eastern edge of the plains where they became traders, operating between the plains and woodland tribes. The Dakota had a woodland-adapted culture based on deer and wild rice, as well as the bison.

SEVEN COUNCIL FIRES (SIOUX)

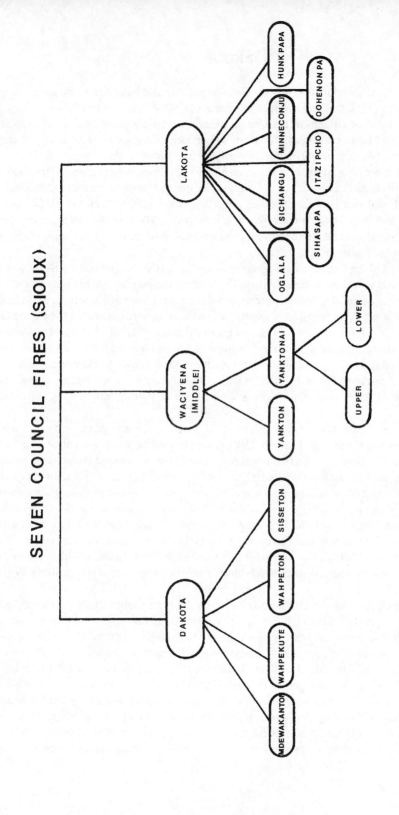

Figure 6.4. Diagram of the members of the Seven Council Fires.

Dakota

The Dakota, because of their location in Minnesota, Wisconsin and Northern Iowa, were oriented to a woodland-prairie way of life that had stronger similarities to other eastern tribes than to their western relatives. The many different villages of the Dakota tribes were built along major waterways such as the Mississippi and the Minnesota rivers. The diversity between villages was great and what was true for one village of one Dakota tribe may not necessarily be true for all of them.

Some tribes were more able to grow corn, squash and beans than others (Pond 1908:343) while those nearest the prairies had easier access to buffalo. The general subsistence was a combination of hunting, fishing and wild rice harvesting (Pond 1908:365; Jenks 1898). Deer and buffalo were the major food animals, although small animals like rabbits and muskrats were important during the winter. A great variety of wild vegetable foods supplemented the meat and wild rice diet. Maple sugar provided a sweetener for foods and a hot drink.

The yearly activities of the Dakota were organized according to the food resources. Even the type of house depended on the season and the activities. In October, the people left for the fall deer hunt. Living in tipis, the village moved to areas where they had not hunted deer the year before and hoped to find large herds. The winter hunt lasted until January when the deer were too skinny to be good eating. If the hunt had been successful, there would be enough dried meat to last until spring. In March came the time of sugar making and muskrat hunting. The muskrat hunters walked out on the ice and speared the animals in their lodges. In May, the hunters and sugar makers returned to their large, gabled, bark houses in the villages. Summer life in the villages was a time of planting, berrying, repairing, fishing, hunting and ceremonies. After harvest, it was time for wild rice harvesting, fall hunting and cranberry picking.

A Dakota's life was spent surrounded by relatives. At birth a child was given a name which indicated his or her position in the family (Eastman 1849:xxv). The first born son was called Chaske while the second son was called Haparm. The first daughter was Winona, the second Harpen and so on until the fifth son or daughter was reached (Wallis 1947:39; Riggs 1880:358). These names were used until a new name was given in a naming ceremony. Children were raised without physical punishment and were spoken to softly (Keating 1824, vol.I:421; Pond 1908:458). All interaction between individual Dakotas was based on kinship, and children were taught to treat each person as if he or she were a relative. Any person called by a kinship term was unsuitable for marriage, no matter how distantly related. Some cousins were allowed to joke with and tease each other. Grandparents were respected and loved while they in turn taught their grandchildren tribal traditions and values (Landes 1968b:86-100).

The political organization of the Dakota was based on the permanent village. Unlike most other hunting groups who separated into small family units for most of the year, the Dakota remained in their village units all year around. Authority was vested in the hands of a primary chief, a war chief, a council and military police. The primary chieftainship was hereditary, as long as the successor was qualified. In the absence of a qualified individual, the council could appoint a person to fill the position (Dorsey 1897:221-222). When a person succeeded to office, he often took the name of his father or grandfather so that names came to be associated with the position. Several men were called Shakopee, Little Crow, Wabasha and Standing Buffalo. The strength of the villages was such that there were no fraternal societies until recent times. Membership in a society was informal and could vary from one meeting to the next. The primary purpose of the societies was to sponsor dances (Lowie 1913:141-142).

TABLE 6.1. Divisions of the Dakota

MDEWAKANTON

    Kiyuksa (Breakers of the law)
    He-mini-can (Mountain-water-wood)
    Kaposa (Not encumbered with much baggage)
    Maga-yute-sni (Eats no geese)
    Heyata-otonwe (Of it chief Hake-waste or village back from the river)
    Oyate sica (Bad Nation)
    Tinta-otonwe (Village on the Prairie)

WAHPEKUTE

WAHPETON

    Inyan-ce-yaka-atonwan (Village at the dam or rapids)
    Takapsin-ton-wanna (Village at the shinny ground)
    Wayaka-otina (Dwellers on the sand)
    Otehi-atonwan (Village in the thicket)
    Wita-otina (Dwellers on the island)
    Wakpaatonwan (Village on the river)
    Can-kaga-otina (Dwellers in logs)

SISSETON

    Wita-waziyata-otina (Village at the north island)
    Ohdihe (From odihan, to fall into an object endwise)
    Basdetce-sni (Do not split the body of a buffalo with a knife but cut it up as they please)
    Itokah-tina (Dwellers at the south)
    Kahmi-atonwan (Village at the bend)
    Mani-ti (Those who camp away from the village)
    Keze (Barbed like a fishhook)
    Can kute (Shoot in the woods)
    Ti-zaptan (Five lodges)
    Kapozia (Those who travel with light burdens)
    Amdo-wapuskyapi (Those who lay meat on their shoulders to dry it during the hunt)

Source: Dorsey, J. O., Siouan Sociology. 15th Annual Report of the Bureau of American Ethnology.

The Dakota religion was a complex system, entirely different from Christianity and difficult for Euro-Americans to comprehend. Man and nature were not viewed as competing forces, but as elements in the same system controlled by *Wakan Tanka*. The life force that enabled Wakan Tanka to control the universe was shared by man and animals, trees, rocks, birds, all the elements of the universe. In the cosmic hierarchy, the forces held by the animals and other beings were sometimes greater than those held by human beings. With proper devotion and submission, however, the natural beings could be persuaded to share their power and to act as guardians and emissaries to the more powerful forces. A young man would receive this power by fasting, purifying himself in the sweat lodge and humbly begging a medicine man for a "wotawe" or sacred protective spirit. The Dakota held two major religious ceremonies: the Medicine Dance and the Sun Dance. The Medicine Dance initiated people into the ability to cure and to the sacred mysteries of the medicine men (Skinner 1920). The Dakota Sun Dance was more informal than the Lakota ceremony and, according to Samuel Pond (1908:102) was not popular with the Dakota because the tribe did not generally believe in self-sacrifice. Young Dakota men who wanted to become medicine men or warriors who wanted to gain supernatural protection would vow to sacrifice themselves to the sun. Enduring the pain of the Sun Dance prepared the men for the pain of life as a medicine man or warrior. The Sun Dance also provided general protection for all the Dakota (Wallis 1921:325). As was generally true of Tribal Peoples, a Dakota's life was filled with ceremonies which ensured the continuing care and attention of the spiritual realm.

Lakota

In the minds of most Euro-Americans, the Lakota are the classic plainsmen, horsemen and warriors. Although many Lakota believe they originated in the Black Hills, historic records and oral traditions of other tribes suggest that the Lakota moved out of Minnesota in the late 1600s. If this movement is true, then the tribe rapidly changed from the woodland way of life to a totally plains existence. The buffalo not only became the mainstay of their diet but also assumed a religious emphasis. The tipi became their only form of dwelling and the Sun Dance became the major religious ceremony. Their success in adapting brought them the admiration of non-Indians.

Because the Lakota came to represent all Plains Indians, there are probably more accounts of Lakota history and culture than for any other Plains tribes. Early visitors to the plains remarked on Lakota customs and recorded meetings with Lakota leaders. The wars which engaged some divisions of the Lakota have also been reported and discussed many times. With the settlement on the reservations, historians found it easy to interview Lakota men and women and to observe the traditional aspects of the culture.

Abandoning the village way of life, the Lakota were forced to make changes in social organization. In place of the permanent village membership, the Lakota relied on the camp or *tiospaye*. Each tiospaye was further divided into camps that usually represented an extended family. Each unit had a formal order in which the tipis were arranged, and every family knew where its tipi should be pitched in the camp. The names of some of the tiospaye (Table 6.3) indicated their place in the camp circle of the Lakota nation, but most names were based on an event in the group's past.

The tipi and its associated structures represented a nuclear family unit and its relationship to the other Lakota and the universe. The tipi was a cone-shaped house made by covering lodge-pole pine saplings, fifteen to twenty feet high, with hides sewn together. Life in the tipi was highly organized, and a strict etiquette was observed. Women sat on the left of the door; men to the right. Behind the fireplace, facing the door was a (Fig. 6.6) place of honor reserved for guests or the head of the household. Behind the place of honor was a sacred area where bundles, shields, and other sacred objects were kept and offerings were placed. No one was permitted to pass between the fire and a person sitting by the fire, nor was it considered proper to step over another person's legs (Laubin 1957:118-119).

Table 6.2. Organization of the Lakota

SICANJU (Brule, Burned Thighs) ca. 1880

Iyak'oza = Lump-on-a-Horses Leg
Tcoka-towela = Blue-spot-in-the-Middle
Ciyo-tanka = Prairie Chicken
Ho-mna = Fish-smellers
Ciyo-subula = Sharp-tailed grouse
Kangi-yuha = Raven keepers
Pispiza-wicasa = Prairie Dog People
Walega-un-wohan - Boil-food-with-the-paunch-skin
Watceunpa = Roasters
Sawala = Shawnee [descendants]
Ihanktonwan = Yankton [mothers]
Naqpaqpa = Take-down-their leggings (after returning from war)
Apewan-tanka = Big manes (of horses)

ITAZIPCHO (Sans Arcs) ca. 1880

Itazipcho-hca = Real Sans Arcs
Cina-luta-oin = Scarlet-cloth-earring
Woluta-yuta = Eat-dried-meat-from-the-hind-quarter
Maz-peg-naka = Wear-metal-in-the-hair
Tatanka-cesli = Dung-of-a-buffalo-bull
Siksicela = Bad-ones-of-different kinds
Tiyopa-ocannunpa = Smokes-at-the entrance to the lodge

SIHASAPA (Blackfeet) ca. 1880

Siha-sapa-qtca = Real Blackfeet
Kangisunpegnaka = Wears-raven-feathers-in-the-hair
Glagla-heca = Untidy
Wajaje = Kill Eagles band
Hohe = Assiniboin
Wamnuga-oin = Shell-ear-pendant

MINICONJU ca. 1884

Unkce-yuta = Eat-dung
Glagla-heca = Slovenly
Sunka-yute-sni = Eat-no-dogs
Nige-tanka = Big Belly
Wakpokinyan = Flies-along-the-creek
Inyan-h-oin = Musselshell earring
Siksicela = Bad-ones-of-different-sorts
Wagleza-oin = Watersnake earring
Wan-nawega = Broken-arrows

OOHENONPA (Two Kettles) ca. 1884

Oohenonpa - Two Kettles or Two Boilings
Ma-wahota = Skin-smeared-with-whitish-earth

OGLALA (Scattered their own) ca. 1880

Payabya = Pushed aside (Man Afraid of Horses Band)
Tapisleca = Spleen
Kiyuksa = Breaks-his-own
Wajaja = Kill eagle
Ite-sica = Bad Face (Red Cloud's band)
Oyuhpe = Thrown-down
Wagluhe = Followers

HUNKPAPA (End of tribal circle)

Canka-ohan = Sore-backs (of horses)
Ce-ohba = unknown
Tinazipe-sica = Bad-bows
Talo-napin = Fresh-meat-necklace
Kiglaska = Ties-his-own
Cegnake-okisela = Half-a-breechcloth
Siksicela = Bad-ones-of-different-sorts
Wakan = Mysterious
Hunska-cantozuha = Legging-tobacco-pouch

Source: Dorsey, J.O. 1897 Siouan Sociology. *Fifteenth Annual Report of the Bureau of American Ethnology*.

The major food resource of the Lakota was the buffalo. The buffalo was so important that many of the ceremonies were directed to thanking the buffalo for caring for the Lakota, and one of the major religious figures was White Buffalo Cow Woman who brought the sacred pipe and the seven ceremonies to the Lakota (Black Elk 1953). The buffalo has been called a walking department store because every part was used by the Lakota. Food, shelter, clothing, bone for tools, sinew for sewing, materials for making containers, and sacred objects were gifts of the buffalo to the Lakota.

The Lakota conceptualized life as a series of circles (Hassrick 1964:216). There was the yearly circle of the seasons, the monthly cycle of the moon, the daily cycle of the sun and the circle of life within which all creatures were related. A Lakota was born into a circle of close family, relatives and other Lakota. The camp, the tiospaye and the nation were other circles which surrounded a Lakota. The closest and smallest circle was the immediate family. Within these circles kinship relations based on age, sex and generational distance from the speaker structured all the social interrelations between individuals. In general, one behaved with respect toward older and younger relatives and maintained a strict respect relationship toward individuals of the opposite sex. Different terms were used by men and women, since the behaviors depended on whether the person was the same sex or the opposite one to the speaker. Brothers were very close while brothers and sisters had to avoid being alone together (Hassrick 1964:103-110).

Men and women also sought to attain membership in societies which brought them recognition. The men's societies were the Kit Foxes, Badgers, Brave Hearts, White Badges, Crow Warriors, Silent Eaters and Bare Lance Owners, although new societies were created from time to time. Women joined the White Buffalo Calf society (Walker 1982:62-63). The men's societies were either military societies whose main functions were control and protection of the camp or leadership societies whose men formed the political authority of the camp or tiospaye.

Lakota religious beliefs included a hierarchy of spiritual beings representing birds, animals, plants and natural phenomena that could be persuaded to aid humans and a universe filled with power which could be used for good but required constant attention lest it become evil (Walker 1980; Powers 1977; Hassrick 1964: 216). *Wakantanka*, the Great Spirit, encompassed four groups of four beings. The first group is composed of the Sun, the Sky, the Earth and the Rock. The second group consists of the Moon, the Wind, the Falling Star and the Thunderbird. The third group is called the lesser beings and includes the buffalo, the bear and man, the four winds and the whirlwind. The last four are the four souls or life forces (Powers 1977:54). Although these sacred beings are arranged in an hierarchical order, they were closely related. The buffalo and the Sun were friends and talked together (Walker 1980:67). Other beings also worked together to assist or harm humans.

The Lakota recognized that too much of any good thing was bad, and they sought to keep a proper balance in the universe. The seven major ceremonies, the sweat lodge, keeping the ghost, seeking a vision, sun dancing, making relatives, preparing a girl for womanhood and throwing the ball, along with many individual rituals were the means by which the Lakota received spiritual benefits and helped to maintain the harmony in the universe.

The ritual intensity, personal sacrifice and great symbolism of the Sun Dance attracted the attention of Euro-Americans who failed to understand its importance to the Lakota. The Sun Dance was a four day ceremony filled with prayers and dances seeking the continuation of the buffalo and the safety of the people. The rituals involved everyone, but the greatest sacrifices were made by men who tied themselves to the Sun Dance tree with thongs that were fastened to skewers through their chest or dragged buffalo skulls by thongs attached to skewers in their back or hung suspended from four poles by thongs or cut pieces of their own flesh and placed them at the foot of the Sun Dance pole. Women were also encouraged to give pieces of flesh from their arms and infants had their ears pierced as a small sacrifice. Euro-Americans viewed these self-sacrifices as tortures imposed on the young men, but sacrifices were actually made in order to strengthen the people and secure the protection of the sacred beings. By this ceremony, harmony was restored to the universe.

Yankton and Yanktonai (Middle Sioux)

The Yankton and Yanktonai, sometimes called Middle Sioux because of their geographical position between the Dakota and Lakota, have not received the same kind of attention that has been given to the Dakota and Lakota. Occupying the area between the James and Missouri Rivers, the Yankton-Yanktonai escaped the early settlements by non-Indians that so drastically affected the other Siouan peoples of the region.

The Yankton were divided into seven or eight family groups (Table 6.2) and the Yanktonai were divided into two major divisions: Upper and Lower or Hunkpatina, according to their geographical location north and south of each other. The Upper Yanktonai, living along the James and Sheyenne rivers in central-eastern North Dakota, were divided into seven family groups. The Lower Yanktonai,

Figure 6.5. Lakota tipi village at Standing Rock. (Courtesy State Historical Society of North Dakota).

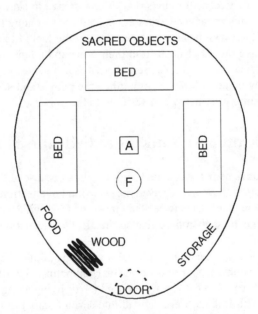

Figure 6.6. Diagram of the interior of a tipi. (After Laubin 1957).

who referred to themselves as Hunkpatina and are not to be confused with the Hunkpapa division of the Lakota, were also divided into seven named family camping units.

The traditional culture of the middle tribes is indicative of their position between the Lakota, the Plains tribe without equal, and the Dakota, a woodland-oriented tribe. The Yankton and Yanktonai lived in a combined riverine and tall grass plains environment which provided a wide variety of resources. In adapting to their environment, the Middle Sioux learned the ways of other tribes like the Ponca, Arikara, Mandan and Hidatsa who were occupying similar riverine-plains locales (Howard 1966a). The buffalo were as important to the Yankton and Yanktonai as they were to all of the Plains tribes, but these two groups also supplemented their diet with corn, squash, beans and fishing. Even the house types show the adaptability of these tribes. From the woodlands, the Yankton-Yanktonai brought with them the dome-shaped house but learned to cover it with hides instead of bark. From the other tribes, they learned to build earth lodges in their permanent villages, and they used the tipi on their hunting trips away from the villages (Hurt and Howard 1950). Because of their close association with other earth lodge users, the Yankton and Yanktonai made pottery, basketry, bullboats, and wooden mortars like those used by the Missouri River tribes (Howard 1966a:11-13).

Family life and kinship were the basis for Yankton and Yanktonai behavior and social organization. Like the Dakota and Lakota, kinship terms were extended to all relatives so only a few terms identified most of the people with whom a person would normally interact. The terms for father and mother were also used for father's brother and mother's sister suggesting a marriage system that included sororal polygyny (a man marrying sisters) and the practice of a man marrying his dead brother's wife. Children of anyone called father and mother were called brother and sister and treated as if they were siblings. Because there were so many people that could be called aunt and uncle there could be many cousins and close relationships existed between them (Morgan 1871:293-382). On the basis of the names of some of the Yankton and Yanktonai divisions, a suggestion was made that the Middle Sioux were at one time organized into clans, but this idea has been disputed by others who point out that there is no real evidence of clans and that band names originated in different ways (Howard 1966a:13; Stipe 1971). Each division or band was an autonomous political unit with its leadership vested in a chief and a council. The chieftainship usually passed from father to son, but this practice was not mandatory (Keating 1824,vol.I:404; Howard 1966a:14). Military police took control during hunts, and all the young warriors formed a "soldiers' lodge" to protect the camp during emergencies (Deloria 1967:19; Howard 1966a:13).

The Yankton and Yanktonai share the religious beliefs of their Lakota and Dakota brothers. The major deity was *Wakan Tanka*, the Great Spirit who created the universe, while some natural phenomena, animals and objects were thought to have sacred powers which could help humans. Some of the religious practices of the Middle Sioux were like those of the Dakota, but others were apparently learned from the Missouri tribes. The Medicine Lodge, Soul Keeping, *Yuwipi*, Snowshoe Dance and Sun Dance were similar to dances performed by other woodland tribes (Gillette 1906; Howard 1952b, 1953, 1955a, 1966a; Howard and Hurt 1952). The Sun Dance, however, appears to have differed from the Lakota practice in that it could be performed by one man without the involvement of the whole group in building a lodge or witnessing the ceremony (Keating 1824, vol.I:449). Other descriptions of the Yanktonai Sun Dance mention the use of sacred bundles by some of the participants.

It is unfortunate that the traditional culture of the Yankton and Yanktonai is not better known, because their position as middle men made them very powerful. They were traders who moved throughout the plains and this gave them an opportunity to learn about new technologies and ideas before other people did. They selected those ideas that benefited them and it would be interesting to know more about the changes that took place in their culture.

Table 6.3. Organization of the Middle Tribes

YANKTON

    Tcan-kute = Shoot in the Woods
    Tcaxu = Lights or lungs
    Wakmuha-oin = Pumpkin-Rind Earrings
    Ihaisdaye = Greasy mouths
    Watceunpa = Roasters
    Ikmun = Wildcat or panther
    Oyate-citca = Bad nation
    Wacitcun-tcintca = Sons of white men

YANKTONAI

    Upper Yanktonai
        Tcan-ona = Shoot at trees or Wazikute, Shooters among the Pines
        Takini = Improved in Condition
        Cikcitcena = Bad ones of different sorts
        Bakihon - Gash themselves with knives
        Kiyuksa = Breakers of the law or customs
        Pabaksa = Cutheads
        Name now forgotten
    Lower Yanktonai (Hunkpatina) = Those camping at one end of the tribal circle
        Pute-temini = Sweat-lips
        Cun-iktceka = Common dogs
        Taquha-yuta = Eat the scrapings of hides
        Sanona = Shot at some white object
        Iha-ca = Red lips
        Ite-xu = Burned face
        Pte-yute-cni = Eat no buffalo cows

Source: Dorsey, Siouan Sociology. *15th Annual Report of the Bureau of American Ethnology*. Washington: U.S. Government Printing Office. p.218.

Turtle Mountain Band of Chippewa

The people who refer to themselves as Turtle Mountain Chippewa are different from all the other tribes in North Dakota, because they are composed of Algonkian-speaking peoples who were once members of other tribes, primarily Cree and Chippewa, and the descendants of some of the members of these tribes who intermarried with French, English, Scottish and other European traders. Because of the mixture of so many peoples, some Turtle Mountain Chippewa identify more with their Chippewa or Cree ancestors while others are interested in their European ancestry. The intermarriage between the groups is so extensive that identity is a personal choice on the part of the individual. The tribal identity recognized and accepted by all is Turtle Mountain Band of Chippewa.

Figure 6.7. Metis camp with tipis and Red River carts. Painted by a member of the U.S. Northern Boundary Commission. (Courtesy of State Historical Society of North Dakota).

Describing the traditional culture, however, it becomes necessary to distinguish between the origins of the various groups that melted into the Turtle Mountain Chippewa. One part of the modern tribe draws its ancestry and traditional culture from the Minnesota Chippewa who moved into this region during the fur trade (Hickerson 1956). These Chippewa adopted so many Plains Indian characteristics, including the tipi, the buffalo hunt, and the Sun Dance, that they are often referred to as Plains Chippewa. Other groups in Canada who made similar adaptations to the plains are called Plains Ojibwa or Saulteaux, and some of the Plains Ojibwa called themselves Bungi (Howard 1966b). A similar move to the plains was made by some of the Canadian Cree who became distinguished as Plains Cree (Mandelbaum 1940). The cultural and linguistic similarities between Plains Chippewa and Plains Cree were so great that much interaction could take place. Some Plains Chippewa and some Plains Cree married non-Indians, particularly French fur traders and added some of the fur traders' ways to their culture. These people are known in Canada as Metis and recognized as a distinctive ethnic group, but in the United States the Metis are part of the Turtle Mountain Chippewa tribe. Other Plains Cree and Plains Chippewa and their French-Indian relatives live at Rocky Boy Reservation in Montana.

All the tribes that make up the modern Turtle Mountain Chippewa were buffalo hunters who utilized the buffalo in the same way that other Plains tribes did. They dried the buffalo meat, used the hides for tipis and clothing, the bones for tools and the sinew for sewing. Like the other Plains tribes, the ancestors of the Turtle Mountain Chippewa used round shields, employed the horse and dog travois to transport their goods and wore hardsoled moccasins decorated with either floral or geometric designs (Howard 1966a, 1966b). The variations on this pattern introduced by the fur traders were the use of a two-wheeled cart in place of the travois and guns to replace the bow and arrow. Wool cloth was used by Metis women to make dresses for themselves and coats for their men, but these articles of clothing were often decorated with traditional quilled and beaded floral and geometric designs, although some of the women took new ideas for designs from the vestments worn by Catholic priests and from the paisley shawls and printed cotton fabrics worn by non-Indian women. Some of the Metis men created a distinctive clothing style that included a wide woven sash wrapped around a cloth coat and shirt. Leggings and moccasins were worn with this outfit. Some Metis were indistinguishable from the other Indians in dress and habits (Brasser 1975, 1976).

The traditional kinship system and its terminology continued to operate long after people settled on the reservation. Father and father's brother were called by the same term which meant father. Mother and mother's sisters were called mother and the children of anyone called mother and father were called brother and sister (Howard 1966b). In this way a Plains Ojibwa or Plains Cree child had a large family of close relatives to live with and care for. Some Turtle Mountain Chippewa with French ancestry added French terms to their system.

In addition to family ties, people were related to each other by clan ties, a carry-over from the Chippewa system. The clans or totems were named after birds, animals, snakes, fishes, and plants. A child was born into the clan of his or her father and kept that clan throughout his/her life. No one could marry a member of the same clan, but the clans provided relatives in different bands so that a person would be welcome wherever he or she went (Skinner 1914b:481; Howard 1966b:73-74). Because the French and English men who married Chippewa or Cree women did not have clans to pass on to their children, the clan system was not used by the people of mixed ancestry, unless a woman married a man who had clan membership to pass on to their children.

The Plains Cree and Plains Chippewa were organized into bands or loose confederations of families, usually named for their leader or their location. People moved from one band to another to take advantage of hunting and social opportunities. Leadership of the bands was partially hereditary, but any leader who did not provide for his people soon found himself without anyone to lead. Assisting the head chief were subchiefs, the military police and the camp council (Howard 1966b:74-75). The Metis, despite their acquaintance with European forms of government, preferred the Indian style and referred to their leaders as chiefs. During the major buffalo hunts, the Metis' military police were in charge just as they were among other Plains tribes (Howard 1972:78).

The religious beliefs and practices of the Plains Chippewa and Plains Cree reflected their original woodland location and their adaptation to the plains way of life. The Great Spirit, or *Gitche Manitou*, was the supreme being who made all things possible. The Midewiwin, or Medicine Lodge, of the woodland tribes, and the Sun Dance or Thirsting Dance, were two ways in which the tribes sought the aid of the Great Spirit (Howard 1966b, Hilger 1959). The Medicine Lodge taught people how to cure illness by using rituals and plant medicines. Other ceremonies included vision quests and dreams in which the Indians received knowledge and assistance from their spiritual beings. To the traditional religious beliefs and practices, the French traders contributed their Catholic beliefs and practices. Today many Turtle Mountain Chippewa are Catholic, although they may also be followers of traditional Indian religions.

Many of the most obvious elements of traditional culture no longer exist, but most tribes have retained some aspects of their language, their kinship system and their traditional religious beliefs and practices. The current attitude of educators and government officials is to encourage Natives to recall and revive as much of the ancient culture as is practical for these times.

BIG WHITE (SHEHEKE)

One of the more interesting people mentioned in the journals of the Lewis and Clark expedition is the man who came to be known as Big White. He not only assisted the Corps of Discovery, but later visitors to the Mandan/Hidatsa villages shared his friendliness and hospitality (Thwaites 1904:151-152).

Sheheke or Shahaka, which means Coyote in Hidatsa, was more commonly known by the name Big White, which had apparently been given to him because of his large size and light coloring. When first met by Lewis and Clark, Sheheke was head chief of Mitutahanka, the lower Mandan village. Because of his position as chief, Sheheke naturally received attention from the leaders of the expedition, but it is clear that his personality caused them to regard him with friendship as well as respect.

The first meeting between Big White and Meriwether Lewis is recorded as October 30, 1804. Big White and another chief who had missed the "chief-making" ceremony were given the presidential medals identifying them as head chiefs. Clothes and a flag had already been delivered to them.

November 1, 1804, Big White and two other headmen spoke with William Clark about making peace with the Arikaras. Ronda (1984:87-88) points out that Shehaka's speech about peace was politically astute because it agreed with the interests of the expedition leaders without really committing the Mandan to a permanent agreement. Big White agreed to make peace but pointed out that the Arikara had violated earlier accords. Big White was more interested in the location of the expedition's winter camp because it would mean trading opportunities. When he learned that the camp would be near the villages, he promised to send them food (Moulton 1987:224-225). Big White kept his word and on November 12 he arrived with 100 pounds of meat packed on his wife's back. She received a small ax and other small gifts for her work (Moulton 1987:233). Throughout the winter, Sheheke sent meat and corn to the men.

Among other services rendered by Big White was a description of the country between the Missouri and the Rocky Mountains. Whether Big White drew maps or gave directions while Clark drew the maps is not clear from the journals, but two maps drawn by Clark and attributed to Big White may be seen in the *Atlas of the Lewis and Clark Expedition* (Moulton 1983:31a,31b). During the trip down river, Big White told Clark the Mandan origin tradition and described some of the former villages of the Mandan (Moulton 1984:308).

When the expedition returned to the villages, Lewis and Clark proposed that some of the Indian leaders accompany them to Washington, D.C. to meet President Jefferson. Big White was the only one who accepted the invitation.

August 17, 1806 the return party, including Big White, his wife and son, with the interpreter Rene Jusseaume and his family, left for St. Louis. When Clark arrived at the Mandan chief's house he found friends and family had gathered to say goodbye. People cried out loud as the family headed for the boats.

One of the first major stops on the return trip was at the Arikara villages on the Grand River. Here the expedition leaders and Big White engaged the Arikara in peace negotiations. From this point on, there are few mentions of the chief, but on September 6, 1908 Clark noted in his journal that the chief, women and children were weary of the journey. "Children cry &c." (Moulton 1993:352).

Two months after reaching St. Louis, Big White was introduced to President Jefferson at the White House. Jefferson asked him to encourage the tribes to live in peace with each other. Big White seems to have enjoyed the attentions of Washington and Philadelphia society. He attended the White House dinner Jefferson held for Lewis and Clark, posed for his portrait, and entertained foreign ambassadors (Horan 1986:45).

In May 1807, a small convoy led by Nathaniel Pryor was assigned to return Big White and his family to their home, but the group was attacked by the Arikara with such violence that it was forced to retreat and it was not until 1809 that Big White accompanied a group of Missouri Fur Trade Company employees and finally reached his home.

In 1811 John Bradbury and Henry Marie Brackenridge joined Manuel Lisa and other Missouri Fur Trade Company men on a trip up the Missouri. Both men met Big White and reported something of his life after returning home. Brackenridge (1816:137) informs the reader that Big White had returned home laden with presents, but his stories of life among the Whites were not believed. As Brackenridge reported, "The Mandans treat with ridicule the idea of there being a greater or more numerous people than themselves." The well known chief Le Borgne called Big White a "bag of lies."

Bradbury is a little more generous in his description of Big White, commenting on his use of English and his hospitality (1904:151). Big White and Bradbury generally conversed by means of Rene Jusseaume, the interpreter (1904:156). In one of the conversations, Big White noted that he would like to go and live among the Whites and that he had persuaded others to accompany him. On another visit to Big White, Bradbury gave him silver ornaments and was feasted in return. When Bradbury asked to buy some moccasins, Big White informed the village and so many women brought pairs to sell that Bradbury got a dozen pairs quite inexpensively (Bradbury 1904:164).

The next twenty years pass with little notice of Big White. Visitors like Prince Maximilian and George Catlin do not mention him and it is probable that he died before they visited the Missouri villages. Francis Chardon, clerk at Fort Clark from 1834-1839, recorded in his journal for January 7, 1835 the death of "the old Mandan chief (The White Head) regretted by all who knew him" (Abel 1932:20). Annie Abel, Chardon's editor, believes this refers to the death of Big White (Abel 1932:294). A different, earlier, death is recorded by John C. Luttig, a fur-trader who kept a post at the Arikara villages from 1812 to 1813. He reports (Drumm 1964:68-69) that some Mandan had brought the news that Big White and another man had been killed in a battle with Hidatsas.

Chapter 7

Federal Indian Policy

Native Americans have a unique relationship with the Federal government. No other American ethnic group has the special legal status possessed by native peoples nor does any other group have cabinet-level representation in the Federal government. This special status has grown out of aboriginal sovereignty and land rights. While some non-Indians continue to press for the abrogation of these special rights (Costo and Henry 1977), most Americans remain unaware of the reasons for the Indians' special legal status.

The current American Indian-Federal relationship has developed out of a series of historical and legislative acts. The Federal government has had no consistent policy for dealing with aboriginal land rights or tribal sovereignty but has usually changed policies to meet public demand. After four hundred years it is possible to point out general characteristics of policy, but historians and lawyers do not agree on the exact identification of the attitudes which helped to shape such policies. In general, policies have alternated between support for tribal rights and sovereignty and the abrogation of such rights. Views toward the proper way of obtaining Indian lands have also changed, as have attitudes regarding reservations and the rights of Indian tribes to retain their reservations and to administer them. One of the long term debates is between assimilationists and separatists. Assimilationists believe that Indians should be absorbed into the general non-Indian population and point out that Europeans and other settlers have given up their traditional languages and customs to become "American." According to this point of view, Indians should be required to do the same. On the other hand, separatists claim that Indians, as original inhabitants of the continent, have the right to retain their language and culture and that the continuation of reservations is part of the maintenance of their ethnic identity. From the separatist point of view, Indians should be able to decide for themselves which aspects of American culture they wish to adopt and those aspects which they wish to avoid. The history of Federal Indian policy shows changes in attitude as the proponents of these two opposing viewpoints gain or lose political power.

Complicating the situation is the way in which Federal policy is developed. The executive branch of the Federal government, which includes the Bureau of Indian Affairs, may suggest policy and may, under certain circumstances, make policy. The Federal legislative branch may also pass laws and acts which directly affect Indians. These laws and acts may provide funds for tribal needs or remove funds from tribal projects. Indians and non-Indians are often in political conflict with each other, and the resulting policy may not be exactly what either group wanted. The Federal judicial branch is charged with interpreting the laws made by Congress and the states. In interpreting laws affecting tribal people, the justices of the Supreme Court must be aware of legal precedents involving Indians, as well as any previous laws which have established Indian policy or Indian legal status. Interpretation of the law does not always coincide with tribal interests or with the Federal desires. President Andrew Jackson in

1832 ignored the Supreme Court's decision in the case of *Worcester vs. Georgia* because it did not agree with his Federal Indian policy.

The general public has not always upheld Federal Indian laws, either. A constantly recurring event in tribal history is the passage of Federal laws to protect tribal lands and the ignoring of these laws by settlers. Since 1964 the Civil Rights Act has prohibited discrimination on the basis of race, sex and religion, but discrimination continues.

Colonial Indian Policy

Although this chapter is concerned with Indian policy from 1775 to the present, the French, Dutch, Spanish and British policies that preceded the establishment of the American government directly influenced the way in which United States Federal Indian policy developed. Generally these policies reflected the idea that the tribes were sovereign political units (American Indian Policy Review Commission 1977:51) with aboriginal rights to the land. By recognizing that the Indians were the rightful owners of the land, the European powers were forced to make provisions for tribal people. Each European government solved the problem in its own way, according to its own interests (Tyler 1973). The Spanish assigned both land and the Natives living on the land to individual landlords and missions. The Spanish made no treaties with the Indians but regarded them as pagan souls to be converted to the glory of God and the Spanish crown. The Dutch settlers recognized Native rights to the land and acquired the land by purchase from the Indians (Tyler 1973:27). One of these properties is the well-known purchase of Manhattan for $24.00 worth of beads and other trade goods. The Dutch generally followed a policy of separation between Indian and White and made little attempt at culture change. The French were more interested in furs and other natural resources than they were in land and permanent settlements, and so they were not too concerned about acquiring land. Instead they often settled in the Indian villages where they married Indian women, finding it easier to live and work among relatives. These marriages resulted in the part Native-part French individual who knew both the land, the natives and their languages, as well as French customs. These people became traders, interpreters and expedition leaders. Some of these men led the way into what is now North Dakota and were responsible for the establishment of trading posts in the Red River Valley and on the Missouri River.

In general, however, the success of the British in the struggle for domination of the continent, meant that British policy had the greatest impact on modern Indian policy. The earliest British policy permitted the colonists to negotiate for land. Like the other governments, the British recognized aboriginal rights to the land but never settled on a specific way of acquiring the land. Each colony negotiated its own land acquisition terms with the native peoples. During this time, the Indians had the upper hand in determining general terms since the colonies were small in comparison to the tribal population.

The struggles between the European powers for control of the continent caused the Indians to be used as pawns. Between 1689 and 1763, four major wars, begun in Europe, were carried out in North America. In these wars the European powers tried to enlist the more powerful tribes as allies. Failing to attract the tribes to their side, the Europeans would try to win an agreement of neutrality. The native leaders took advantage of the needs of the Europeans and tried to negotiate treaties and trade agreements that would benefit their tribes. Eventually, tribes were pitted against each other (Hagan 1961:17-18).

During the French and Indian War, many Indians sided with the French because they were relatives or because the French appeared to be less interested in acquiring land. Others sided with the British because they thought the British would be easier to get along with. The Treaty of Paris that ended the

French and Indian War in 1763 resulted in a major change in Indian policy. The French were removed from power in North America and the British began to move into areas formerly held by the French. Finding the British less generous and forgiving than the French antagonized a number of tribal leaders (Vogel 1972:55). In an attempt to remedy the situation, the confederated tribes under Pontiac captured a number of British forts. The success of the surprise attack forced the British to pay more attention to Native demands, but it also increased the settler's opinions of Indians as enemies, not to be trusted.

In order to control both Indians and Whites, in 1763, King George III issued the Proclamation of October 7, also known as the Royal Proclamation. The Proclamation established an area that would be considered "Indian Country" free from White settlement. Any non-Indians living in "Indian Country" were to be removed and no land could be sold to White settlers. Trade with Indians was to be licensed (Vogel 1972:56). By setting aside land, reserving land, for Indian use and regulating land sales, trade and other aspects of Indian-White relations, King George created the model for subsequent Federal policy. The role of local settlers also proved to be prophetic of future problems as both settlers and administrators ignored the provisions of the Proclamation. Governor Dunmore of Virginia commented on the situation (Hagan 1961:27) "Nor can they (the settlers) be easily brought to entertain any belief of the permanent obligation of Treaties made with those people, [the Indians] whom they consider, as but little removed from brute Creation." Since the authorities made little attempt to support the provisions of the Proclamation, settlement by White people usually resulted in resistance by the Indians. Tribal leaders also addressed frequent complaints regarding the encroachments to King George's representatives, but no satisfactory means of dealing with the problem ever developed. The most frequent solution was to remove the Indians from the area. Thus while the British crown was publicly advocating a policy of land acquisition by purchase, the general public was following a policy of acquiring land by conquest. (Some would argue that this policy was acquisition by theft since colonists broke the law by occupying tribal lands and were not only never punished for the transgression but in fact attained their goal of getting the land.)

This general state of affairs continued under U. S. Federal policy.

United States Indian Policy

The Continental Congress generally followed the Indian policy established earlier by Great Britain. Concern over Native reactions to American independence led the writers of the Articles of Confederation to include Indian affairs in the document (Vogel 1972:64). In July 1775 the Continental Congress established a Committee on Indian Affairs, and three administrative departments, a northern, middle and southern were organized (Tyler 1973:33). The men assigned to these departments were told to solicit tribal support for the Revolutionary cause and to be alert for British agents inciting Indians against the Americans (Vogel 1972:64). The Articles of Confederation which were finally effected in 1781 gave the Congress the right to regulate trade and manage Indian affairs so long as such practice did not infringe on states' rights. The necessity to attract Indian allies to the American cause brought about the first treaty between an Indian tribe and the Continental Congress.

In 1778, the Delaware signed a treaty of "peace and friendship" in which they agreed to aid the United States in the war with Great Britain. In exchange for their assistance, the Delaware were offered the opportunity to form their own state and the Ohio River was agreed upon as the permanent western boundary for White settlement. As Vogel (1972:65) points out, however, not only was this the only treaty of alliance made between the United States and an Indian tribe during the Revolutionary War, but it only lasted a year. Some states negotiated treaties of assistance with their local tribes and some tribes sided with the struggling colonists without formal relationships.

The end of the Revolutionary War did not change the situation between the Federal government and the native peoples. The British were still a force in North America and Indian leaders maintained sufficient power to require Congressional attention. Although the Continental Congress issued a proclamation barring Whites from purchasing Indian lands and prohibiting White settlement in Indian country, constant complaints from Indian leaders about encroachment on Indian land indicated a need for stronger solutions. Treaties defining boundaries and providing for payment of goods or money continued to be the primary means of pacifying unhappy Indian leaders, but the Continental Congress also began to consider legislation to solve the problem (Tyler 1973:34).

Henry Knox, Secretary in the War Office from 1784 to 1789, was given responsibility for Indian affairs. Under the new Constitutional government, Knox was made Secretary of War in 1789, a post he held until 1795. Knox attempted to rectify the situation by returning to a strict policy of honesty and fairness in Indian affairs. He presented a proposal to Congress that would have prevented non-Indian settlement on Indian land by force, if necessary. Knox also advocated rigid enforcement of treaties and desired to give Indians the opportunity to become Christian, to learn to farm and to own land, believing that this was one way to protect them from greedy settlers. The response of Congress, however, was to pass more laws rather than to provide for the enforcement of existing laws and treaties.

By 1786, the Indians were so angry about the continued encroachment on their lands that they threatened to repudiate all the treaties and agreements. Believing that British rule was preferable to the problems with the American settlers, Indian leaders attempted to confederate the tribes in order to end American domination. Congress then passed the Northwest Ordinance of July 13, 1787 which stated, in part:

> ...The utmost good faith shall always be observed towards the Indians; their lands and property shall never be taken from them without their consent; and in their property, rights and liberty, they never shall be invaded or disturbed, unless in just and lawful wars authorized by Congress; but laws founded in justice and humanity shall, from time to time, be made, for preventing wrongs being done to them, and for preserving peace and friendship with them (Vogel 1972:74).

Despite these affirmations of good faith, Congress did not provide for the punishment or removal of those who invaded tribal territory. The policy of acquisition by conquest (or theft) continued. Congress also passed a number of new laws aimed at regulating trade between Indians and non-Indians.

Under the Constitution, Congress preserved the right to administer Indian affairs. Indian affairs was placed under the jurisdiction of the War Department (Prucha 1975:14). In 1790 Congress passed the first of a series of Trade and Intercourse Acts. All traders in Indian country must be licensed and pay penalties if they operated without a license. The first Trade and Intercourse Act also stated that the purchase of lands from Indians was invalid without a treaty. This ruling was aimed at protecting Indian land from unscrupulous purchasers and protecting the Federal interest in Indian property. Finally, the Act contained provisions for the punishment of Whites who committed crimes against Indians while the Whites lived in Indian country. This Act was a preview of much of the later legislation and has become relevant in the present day as some tribes have regained lands illegally bought from them after the Act was passed. The Trade and Intercourse Act of 1793 was much stronger than the Act of 1790. It prohibited settlement on Indian lands and provided for the removal of such settlers by force, if necessary. In addition to the crimes previously listed in the earlier Act, those involving horse thieves and traders were added. Finally, the Act prohibited Indian agents from trading with the Indians in order to prevent conflict of interest charges.

Between 1783 and 1800, Congress continued to make treaties with individual tribes and attempted to negotiate settlements satisfactory to both sides. These treaties began to contain the idea of annuities, money or goods to be paid to the Indians every year for a specified number of years. In 1790 a Congressional treaty with the Creeks contained a $1500 annuity. Between 1778 and 1809, forty-nine treaties were made (Costo and Henry 1977:208-209). Some of these treaties were rewrites of existing treaties as changing relations necessitated new provisions, and some of these were treaties with new nations as westward expansion caused more Indian-White contact. In addition to treaties, Congress also made agreements or contracts with separate nations. The agreements were sometimes contracts between an individual and a tribe, sometimes unratified treaties and a variety of other miscellaneous agreements between Indian nations and non-Indians.

The War of 1812 was an important event in the development of Indian policy because the Indians became "enemies" to be feared and to be dealt with harshly. The presence of the British in Canada and around the Great Lakes had given the native peoples another party to play off against the Americans. A number of Indian tribes sided with the British, believing that the British would give them back their land once the Americans were removed. Tecumseh the Shawnee, and Black Hawk the Sac joined with the British and were successful in defeating a number of American armed units. The Indian success was such that when the Treaty of Ghent which ended the war was signed in 1815, the Indians refused to believe that the war was over. They were winning, and the British had surrendered to the Americans (Hagan 1961:63-64)!

In an unusual move, the British negotiators of the Treaty of Ghent succeeded in obtaining an agreement that the United States would not only not punish the hostile tribes but would sign treaties with each of them guaranteeing them the lands they held before the War (Vogel 1972:68).

Despite the British efforts and the American agreement, the Indians lost more than they gained. The surrender of the British and their relinquishing of holdings in North America meant that the native peoples had no buffer between them and the Americans and that they were no longer able to play political games by alternating between the British and the Americans. The holdings of the British were opened to White settlement. As punishment for their part in the war, many tribes were forced to cede lands and move west of the Mississippi.

After 1815, the idea of an Indian country west of the Mississippi took hold. With the Louisiana Purchase in 1803, a vast "empty" territory had been acquired, and some tribes had already moved there years before in an attempt to get away from the White settlers. Others were "encouraged" by bribes or tricks to cede their lands in exchange for lands in "Indian Territory." Many smaller tribes, including the Delaware, the Shawnee, the Miami, the Piankashaw and the Wyandot took lands in Oklahoma in exchange for their traditional homelands in the east. Between 1815 and 1830, one hundred treaties were made. The larger tribes, the Creeks, Cherokees, Chickasaws, Choctaws and Seminoles of the southeast resisted cession, but the election of Andrew Jackson as president meant the end of Indian tenure east of the Mississippi.

Before 1830, however, two other Federal actions affected native peoples. In 1819, Congress passed the Civilization Act which provided money for religious organizations to provide schools for Indians. Education had long been a concern, but not until this Act did Congress officially take a stand on the necessity of providing education for Indians. One passage set out the specific content for the education of the Indians:

...The President of the United States shall be, and he is hereby authorized, in every case where he shall judge improvement in the habits and conditions of such Indians practicable, and that the means of instruction can be introduced with their own consent, to employ persons capable of good moral character, to instruct them in the mode of agriculture suited to their situation; and for teaching their children in reading, writing and arithmetic, and performing such other duties as may be enjoined...(Prucha 1975:33).

Although the bill provides for the tribal people to consent to education, because it placed the education in the hands of religious groups, it also included conversion as part of the education. This uniting of religion and education created problems for native peoples for many generations.

The second event was the establishment of the Bureau of Indian Affairs in the Department of War in 1824. Secretary of War, John C. Calhoun set up the Bureau and appointed Thomas L. McKenney to be in charge. In 1832 Congress finally confirmed the position and designated a Commissioner of Indian Affairs. The job originally was designed in order to have someone be in charge of administering the Civilization Fund, hearing complaints from tribes regarding violations of various acts and supervising the distribution of the annuities guaranteed to the many different tribes in their treaties (Prucha 1975:33-37).

Removal and Reservations

Andrew Jackson had grown up on the frontier and had earned a reputation as an Indian fighter. He believed in the acquisition of land by conquest, if necessary, and regarded Indian claims to sovereignty as impossible. In an address to Congress in 1829 Jackson stated:

Actuated by this view of the subject, I informed the Indians inhabiting parts of Georgia and Alabama that their attempt to establish an independent government would not be countenanced by the Executive of the United States, and advised them to emigrate beyond the Mississippi or submit to the laws of those States (Prucha 1975:48).

Jackson also suggested that a large area west of the Mississippi be set aside for the use of the tribes. Because of his feelings about sovereignty, Jackson refused to enforce the Supreme Court ruling in favor of Cherokee sovereignty in the case of *Worcester vs. Georgia* and proposed to remove the tribes to the West.

In the debate over the Indian Removal Act, a number of congressmen supported tribal sovereignty. Senator Frelinghuysen of New Jersey spoke at length on the issue of aboriginal land rights and Indian claims. He also pointed out that the United States had acquired much more land than could be profitably used by its citizens and that the necessity to acquire the remainder of tribal land was not proven (Prucha 1975:49-52). The Indian Removal Act was passed in 1830, and President Jackson took this as a mandate to force removal of the tribes to Indian territory.

The Indian Removal Act of 1830 gave the President the right to exchange lands in the west, that is, Oklahoma, for those held by Indians in the east. The tribes were allowed $500,000 to assist them in their move. The President was also given the authority to provide protection for the tribes against other tribes already residing in the new territory. Thus Congress recognized that the tribes already living west of the Mississippi might not welcome the new settlers.

Since most of the small tribes had already moved, Jackson concentrated on moving the major south-eastern tribes the Cherokee, the Creek, the Choctaw, the Chickasaw and the Seminole, to Indian Territory. The members of these tribes were farmers and had adopted many customs of the White settlers who lived around them. The Cherokee had a system for reading and writing the Cherokee language, and a legislature and court system patterned on the Federal system. The Cherokee did not willingly give up their lands and struggled for a number of years to avoid removal.

The Choctaw were the first to sign a removal treaty. Some Choctaw had moved years before to escape persecution, and so the majority of the tribe agreed to join them. From 1831 to 1834, a majority of the Choctaw left Mississippi and moved to Oklahoma. Not all Choctaw agreed to the treaty. Some, however, stayed behind and have since sought recognition for themselves as the Choctaw Tribe of Mississippi. The Federal government has attempted to avoid recognition of the Choctaw Tribe of Mississippi on the basis that they chose to give up their Indian status when they stayed behind. However, the Choctaws of Mississippi were successful in their request for Federal recognition while other tribes in similar circumstances have not been so fortunate.

The Creek and Seminole were forced into removal in 1832. The Creek Treaty of 1832 provided for allotments to individual Creek. These allotments were soon lost through fraud, and it was evident to the Creek that their only chance of survival as a group was to migrate (Hagan 1961:78). The Federal government provided moving assistance by contracting with private companies.

These companies did not care whether the Indians were warm and safe, and so many Creek died on the way to Oklahoma. The Seminole at first agreed to join their Creek relatives in Oklahoma, but some decided to fight and thus began the Seminole Wars. The war lasted seven years, ending in 1842 when the Federal troops violated a flag of truce and finally captured Osceola, one of the Seminole leaders. The government eventually ceased formal military operations and let the Seminole remain in the swamps of Florida.

The Cherokee removal has been called the "Trail of Tears" because so many Indians died. The Cherokee had petitioned Congress not to ratify a treaty which had been signed by a small number of Cherokee. When the treaty was ratified, the Cherokee simply refused to move. As many as fifteen thousand Cherokee were then rounded up by Federal troops and marched to Oklahoma during the late fall. The Cherokee were forced to march with no chance to bring in the harvest and no time to prepare for the move. Provisions often failed to arrive and cold winter weather caused many people to be ill. Estimates are that perhaps four thousand Cherokee may have died on the trek. A few Cherokee hid in the hills of North Carolina and Tennessee, and today they are known as the Eastern Cherokee and live on a small reservation in North Carolina.

Despite the guarantee of the Indian Removal Act that "the United States will forever secure and guaranty to them, [the Indians] and their heirs or successors, the country so exchanged with them" White settlers were already moving west of the Mississippi, and the pressure on Indian land continued. By 1850, the Federal government realized that the establishment of an Indian Territory was not possible. Instead of the whole central part of the country being "Indian Territory," the needs of White settlers demanded that some parts be opened for settlement. The need for settlers to cross the central plains and reach the west coast also put pressure on Congress to reduce the size of Indian country.

Before 1850 a large section of land was set aside as Indian Country for the Plains and Removed Indians. This region included what is now North and South Dakota, Montana, Nebraska, Kansas, Wyoming, Eastern Colorado and Oklahoma. This territory was to be a vast reservation where all the tribes would be settled. Statehood, however, interfered with this plan. Oregon was settled in 1841; Texas joined the Union in 1846; and California, New Mexico and Arizona became part of the United States in 1848. The discovery of gold on the west coast and in the Black Hills saw more and more settlers heading west. As these migrants crossed the plains, they destroyed timber, bison and other resources needed by the Natives. Because Indians desired to protect these resources, the Whites demanded protection from what they viewed as unreasonably hostile Indians. In order to provide for the people moving west, treaties were made with the Native Peoples. Between 1852 and 1856, fifty-two treaties were negotiated. In 1867, Congress created a special Commission to study the situation and to determine how to proceed. The commission known as the Peace Commission, was instructed "to insure civilization for the Indians and peace and safety for the Whites" (Tyler 1973:78).

The Peace Commission of 1867 made a number of recommendations. Some of these referred to specific situations, and some were more general. Most of their findings were critical of the Whites, and one result of the criticism was the abandonment of the Bozeman Trail. The Commission also recommended that Kansas and Nebraska be cleared of native inhabitants by removing these peoples to some other Indian territory. The Treaty of Fort Laramie of 1868 and the Treaty of Medicine Lodge of 1867 with the southern plains tribes established reservations for the tribes and authorized the division of the land into allotments for individuals. Also provided under these treaties were farm tools, farm animals, and educational facilities. The Commission also called for changes in the laws permitting the governors of states to call out troops against the Indians and for a complete change in the agents, superintendents and other administrative personnel of the Bureau of Indian Affairs. The Treaty of Fort Laramie, 1868, established the Great Sioux Reservation and identified unceded lands which were to be buffalo hunting grounds for the various tribes. Some of the issues raised by the Commission and others created by the Treaty continue to be relevant.

From 1867 to 1876, the last of the Plains Wars was fought. The Treaty of Fort Laramie had guaranteed that the Indians could hunt off the reservations and that they would be protected from White people settling on tribal lands, but the discovery of gold in the Black Hills made it impossible to prevent White encroachment, and the Indians, believing that the Whites had broken the treaty, felt it necessary to fight once again for their rights. In 1874, Federal troops were sent into the Black Hills to protect, not the rights of Tribal Peoples which the treaties had claimed would be protected, but the goldseekers (Hagan 1961:117). The Federal government attempted to purchase the area, but the tribes refused to sell because the land was sacred. After the wars, the Great Sioux Nation was divided into smaller reservations in North and South Dakota. In 1871 Congress passed a bill prohibiting further treaty-making with Indians. Subsequent reservations and alterations in reservation size were made by executive order or executive agreement rather than by treaty.

In the years following 1850, federal policy had a two-pronged approach. Tribes which refused to settle on the reservations came under the control of the army, whose job was to force them to move to the reservations. The army established forts for their work. Tribes who settled on the reservations were provided with agents selected by various religious denominations.

In 1869 a Board of Indian Commissioners was established. In its first report the Board blamed the White people for most of the aggression and pointed out that the Indians had been cheated and tricked by unscrupulous soldiers, traders and agents. In their recommendations, the Board stressed the need for Christian education and for the allotment of land in severalty to those Indians who were able to manage the land. They recommended the teaching of English in order to avoid misunderstandings due to language difficulties (Prucha 1975:131-134). Most of the recommendations made by the Board were subsequently implemented by the Board or by Congress. In 1872, the Board divided the reservations among the various religious denominations in order to provide for the education and Christianization of the Tribal Peoples, without the competition between denominations. In 1879 Carlisle Indian School in Carlisle, Pennsylvania was established. In 1887 Congress passed the General Allotment Act to provide for the allotment of lands to individual Indians.

Allotment

The idea of allotting lands to individual Natives was present in many treaties and recommendations to Congress, but by the later 1800's a number of influential people began to press for the distribution of land. Some people felt that individual ownership of land would protect native rights by removing land from the control of Congress and the Federal government. Since most Euro-Americans dreamed of owning land and regarded land ownership as the ultimate achievement, most people thought that giving land to each Indian was a wonderful idea. Other people recognized that this land grant would be a means of gaining access to tribal lands because after the land allotments had been made, the remaining lands were to be opened to White settlement. Opposing forces recognized the opportunities for land loss and felt that the success of such a scheme would mean the total assimilation of Indians into White culture.

Senator Henry Dawes was the primary force in the passage of the General Allotment Act of 1887, sometimes known as the Dawes Act. He was single-minded in his determination, as indicated by the following excerpt from one of his writings:

> The head chief told us that there was not a family in that whole Nation that had not a home of its own. There was not a pauper in that Nation, and the Nation did not owe a dollar. It built its own capitol...and it built its own schools and its hospitals. Yet the defect of the system was apparent. They have not got as far as they can go, because they own their land in common. It is Henry George's system, and under that there is no enterprise to make your home any better than that of your neighbors. There is no selfishness, which is at the bottom of civilization. Till this people will consent to give up their lands, and divide them among their citizens so that each can own the land he cultivates, they will not make much more progess (Lake Mohonk Conference Proceedings 1885:43).

Today we have to marvel that Senator Dawes' could not recognize the absurdity in believing that a tribe that had schools and hospitals and no poverty needed to be changed. If native peoples had been allowed to keep their land and use it as they had always done, conditions might be very different.

The original Allotment Act of 1887 provided that each head of an Indian family would receive one-quarter section (160 acres); each single person over eighteen years of age, one-eighth section (80 acres); and all other single persons under eighteen years of age, one-sixteenth of a section (40 acres). This land was to be held in trust for the owners or the owner's heirs for twenty-five years. If the owner "adopted the habits of civilized life, " i.e., settled on his or her allotment, he or she was declared to be a citizen of the United States with all the rights and privileges (Prucha 1975:171-174). These rights included the protection of the law and the privilege of paying taxes. Lands that were not allotted were to be opened for homesteading to non-Indians. In 1891, the Act was amended to provide for allotments of 80 acres to Indians not covered in the original Act and to include children born since the first allotments were made. Allotments of grazing land would be double that of the acreage for agriculture. The Burke Act of 1906 considerably modified the Allotment Act by making it possible for agents to make citizenship coincident with receiving title to the land. Once the title was received, the land could be sold, leased or disposed of by the title holder.

Allotment continues to have repercussions. The immediate effect of the Act was to reduce the total acres of Indian land by 65 percent. Before allotment 139 million acres were held in trust for Indians. In 1934 when allotment was officially repealed, only 48 million acres of land were left, and many Indians were without land. This alienation of tribal trust lands occurred in two ways. First, after the reservation

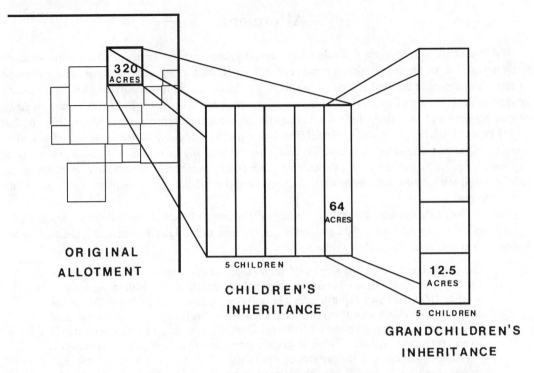

320
ACRES

ORIGINAL
ALLOTMENT

5 CHILDREN

64
ACRES

CHILDREN'S
INHERITANCE

12.5
ACRES

5 CHILDREN

GRANDCHILDREN'S
INHERITANCE

Figure 7.1. Diagram illustrating the problem of fractionated heirship. When children inherit equal shares of an allotment, in only a few generations, there will only be fractions left.

lands were allotted, surplus lands were opened for White homesteading. Most reservations today have White residents who own land on the reservation. In North Dakota, more than 75% of the land on some reservations is owned by non-Indians. The presence of these non-Indians causes problems of jurisdiction. Do these people have to abide by tribal laws or are they subject to White laws, even though reservations have their own legal system? Second, land was alienated by agents declaring Indians competent to manage the land and giving them title to it. Since this decision meant that the land could be sold, it was often sold to a non-Indian. Title also meant that the land was taxable, and much land was taken when Indians were unable to pay the property taxes. The courts have recently ruled that this land should not have been taxed and have made it possible for some of the lands to be returned to Indian ownership, but a long and difficult legal process is involved.

A more long-term affect of allotment has been the fractionation of Indian-owned land. Under the original Act, the lands were to be divided evenly among the allottee's heirs: a single 160 acre tract might be divided between the five or six or more children of the original recipient. Since those children have had children of their own and those children have had children, the original 160 acres may now be shared by several hundred heirs. No one has a large enough share to use the land efficiently although there may be a large enough tract to provide land for a home. Deciding which site belongs to which person is another issue which can cause quarreling and disagreement between relatives. Today many Indians own land on a number of different allotments, sometimes even on reservations in different states, and the disposition of these lands is very difficult. If all the heirs can be convinced to sell, it

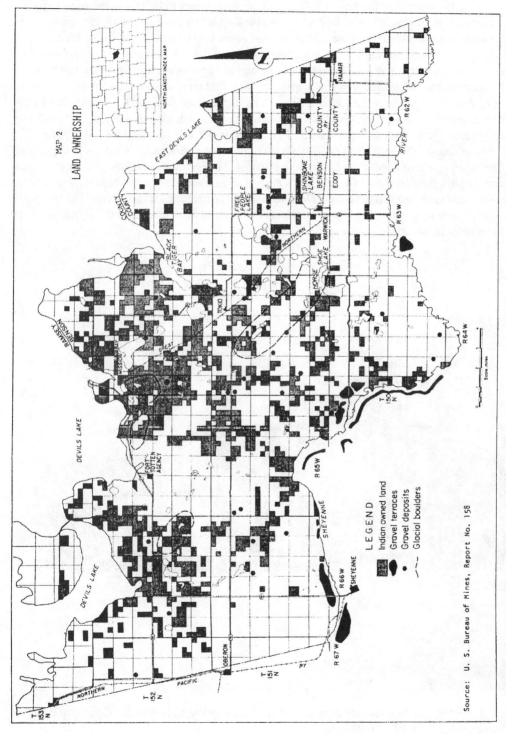

Figure 7.2. Map showing how allotment and opening reservations to non-Indian ownership has affected Fort Totten reservation. (Source:U.S. Department of Interior 1976).

103

may be possible to consolidate the land, but if one of the heirs wants to build a home or to keep the share for sentimental reasons, then the only way to use the land is to lease it. Dividing the income from a lease between several hundred heirs means that no one receives very much income from the property.

By 1920 it was obvious that allotment, rather than providing Indians with a means of self-development and self-support, was a disaster. Cases of fraud in land-dealings were numerous and perhaps 100,000 Indians were landless and unhappy when they were told there was no land for their children. The reservations which had been guaranteed "for as long as the grass shall grow" were rapidly being owned by non-Indians. The sums received from the sale of lands which were to be spent for health and education benefits for the Indians were tied up in Congressional discussions and federal bureaucracy. The sad state of Indian life, health and education caused constant agitation for a change in the law. In 1926 a Commission was ordered to investigate the situation. The report of this Commission, known as the Meriam Report, but officially titled *The Problem of Indian Administration* (Meriam et. al. 1928), was highly critical of Indian policy and revealed the plight of Tribal Peoples nationwide. Poverty, poor education, poor health and numerous other problems were documented. Eventually legislation was passed to remedy the situation.

Figure 7.3. Fort Yates Agency building, ca.1900. Photo by Frank B. Fiske. (Courtesy of State Historical Society of North Dakota).

Indian Reorganization Act

The Indian Reorganization Act of 1934 or the Wheeler-Howard Bill was the policy of John Collier, Commissioner of Indian Affairs from 1933 - 1945. Collier had worked with Tribal People and had seen their problems. In an attempt to change earlier policies for the better and to give Tribal People participation in their own government and in solving their problems, Collier devised a multi-pronged policy. Collier's first act was to halt the sale of tribal lands and to revoke the agent's right to issue titles to land. Second, he declared that there should be no Federal interference with tribal religion and culture and that language and culture should be encouraged in the schools. This was a direct attack upon the efforts of agents, schools and missionaries to forceably change tribal culture through prohibition of religious activities and language.

The Johnson-O'Malley Act of 1934 authorized the Secretary of the Interior to contract with the states or authorized agencies to provide education, medical services, agricultural assistance and social welfare to Native people. The greatest impact has been in education where the Johnson-O'Malley funds are still used to provide assistance for Indian children in public schools.

The Indian Reorganization Act and the Oklahoma Indian Welfare Act were aimed at restoring the land base and making Indian reservations economically viable. The Reorganization Act officially ended the policy of allotment. In order to regain some of their lost reservation lands, Indians were provided funds to assist them in the purchase of land. Any lands that had not been sold or homesteaded were returned to the reservations. Provisions in the Reorganization Act allowed the tribes to incorporate and to establish tribal constitutions and constitutional forms of government. The establishment of constitutional forms of government was, and still is, controversial. Some Indian people regard the establishment of tribal councils under constitutional forms of government as an attempt to degrade the traditional tribal leadership. Collier, however, viewed it as a means of giving Native leadership recognition that would permit the tribes to establish business, conduct their own affairs and eventually be free from government control. The Act also provided for Native People to be given preference in the Bureau of Indian Affairs, but this provision was not enforced until the mid-1970's.

The Indian Reorganization Act was never unanimously acclaimed, and there was constant pressure from Indians and their supporters for repeal. Despite the inability of the Act's opponents to pass repeal measures, other changes in Indian policy were made by later Commissioners.

Termination and Relocation

The 1950's saw a return of the earlier policy of forced assimilation through removal of Federal services to Tribal People. The end of these services was to be accomplished through a variety of means. First of these was relocation.

Relocation encouraged Indians to move from the reservations to urban areas. The encouragement took the form of Federal financial assistance, help in finding a job and in locating housing in the urban areas. The basic idea of relocation was to find permanent employment off the reservation for those Indians who had employable skills but were unable to find work on or near the reservation. It was assumed that once people had jobs, they would no longer need the educational and medical benefits that were provided for them on the reservation. Between 1952 -1967, 60,000 Indians were relocated. How many of these people returned to the reservation is not known, but the indications are that many did. The early relocation programs were not well designed. Applicants were not carefully screened for their ability to adapt to the urban environment. Often the job skills that applicants possessed were not those which would provide sufficient income for a large family, and the poverty was often worse in the urban areas than on the reservation. Program officials did little follow-up. After relocatees were found jobs and houses and given initial information about the city, not enough further contact was made to determine whether additional assistance was needed. Originally, relocatees were moved as far away from their home reservation as possible because officials believed that the relocatees would be discouraged from returning to their reservation. Once in the city, relocatees were not placed in jobs or housing near other Indians but were encouraged to assimilate by living among non-Indians. Many Indians felt lost and out of place and returned to the reservation where their friends and families were. Today, the relocation program has been changed to recognize the need for more assistance in making the transition. The idea that these moves are permanent has been discarded, and people are encouraged to find work near their home reservation so that familial contacts can be maintained. Educational assistance is provided to help Indian people obtain marketable skills. Large numbers of Indians in urban areas have resulted in the organization of tribal centers, clinics, day-care centers and other organizations which help Indian families adjust to the urban environment. However, most Indians who

Figure 7.4. Issuing wagons and plows at Fort Yates. Photo by Frank B. Fiske. (Courtesy of State Historical Society of North Dakota).

move to the city give up the educational and medical benefits that are available to them on the reservation.

A more disastrous policy of the 1950's was Termination. The House Concurrent Resolution 108 made a policy to free all tribes "from federal supervision and control and from all disabilities and limitations especially applicable to Indians." The Resolution named specific states and tribes which were to be "freed" immediately. One of these tribes was the Turtle Mountain Chippewa of North Dakota. Under Termination policy, tribes would be declared self-sufficient. All the trust lands would be sold and the proceeds would be divided among the people. No reservation and no further government services would be offered. Eventually, with all reservations terminated and all treaties abrogated, the Federal government would no longer be responsible for Indians. Opponents of the policy pointed out that this idea completely disregarded the treaty provisions which established reservations as permanent homes for Indians and that the results would be similar to allotment, further loss of Indian lands. Proponents of the policy said that Indians would have equality of opportunity and freedom denied them under the Federal paternalistic approach.

A number of tribes were terminated. Termination proceedings were different for each tribe because it was necessary to take into account the economic situation of the reservation, its resources and the capabilities of the people. The Klamath Reservation of Oregon was terminated and the lands allotted to individual Klamath. For some Klamath the proceeds were placed in trust and administered by the National Bank of Portland, until the trusts were liquidated in 1973. For the remaining Klamath, the funds were received directly and used at the discretion of the recipients. Many used the money to buy and furnish new homes. Large sums of money appeared to diminish very rapidly, and many Klamath were soon dependent upon social welfare and other services. Some Federal services were available to the Klamath under specific education and health acts, but the terminated tribes were ineligible for the majority of Federal programs. The Menominee Reservation in central Wisconsin was turned into Menominee County and the Menominee Tribe was given the administrative seat of Menominee Town. The Menominee had difficulty operating as a county because they were unused to county management, which includes the necessity to tax county residents, allocate funds and govern the county. The once-prosperous Menominee Reservation was taken over by non-Indians, and the Indians became a minority. The Menominee felt discriminated against and formed the lowest socio-economic level in the county. In 1973, the Menominees successfully sued to have the reservation restored. Other terminated tribes have followed the lead of the Menominee and asked for restoration.

One other effort to shift responsibility for Indians away from the Federal government was Public Law 280, passed by Congress in 1953. This law required some states and permitted other states to take jurisdiction over civil and criminal offenses committed on Indian reservations. Under the law, three different situations were defined. Some states, including California, Minnesota, Nebraska, Oregon and Wisconsin had to take jurisdiction. Arizona, Montana, New Mexico, North Dakota, South Dakota, Utah and Washington could assume jurisdiction if they amended their state constitutions to permit such action. Other states could decide for themselves whether they wanted to take jurisdiction or not. State jurisdiction did not include taxation of reservation property or any supervision related to hunting, fishing or trapping rights. Public Law 280 has had a negative impact on tribal judicial issues because of the disagreement over who has jurisdiction in what areas. For example, North Dakota takes jurisdiction only when the tribe or the individual consents; otherwise the case is a Federal or Indian case, depending upon the crime. Problems have developed in working with state law enforcement officials since the tribes pay no taxes to support the state law enforcement program. Some states would like to interpret Public Law 280 to mean that the state has jurisdiction over land use, zoning and building codes on the reservation; however, most tribes steadfastly maintain that these are tribal rights.

Compounding this problem are the Supreme Court rulings which provide certain rights to Indian tribes which appear to be in conflict with state's rights.

In 1968 the Indian Civil Rights Act was passed. Although Indians became citizens in 1924 and came under the general Civil Rights Act when they appear in Federal court, this was not the case in the tribal courts. The Indian Civil Rights Act provided that Indians should receive the same rights in tribal courts as they would in state and Federal courts. These rights include freedom of religion, freedom of speech, press and assembly; protection from unreasonable search and searches without warrants; security from double jeopardy; protection against self-incrimination; security from seizure of property without just compensation; the right to a speedy and public trial, with confrontation of witnesses and counsel but without the right to free counsel. Under the Act, the tribal courts are limited to sentences of less than one year or a fine of less than $5000 or both. Sec. 203 guarantees the privilege of *habeas corpus* to test the legality of a person's detention by an Indian tribe. Other sections of the Act established a model code for Indian offenses and attempted to solve some of the state jurisdiction problems by allowing for retrocession by the states and making assumption of jurisdiction contingent upon the approval of the tribes involved.

Relocation, Termination and Public Law 280 were aimed at ending Federal responsibility to Native Peoples by assimilating them. A new approach, Self-Determination, reversed these goals.

Self-Determination

Throughout the 1960's the policy of termination was questioned. The results of the Menominee and Klamath cases, as well as the obvious unreadiness of other tribes to be terminated, caused concerned individuals to question the reality and the legality of Termination. In 1966 when Congress interviewed Robert La Follette Burnette for Commissioner of Indian Affairs, the Congressmen asked him specifically about Termination. Burnette identified a change from Termination to self-control, suggesting that at some point in the future tribes would be ready to assume control over their affairs, without bureaucratic intervention, but that this did not mean that the Federal government would lessen its responsibility to Indians nor would it mean the end of the Federal Indian relationship.

President Lyndon Johnson first proposed the idea of Self-Determination in a Congressional address in March, 1968. In this address President Johnson recommended "A policy of maximum choice for the American Indian: a policy expressed in programs of self-help, self-development, self-determination" (Prucha 1975:248). To push this policy forward Johnson established a National Council on Indian Opportunity and asked Congress to appropriate one-half billion dollars for programs. Nixon continued the requests to Congress to support Indian self-determination, and finally in 1975 Congress passed the Indian Self-Determination and Education Assistance Act (Public Law 93-638) which formally established Self-Determination as a policy.

The Self-Determination Act is comprehensive in its approach to Indian policy. Not only did this Act recall the days of the Indian Reorganization Act, and officially end Termination as a policy, it reorganized the Johnson-O'Malley Act and others. One of the primary features of the Self-Determination Act was the provision for tribes to contract with the Bureau of Indian Affairs to administer their own programs. Previous Acts had always assumed that the Secretary of the Interior (or his authorized representative) would have to approve any attempts at Indian control of their affairs. This Act does not require such approval, only that the tribe indicate its readiness to assume such control. A number of tribes have taken the opportunities provided by Self-Determination to assume control over their schools, and the result has generally been an increase in tribal and parental support for education. Other opportunities exist, but tribes need to move slowly in order to build the necessary skills and confidence in their abilities to make decisions. A constant difficulty which the tribes face is the lack of sufficient funds to support their programs. The Federal government remains the primary source of funds, and the tribes are constantly faced with the need to defend their allocations from Congressional cuts. What the future holds is still uncertain, but Federal Indian policy has a record of changing approximately every twenty years. If the trend continues, Indian people will be forced to deal with another change in policy sometime around the beginning of the next century.

New Approaches to Self-Determination

The latest trend in Federal policy has been to make laws determining how Indians and non-Indians relate to each other over certain issues. One issue is Native child adoptions. The other issue is Native American religious rights. Another issue which caught the attention of many was the presence of Native American skeletons in museum collections.

In 1978 Congress took up the issue of the placement of Native American children in non-Indian foster or adoptive homes. For many years, large numbers of Indian children had been removed from their reservation homes and placed in care of non-Indian parents. Social workers and legal authorities argued that these children were better cared for by non-Indians than by Indians, but the tribes argued that this process prevented Native children from learning their culture and caused much hardship if the grown-up child wanted to return to the reservation to live. Many people were never able to learn their tribe of origin and spent their adult years searching for a home. In response to the strong tribal lobby, congress passed the Indian Child Welfare Act in 1978, giving tribal courts the right to determine where an Indian child should be placed if the child's home was considered unsuitable. Tribes may take into account traditional child rearing practices and other kinds of information that were ignored by outside authorities. It has been difficult for tribes to implement the Indian Child Welfare Act because non-tribal courts and other authorities do not always recognize tribal jurisdiction. In some cases tribes would like to keep a child on the reservation, but there is no place for the child. Tribes have not received sufficient funds to provide enough foster families or group homes to meet the needs. Tribes also lack funds to hire as many social workers and other officials as they need. These problems are not so critical as to question the utility of the Act, but they are representative of the difficulties inherent in establishing new policies and programs.

In 1978 Congress also passed the Native American Religious Freedom Act (Vecsey 1993) guaranteeing tribal members the right to practice their religion without interference from non-Indian authorities. The problems that drove Native Americans to seek redress in the form of a congressional act were numerous and still have not been resolved. Vecsey (1993:9) summarizes the past and continuing problems as

- the degradation of geographical areas deemed sacred sites

- the maltreatment of Indian burials, particularly bodily remains

- the prohibition against capture, kill, and use of endangered or protected species

- the regulations regarding the collection, transport, and use of peyote

- the alienation and display of religious artifacts

- the prevention of Indian rituals and behavior, particularly in authoritarian institutions

This summary only suggests the extent of the problem, it does not convey the differing legal aspects of specific cases associated with each issue. For example, the last mentioned refers, among other things, to the question of whether Native Americans should be permitted to use Peyote in prison. Obviously, this is a complex issue involving religious rights, the nature of the prison and the prisoners, the fact that Peyote is a controlled substance, the warden's attitude and many known concerns. Non-Indians have been hesitant to accord Native Americans unequivocal religious rights if these rights contravene the rights of non-Indians. The Native American Religious Freedom Act has been strengthened by more recent legislation, but much work still needs to be done to arrive at a position where all sides can feel comfortable.

An outgrowth of some of the religious problems was the passage, in 1990, of the Native American Graves Protection and Repatriation Act (Sockbeson 1990) which gave tribes the opportunity to have skeletons and associated burial objects returned to them. Museums and other institutions that receive federal funds must inventory the appropriate collections and, if the items can be determined to be associated with a specific tribe, the tribe must be notified. If the "tribe can prove cultural affiliation or prove prior ownership or control and also provide some evidence that the museum did not acquire the item with the consent of the legal owner" (Sockbeson 1990:2), the museum must return the item. As with other recent legislation, working out the details has been a torturous process which sometimes involved museums and tribes in court cases.

While recent federal policies have resulted in difficult decisions, the direction of these policies, away from managing Indian affairs, toward protecting Native American rights is a significant shift. These acts no longer treat Native Americans as children who need to be protected, but give them the right to be treated as equals with their own ideas about the direction their lives should take.

SITTING BULL

Sitting Bull's life, like that of other well known Native American leaders of the last century, has become a mixture of fact and myth. Numerous books and films have described his life, but too many depict him as either a hero or a monster, not as a human being. Because of these depictions, many people believe that Sitting Bull hated all non-Indians, but that is a myth.

Keeping track of dates was not as important to the Lakota as it is to us, but it seems that Sitting Bull was born in March 1831. At the time, his family was living with other Hunkpapa Lakota on the Grand River, near present-day Bullhead, South Dakota. His father was Tatanka Ptaica (Jumping Bull) and his mother was Umpan Wastewin (Lady Good Elk) (Carroll 1986:153). His first name was "Slow" because he did not make decisions quickly, but took time to think. From information gathered by Stanley Vestal (1932) it seems that Sitting Bull was an only son. He had two sisters, Good Feather Woman and Brown Robe. The sons of Good Feather Woman were well-known warriors. In later years one was known as Chief Joseph White Bull and other as Chief Henry Oscar One Bull.

Not until he was fourteen and a good rider did Slow have a chance to earn a new name. His father and other men had already left on a war party when Slow decided to join them. He told no one, just collected his goods, saddled his horse and rode away. His opportunity to demonstrate his bravery came when the men sighted an enemy some distance away. The group decided to wait until the enemies were closer and then surprise them. Slow painted himself yellow and his horse red. As soon as the signal was given he rode toward the enemy. When the enemy saw the Hunkpapa, they turned and rode away from the Lakota. After a breath-taking ride, Slow caught up with the last enemy rider. The man dismounted and attempted to defend himself, but Slow charged in and counted coup before the man could release his arrow. In honor of his accomplishment, Jumping Bull renamed his son Sitting Bull and that name he carried proudly until his death (Vestal 1932:3-13). Soon after this success he completed his training for manhood by going on a vision quest and earning a spiritual protector.

Sitting Bull drew several autobiographical accounts of his war exploits (Vestal 1932:316-320) and some of these have been published. They do not agree in all details, but they do illustrate the significance of warfare in determining Sitting Bull's rank and role. These exploits led, in 1856, to his joining the Strong Heart Society, a group of warriors who acted as camp police and patrolled the tribal hunts.

Sitting Bull did not come to the attention of Whites until 1863 when Generals Henry Hastings Sibley and Alfred Sully intruded on Hunkpapa country. Sitting Bull refused to attack Whites until they interfered with his people's ability to sustain themselves as buffalo hunters. The first such conflict came in the Killdeer Mountains, July 28, 1864. Some of the Dakota, including Inkpaduta, had joined Sitting Bull's camp and these all engaged in defending themselves against the troops led by General Sully.

In 1866, the military arrived in greater numbers in Hunkpapa territory and began construction of Fort Buford. Further west, the army began erecting Fort Phil Kearney and other forts to protect the Montana trail. The Strong Hearts, led by Sitting Bull, terrorized the region around Fort Buford, intending to force the military to withdraw (Hoover 1980:155-157). From time to time, Sitting Bull, Gall, Black Moon and others also joined the Oglala Lakota leader Red Cloud (Robinson 1904:360). The result of the constant harassment by Sitting Bull's and Red Cloud's forces was the Treaty of Fort Laramie of 1868.

The Treaty of Fort Laramie of 1868 essentially gave the Lakota what they wanted. The troops were to be withdrawn. The Lakota were allowed to hunt buffalo off the reservation, and those who wanted to farm would be assisted to do so. Unfortunately, the discovery of gold in the Black Hills brought government attention and hordes of gold-seekers in violation of the treaty. Again, the tribes determined to fight for their rights.

By the time of the Battle of the Little Big Horn Sitting Bull had attained a position of leadership, although his was more spiritual than defensive. The Battle of the Little Big Horn seemed to suggest success for the Indians, but the full force of U.S. military might prevented the Indians from reaching their goal. As other Indian leaders signed treaties agreeing to return to the reservation, Sitting Bull found himself with a dwindling force.

Only a few months after the stunning success on the Big Horn, Sitting Bull led his remaining followers into Canada. He apparently hoped that either the Canadian government or relatives of the Dakota who had fled to Manitoba would aid him, but he was given little help. Under pressure of starvation, Gall, Crow King and others returned to the United States. Finally, in 1881, Sitting Bull journeyed to Fort Buford and surrendered his horses and weapons. A few families remained in Canada and today their descendants live at Wood Mountain and Cypress Hills (Howard 1984:15).

Sitting Bull and his party spent two years in prison at Fort Randall before being allowed to return to Fort Yates. At Fort Yates, James McLaughlin, the Indian agent, had managed to attract many of the Indians to education, agriculture and Christianity.

Sitting Bull was not adverse to education or agriculture, and he willingly discussed religion with various missionaries, but he did not believe it was necessary for him to give up his Indian ways. Because of his character, McLaughlin was concerned that Sitting Bull would distract other Indians, so he arranged for Sitting Bull to travel with wild west shows for several years. By 1886, however, Sitting Bull was living on Grand River, planting a small garden and receiving visitors.

One of the moves that McLaughlin made was the establishment of an Indian police force. The Indian police were young men whose primary task was to arrest Indians who practiced traditional ways. They also carried out the orders of the agent.

The one issue that brought Sitting Bull back into conflict was the decision by Congress to open reservation lands for sale to non-Indians. Attempts had been made for many years to get the Lakota to break the Diminished Sioux Reservation into smaller reservations and sell the left-over land. No one would agree to the sale, which required approval of ¾ of the adult males. Eventually, the commission found ways to persuade the Indians to agree to the division and sale, but Sitting Bull resisted and did not sign.

Sitting Bull became interested in the Ghost Dance, a new religion which was sweeping Indian country. The Ghost Dance taught that if a person gave up non-Indian ways, dressed in special dress and danced until he/she had a vision, that some day the Great Spirit would remove all White people and return the buffalo. Whether Sitting Bull actually believed the message or simply saw the dance as a way of getting people together is open to discussion, but local Whites believed the Indians were again preparing for war.

The outcome was that as Sitting Bull prepared to join the Ghost Dancers, McLaughlin issued a warrant to the Indian police to arrest Sitting Bull and bring him to the agency. The police went to Sitting Bull's house on Grand River where they found him in bed. Sitting Bull agreed to accompany the police, but before he could get dressed, a shot was fired and in the ensuing melee Sitting Bull and several Indian police were killed. The descriptions of the fighting are confused, but seven policemen and eight of Sitting Bull's followers died or were seriously wounded.

Sitting Bull's death was reported by newspapers throughout the country. Some blamed McLaughlin for the shooting, others thought McLaughlin was a hero for ridding the country of a problem.

Today Sitting Bull is probably the most highly respected of all Indian leaders, by both Indians and non-Indians. He has become a symbol of resistance and an example of how Indians were treated. He is looked upon as a wise man and brave fighter and his words are included on posters and in teaching units for Native American children. Sitting Bull was a man who knew what was right for Indian people and never wavered from his vision.

Chapter 8

Reservation Government and Law

The governing of any group of people is a complex issue often not fully comprehensible to outsiders. Government involves social organization, ideology and values, and overt and covert sanctions on human behavior. In the case of reservation government, the issue is made more involved by the presence of state and Federal interests and by the carry-over of traditional tribal styles of government. The subject of government can be broken down into a consideration of the organization and administration of day to day activities, and law and order, including courts, codes, crimes and jurisdiction. Each of these components must be considered separately, although all of them form part of the general system of governmental organization. In addition, one must also consider Federal and state relationships to these components.

Two major blows to the traditional form of tribal government were 1) settlement on reservations and the subsequent policy of assimilation and 2) the establishment of constitutional governments with elected representatives. Both of these took place as part of Federal policy, not as a natural outgrowth of Indian government, and the results have been long-lasting.

Traditional Tribal Government

The details of Plains Native governments varied from tribe to tribe, with general similarities throughout the region (Provinse 1937). In the earliest times Indians had no chiefs (according to the *American Heritage Dictionary of the English Language*, "chief" is an Indo-European word meaning "head"), in the sense of permanent leaders. For most of the year, Plains peoples lived in small family groups with leadership vested in one of the older men. Among the Lakota, these family groups were called *tiospaye* (Hassrick 1964:12). The Hidatsa and Mandan family units were earthlodges shared by related women (Bowers 1950:26). Individual family heads were accorded status and prestige on the basis of an intricate system of partly hereditary and partly achieved accomplishments. A successful headman would attract people, distant kin and friends, to his camp. Alternatively, people would leave an unsuccessful leader who would gradually find himself without constituents or without enough men to protect the group. Scattercorn, an old Mandan woman, told Bowers of a time when some of the Mandan women were unhappy with the location of the village. When the leaders refused to move the village, these women moved to another village (Bowers 1950:28). The headman had no power to coerce people. As long as he was able to lead wisely, to keep his people satisfied and safe, he was listened to and followed. He led by example, and so he always had to set a good example for others to follow. The headman was the most generous because he wanted people to follow his lead and be generous, too. If something needed doing, the headman would do it, anticipating that others would join in. In this way, people did what needed to be done without pressure or restraint.

When important decisions had to be made, the men of the camp would be called together in council. The issue would be debated, with all men giving their view, and then the men would go back to their families and discuss the matter with them. This system is decision-making by consensus. When all points of view had been heard, the council would arrive at a decision that was satisfactory to everyone. Such a decision might be arrived at after considerable debate. If people were unhappy with the decision, they would leave the group. This act would weaken the group, and so unanimity was desirable. The fact that most of the people in a camp were related also strengthened the idea that agreement was desirable so that relatives would not be divided over issues. No vote was taken. No one was forced to accept the decision, but since everyone had been heard and a sincere attempt had been made to accommodate all points of view, most people were satisfied with the outcome of the council meeting and would follow the headman as he carried out the council's will. Bowers (1965:34) notes, however, that when a dissatisfied group of Hidatsa established a separate winter camp, religious sanctions, namely requesting the gods not to send buffalo to the other village, were used to bring the dissidents back to the main village.

At certain times of the year, strong control was necessary (Provinse 1937). At these times, the military police took control. One of these times was during the performance of a major ceremony, when large numbers of people came together and sacred conditions had to be maintained. Feelings often ran high during these times, and strong pressure was sometimes necessary to maintain the peace and harmony required for a successful ceremony. Another time was during the large tribal buffalo hunts when misbehavior on the part of a single individual would jeopardize the success of the hunt and endanger all the people. Each tribe had military or police societies. Membership in these societies was by achievement. An individual would be invited to join a society because he appeared to have the necessary qualities to become a leader. If he did not develop these abilities or later showed some fault, he would be dropped from membership in the society, and he would lose all chance to become a leader. The Lakota passed the policing duties around from society to society, but the Mandan and Hidatsa gave police duties to only one society, the Black Mouths (Bowers 1965:184). In general, the police had the right to punish any individual who did not behave in an appropriate manner during tribal ceremonies or on the hunt.

The lack of formal tribal government should not be taken to mean that Tribal Peoples had no law. Early observers of the Plains Indians frequently assumed that they were lawless, since there were no police or court system and no written laws. Native law was unwritten and based upon ideals of human behavior and recognition of human frailties. Native men were expected to be brave, generous, wise and strong. Native women were expected to be brave, generous, truthful and hospitable. Other expectations were that people would work hard, be loyal and faithful, courteous, and gracious in receiving gifts. Strong feelings were held against promiscuity and gossip, but gossip might be used to direct a person into more appropriate behavior. Most people who strayed from good behavior were dealt with by the family. Someone would point out the error of a relative's ways and suggest that he/she change for the better. Teasing and shaming were used when necessary. More serious offenses were also dealt with by the families who were directly concerned.

Tribal law was generally private law; that is, it took place between individuals and the parties involved were expected to settle the issue. The major concern in Indian law was to maintain the harmony of the group. Theft was a rare crime because generosity demanded that if a person admired someone's possession the object should be given to the admirer. In addition, everyone knew everyone else which made it impossible for someone to hide a stolen object. Most complaints centered on the personal relationships between men and women. The Lakota maintained a high premium on fidelity but also permitted men to steal other men's wives (Hassrick 1964:45-47). The most important men often had two or more wives who were sometimes the objects of theft or abduction. If a man was cruel to his wife, the wife's family might become involved in a dispute with the husband. Murder was an appalling crime, but it, too, was a crime between families and not one that involved the welfare of the entire group. Murder could be settled by the aggrieved family killing the murderer or accepting compensation for their loss. Sometimes the murderer was made responsible for the family of the murdered person, either by marriage or adoption into the family (Deloria 1944:34-36). A murderer, however, was sometimes ostracized for his crime. If the dispute could not be settled by the families, the headman or village council might be called in to prevent disruption of village harmony. If necessary, the police societies could be called upon to administer justice, but this was rare and was done only by the members of the society to which the criminal belonged.

European Impact on Tribal Government

The European traders who entered the plains found it difficult to understand a people without permanent leadership. The traders expected that if one man gave them permission to build a trading post or to hunt in the area, this man spoke for the tribe as a whole. The nature of tribal government in these times was indicated in several ways. The Hidatsa told Bowers that there had been no tribal council until the late 1700's, when the three villages established a council of war leaders to deal with matters of defense (Bowers 1965:26-27). Tabeau held a council of Arikara leaders and ended up with forty-two "chiefs" (Abel 1939:124). When the traders and other visitors became aware that different tribal divisions had different leaders and that leaders changed as situations changed, they decided to identify specific individuals as chiefs by a process known as "making of chiefs" (Prucha 1971:18). The Spanish, British, French and American governments followed the procedure of distributing medals, flags, clothing and other symbols of authority to individuals identified as leaders of their tribesmen. Lewis and Clark distributed medals of three different sizes to headmen of different ranks and smaller medals to other individuals (Prucha 1971:17). At a meeting with some Teton, Lewis and Clark gave a medal, a red coat, a cocked hat and a feather to Black Buffalo, the great chief, and medals to The Partisan, second chief, and Buffalo Medicine, third Chief (Prucha 1971:19). Similar procedures were followed with the Arikara, Mandan and Hidatsa.

The journals of the expedition recorded the following for October 29th, 1804.

> The following Chiefs were made in Council to day
>
> *Ma-tto-ton-ha* or Lower Village of the Mandans
> 1st Chief *Sha-ha-ka* or *Big White*
> 2 do *Ka-goh-ha-mi.* or *Little Raven*
>
> *Roop-tar-hee* or Second Village of the Mandans
> 1st and Grand Chief, Pose-cop-sa-he. or *black cat*
> 2nd Chief Car-gar-no-mok-she raven man Cheaf [sic]
>
> *Mah-har-ha* 3rd Village
> 1st Cheaf Ta-tuck-co-pin-re-ha white Buffalow robe unfolded
>
> *Me-ne-tar-re Me-te-har-tan*
> 1st Cheif —*Omp-he-ha-ra.* Black Mockerson
> 2 do *Oh-harh* or *Little fox*
>
> We sent the presents intended for the Grand Chief of the *Min-ne-tar-re* or Big Belley, and the presents flag and Wompom by the old Chief and those intended for the Chief of the Lower Village by a young Chief (Reid 1947-48:49-51).

The medal given to Big White was still in the possession of his great-grandson, Gun-that-Guards-the-House, in 1908 (Gun-that-Guards-the-House 1908).

Lieutenant Zebulon Pike followed a similar process in his meetings with the tribes in Minnesota in 1805, except that he did not have medals to distribute and had to promise they would be sent to the chiefs. He informed the Leech Lake and Red Lake Chippewa, gathered in council, that the traders did not have the authority to make chiefs, that only certain people, appointed by the Great Father, had such power. The Chippewa responded that the medals had been given to them for good performance of their duties, not as symbols of authority (Prucha 1971:27).

The making of chiefs was a complicated process and one which was not always successful. Lewis and Clark came to regret giving a medal to The Partisan, complaining that he was a "Great Scoundrel" (Prucha 1971:19). Near the Yellowstone, Lewis and Clark gave a medal to a man who was killed the next morning when he attempted to steal guns from the party (Prucha 1971:23). Some Indian men who went to Washington to meet the President were given medals in commemoration of their Washington visit. When they returned home, they found that they were scorned by their tribe, because they were considered too young to be chiefs (Prucha 1971:32). Traders used medals as gifts and to create "chiefs" more friendly to their plans. Tribal leaders then complained that the medals had flooded the market and destroyed the authority of the old men (Prucha 1971:53). Eventually, medal-giving came under the control of Indian agents who used the medals to reward good behavior.

Medals, flags and clothing became symbols of chiefly authority, but probably the presents given to the chiefs to be redistributed to their followers helped most in establishing leadership and authority. Presents were always given to leaders who came in contact with explorers, traders, and agents. Since one of the signs of a leader was the ability to give away many things and the objects brought by the white men, cloth, beads, needles, guns, thread, and knives, were rare and valuable, the distribution of these items by the chiefs was a sign of their success. Treaty-signing was always accompanied by the distribution of gifts to the signers. In 1805, Pike signed a treaty of cession with seven Dakota chiefs, although only two men actually signed the treaty which took about 100,000 acres in exchange for some presents and $2,000 in cash or merchandise (Meyer 1967:25). Early treaties provided for goods and annuities to be given to the chiefs to distribute. The Treaty of Traverse des Sioux in 1851, by which the Sisseton and Wahpeton ceded most of their land in Minnesota, called for $275,000 to be paid to each of the chiefs, in a manner to be decided by them, after the Indians had settled on the reservation. This sum was to be used to provide subsistence to the bands for the first year (Kappler 1904:591). Treaties establishing reservations also provided for food, clothing, and other necessities to be distributed to people who settled on the reservations.

The establishment of reservations brought Tribal Peoples under the control of the Federal government and paved the way for many changes in tribal government and politics. Up until reservation times, Native chiefs were able to deal with the Federal agents as equals. Once on the reservation, however, the power of the chiefs weakened as the agent assumed more and more authority.

Reservation Government and Politics, 1870-1934

Probably the greatest impact on tribal government came with the establishment of reservations. By this time, the chief and council form of government had stabilized, and leadership was vested in the hands of older men. The traditional way of dealing with disagreements, separation from the group, continued to create problems for agents. In 1870, Crow Flies High, Hidatsa, left Fort Berthold Reservation and established an independent village near Fort Buford. Since Crow Flies High was out of the control of the agent, he and his followers were forced to return to the reservation in 1886 (Meyer 1977:139-140). The movement of Lakota bands on and off the Great Sioux Reservation is well documented in agent's reports. Eventually, the agents' need to control these movements brought the army into the area.

Between 1876 and 1890, a number of Federal policies increased the power of the agent and concomitantly decreased the power of the chief (Mattison 1955:160). The practice of distributing rations to the chiefs was stopped on most reservations. Rations were given directly to the families at weekly or bimonthly occasions. At Standing Rock, however, the practice of distributing to the chiefs continued until 1876 when it was stopped by Captain R.E. Johnson. That the chiefs recognized they were losing power is demonstrated by Sitting Bull's attempt to gain authority over Agent James McLaughlin. Shortly after McLaughlin's appointment as agent to Standing Rock, Sitting Bull approached McLaughlin and informed him of "...a code of regulations by which he and his people desired to be governed" (Seymour 1941:301-302). Among other requests, Sitting Bull asked that all rations be given to him for distribution.

With rations distributed to individuals, the agents were able to withhold rations from those individuals who did not adhere to the agents' ideas of appropriate behavior. At Devils Lake, the agent issued basic rations—pork, flour and tobacco—to those who did not work and additional rations of soap, sugar, coffee, tea, candles and kerosene to those who did work (Meyer 1967:230). At Standing Rock in 1883, McLaughlin reported that he was able to attract Indian children to school only by withholding their rations (House Executive Documents, 2nd Session, 48th Congress, 1884-1885:99). In 1874, 1875, 1876 and later, the Arikara made official complaints to President Grant that their rations were being withheld (Mattison 1955:159, note 87) and a letter making a similar charge signed by Mandans—The Bold Eagle, Rushing Eagle and Scared Face—is reproduced in the North Dakota State Historical Society Collections of 1908 (Bad Gun 1908:467). Indians identified as "hostiles" or "conservatives" by the agents suffered most often from the withholding of rations and loss of hunting privileges because the agents punished them for not cooperating. The "progressives," who were often hated by the conservatives for having "sold out," received the support of the agent, including extra food and other necessities.

The control of the agents was so strong that Agent A.J. Stephan at Standing Rock was able to depose Running Antelope, whom he described as "the politician Indian of this agency" (Hagan 1966:95), for his association with Lieutenant Colonel W.P. Carlin, commanding officer at Fort Yates. Similarly, at Fort Berthold, Agent Mahlon Wilkinson deposed White Shield as chief of the Arikaras because of White Shield's complaints about the agent's not delivering the annuities correctly (DeTrobriand 1951:136). Unlike Running Antelope, however, White Shield continued to be chief in the eyes of the Arikara and the Federal government (Meyer 1977:122).

Further complicating relations between Tribal Peoples and agents were the other White men who lived on or near reservations. Some of these men had married Native women and lived legally with their wives. Other men, however, had moved west to escape punishment for breaking the law and continued their criminal activities after they settled in Indian country, cheating the Indians at every opportunity. These men were constant sources of friction between Indians and the agents responsible for the protection of the Tribal People. Traders were also attracted to the reservations, finding it profitable to sell liquor and other illegal goods to the residents, despite the agents' demands that they cease these activities. The army provided the only law available to the agents, but that, too, caused problems for the agents. Some of the problems were apparently personality conflicts between commanding officers and agents, as in the case of agent Stephan, Captain Carlin and Running Antelope. Agent Stephan also complained that the army supported off-reservation hunting and the Sun Dance (Hagan

1966:95) and that the soldiers bothered the Indian school girls (Rahill 1953:303). A study of disease in the military forts of the Upper Missouri found that syphilis was the fourth most common disease at Fort Randall, Fort Buford and Fort Stevenson. The surgeon at Fort Stevenson blamed this on the soldiers' relations with Indian women (Mattison 1954:30). Another group of White men who caused friction between Indians and agents were the missionaries. The missionaries did not always find the agents sympathetic to their cause, particularly if the agents were of a different denomination than that which had been assigned to the reservation.

Indians also broke laws established by agents. Many of the rules which the agents set up were aimed at "civilizing" the Indians. When these laws were incomprehensible to the Tribal People, they ignored them. At other times, Native Peoples found violence to be the only way to attract attention to their point of view. Woodhawks, men hired to cut wood for the steamboats and trading posts, were frequent targets for Native anger. These men were not above cutting timber on tribal land or cheating the Indians out of timber they had cut. Joseph Henry Taylor became a woodhawk in 1867, working on the Missouri between Standing Rock and Fort Berthold. Taylor's book, *Frontier and Indian Life and Kaleidoscopic Lives*, (1932) gives many examples of the relationships, many verging on the illegal, between White men and Indians during these times.

All of these problems, which the agents had little power to deal with, brought about the establishment of Indian police forces. The idea had been tried successfully on some reservations, and Congress finally authorized pay for Indian policemen on all reservations in 1878. The duties of the Indian policemen were defined by the agents.

> The Indian policeman was the reservation handyman. He performed housekeeping duties on the reservation, tried to preserve law and order, and served as an agent of the civilization program. Maintenance and housekeeping occupied most of his time; he supplemented the agent's labor force by cleaning out irrigation ditches, killing beef cattle for the meat ration, taking the census, building roads, carrying messages, and performing a dozen other chores (Hagan 1966:51).

Additional tasks were expected of the Indian policeman. He was to be the eyes and ears of the agent, keeping the agent informed of the happenings on the reservation. He was to be a model of a progressive Indian, wearing short hair, boots and a uniform, similar to army uniforms. The police also had to enforce the directives against drinking, gambling, dancing, practicing traditional medicine and similar ceremonies which the agent deemed wrong. Needless to say, the role of policeman was not popular with many Indians, and the conservatives regarded the Indian police as spies. To some residents, however, the Indian policemen were the same as the former societies that had police duties, a force to be respected even though they were not selected in the same manner as in earlier times.

The establishment of the Indian police force was followed by the establishment of the Courts of Indian Offenses in 1883. At first, the courts were headed by either the three leading tribal policemen or three men selected by the agent. By 1892 the court system had become a little more complex. The reservations were divided into districts based on population, and a judge was assigned to each district. These judges were to be "men of intelligence, integrity, and good moral character, and preference shall be given to Indians who read and write English readily, wear citizen's dress, and engage in civilized pursuits, and no person shall be eligible to such appointment who is [a] polygamist" (House Executive Document no. 1, 52d Congress, 2d Session, serial 3088:28-31).

Despite this directive, selecting judges was not easy. Obviously the judges would be responsible for further acculturation of other Indians, and so they had to come from the progressive faction. Since the medicine men and traditional leaders formed the conservative faction, judges often refused to serve because of fear of the power of the medicine men. Other judges found it difficult to support Federal restrictions on tribal traditions (Hagan 1966:115). As late as 1890, the agent was still deciding cases at Fort Berthold (Brown 1976:25-26).

The courts, despite the basic problem with comprehension of the White man's legal system and difficulties with the hiring of judges, appeared to work fairly well. A variation of the Courts of Indian Offenses is still in existence in the modern tribal courts. The basic system of the Courts of Indian Offenses was that each district had a judge, and each reservation had a court composed of all the district judges. The reservation court was to meet at least once a month and to act as final arbiter in cases appealed from the district courts.

The duties of the judges were numerous and varied. Most dealt with civil cases, drunkenness, theft and damage to property. Other crimes specified by the Bureau of Indian Affairs, such as attendance at tribal dances, practice of traditional medicine, polygamy and destruction of property by mourners, were also heard in these courts. The judges performed marriages for which they were permitted to charge a fee of one dollar. In 1891, the court at Devils Lake Reservation was held every Saturday. The arresting officer and the defendant made statements, and then the judges conferred and arrived at the decision. In one year, the court handled six cases of damage done by stock, six for drunkenness, ten for gambling, three for desertion, three for adultery, six for assault and battery, one for theft, one for rape and one for bastardy (Meyer 1967:236). Since the judges were familiar with the defendants, they had an inside edge in deciding cases.

Most of the punishments were mild, either fines or hard labor (Hagan 1966:121), and showed some retention of traditional legal mores. The agents preferred hard labor since it accomplished necessary work about the reservation and did not deprive families of their relatives. Ella Deloria commented on how Indian people regarded the punishments handed down by the Courts.

> Of course prison life was really only symbolic, for the prisoner lived with the police staff and worked certain hours at raking the superintendent's yard or at some such task. He chatted as he pleased in a leisurely and friendly way with passers-by. Imprisonment was without stigma to the Dakotas, who never imprisoned one another in the old life. One man did not arbitrarily keep another from his freedom. You did that only with horses and other animals, not fellow men. So there was actually no name for it but "to be tied up." "Yes," a woman camping near the agency during her husband's term might explain, "We are waiting here because their father (indicating the children) is tied up just now" (Deloria 1944:87-88).

Guilty Indians did not usually contest the charges and accepted their sentences with equanimity. Jail breaking was rarely a problem, and so jails were often old buildings with little security. The jail at Devils Lake Reservation did not even have a lock in 1898 (Hagan 1966:121).

Although the reservation judicial system seemed to be working, many non-Indians were still concerned about the legal position of American Indians. Tribal People were not permitted to vote even if they had established residence off the reservation, and they had no constitutional rights since they were not American citizens. Unlike the situation with immigrants, Tribal People could not even apply for naturalization, and so even after a century or more of "civilization," Natives remained outside the mainstream. Crow Dog's case, however, shocked the nation into action. Crow Dog was found guilty of the murder of Spotted Tail by a non-Indian district court. On appeal to the Supreme Court, the case was over-turned on the basis that state and Federal courts had no jurisdiction over crimes committed by Indians against Indians in Indian country (Ex parte Crow Dog, 109 U.S. 556 (1883)). The idea that a man could murder someone and not be tried so outraged people that in 1885, Congress passed the Major Crimes Act, which required that crimes like murder, even when committed by Indians against

Indians on a reservation, be brought into Federal court for trial. This decision satisfied some people, but others were still concerned about providing Constitutional rights to Indian people. Still others recognized that while Tribal People could be tried in Federal courts for some crimes, most Natives had little opportunity to bring cases against non-Indians.

A remedy to the situation was found in the Allotment Act. By providing for individual Indians to own property, the Act made it possible for Indians to become citizens. As citizens, Indians would be protected by the United States Constitution and come under the jurisdiction of state and Federal governments. Of course, citizenship under the Allotment Act also meant that Tribal People would pay taxes and have to follow the same laws as other Americans. Not all Indians could become citizens. Only those Indians who were considered competent according to White standards to own land and understand the rights and obligations of citizenship became citizens. Other Natives remained under the reservation legal system, without constitutional rights, until the Indian Citizenship Act of 1924.

The Allotment Act brought some major changes in the Indian legal system. One issue that developed concerned Tribal People whose land was alienated after they had received title to it. If a tribal member sold his/her land or had it taken for non-payment of taxes, how did this affect his tribal rights? Many of these landless Natives continued to live on the reservations and believed that they were protected by reservation laws, but the Federal government believed that, since these people had become citizens, they were now subject to both state and Federal laws. The Major Crimes Act, along with the Allotment Act, took much power away from the reservation courts, and so the Indian police and judges found themselves with less to do. The issue of jurisdiction and powers of the tribal courts is still problematic today.

One of the long-lasting effects of reservation government was the development of factions, which are political divisions that seek power at the expense of other divisions. The factions developed along many different lines. One obvious division was between conservative and progressive Indians. The two attitudes were irreconcilable and often resulted in bloodshed. The Indian police, a progressive faction, was responsible for the death of Sitting Bull, leader of the conservative faction at Standing Rock. Historical incidents resulted in the creation of groups who refused to work together. Signers of treaties, for example, took sides against non-signers. Another divisive factor was the presence of different tribal groups on the same reservation (Taylor 1980:45). Fort Berthold Reservation brought together Mandan, Hidatsa, and Arikara, who, although living together in a single village for many years, retained their distinct languages and leadership. At Standing Rock, Hunkpapa, Yanktonai and Blackfeet Sioux came together. Cuthead, Sisseton and Wahpeton settled at Devils Lake. The Chippewa and Metis who came together at Turtle Mountain represented very different cultural backgrounds. Each of these tribal groups was composed of divisions, each with its own leadership and struggling for leadership on the reservation.

Another difference developed along age lines. Young Tribal People, particularly those educated in mission schools or at Carlisle or Hampton Institute, had ideas that were different from those of the older Indians. The young ones found jobs working for the agent and this responsibility gave them knowledge of the Federal system that gave them authority over the older people. Distinctions between Indians who had some Euro-Americans ancestors and those whose ancestors were all Native, also developed. It seemed as if those persons who had Euro-American ancestors were more likely to get jobs at the agency, since they spoke English better and had a better appreciation of the White man's ways although some agents believed that the mixed-bloods were mentally and morally inferior to full-bloods (Taylor 1980:168 note 75).

Religious differences also influenced the development of factions. When the various denominations were assigned to the reservations, it was assumed that all Indians would eventually become

Christianized into that denomination, but this overlooked the earlier efforts of other denominations. The Catholics had made many converts among the Lakota, and yet most of the Lakota reservations were not assigned to the Catholics. Catholic Lakota did not get along with Protestant Lakota. When the reservations were opened to all denominations, the competition became even more intense.

If the reservation was conducive to the development of factions, the agents and other White people helped to maintain the factions by manipulating them to their own advantage. The personality conflict between Sitting Bull and James McLaughlin brought Gall and John Grass to power. When Sitting Bull opposed the agreement of 1888 to reduce Sioux land holdings and allot land individually, McLaughlin turned to Grass and persuaded him to sign the agreement and to convince the others. Other Lakota followed Grass's lead and the necessary signatures were obtained. Other non-Indians took advantage of differences between factions to press their own advantage. When a dispute arose between the Agency physician at Fort Berthold, Dr. J.J. Best, and the agent, Thomas Jones, Best charged the agent with defrauding tribal teamsters and cited a number of the teamsters as witnesses (Brown 1976:22-23). In this instance, the doctor sided with the Indians in an attempt to win his own case against the agent.

Tribal People, too, were politically astute, and they took advantage of factions to promote their own causes. Sitting Bull's position as a conservative and his personality conflict with McLaughlin made it necessary for him to seek support for his ideas from other sources. After the opening of the reservations to all religious denominations in 1882, Sitting Bull found this support in the missionaries, Catholic, Congregational and Episcopal (Hoover 1980:167). Since the denominations were competing for converts, Sitting Bull was a worthwhile prize, and the missionaries were willing to assist Sitting Bull in different ways.

Colson (1971:11) has suggested that the presence of factions worked to maintain tribal culture and to preserve the reservation. If only one point of view had existed, the frequent changes in Indian agents and Indian policy would have made it difficult for Tribal People to adjust to the changes. As it happened, every change in policy found a group ready to accept the change and to work with the government officials in charge. Carrying the argument further, if all the Tribal People had been progressive, the policies of assimilation would have succeeded and today no tribal cultures would remain. The presence of progressive Indians convinced the government that assimilation policy was succeeding and allowed the conservatives to maintain traditional ways. The presence of individuals with whom the agent could work permitted others to remain away from the agency. Factionalism, despite its apparent contribution to unstable tribal government, has also contributed to the maintenance of Indian identity.

Modern Tribal Government

The tribal council, composed of elected representatives, that exists on North Dakota reservations today, was created by the Indian Reorganization Act (IRA) of 1934. In the years between the Allotment Act and the Reorganization Act, reservation governments made few changes. The chiefs, now usually the descendants of original chiefs, remained in nominal charge, but the agents had actual control of all decision-making. Among other matters, the Indian Reorganization Act aimed to put decision-making and law and order back into tribal hands, but traditional tribal government has not returned. Although the phrase tribal council suggests a traditional form, the present tribal governments more closely resemble constitutional democracies.

The Indian Reorganization Act called for each tribe to vote on acceptance or rejection of the Act. Acceptance of the Act enabled the tribe to prepare a constitution, which was to be voted on by members of the tribe and approved by the Secretary of the Interior. Once the constitution had been approved, the tribe could then elect a tribal council. The council was given certain rights, including negotiations with other governmental agencies, employment of legal council and review of tribal budgets (Prucha 1975:224). If one-third of the tribal members so requested, the tribal council could organize as a business corporation, receive a charter and conduct tribal business.

Although the Indian Reorganization Act appears to be fairly simple, it was and is controversial. Many Tribal People did not understand the basic issues which were involved in the Act, although the Bureau of Indian Affairs sent out people to explain it. Voting was a concept foreign to tribal leaders who were unable to advise their people on the correct action to take. In North Dakota, only the Mandan, Hidatsa and Arikara voted to accept the Act. Reasons for rejection vary, but factionalism undoubtedly played a role as did the agents' concerns that strengthening the tribal government would weaken their control. The controversy continues today. Some tribal members feel that the Indian Reorganization Act weakened the power of the traditional leaders and paved the way for termination. Younger people were brought into positions of leadership, and the elders felt unwanted. Many Indians point out that voting was not the Indian way and that voting caused more factionalism. Since representative democracy can result in a large segment of the population being unhappy because its point of view did not win the election, this group acts as a negative force, and reservations have become politically unstable. Others feel that the tribal constitutions written under the Act gave too much power to the Secretary of the Interior. The American Indian Policy Review Commission (American Indian Policy Review Commission 1977:15) pointed out that tribes that rejected the Act in 1934 and are now operating under non-IRA constitutions may be receiving services to which they are not legally entitled. The Commission suggested that there needs to be a new opportunity to vote on acceptance of the Act.

The Arikara, Hidatsa and Mandan approved their constitution in 1936 and organized as the Three Affiliated Tribes. They also incorporated as a tribal business, and today, the governing body is the tribal business council, a corporation in which all members of the tribe are partners. The advantages in incorporation are mainly economic. A corporation has a legal life beyond the life of any of its individual members. If one of the members dies, provisions for replacement without interruption of the conduct of business are already set up. Individual members of the corporation are not liable for the corporation's debts nor for taxes, although they are responsible for their own debts and taxes on their income from the corporation. The corporation can be sued, but individual members are not liable to suit. Incorporation is a way for tribes to overcome the problem of borrowing money and credit and to expand tribal business opportunities.

The Standing Rock Sioux, Turtle Mountain Chippewa and Devils Lake Sioux developed constitutional forms of government outside the Indian Reorganization Act and have not been able to incorporate the whole tribe as a tribal business in the same manner as the Three Affiliated Tribes. Tribal corporations have been established, such as Devils Lake Sioux Manufacturing and Standing Rock Housing Corporation, but these companies are not the whole tribe.

All four North Dakota tribes are organized along similar lines. The basic model for tribal constitutions was provided by the Bureau of Indian Affairs and is basically similar to the United States Constitution. Each reservation is organized into districts on the basis of population. Each district elects representatives to the tribal council. The tribal council has officers, a chairman, a secretary and a treasurer, who may be elected by the tribe as a whole or may be elected from among the council members. The council has control over many functions, some requiring review by the Federal government while others do not. The powers of the council have been increased under the Indian Self-Determination Act, since tribal councils may now contract to carry out many of the functions previously handled by the Bureau of Indian Affairs. Specific duties of the council are described in the constitution and tribal code of each reservation. Generally, however, these include: review of Federal appropriations, encouragement of arts and crafts, employment of legal counsel, creation of education departments, administration of tribal lands, establishment of civil and criminal codes, levying of taxes, issuance of licenses and permits, regulation of inheritance of property and determining tribal membership, and authorization of tribal colleges (Taylor 1980:102). Through various court actions, the powers of the tribes have been determined to resemble those of state governments (American Indian Policy Review Commission 1977:102-103), although not all tribes utilize all of these powers. For example, none of the North Dakota tribes levy income or property taxes on either their members or the non-Native residents of the reservation, although the courts recently ruled that tribes can tax non-Indian-owned businesses operating on the reservation. This power will become more crucial as funds from Federal sources become scarcer.

The primary difference between the organization of tribal governments and the organization of state and/or Federal governments is that there is no separation of powers. The tribal council makes the laws, administers them and enforces them through the tribal court, which is appointed by the tribal council. The problems inherent in this situation are made clear by the firing of the chief tribal judge, Richard Frederick, by the Turtle Mountain Chippewa Tribal Council in 1979 (Kofski 1979:3A; Valentine 1979:1D). Frederick was apparently relieved of his position after he signed arrest warrants for five members of the tribal council. Because the tribal council makes the laws and carries them out, reservation residents often feel the council takes advantage of its powers to promote its own interests rather than promoting the affairs of the whole tribe. The only way the people can influence the tribal council is through attending meetings, speaking to individual representatives and/or by recalling their representatives. Because charges of misconduct are common, people are reluctant to run for election to the tribal council. When sufficient candidates are available to represent different interests, tribal elections become hotly contested political events with much discussion of individual qualifications via public debate. A great deal of interest is shown in the results of the election because reservation politics will be influenced for several years.

Recent changes in Federal policy have mandated that tribes create separate branches of government. The Turtle Mountain Band of Chippewa have made the greatest progress by voting to establish a separate court system in which judges would be elected by tribal members. So far, however, the tribal council has been reluctant to press for total separation of powers.

The Federal government has plenary power over Indian affairs, including tribal government. The authority of the Federal government over Indians is found in Article I, section 8, clause 3 of the United States Constitution and in treaties signed with tribes. The tribal constitutions support this authority by requiring approval of the Secretary of the Interior. The Constitution assumes the right of Congress to pass laws, make treaties and otherwise regulate Indian affairs. Treaties established the Federal government as a trustee of Indian land. In addition, many of the treaties carried provisions for annuities and services, particularly health and education, which require agencies to administer. Most Indians do not want this Federal supervision terminated. The presence of the Federal government provides a measure of security within which tribes are free to operate. The special provisions under which services are given provide basic needs for many Indians. The presence of the Bureau of Indian Affairs also indicates that the treaties are in force and are being upheld by the Federal government. The Bureau of Indian Affairs (BIA), a division of the Department of the Interior, is the agency entrusted with maintaining Federal obligations to the tribes.

Some Tribal People feel that the Bureau of Indian Affairs takes its supervisory powers too seriously and steps in where it should not. The American Indian Policy Review Commission found numerous cases where the Bureau of Indian Affairs had interfered in tribal matters, particularly in the election of tribal officials (American Indian Policy Review Commission 1977:189-191). The paternalistic approach of the Bureau of Indian Affairs is expressed in the view that the Bureau is responsible if something goes wrong and that it needs to take action to prevent such occurrences. The opposing view is that Tribal People are being prevented from developing their administrative capabilities through learning from their mistakes. The Self-Determination Act has given tribes the opportunity to take control of many of the services formerly performed by the Bureau of Indian Affairs. More recently, the Bureau has taken a "hands-off" approach even when the resulting inaction has caused threats of violence.

Greater dissatisfaction with the Bureau of Indian Affairs is found in the bureaucracy which it represents. As part of the Department of the Interior, the Bureau is included in the executive branch of the Federal government (Fig. 8.1). The head of the BIA is appointed by the Secretary of the Interior, and the position is entitled Deputy Secretary of the Interior for Indian Affairs. Unique to the Bureau is the presence of the Deputy Secretary for Indian Affairs at cabinet meetings, which provides Tribal People with cabinet-level representation, something that no other ethnic group has. But this is no particular advantage because policy and laws affecting Indians are made in Congress and for Tribal People to be heard in Washington and to make changes in Indian policy, they must have elected representatives to Congress or lobby in Congress. Since it has been almost impossible for an Indian to get elected to Congress, most major tribal organizations and many small ones have full-time lobbyists to make sure that their interests are represented when policy and budgets are being determined by Congress. Unfortunately, Tribal People make up less than 4% of the total population, and so their impact tends to be minimal. To Tribal People on the reservation, the Bureau can appear unresponsive to requests for change since such requests must move upwards from local level to cabinet level and then must wait for the Bureau to make a presentation to Congress.

The Bureau of Indian Affairs is organized as a hierarchy. As with many other governmental agencies, the major administrative center or head office is located in Washington and Denver. The BIA has eleven regional offices. The one for North Dakota is in Aberdeen, South Dakota, and covers Nebraska, North and South Dakota. There are eighty-two agency offices. Each of the North Dakota reservations has an agent, called a superintendent, in charge of administering Federal policy. Each of these offices, head, regional and agency, has numerous divisions, including health, education, land, planning, economics and record keeping. Suggestions have been made that some of these duties could be transferred to other Federal agencies just as responsibility for the provision of health services was transferred from the Bureau to the Public Health Service in 1955. The Bureau is currently under orders to examine its educational services and to show why they should not be transferred to the Department of Education. Indians are generally against the transfer of services from the Bureau because they feel that the Bureau is more familiar with their needs and interests. They fear becoming a minority in a large, general administrative program in which they would have to compete for funds with other minorities.

Most financing of tribal government and tribal programs comes from the Federal government. Tribes, because of Federal control, have few independent sources of income. Fees from licenses and some leasing go directly to the tribe, but these funds are a minor portion of the amount needed to run tribal programs. Money owed the tribes from land sales and land claims, except for sums paid directly to individual tribal members, are kept for the tribe and administered by the BIA. The American Indian Policy Review Commission found that most tribes did not have enough money to pay tribal officials and were using overhead from grants to pay the people actually running the tribe. Many tribal offices were run by people paid from Federal programs. As long as tribes do not have money to support themselves apart from the Federal government, they will be in a dependent position. The government can withhold funds until the tribe conforms to Federal policy, even though it is against the wishes of the tribe.

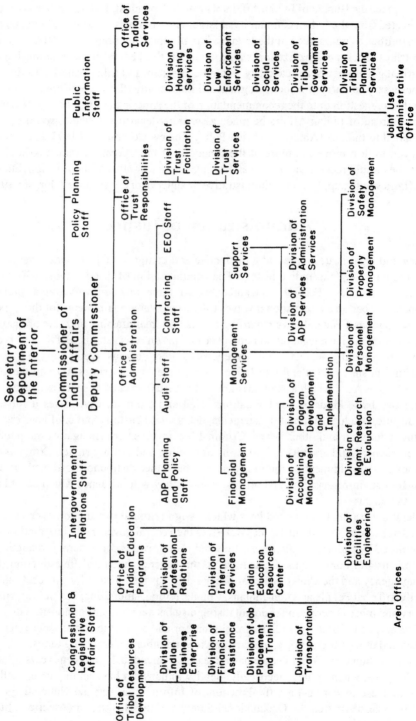

Figure 8.1. Organizational chart of the Bureau of Indian Affairs.

In 1974, the National Congress of American Indians passed a resolution suggesting that the Federal government replace the Bureau of Indian Affairs with an independent, Federal Indian commission, run by Indians elected from the Indian community at large. This commission would administer the Federal trust responsibilities as guaranteed in the treaties, but all other functions of the BIA would be turned over to the tribes. Such an organization would maintain the Federal-tribal relationship but would strengthen tribal governments. Bureaucracy would be lessened, and tribes would have direct access to the funds necessary to carry out their programs. Until recently, the Federal government paid little attention to this suggestion or to the recommendation of the American Indian Policy Review Commission that the Bureau of Indian Affairs be made a separate department which would consolidate all programs related to Indians (American Indian Policy Review Commission 1977:22). There is a new move, however, to turn more and more of the functions of the Bureau of Indian Affairs over to the tribes. The tribes would receive the money and be in complete control of the function, but the Bureau of Indian Affairs would supply some administrative or supervisory assistance (Dorsher 1989).

Administration of Justice

Tribal law and legal issues represent a distinctive and complex subject matter involving treaties, legislation, Indian policy and Indian history. The administration of justice involves Tribal People in three different legal codes—Federal, state and tribal. All three may be involved in a single issue. For example, opening a bar on a reservation involves tribal laws, state requirements for the dispensation of alcoholic beverages and Federal laws regarding production, manufacture and sale of distilled spirits. In general, states do not have legal jurisdiction over Indians on reservations. Off the reservation, however, Indians are generally subject to the same laws as other citizens. Exceptions to these two principles are found in specific Federal legislation, such as the Major Crimes Act and the General and Assimilative Crimes Acts, which assign jurisdiction for certain crimes to specific courts.

There are two basic kinds of legal situations: civil and criminal. Civil cases involve private or individual disputes, such as automobile accidents, debts, child custody and civil laws regarding zoning, planning, education and other issues. Criminal law involves crimes against the public, ranging from murder, robbery and assaults to violations of hunting and fishing rights. Criminal cases often result in fines or imprisonment of the guilty party. Four other distinctions are made in Indian law: Indian, non-Indian, on-reservation, and off-reservation; they will influence which court has jurisdiction in a particular case.

The Federal government has passed laws which assign criminal jurisdiction over Tribal People to state and Federal courts. The Major Crimes Act gives the Federal government jurisdiction over certain crimes committed by Indians on the reservation and also provides for Federal jurisdiction in crimes involving Indians and non-Indians. In such cases, the Federal Bureau of Investigation (FBI) is the investigating agency and the United States attorney's office is responsible for prosecution. Some laws apply equally to Tribal People and non-Indians. Counterfeiting, smuggling, interfering with the mails, bank robbery and other Federal crimes do not distinguish between Indians or non-Indians, on-reservation or off-reservation. Similarly, Indians are eligible for and subject to social security taxes, Federal income taxes and other Federal taxes, military service and other Federal obligations.

Federal jurisdiction over Tribal People has increased tremendously in recent years. Many laws are passed by Congress which do not specifically identify Indians but have an impact upon them as citizens. Some of these recent acts are the Freedom of Information Act, the National Environmental Policy Act, the Clean Air Act, the Occupational Safety and the Health Act (American Indian Policy

Figure 8.2. The "Blue Building" is the administrative center of the Devils Lake Sioux tribe. The building also houses the bureau of Indian Affairs and other offices.

Review Commission 1977:177). The Indian Civil Rights Act limited the powers of tribal courts and gave them the right to file a petition of *habeas corpus* in Federal court in order to test the legality of detention by the tribe. (The Native American Religious Freedom Act is a recent act granting religious freedom to Indians.)

Generally, state and local governments have little jurisdiction over Indians on reservations. The General and Assimilative Crimes Act extended state laws to cover actions in Federal enclaves, taken to include reservations, that were illegal or immoral under state law but for which there were no Federal prohibitions. These include gambling and prostitution. The idea behind the Act was to make it impossible for Federal areas to become havens for behavior which was illegal under state laws. For example, if gambling is prohibited by state law, gambling is also illegal on reservations, on military bases and in national parks located in that state. The issue has become more complex in recent years as tribes have promoted bingo and other gambling operations on the reservations. Courts have decreed that tribes do not have to abide by state laws regulating bingo games, and so the tribes can run the games as often as they wish and offer prizes as large as they can afford. In response to state concerns about their lack of control over tribal gambling, Congress passed the Native American Gaming Regulatory Act. The Act required states to form agreements or compacts with tribes outlining the gambling that would be allowed, defining the betting limits, if any, and describing how proceeds would be spent. Some states are now asking Congress to rewrite the Act to give them more control, but tribes are resisting this.

The inability of state and local governments to prosecute Indians for minor crimes has caused problems in recent years. One major issue has been the prosecution of Indians for writing checks on insufficient funds. Even though the crime is committed off the reservation, if the perpetrator returns to the reservation, neither the state nor local authorities can arrest the offender. The city of Bismarck and the Standing Rock Sioux Tribal Council worked out an extradition agreement to return Indians to Bismarck for prosecution on bad check charges (*Grand Forks Herald* 1980a).

The growth of gaming on reservations has resulted in a new twist to the jurisdiction problem. Non-Indian gamblers may write checks on insufficient funds and the tribes find it very difficult to get the off-reservation courts to issue warrants for the offender. Generally tribes do not have jurisdiction over non-Indians and must rely on county courts to prosecute non-Indians who commit crimes on the reservation. Local courts are reluctant to deal with the issue (Wood 1993:1A).

Another problem area is the collection of state sales taxes. Tribal People living on the reservation are exempt from state taxes but are usually required to pay sales taxes on items bought off the reservation. Some North Dakota Indians are refusing to pay sales taxes on items bought in communities that are off the reservation but near enough to receive much reservation business. North Dakota Legal Services, Inc. took the position that state excise taxes on motor vehicles were not valid for Indians. This stand was based upon the Supreme Court decision in the case of *Washington, et al. v. Confederated Tribes of the Colville Indian Reservation*. North Dakota Legal Services, Inc. sought an exemption from state sales taxes for North Dakota tribes (North Dakota Legal Services, Inc. 1980:8). Some Minnesota tribes successfully defended their right to make and sell their own license plates instead of using state plates and two North Dakota tribes, the Devils Lake Sioux and the Turtle Mountain Band of Chippewa, followed their lead. From time to time, states have attempted to enforce jurisdiction over zoning, hunting and fishing, but these decisions have been struck down by Federal courts.

One of the greatest jurisdictional issues of the present-day concerns jurisdiction over non-Indians on Indian reservations. Do the tribes have jurisdiction over non-Indians? The question has arisen out of attempts by tribes to assert their sovereignty and out of Supreme Court decisions that uphold some facets of that sovereignty. Non-Indians do not want to be tried in Indian courts, but Indians point out that treaties and laws give them jurisdiction. In the case of *United States v. Mazurie* (419 U.S. 544), the Supreme Court upheld the right of Indian tribes to regulate non-Indians insofar as their business transactions are concerned (Getches, Rosenfeldt and Wilkinson 1979:263). In 1978, however, the Supreme Court came to the conclusion that Indian tribes do not have jurisdiction over non-Indians. In the case of *Oliphant and Belgarde v. the Suquamish Indian Tribe et al.* (435 U.S. 191), the court ruled that the tribe did not have the right to try non-Indians for criminal offenses (46 *Law Week* 4297-4306). In 1990 the U.S. Supreme Court further weakened tribal jurisdiction by ruling in the case of *Duro v. Reina* that a tribal court does not have jurisdiction over non-member Indians. These recent decisions limit Indian jurisdiction to civil cases or to cases involving only tribal members, while criminal cases are to be handled in state and Federal courts. Concern over their diminishing jurisdiction prompted tribal leaders to ask Congress to help solve the problem. Congress responded by amending the Indian Civil Rights Act to extend jurisdiction to all Indians and is now considering legislation to return jurisdiction to tribes.

The Courts

Depending upon the circumstances, cases involving Indians may be tried in Federal courts, state or local courts or in tribal courts. Major crimes are tried in Federal courts. Civil cases and minor crimes committed by Indians off the reservation are tried in state or local courts, and cases occurring on the reservation are tried in tribal courts.

One of the issues of concern to Tribal People is their receiving a fair trial. Although Indians have all the rights and obligations of other American citizens, when they enter non-Indian courts they are often at a disadvantage (*Native American Justice Issues in North Dakota* 1978). One of the problems faced by Tribal Peoples is stereotyping and discrimination. Many non-Indians have been raised on Hollywood movies that depict Indians as violent or lawbreakers, and so when an Indian is brought to trial, non-Indians assume that he or she is guilty. An unbiased jury may be easier to select in a Federal case since the jury is drawn from a wider area and a change of venue may help, but finding an unbiased jury is difficult in Indian cases. Since Tribal People are a minority in North Dakota, they are rarely called to serve upon juries, although increasing urbanization should increase the chances of Indian jury representation. Tribal People may find themselves at a disadvantage because they do not fully understand

Figure 8.3. A small building near the administration building houses the tribal court of the Devils Lake Sioux.

the non-Indian legal system. Another problem some Indians face is linguistic and cultural differences which may make communication between Indian and non-Indian awkward. If an Indian is provided with court appointed legal counsel, a lack of understanding on the part of the counsel could make defense uncertain. In testifying, an Indian may have trouble expressing him/herself and may make an unsatisfactory impression upon a jury. Whatever the cause, statistics show that many more Indians are in jail in North Dakota than the proportion of their population justifies. In 1975 the inmate population of the North Dakota State Penitentiary was 275, of whom 17 percent were Indian (*Native American Justice Issues* in North Dakota 1978:3). A recent study of the juvenile detention facility in Mandan showed that 30% of the population was Native American (Schmidt 1994:1A).

Treatment of Tribal People by the non-Indian legal system has improved in recent years as states have become aware of the problems. Indians now have access to legal aid programs which will help them obtain adequate defenses, find bail, and explain their rights to them. Tribal People with law degrees are available for counsel. Indians themselves are more knowledgeable about non-Indian laws and are more aggressive in demanding their civil rights. Overt discrimination is no longer seen because it would be challenged, and hidden discrimination is hard to prove. Hidden discrimination against Indians may be seen in the treatment they receive before and during arrest. An Indian may be arrested for drunk driving while a non-Indian would be warned. After arrest, an Indian may find it impossible to post bail, and bail may be set higher for Indians than for non-Indians. Austin Gillette, former tribal council chairman of the Three Affiliated Tribes, alleged that county authorities set excessive bonds for Indians charged with writing bad checks (*Grand Forks Herald* 1980b:10B). Once in court, Indians may receive the same fines and/or sentences as non-Indians. Unfortunately, few court records can be examined to identify differential treatment of Indians since most law enforcement agencies do not identify cases by race.

Most cases involving Tribal People are heard in tribal courts. The main differences between the modern tribal court system and the Courts of Indian Offenses is that these courts are under the control of the tribal council rather than the BIA. The courts are based on a non-Indian model and on non-Indian concepts of law and justice, although current tribal law continues to follow some traditional patterns. The basic tribal court consists of a chief judge and as many associate or trial judges as necessary. The chief judge may be purely administrative or may also hear cases, depending upon the case load (Brakel 1978). All proceedings are recorded by a court recorder. Other legal personnel which may be involved are probation and juvenile officers, advocates, prosecutors and attorneys. Selection of judges varies from reservation to reservation, and only recently has it been possible to have judges with legal training. More and more Indians are obtaining law degrees and returning to work on reservations as judges and lawyers. Most tribes have at least one bar association lawyer in their tribal court system. The tribal courts continue to be less formal than the Federal and state courts, and the justice dispensed is still related to individual cases rather than to an impersonal law since judges usually know the people and the issues involved. Advocates may have some background in law although a legal background is not considered necessary for an advocate to appear before a tribal court. This practice can be viewed as a carryover of a traditional custom of asking a well-known orator to represent one's wishes in a public setting. (Today, this is seen most often during ceremonies, where an announcer publicly represents the family or individual).

Most of the cases handled by the tribal courts involve "disorderly conduct, assault and battery, intoxication and drinking while driving" (Kingman 1991). Differences in the nature of crimes may also be related to traditional tribal customs. In 1966, McCone suggested, based upon data from 1955, that the traditional Indian pattern of crimes against property continued to show up (McCone 1966:150). Using 1972 statistics from Standing Rock (Brakel 1978:34) and 1977 statistics from Burleigh County

(*Native American Justice Issues* 1978:2), a similar situation was demonstrated. The non-Indian arrest rate for crimes against property (burglary, larceny, theft, auto-theft) is six times greater than the arrest rate for crimes against the person (murder, rape, robbery and assault). The Indian rate for Burleigh county showed crimes against property to be four times the rate for crimes against the person. The data from Standing Rock showed crimes against property to be half that of crimes against the person. McCone had found the same rate for a period almost twenty years earlier (McCone 1966:149).

Samuel J. Brakel (1978) investigated the operation of tribal courts and identified a number of problems, which included poorly trained judges, overzealous arresting officers, weak codification of tribal laws, interference from tribal council, poor facilities and a general feeling on the part of both Indians and non-Indians that the tribal courts were ineffective. As a trained lawyer, he found an abundance to complain about. Many of the problems Brakel identified can be related to control of the court system by the tribal council and to lack of funds for hiring and training competent personnel. The lack of funds is probably the most significant element. If salaries were higher and tribal councils less able to intervene in the courts, more knowledgeable judges might be hired. If judges were more knowledgeable about the law, they would find it easier to recognize situations which do not require legal intervention and to make more coherent decisions in those cases which they do hear. Perhaps the gravest criticism of the tribal court system is the lack of appeal procedures. In some cases tribes have established appeal procedures, but most have not, and a decision by the tribal court is final.

Despite the problems identified by Brakel, the system does appear to serve an important function. Reservation residents are provided with quick access to a legal system that is not overwhelmingly formal. These courts are more familiar to Indians. The judges are known to them. Justice may be more related to individual needs and perceptions than would be the case in off-reservation courts. Traditional forms of justice may be applied when they are relevant. Indians living on reservations feel free to bring cases to court because the costs are small. Because counsel and juries are not required, many cases are solved quite simply, with the judge acting as mediator. Juries and counsel are available when they are requested. With Indians becoming better educated, the training of judges and lawyers will improve as will the use of the system. A training program sponsored by the National American Indian Court Judges Association helps to prepare judges for their work. Legal training programs and legal aid provide people with an understanding of reservation law. The authority of the tribal courts has been upheld in Federal courts and this authority has increased respect for the tribal courts. Finally, tribal courts, like tribal councils, are a visible indication of tribal sovereignty and a continuing reminder of the unique relationship between Indians and the Federal government.

The relationship between tribal governments and the Federal government is based in aboriginal sovereignty. Over the years the relationship has changed as tribal governments have asserted their rights to determine the legal direction of the tribe. Today state, local and Federal governments show an increasing recognition and acceptance of the authority of tribal governments and tribal courts. Better economic bases and better education will undoubtedly provide additional sovereignty to tribal governments.

LITTLE SHELL (AIS-SANCE)

Because several well known Chippewa men were named Little Shell there is a great deal of difficulty in distinguishing between particular individuals. Charles Gourneau (1988:23-29) studied the historical documents and identified the different men as Little Shell 1, 2, 3, and 4.

The first Little Shell was among the Chippewa who moved from central Minnesota into the Red River valley to take advantage of fur trade opportunities. This move established a new division of Chippewa, the Pembina Band, which now comprises part of the Turtle Mountain Band of Chippewa. Alexander Henry found Little Shell to be a difficult man, easily irritated and violent when angry. Henry records several instances of Little Shell's murderous temper. But the man was a brave warrior on whom others could depend and that made him a powerful leader.

The first Little Shell was killed around 1810. Tanner (James 1956:170) recorded the incident. Little Shell invited Tanner and others to accompany his group on a hunting trip to the region around Devils Lake. Tanner refused and later learned that the party had been attacked by the Sioux. Most, including Little Shell, were killed in the battle. In later times, Chippewa claimed the region north and west of Devils Lake as their traditional hunting grounds.

Except for a brief mention by William Warren, nothing is known about Little Shell 2. "Weesh-e-da-mo, son of Aissance (Little Clam), late British Ojibway chief of Red River, is also a member of this family. He is a young man, but has already received two American medals, one from the hands of a colonel of our Army, and the other from the hands of the Governor of Minnesota Territory. He is recognized by our government as chief of the Pembina section of the Ojibway tribe" (Warren 1885:46-47).

The most famous of the dynasty was Little Shell 3 who was present at several treaty signings, visited Washington, D.C. and fought to get land and a fair settlement for the Turtle Mountain Chippewa. According to Charles Gourneau, Little Shell 3 was born in 1829 (Gourneau 1988:28). Laura Law (Law 1953:22) says he was born at Iron Mountain, Manitoba. His life is unknown until 1863 when he signed the Red Lake and Pembina Treaty. When Major Woods' inspection expedition reached Pembina in 1849 the commander found the Pembina Chippewa well established, but maintaining strong ties with other bands of Chippewa in Minnesota (Woods 1850:22-23). Father George Belcourt, the Catholic priest at Pembina, informed Major Woods that the Pembina claimed the land as far west as the Mouse River and Moose Mountain, Saskatchewan (Woods 1850:37). Little Shell was not present in Pembina to meet with Major Woods so it is likely that he and his followers had moved west to hunt buffalo. Father Belcourt's description of Chippewa life leaves no doubt that people still followed traditional ways, having adopted little Euro-American culture.

In 1863, Alexander Ramsey and Ashley C. Morrill met with representatives of the various Minnesota Chippewa bands to discuss a treaty. The treaty resulted in a cession of most of the lands in Minnesota and some in what is now eastern North Dakota. The Pembina, led by Red Bear, Little Shell, Summer Wolverine, Joseph Gornon and Teb-ish-ke-ke-shig, agreed to give up their claims to this land, but did not discuss their claim to land in what is now North Dakota.

Claims to North Dakota land occupied Little Shell for much of his later life. As more and more people moved into the area claimed by the Chippewa it became clear to the leaders that something needed to be done. In 1873 representatives of the Turtle Mountain Band of Chippewa, as the group came to be known, asked Congress to establish a 3000 square mile reservation for them (Murray 1984:21). This attempt was futile, but it did indicate that the Chippewa had a claim and they intended to fight for their rights. As long as there were buffalo and tribes were free to hunt them, there was little concern for land ownership. But by 1882 the buffalo were gone and land hungry farmers were moving into the region.

In July 1882, Little Shell and others put up signs forbidding "Any white man to encroach upon this Indian land ...before a treaty [is] made with the American government." The result was not the desired treaty, but an order from the Secretary of the Interior opening the Chippewa claim to settlement by non-Indians (Murray 1984:23). Following lengthy protests by the Chippewa, President Chester A. Arthur established a twenty-four by thirty-two mile reservation, approximately twenty-two townships, by executive order. In 1884, the reservation was reduced to two townships and most land was restored to public domain, leaving many Turtle Mountain Chippewa with off-reservation farms or no land at all. Little Shell protested the reduction of the reservation and continued to press for settlement of land issues and compensation for the land.

In 1891 Little Shell agreed to consider removing the Turtle Mountain Chippewa to Montana, if the Federal government would provide sufficient land for the whole group. He wrote to the Commissioner of Indian Affairs asking for a reservation twenty-five miles wide by thirty miles long. At the same time, the Turtle Mountain Chippewa were claiming 446,670 acres (U.S. Senate 1898:19). Others, however, refused all suggestions, demanding a larger reservation in the Turtle Mountains and asking that the pressing issues be settled. At a special meeting, the tribal council, supported by many others, passed a series of resolutions (Murray 1984:25). One of the decisions was to hire John B. Bottineau to represent them in Washington, D.C.

John Waugh, Indian agent at Devils Lake, had primary responsibility for the Turtle Mountain people, but he was assisted by E. W. Brenner, sub-agent for the Turtle Mountain Band. Both men became involved in the treaty negotiations when they appointed a new tribal council of 32 men to draw up a tribal roll. Little Shell returned from a visit to Montana to find that he and the regular council of 24 had been supplanted. A major source of disagreement between the tribe and the government was whether only full-blooded Chippewa should be placed on the roll or whether Metis should be included. The tribe considered the Metis to be members of the tribe, but the Federal government always tried to prevent mixed-bloods from being included. As negotiations dragged on, Little Shell and his followers became more and more concerned and eventually they withdrew from the process. On October 22, 1892, a majority of the Turtle Mountain Band of Chippewa agreed to a monetary settlement of $1,000,000 for their claim. (In later years this came to be known as the Ten Cent Treaty, because the money came to about 10 cents an acre.)

Little Shell charged that the settlement would not benefit the tribe, that the money was inadequate and that issues concerning land had been ignored (Murray 1984:27). In 1893 Little Shell and his followers petitioned Congress not to ratify the agreement. Congress listened to the traditional leaders and, at first, did not approve the treaty, but in 1904 it was ratified.

In 1898 Little Shell, Sasswain (Henry Poitrat), Gourin (Baptiste Champagne) and Bay-riss (Cuthbert Grant) wrote to Attorney John Bottineau: "In regard to the affairs and doings of the three commissioners—the ten-cent treaty commissioners—we are very much troubled in here about it; but I repeat to you here again, as I did say while in Washington—to the House Committee on Indian Affairs—that I would never sign their affairs, the ten cent treaty; I am all the same yet and now" (U.S. Senate 1898:26).

When Little Shell died in 1900 he left a legacy of never agreeing to settle for less than what was right. In recent years, his descendants have argued against the proposed settlement of the Ten-cent Treaty claim in which the government agreed to compensate the Turtle Mountain Band of Chippewa and descendants of the Pembina Chippewa for paying only ten cents an acre for land that was worth much more. The "Little Shell" band points out, as did Little Shell, that other lands claimed by the western Chippewa had never been included in the settlement.

Chapter 9

North Dakota Reservations

A close examination of most North Dakota road maps will show five reservations in the state. Two of them, Sisseton and Standing Rock occupy lands on both sides of the North and South Dakota border. Such situations cause problems for these states because they need to know which state government has the authority to deal with the reservation. The determination is based on the location of the administrative center for the reservation. Sisseton, the administrative center for Sisseton Reservation, is located on the South Dakota side of the border, and so Sisseton is considered to be one of the many reservations in South Dakota. On the other hand Fort Yates, the administrative center for Standing Rock Reservation, is located in North Dakota, and so Standing Rock is considered a North Dakota reservation even though most of the land is on the south side of the border. Technically, then, Standing Rock, Fort Berthold, Devils Lake and Turtle Mountain are the only reservations in North Dakota (Fig. 9.1).

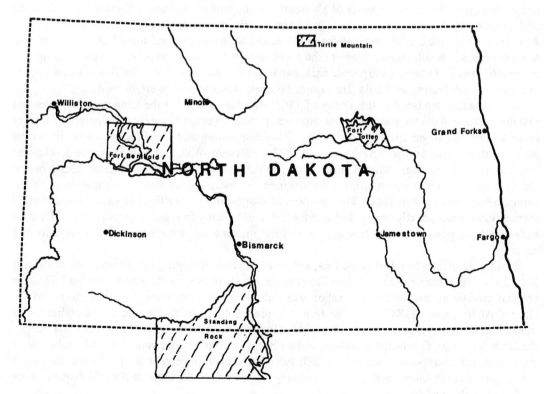

Figure 9.1. Map showing North Dakota Indian reservations and related communities.

Each of the four reservations in North Dakota was established under different circumstances, although all share the common heritage of having been established in locations that White settlers thought were not desirable for living. Subsequent events which usually resulted in the reduction of the reservation land base have shown that this perception was not accurate, but the location of the reservations in remote areas has influenced their present economic and social development.

Modern reservations in the Dakotas are not fenced or marked to distinguish them from other land. The casual visitor would not know that he was on a reservation except for a sign identifying the land as an Indian reservation. All the reservations were opened to non-Indian settlement during the allotment years, and so all the reservations today have non-Indians and Indians living on them. This division of reservation land has had a tremendous impact on tribal settlement patterns, tribal economics and contemporary tribal culture.

Fort Totten Reservation

Tribe: Devils Lake Sioux (Dakota, Cuthead Band of Yanktonai)

Reservation size: 245,140 acres (59,900 acres owned by Indians, tribe and federal government)

Fort Totten Indian Reservation, home of the Devils Lake Sioux Tribe, is the easternmost reservation in North Dakota and was originally established in 1867 by a treaty with the Cuthead band of Yanktonai, and the Wahpeton and Sisseton Sioux of Minnesota. At the time of the Dakota Conflict of 1862, some of the Dakota were living on reservations in Minnesota and others were living in the Dakota Territory. After the conflict, the Dakota reservations in Minnesota were reduced, and some Dakota were moved to a reservation in South Dakota. Many of the people who did not want to take part in the uprising fled to Canada. In order to bring these people back, two reservations, Devils Lake, the first one in what was to become North Dakota, and Lake Traverse or Sisseton-Wahpeton, were established.

As originally established in the Treaty of 1867, the reservations for the Cuthead, Wahpeton and Sisseton Sioux and others who wished to join them included a claim to eight million acres of eastern Dakota Territory (Meyer 1967:207) (Fig. 9.2). Other than setting aside land for the use of the Native people, little else was done for several years. In 1872 the Sisseton-Wahpeton agreed to cede the claimed land between the two reservations. Until 1871, when there were finally enough Indians settled on the Devils Lake reservation for an agent to be assigned, the Indians were under the supervision of the commanding officer of Fort Totten. The assigning of an agent from the Office of Indian Affairs brought the reservation more directly into contact with the Office of Indian Affairs and its regulations. Difficulties with agents, distribution of annuities, educational facilities and White settlers ensued in the following years.

By 1883 homesteaders had settled 64,000 acres of land belonging to the reservation (Meyer 1967:237). Rather than move the settlers Congress decided to reimburse the tribe for the land. Thus the original acreage granted to the reservation was reduced to 166,400 acres. Under the terms of the General Allotment Act (1887) the tribe agreed to open 100,000 acres for sale to non-Indians. The funds from this sale were to be used to benefit the Indians living on the reservation. The remainder of the lands was to be distributed to individual families. The Federal government would retain title to these lands for twenty-five years after which the allottee could receive a fee patent and become a voting citizen of the United States. Upon receiving the fee patent, the individual could dispose of the land as he or she wished.

INDIAN LAND CESSIONS IN NORTH DAKOTA

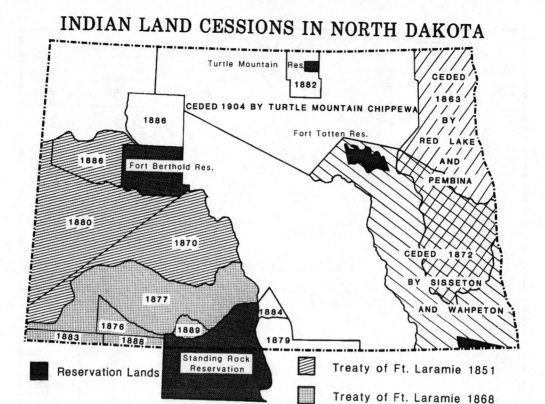

Figure 9.2. Map showing Indian land cessions in North Dakota.

By 1934 when Allotment was officially repealed as a policy, the land owned by the Devils Lake Sioux had been diminished to less than 50,000 acres, its size today. Some of this land is not suitable for agriculture or housing and is presently unused. The reservation itself is checkerboarded with White-owned farms. Since 1934 an official Federal policy of retrocession, that is, buying back land for the tribe, has been extremely slow, and only a small amount of land, approximately 6077 acres is tribally owned (North Dakota Indian Affairs Commission 1981).

Today, the reservation lies about 15 miles south of the city of Devils Lake (Fig. 9.3). This proximity to an urban area is the nearest of any of the reservations in the state. The nearest large city to the reservation is Grand Forks, a little more than 100 miles east. The reservation is located between Devils Lake, the largest natural body of water in the state, and the Sheyenne River. Most of the land is gently rolling although Sully's Hill, Devils Heart Butte and Lookout Mountain are high spots. Low areas are marshy, and many small lakes, used by non-Indians as places for summer homes, dot the reservation. Intermittent streams drain these lakes. Around these streams and lakes are non-commercial timbers, mostly birch, elm, and oak. Soil on the reservation tends to be sandy and rocky.

The reservation is connected to Devils Lake and other parts of North Dakota by major highways. US 281 runs north and south through the western part of the reservation but does not pass through any large Indian communities. State Highways 57 and 20 serve most of the reservation's more populated areas, including the agency town of Fort Totten. Except for the roads around Fort Totten, the roads on

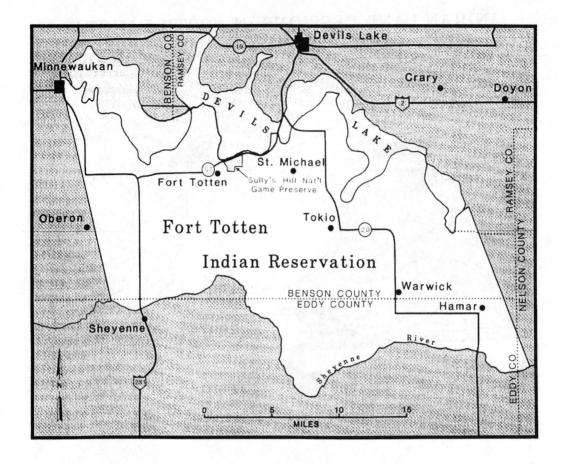

Figure 9.3. Fort Totten Reservation. (Map drawn by Scott Williams).

the reservation are gravel roads. A Burlington-Northern rail line crosses the reservation but does not provide passenger service. The nearest air connections are at Devils Lake, and several airlines serve the region from that point. The nearest bus connections are also in Devils Lake.

Fort Totten Reservation consists of small communities and a widely spaced settlement pattern. People are not crowded onto the reservation, although some areas appear crowded. Communities are separated by distances of thirty miles or less (Albers 1974:72) which makes communication easy. The larger tribal communities developed around Euro-American settlements on the reservation. Fort Totten was originally a fort built to protect settlers from Indians, but the fort was never put to the test. The Indian Agency was eventually established at the fort, and then a school was added. Settlers' homes and Indian homes gradually filled in around the fort buildings until today the community has some eight hundred residents. The original fort buildings and square still remain on the edge of the community and are administered as a historic site by the State Historical Society of North Dakota. However, alternative sources of support are being sought. A few miles east of Fort Totten is St. Michaels. Between Fort Totten and St. Michaels is a densely populated area with many Indian homes. St. Michaels began as the location of a Catholic mission church and school. A small store there sells groceries, cashes checks and acts as a post office for the local residents. South of St. Michaels is the Indian community of Tokio. Tokio is large enough to have a post office, a grain elevator, a school and other buildings. Other areas that are identified as Indian communities are Crow Hill and Wood Lake. These represent not only settlement areas but voting districts on the reservation. These areas are not indicated on any of the small scale maps, but can be seen on the larger scale maps. Residents of these areas are often related by kinship and regard themselves as a community. Outside the areas of dense settlement, most homes are located in areas where trees provide shade. Clumps of trees can usually be assumed to have one or two homes located among them.

In addition to the Indian communities on the reservation, several communities are predominantly White. The largest of these is Warwick. While Tribal People may live in these communities, they are in the minority and take little part in community activities. Particularly they do not form Indian organizations or sponsor Indian events (Albers 1974:92), although they may participate in events sponsored by other Indian communities.

The agency town of Fort Totten is tribal headquarters, as well as Bureau of Indian Affairs administrative headquarters, for the tribe. The actual fort buildings are maintained by the state as a tourist attraction. Like other agency towns in North Dakota, Fort Yates, New Town and Belcourt, Fort Totten represents the interface between Indian and White, between tribal and Federal government.

The Fort Totten community sits on a hill above Devils Lake. Entering Fort Totten, the first building one sees is a large, fairly new community building called the Blue Building because of its blue tile surface. This Blue Building houses the federal and tribal administrative units, a public health clinic, a lunch counter, bank, post office, Indian store, a community room and a wide variety of program offices, such as the Community Action Program and Women, Infants and Children Supplementary Nutrition (WIC) program. The Blue Building is a popular spot, because so much business is conducted there that it is a good place to meet friends, to visit and to pick up information about reservation activities. The interior of the building is cool on a hot day and warm on a cold one, and although people are frequently reminded not to loiter, the Blue Building is still the best place to find out what is happening and the best place to be when the weather is uncooperative.

Across the road from the community building is the building which originally housed Little Hoop Community College. This small building now serves as the tribal courthouse, while the community college has taken over the old high school. Behind the court building is a powwow ground and rodeo arena. Unlike the smaller powwows which are sponsored by communities primarily for their own pleasure, the Fort Totten Powwow is part of a regional tourist promotion known as Fort Totten Days. For the most part, this promotion is carried out by non-Indian residents in Devils Lake and centers around the Fort, but the Indians have become part of this and benefit from the promotional activities of the other events. Fort Totten Days attracts large Indian and non-Indian audiences. The rest of the agency town consists of houses, schools and the Devils Lake Sioux Manufacturing Company. The housing is new, ranch-style single family or four-plex apartment structures. The school, completed in 1984, educates all the reservation children from kindergarten through high school. Most of the people who live in the community are employed by the tribal or Federal government and work in the Blue Building, or work for Devils Lake Sioux Manufacturing or are employed by the school.

The reservation has no commercial or business district. People must drive to Devils Lake in order to shop. A grocery store-general store is available at St. Michaels and smaller stores elsewhere, but the selection is small and the prices are higher than in Devils Lake. An industrial park is currently occupied by one industry, the Devils Lake Sioux Manufacturing Company, that makes camouflage nets and other products. The business was originally under contract to the Federal government but now has contracts with other industries.

Fort Berthold Reservation

Tribe: Three Affiliated Tribes (Arikara, Hidatsa, Mandan)

Reservation size: 981,215 acres (63,624 Indian, tribal and Federal owned)

Fort Berthold Reservation (Fig. 9.4), home of the Three Affiliated Tribes (Mandan, Hidatsa, Arikara) lies along the Missouri River in the west-central part of the state. Originally a vast area of more than 12 million acres, extending from east of the Missouri River into Montana as far as the Yellowstone River, was defined in the Treaty of Fort Laramie in 1851 as the boundaries of the Arikara, Mandan and Hidatsa (called the Gros Ventre in the treaty) tribes. This area was never claimed by the tribes, and by 1870 a new agreement was drawn up and made legal by an executive order signed April 12, 1870 (Meyer 1977:112). In 1880 another executive order reduced the reservation to less than 3 million acres. In 1894, allotment of the reservation began. One of the main differences between the allotment

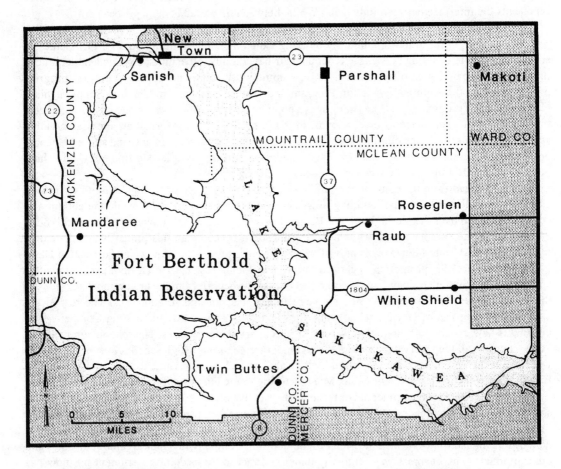

Figure 9.4. Fort Berthold Reservation. (Map drawn by Scott Williams).

proceedings at Fort Berthold and those at Fort Totten was the provision to hold surplus lands in trust for the Three Affiliated Tribes rather than to sell them to non-Indians. By 1901, however, pressure to sell off the surplus lands was critical and though the Indians successfully resisted this pressure for some years, in 1910 they signed an agreement to reduce the size of the reservation once again. In 1948 an investigator for the Bureau of Indian Affairs filed the following report concerning Indian land at Fort Berthold (Macgregor 1948:2).

> Its gross acreage is 643,368 acres from which 63,150 acres have passed into non-Indian ownership. The remaining 579,858 acres of Indian lands are held in trust by the United States. The great majority of this acreage, 550,269 acres, has been allotted in different size tracts, patterned after the homestead system, to individual members of the tribe. The residue of 27,729 acres after allotment was discontinued and has remained tribal land, also held in trust, and in a governmental reserve aggregating 1,860 acres. No allotments have been made since 1929.

The construction of Garrison Dam in 1954 and the subsequent inundation of the Missouri River bottomlands reduced the land base by another 150,000 acres. Alienation of land through sales continued, and by 1959 the reservation acreage stood at 426,413 acres (Meyer 1977:241). In 1970, a decision was handed down that the 1910 agreement did not take land away from the reservation but merely opened the land to White settlement. This meant that a section of land east of the Missouri was returned to the reservation although few tribal members lived on the land. Currently, the reservation acreage is slightly more than 980,888 acres, of which 356,998 acres are individually allotted, 353,790 acres are in the returned homestead area and 152,000 acres are in the reservoir taking area (North Dakota Indian Affairs Commission 1985). The tribe is presently attempting to prevent any further erosion of the land base by purchasing land that is put up for sale by either tribal or White owners. The tribe is also negotiating with the Army Corps of Engineers and the Bureau of Land Management to have access lands around the reservoir returned to tribal control.

The Fort Berthold Reservation used to offer a more varied topography than it now does. The Missouri River and the Little Missouri bottomland offered rich soil and protected spots for homesites. For hundreds of years before inundation, the Arikara, Hidatsa and Mandan people had lived and farmed along the river bottom. When the lake was created, the people were moved from these rich bottomlands to the uplands overlooking the lake. The upland area is either rolling hills or a rough terrain with buttes and gulleys. The east bank of the reservation is more rolling, and the land is suitable for small grain growing, while the central and southern parts are used for stock ranching. The highest point of land on the reservation is Saddle Buttes which can be seen from a great distance. A few permanent creeks flow into Lake Sakakawea, but most of the gulleys are full only during spring rainy seasons and summer storms. Precipitation ranges from 14 - 16 inches with the normal annual precipitation less than 15 inches on the west side of the lake and more than 15 on the east side of the lake. Most of the precipitation falls during the growing season, thus preventing real drought. This summer rain is primarily from thunderstorms which develop suddenly and intensely in this part of the country.

The average number of growing days is 110-119 with approximately 130 - 139 days of 28 degrees and above temperatures (U.S. Dept. of Interior 1971:117). Not only is the terrain in the western and southern part of the reservation too rough for efficient farming, but the soils are thin and not suited to agriculture. Soils in the northern and eastern segments, however, are deep, glaciated soils suitable for agriculture. The vegetation of the western and southern segments is mainly grasses suitable for grazing: western wheatgrass, little blue stem, blue grama, sand reed grass, plains muhly, green needlegrass, and needle and thread (U.S. Dept. of Interior 1971:5). In the gulleys berries from shrub trees, such as juneberry, buffaloberry and chokecherry are a food source for reservation residents. Trees on the reservation are noncommercial species: burr oak, box-elder, birch, green ash and cottonwood.

The building of the Garrison Dam and Lake Sakakawea disrupted social and economic patterns and required many new constructions, such as roads, bridges, and homes. Lake Sakakawea divided the reservation into five segments which are now identified as administrative units. Communication between these segments is difficult because only one bridge at the northern end of the reservation crosses the reservoir. To reach the southern segment, one must drive many miles around the reservoir. Original plans to bridge the southern part of the reservoir have been tabled for lack of demonstrated need. The new roads that were put in to replace old roads are also on the edges of the reservation boundary, and most residents must drive over dirt roads or tracks to reach major highways or towns. Distances between communities, which may be as much as 100 miles, require a car. Towns on the reservation provide some commercial and business establishments, but most people go to Minot or Bismarck for large-scale shopping. Train and plane service is available in Minot and Bismarck. New Town and Williston have small airports, accessible by small private planes.

Figure 9.5. Modern housing at Twin Buttes, North Dakota. (Fred Schneider Photo).

The major reservation communities are New Town, Parshall, White Shield, Mandaree and Twin Buttes. New Town was built to replace the former agency town of Elbowwoods and to accommodate citizens of the towns of Sanish and Van Hook which were inundated by the reservoir. Some of the buildings in New Town were moved from their previous locations, but many were newly built and new buildings have been added since the move. The main street, which is also state highway 23, is double wide with the center part for through traffic and a lane on each side for shop traffic. Stores, banks, bars, post office, motels and entertainment facilities line the main street. All of the buildings on this street are low, one or two story buildings, and the town has a western atmosphere. The lack of trees along the main street contributes to a feeling of spaciousness. On streets paralleling the main street are private homes, schools and churches. On the eastern edge of town is a housing complex of single family dwellings and the new campus of Fort Berthold Community College.

Right after the move to New Town, the tribal administration occupied a building with the Bureau of Indian Affairs Federal administration. Subsequently, the tribe moved to its own temporary office in a small building on the main street. In 1979, the tribe completed a new tribal office building across the river (reservoir) from New Town. New Town was established on land not believed to be part of the reservation and so New Town was a non-Indian town. The Natives who lived in New Town were those who worked for the tribal or Federal administration. In 1990 the population of New Town was estimated at 1338 (U.S. Bureau of the Census 1992). Of these residents, 719 were Indian. New Town is now considered to be on land that is part of the reservation, but it is still a non-Indian town because the Indians who live in New Town do not participate in town politics and have established their own organizations.

About three miles west of New Town on state highway 23 is the Four Bears complex. This complex was originally designed as a tourist attraction to provide income for the tribe. A 40-unit motel with restaurant and convention facilities, a service station, camping area and docking facilities were constructed. The motel was completely remodeled and reopened in 1993 as the Four Bears Casino. Next to the motel is the Four Bears Tribal Museum, a small building that houses artifacts and books relating to the history of the Mandan, Hidatsa and Arikara. This area is rapidly developing as a tribal community. The new tribal office building is located near the motel complex. The Public Health Service clinic is located across the road from the motel, as are the powwow grounds which have a permanent arbor built in 1977. A short distance away is Drags Wolf village, a new housing complex for Indian families.

Parshall, unlike New Town, was established by White settlers long before the reservoir was put in. The act of 1910 that opened the reservation land to White settlement allowed the establishment of townsites. One of these was Parshall, established in 1914 as a commercial center for farmers in the area (Meyer 1977:165). Parshall also attracted Indian business and a few Indian families settled on the edge of town. In 1990 Parshall was estimated to have a population of 943 which included 336 Indians (U.S. Bureau of the Census 1992). Like New Town, Parshall is not an Indian town even though it is now located on land belonging to the reservation. The Indian population of Parshall is growing and the nature of the town may change.

The real tribal communities are White Shield, Mandaree and Twin Buttes, each of which is identified with one of the three tribes. White Shield is Arikara; Mandaree is Hidatsa; and Twin Buttes is Mandan. These towns were built by families who were moved out of the river bottom and represent composite populations from a number of other communities. Each town is also the location of a tribal-Federal subagency for the segment. Before the reservoir was built, 289 out of 357 households were located in the reservoir area. These households formed residential communities, distinguished by tribal and kinship affiliations. Nishu and Beaver Creek were Arikara communities. Charging Eagle and Red

Butte were Mandan communities, and Independence, Shell Creek and Lucky Mound were Hidatsa communities. Members of all three tribes and non-Indians lived at Elbowwoods.

White Shield, the new community of the Arikara people, is the largest community in the eastern segment, housing over 200 people. White Shield is a primarily residential community consisting of the eastern segment subagency, a school, churches, community hall and powwow grounds.

The northeastern segment has no real community center. The location of Lucky Mound School, now closed, has been turned into the northeastern segment subagency to serve those families that live in the district, but there is not a permanent community near the agency itself. Lucky Mound was originally a Hidatsa Community, but the residents dispersed into other communities when the reservoir was built. The residents of the northeastern segment sponsor a powwow known as the Santee Reunion.

The people who used to live in the community of Shell Creek, in the northern segment, were removed because of the reservoir. Although Shell Creek no longer exists, the people refer to themselves as the Little Shell people and maintain a sense of community. Each summer the Little Shell people sponsor a powwow in the powwow grounds across from the Four Bears Motel complex. On the east side of New Town, the Little Shell group built a community hall where they hold bingo games and special ceremonies, like the Mid-Winter Ceremony or powwow.

Mandaree is, according to one person, "the heart of the reservation." Located in the western segment, Mandaree is a new community of about three hundred people. Mandaree is a residential community with a school, community hall and churches. The residents of this community sponsor an annual summer powwow and local winter celebrations.

The former community of Independence, inundated by the reservoir, has merged with others in Mandaree and there is little sense of the earlier community. Those communities of the western segment outside Mandaree are often cut off in the winter because the roads are either poor or nonexistent. Families with children or elderly people who may need a doctor's care prefer to move to Mandaree or some place nearer these services.

Twin Buttes, in the southern segment, is the largest tribal community in the area. Twin Buttes has the southern segment subagency, a school, and a clinic, several churches, a community hall and a trading post. The roads in this isolated community are not paved and the lack of grocery and gas stations means that people must travel many miles in order to get the services they need. On the other hand, Twin Buttes reflects the peaceful country life of an earlier time and is the home for many of the more traditional Mandan people.

A major difficulty which all of these communities face is communication. Each segment operates more or less independently. Thus a person may contact the tribal office in New Town for information concerning a powwow to be held in one of the other segments and find that no one knows about the activity. The long distance which one must drive to get from one community to another also prohibits close contacts and the division of the reservation into segments has enhanced some of the cultural distinctiveness between the Mandan/Hidatsa and the Arikara people.

Standing Rock Reservation

Tribe: Standing Rock Sioux (Lakota and Yanktonai)

Reservation size: 2.3 million acres (849,989 Indian owned,
1,483,000 non-Indian owned, 55,993 acres in reservoir taking area)

Standing Rock Reservation (Fig. 9.6), home of the Standing Rock Sioux Tribe, straddles the North Dakota-South Dakota border. The northernmost part of the reservation is about forty miles south of Bismarck. The southernmost part of the reservation stretches into South Dakota until it joins the Cheyenne River Reservation. Standing Rock is the largest reservation in land area although it does not have the largest population. Unlike the other reservations in the state, the North Dakota section of the reservation forms a single county, Sioux County.

Originally, Standing Rock was part of the Great Sioux Nation which was established by the Treaty of Fort Laramie in 1851. The Great Sioux Nation then included all of South Dakota west of the Missouri, part of western North Dakota, eastern Montana and Wyoming and western Nebraska. The center

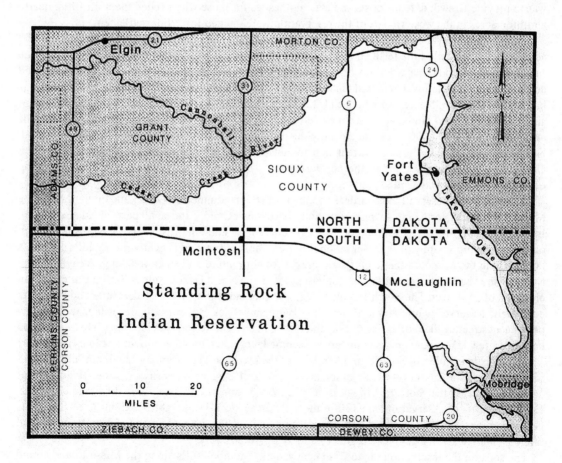

Figure 9.6. Standing Rock Reservation. (Map drawn by Scott Williams).

of the reservation was the Black Hills, an area sacred to all Lakota. In 1868, at another Fort Laramie meeting, the land base was reduced to all of South Dakota west of the Missouri River. Montana and Wyoming were left unceded as open hunting territory for Indians from many nations. When gold was discovered in the Black Hills, the Lakota objected to the presence of Whites and soldiers, a direct violation of the treaty, and eventually began to make wars to get the Whites to leave the territory. Because the Federal government maintained that the Lakota had broken the treaty, the government punished the Lakota by dividing and separating the Great Sioux Nation into smaller units.

From 1882 - 1889 a series of treaties were made with individual Sioux tribes and bands. These treaties broke up the large reservation into smaller ones to be used by different groups. The Act of 1889 which created these reservations provided over two million acres for Standing Rock Reservation. Most of the reservation's inhabitants were members of the Hunkpapa band although descendants of the Oglala, Yanktonai and other divisions lived there. At the time of its establishment, the reservation was approved for allotment. Heads of families were to be allotted 320 acres and 160 acres to other Indians. In addition, each family was to receive $50 in cash, a span of horses, farming equipment and a two year supply of seed. Allotments began in 1906 and ended in 1915. In addition to the original allotment, 2,500 timber allotments in the Missouri River bottomland were made to families. Each timber tract was to provide firewood, fence posts and even homesites for those who needed them. In 1908, nearly a million acres in the western part of the reservation were opened for White settlement.

In 1948 the reservation contained over one million acres of land. The Oahe Reservoir took 50,000 acres which consisted of the fertile bottomland and timber areas. The timber had been used to provide fuel, fence posts and other wood for reservation needs. In 1963, the reservation consisted of 869,358 acres, of which 609,457 were allotted (U.S. Dept. of Interior 1964:3). In 1973, the reservation holdings had shrunk to 844,525 acres, of which 511,220 were individually owned. Today, the reservation consists of Indian owned lands, non-Indian owned lands and reservoir taking areas. Indian owned lands are approximately 500,000 acres that are individually allotted and 350,000 acres that are tribally owned. Nearly one and a half million acres are in non-Indian hands (North Dakota Indian Affairs Commission 1985). Like other reservations in the northern plains, Standing Rock is faced with the continuing diminution of Indian controlled lands.

Standing Rock Reservation is bordered on the north by the Cannonball River and on the east by the Missouri River. In North Dakota the reservation is also Sioux County and small parts of Adams County. In South Dakota the reservation comprises Corson County and small parts of Dewey and Ziebach counties. The topography of the reservation is varied. Most of the land is gently rolling hills and grass lands. Along the Missouri gentle bluffs are usable for agriculture and stock ranching. Away from the Missouri are "badland" type areas. The highest point on the North Dakota side is Barren Butte, with an elevation of 2190 feet. The South Dakota side has higher elevations. Rattlesnake Butte and Elk Butte edge Oahe Reservoir while Hump Butte, Clay Butte and Black Horse Butte are further west. A few permanent streams, like Porcupine Creek, and rivers, like Grand River, provide water. The reservation has only a few lakes, but some marshy areas become lakes when the intermittent streams fill up.

The climate is little different from other parts of the Dakotas. The average annual rainfall is 16 - 17 inches in the eastern part of the reservation and 15 - 16 inches in the western part. Most of the precipitation falls during the short growing season. The average number of days without frost is 135 in the eastern part of the reservation and 130 in the western section. Temperature extremes of 50 degrees below zero to 119 degrees above zero have been recorded for the reservation although the normal range is more nearly 11 degrees in January and 72 degrees in July.

The soils on the reservation range from heavy, dark, "gumbo" soils along the Missouri and Grand Rivers, to sandy soils which form the eroded "badland" areas in the higher elevations. Between these two regions, the soils are suitable for farming and are used either as grassland for cattle raising or have been broken up for agriculture. The vegetation is a mixed prairie variety with mid to short grasses. Shrub trees grow in ravines, but cottonwood stands once covered the lowland areas along the Missouri River (U.S. Department of Interior 1973:35).

The reservation is crossed by several major highways, although, because of Oahe Dam, none of the tribal communities are now directly on these highways. Major roads are N.D. Highways 6 and 24 and South Dakota 63 and 65. At McLaughlin, U.S. Highway 12 joins South Dakota 63. Cannonball and Fort Yates are only a few miles from the major highways, but many other tribal communities are located at a distance from major transportation networks. Kenel and Wakpala are on paved roads, but most reservation roads are unpaved, though in good condition. No major transportation facilities exist on the reservation. Distances between Fort Yates, the agency town, and other tribal communities are as much as 40 miles.

Standing Rock, like Fort Berthold was affected by the building of a dam and the subsequent inundation of reservation lands. Oahe Reservoir was part of the same plan to control the Missouri River and to provide water for electricity and irrigation that brought about the building of Garrison Dam and others higher up on the Missouri (Lawson 1982). The location of Bismarck prevented the engineers from taking additional land for Oahe Reservoir. The reservoir could come no higher than the 1620 foot mark because it would flood Bismarck. While it was considered possible to move small communities such as Cannonball and Kenel, approximately 170 families, it was not considered feasible to relocate the city of Bismarck. Consequently, the impact of dam building on Standing Rock was much less than the impact on Fort Berthold Reservation where Lake Sakakawea is much larger than Lake Oahe. Lake Oahe stretches from Pierre, South Dakota, to Bismarck, North Dakota. The lake is neither very wide nor very deep in most places and looks more like a wide river than a lake. Because the river is not very deep, the trees that were standing in the bottomlands were not removed nor have they been moved by water action. Thus along the river great stands of dead cottonwood trees are found in the water. While their stark white trunks may have an aesthetic attraction to some, they also serve as a constant reminder of the changes that have been brought by the White man's struggle to control nature.

Most of the Indian population lives in the eastern half of Standing Rock reservation. A gradual shift in population has been from the North Dakota side of the border to the South Dakota side. The major tribal community on the reservation is Fort Yates, the agency town. Originally, Fort Yates was a fort, built in 1878 to protect White people crossing the area. It later became the administrative center for the reservation, much as Fort Totten became the administrative center for the Devils Lake Sioux. The fort itself was built on a bluff overlooking the Missouri. On the bottomlands below the fort, the tribal community established itself. When the reservoir was put in, the lower Indian community was flooded and had to be rebuilt. The higher buildings which included the old fort, the school and administration building were not flooded, but the area became an island, now connected to the mainland by a causeway.

The modern community of Fort Yates consists of two separate areas; the older area on the island, and the rebuilt community on the mainland. Total population of Fort Yates in 1990 was 1913. Of these 1728 (U.S. Bureau of the Census 1992) were Indian. The administrative area, some houses, stores, gas stations, national franchises and Indian service buildings are located on the island, connected to the mainland by a causeway. The island is about 2 miles long and less than a mile wide. The island has limited space for growth, hence people either build very small houses or build new ones on the mainland. Mobile homes are one solution to the problem of limited space. The old community of Fort Yates is entered by a causeway which bisects the town. The left side has government buildings, some of them new, modular buildings. To the right are gas stations, a grocery store, and other enterprises. Behind these shops to the right is the residential area. The tribal office building is on the left side of the road. At the left end of the island is a new housing complex, called "The Complex," which was built for senior citizens. Not having enough senior citizens to fill The Complex, The Complex is rented out to other people who need a place to live. Nearby The Complex is the public health hospital, a comparatively new building. Fort Yates, old town, is tree-lined, comfortable and quiet with a feeling of last century charm. It is an unhurried, pleasant place to be.

On the mainland, to the north, the new town of Fort Yates, called Sioux Village, was built to house Indian families whose homes were inundated by Oahe. Some houses were moved from the bottomland, but most were newly built. This section of Fort Yates is a fast-growing community with churches, a community college, and a community hall.

Other major tribal communities on the reservation represent tribal districts which are part of the governing system. Cannonball, the northernmost tribal community on the reservation, was relocated from the reservoir-taking area. Some disagreement about the location of the settlement caused the town to spread out north and south along the river. The central part of the community is laid out in residential blocks. A school, a Public Health Service clinic and churches are non-residential structures in the town. Each summer, Cannonball sponsors a powwow. In 1993 the tribe opened Prairie Knights Casino just outside Cannonball.

Other tribal communities, except for the tiny community of Porcupine, located across the Cannonball River from Shields, are on the South Dakota side of the border. Kenel, another community that had to be relocated because of the inundation from Oahe Reservoir, is about one mile south of the old town. The former government day school was moved to use as a community center. House lots were laid out in blocks. The town is primarily residential, although a gas station, a small store and several churches are convenient for the residents.

Little Eagle, population 300 in 1970, is one of the growing communities on the reservation. Although Little Eagle is located on the Grand River, the water supply is tenuous, and considerable effort has been expended to get a satisfactory water supply for the community. A community development committee was able to use funds from the money paid to the tribe for taking lands for the reservoir to drill wells in search of better water. Funds were also used to develop a community/recreation building. North of the town a residential area was laid out, and new houses are being built in this area.

Wakpala, Bullhead and Mission are other small Indian communities of less than four hundred residents. The majority of the residents are Indian. Many non-Indian towns are located on the reservation. Most of these are larger than the Indian communities. For a variety of reasons, Indians who live near these towns do not usually take part in town activities although they may send their children to the town school. Solen and Selfridge are two non-Indian towns whose schools have large Indian populations. In South Dakota, McLaughlin has a growing Indian population. In 1970 its total population was 863, Indian 103; however, this percentage has undoubtedly changed since there are Indian owned and operated businesses, as well as a branch office of the tribal court, an out-patient clinic of the Public Health Service, and a Bingo palace.

Mobridge, located across the Missouri on the eastern edge of the reservation, is a non-Indian town with a population of over 4000. Ten percent of the population is Indian. The size of the town and the location of the former Chief Gall Motor Lodge attracts Indians to the town for shopping, recreation and business.

Turtle Mountain Reservation

Tribe: Turtle Mountain Band of Chippewa (Chippewa and Metis)

Reservation size: 46,080 acres (Indian controlled 33,107)

Turtle Mountain Reservation, home of the Turtle Mountain Band of Chippewa, is the northernmost reservation in North Dakota Fig. 9.7). Located just below the Canadian border, the reservation is part of a large hilly area known as the Turtle Mountains. Also located in the Turtle Mountains are the International Peace Garden, which spans the US-Canadian border, Lake Metigoshe State Park and other tourist attractions. Turtle Mountain was the last reservation to be established in North Dakota, although tribal claims to the area had been recognized long before the final establishment of the reservation.

In 1861, the Act which provided for the establishment of the Dakota Territory recognized the claims of Chippewa and Metis to 10 million acres in northeastern North Dakota. The Metis were a distinct ethnic group composed of the descendants of Indian and Euro-American marriages (Delorme 1955).

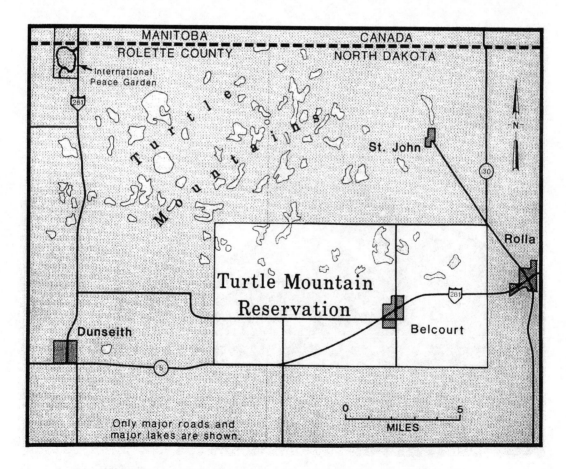

Figure 9.7. Turtle Mountain Reservation. (Map drawn by Scott Williams).

Although the Metis have a separate history in Canada, they have never been recognized as a distinct ethnic group by the United States Federal government. Their affiliation with the Chippewa has permitted them to be classed as Indians, and they have received services from the Federal government under that classification although the Federal government has always sought to remove the Metis from eligibility. In 1863, the Red Lake and Pembina bands of Chippewa signed a treaty which established reservations for them in Minnesota. The Turtle Mountain Chippewa refused to acknowledge the treaty, claiming that their use of the land predated any land use of the other tribes. Although the government had originally agreed to the Turtle Mountain Band's claim to central North Dakota, in 1882 the land was officially opened for settlement.

An executive order in 1882 set aside a tract of land running from the Canadian border to the line between township 158 and 159 (approximately the present boundaries of Rolette County) for the use of the Turtle Mountain Chippewa. This tract was approximately 72 thousand acres. In 1884 the land base was reduced to two townships and the rest of the land restored to the public domain by executive decision. The Turtle Mountain Chippewa protested these actions, and in 1892 a formal treaty was

Figure 9.8. St. Ann's Catholic Church, Belcourt, recently celebrated its 100th aniversary.

drawn up which provided for the sum of one million dollars to be paid to the Turtle Mountain Chippewa for the lands which had been arbitrarily opened for settlement (Murray 1984).

Before this treaty was drawn up, however, the Turtle Mountain band had been enlarged by Metis who had fled from the Riel Rebellion in Canada and now sought a peaceful homeland. Although refusing to enlarge the size of the reservation, the Federal government did agree that those Metis who could establish their claim to tribal ancestry would be able to either settle on the reservation or take homesteads off the reservation. Establishment of Indian ancestry was arbitrarily handled by agents who wanted to lessen the demand for Indian allotments, and so many of the Metis, along with Chippewa for whom there was no room on the reservation, were forced to settle far from the reservation. One group lives near Trenton, North Dakota, and another lives in Montana. These groups have been prosecuting their claim for Indian identity for many years, with more or less success. In addition to providing a cash settlement for the formal abandonment of the claim to northeastern North Dakota, the treaty provided for the allotment of the reservation to individual members. In 1906, Graham's Island, part of the Devils Lake Sioux Reservation was allotted to Turtle Mountain people.

Today the reservation itself consists of two townships, approximately 34 thousand acres, mostly individually allotted. Members of the tribe own another 35 thousand acres of land off the reservation. Most of the land off the reservation is tribally owned. Individual tribe members also own another 60 thousand—70 thousand acres in North Dakota and Montana. Turtle Mountain is the only North Dakota reservation located totally within a single county. The small reservation has a large population of Indians.

Figure 9.9. Wahpeton Indian School, ca. 1910. (Courtesy of State Historical Society of North Dakota).

The Turtle Mountain Reservation has perhaps the most beautiful landscape but is the least suited to human habitation of all the reservations in North Dakota. The Turtle Mountains are gently rolling, wooded hills occupying about 400 square miles on both sides of the United States-Canadian border. Much of the area that is not hilly is covered with water. No important permanent streams are found in the area, but the reservation has at least thirty lakes of various sizes. Between the lakes are marshy areas. The Turtle Mountains were covered by the glaciers which created the lakes and left behind rocky, sandy soil, not suitable for agriculture. The average precipitation for the area is between 16 - 17 inches. The growing season is 118 days between killing frosts. The Turtle Mountains served as wintering places for early Chippewa and Metis families. The hills provided some protection from the cold and deer, rabbits, fur-bearing mammals and wild fowl were plentiful.

Although the reservation appears to be out-of-the-way of commercial transportation routes, US route 281, a major north-south highway in North Dakota, takes a westward turn and passes through the southeast corner of the reservation. Belcourt, the major Indian community on the reservation, is bisected by route 281. Bus transportation is available but not convenient, and there is no passenger train service. The nearest large city to the reservation is Devils Lake, 80 miles to the southeast. Rolla, a town just off the Turtle Mountain Reservation, has a landing strip but no regularly scheduled flights.

Belcourt, with a population of over 2000, is the largest Indian community in North Dakota and is also the largest town in Rolette County, a situation unique in North Dakota. Belcourt is also the agency town for the reservation. In 1968, a new tribal administration building was completed. The Turtle Mountain Housing Authority, established in 1962, has built a number of low rent units in Belcourt. The Community School provides an education for students in grades 1-12. The U.S. Public Health Service recently built a large, new hospital in Belcourt which it plans to make into a regional health center for tribes in North and South Dakota.

South Belcourt is a new community of planned housing constructed by the Turtle Mountain Housing Authority. The town itself serves as a regional shopping center and it has a variety of stores and services, including a grocery store, bar, cafe, gas stations and a Tastee Freeze. Most of the commercial outlets are operated by members of the Turtle Mountain Chippewa tribe. In 1978 a new shopping mall, owned and operated by the Turtle Mountain Chippewa Tribe, was opened. The mall contains a restaurant, a barber shop, a beauty shop, a western wear store, a food store, an appliance store and a general merchandise store. Turtle Mountain Community College provides general education and college level courses for residents of the area. Belcourt has an annual powwow and an annual fete, St. Anne's Days.

Since 50 percent of the population of Rolette County is Indian, it is to be expected that other towns in the area off the reservation, have large numbers of Indian residents. Dunseith is one of these towns. In 1970 the population of Dunseith was 40 percent Indian. In the rural area around Dunseith the population proportion increases to 53 percent Indian. The large tribal population makes possible a tribally operated day school in Dunseith for elementary school children. The rural population tends to be more conservative than the residents of Dunseith proper or of Belcourt.

The area north of Belcourt is the home for a number of the more traditionally-Indian people. The small number of people who claim direct descent from the Turtle Mountain Band of Chippewa tends to be more conservative than those who are descended from Metis people. The customs between the two groups also vary. The greater number of Metis descendants has given them positions in tribal government, but the traditional Chippewa who uphold the Indian customs serve as a reservoir of tribal history and knowledge. East of Belcourt is Rolla, the largest non-Indian town in the area. The Indian population in Rolla has been small but is beginning to grow as housing on the reservation becomes more and more difficult to find.

Wahpeton Indian School

Wahpeton Indian School at Wahpeton, North Dakota, is, like the reservations, Federal trust property but it is unlike the reservations in the manner of its establishment, and in the fact that it is not set aside for the use of a single group. Wahpeton was established in 1908, along with a number of other boarding schools, to help educate Indian boys and girls.

Today Wahpeton Indian School is a boarding school for Indian children in grades one to eight. The school is located on fifty-two acres owned by the Federal government. In 1972-73 383 children were in school. Children are sent to this school by parents who cannot keep the children at home due to illness, financial difficulties or for other reasons. In 1982 the Bureau of Indian Affairs recommended closing the school as part of an attempt to save funds and to keep tribal children in their own communities. The large number of parents and others who spoke against the closing caused the Bureau to reconsider its decision, and so the school has remained open.

General Similarities in Reservations

Although all of the North Dakota reservations are different in terms of natural environment and their relationship to larger, urban areas, they have commonalities. All the reservations have small communities in which people live with little access to commercial enterprises. These communities may be far from major transportation units, off main roads, too small to have more than a local grocery store or gas station and lack any reason for most non-Indians to go there. These communities often house the more traditional members of the tribe because they are removed from the outside world. Communities vary, however, with people choosing to live near those who are more like them. Agency towns like New Town and Fort Yates are more often the residence of people who are less traditionally oriented. On all the reservations people may choose to live very simple lives, without electricity and/ or running water. In some instances, the homestead is too far from the source to make laying in water pipes or electricity lines economical or profitable. But more often the residents in these remote areas do not wish to be burdened with lights, telephones or running water.

Transportation is a major problem for many of the people in the more remote areas of the reservations. The reservations are all accessible by car, but the more remote areas are often cut off by winter storms and spring mud. Most of the reservations are far removed from air, train and bus lines so that a car is necessary. Long distances between reservation and communities may increase feelings of separation and isolation, but there are compensations.

This isolation results in reservation communities developing strong social and cultural identities. People in these communities know each other well, have learned how to get along with each other, or how to control outbreaks of anger, and distrust, and find life more interesting and more fulfilling than living in the urban areas. Community activities like Bingo, powwow clubs, and church events bring people together. Often the people who live in these small, rural communities are relatives who are obligated by tribal values to assist each other in times of need.

The attraction of life on the reservation is evident in recent statistics. In 1979 North Dakota tribal leaders indicated that surveys showed more people moving back to the reservations from the urban areas (Oyaka Newsletter 1979). More than 8,000 North Dakota Indians left the reservations between 1952 - 1969. Those people who have worked long enough or have reached the age to retire are now returning to the reservations. From 1973 to 1979, Standing Rock Reservation experienced a 31 percent increase in population. Leaders at Fort Totten noted a population growth of 29 percent. Only a small proportion of these increases is attributed to births. The remaining increase represents people who once left the reservation but have now returned to live there.

People who return to the reservations to live must adjust to a different way of life. Some returnees find it difficult to be accepted by the long-time residents who fear changes will accompany the influx of people (Weibel-Orlando 1991). People who have lived and worked in urban areas may want to make changes in tribal government, education, and employment. These changes may eventually benefit the tribe, but Indian custom prefers to make changes slowly. The returnees also place additional stress on housing, employment, school and health facilities. On the other hand, people who retire with pension and social security incomes bring much needed funds into the reservation communities.

This chapter has briefly surveyed the four reservations in North Dakota. It has taken a geographic approach, describing the reservation settings and communities, rather than examining social or economic issues. The remaining chapters provide detailed analyses of economics, education and health.

MARIE LOUISE BUISSON MCLAUGHLIN

Marie Louise, called Louise or Lou by her family, was born in Wabasha, Minnesota, December 8, 1842. Her family was part Mdewakantonwan Dakota and part non-Indian. Louise's grandfather, Duncan Graham, a well-known fur trader who received recognition for his military success on the British side in the war of 1812, married Ha-za-ho-ta-win, sister of Wayagoenagee, leader of the Mdewakanton Dakota (North Dakota Historical Collections 1910:216). There is a tradition, recorded by Owen Libby, that Duncan Graham had a trading post near Devils Lake in the early 1800s. Grahams Island is supposed to have been the location of the post, but there is no evidence of such a post in the records of the fur companies. If the Grahams had been there, their grand-daughter and other descendants completed the circle by returning there in 1871.

Duncan and Ha-za-ho-te-win Graham had four daughters: Nancy, Sarah, Jane, and Marie and one son, Alexander. Three of the girls married ambitious businessmen, but Nancy married a fur trader who worked at whatever job was available. Joseph Buisson, born near Montreal, sometimes worked for the American Fur Company (McLaughlin 1913), but sometimes was out of work. All the daughters had numerous children and these generally stayed near the southern Minnesota area of their birth where they maintained close family ties.

The Buissons, Nancy and Joseph, had seven children: Harriet, Henry, Marie Louise, Antoine, Joseph, Cyprian and Mary Jane. The family generally mixed French and Dakota customs, as did most of their friends and relatives. At age 14 Marie Louise was sent to boarding school at Prairie du Chien, Wisconsin (McLaughlin 1913). Marie was a staunch Catholic, although in later life she had an interest in traditional Indian ceremonies at Devils Lake and Standing Rock and provided information on them to visitors (Gillette 1906).

In January 1864, Marie married James McLaughlin, a travelling salesman from Canada. Their first two children, daughters, died soon after birth, but James Henry, born 1868, and Marie Imelda, born 1870, survived.

When Devils Lake Reservation was first established in 1867, there were not enough Indians to formally build an agency, but by 1871 there were. William H. Forbes was appointed as agent and he hired James McLaughlin as blacksmith and some of Marie Louise's cousins, George and Alexander Faribault, as agency employees. Soon after the McLaughlin family moved to Fort Totten another son, Charles Cyprian, was born. He was followed a year later by John Graham. The last son, Rupert Sibley, was born in 1875.

One of the ways in which Marie Louise's tribal heritage showed itself was in the manner in which her relatives accompanied her to Fort Totten. Some went to work for the agency and some visited. Not only were the Faribaults hired, but in 1873 Antoine Buisson, Marie Louise's brother, became the agency carpenter. John Cramsie, married to Mary Louise's sister, Mary Jane, was hired as agency interpreter. Two years later, 1875, Marie Louise herself replaced Cramsie as agency interpreter. At a time when most women, especially married women with families, did not work outside the home, Marie Louise McLaughlin was a paid government employee at $400 a year (Pfaller 1978:385). She held the post of interpreter off and on for many years, receiving both criticism and acclaim for her skills.

In 1876, after a short politically-charged struggle with Paul Beckwith, who had been appointed agent in 1875, James McLaughlin was appointed agent for the Devils Lake Sioux Reservation (Pfaller

1968:29-38). He kept this position until 1881 when he accepted a position as agent for the Standing Rock Sioux. John Cramsie replaced McLaughlin as agent for the Devils Lake Sioux. Antoine Buisson stayed on at Devils Lake; after all he still had a sister married to the agent, but other relatives moved to Standing Rock with the McLaughlins and others joined them there. Agnes, the daughter of Marie Louise's sister Harriet, became a school teacher at Standing Rock. She married and lived there all her live. Cousin Aaron Wells also moved to Standing Rock.

At Standing Rock, Marie Louise continued her work as interpreter. She was originally paid $600 a year, but this was cut in half soon after she started work (Pfaller 1968:169). She was friends with Sitting Bull and one of her assignments was to accompany him on one of his tours. The members of the touring party called her "mother" (Pfaller 1968:102).

Life as an Indian agent was filled with problems. Unhappy agency employees, representatives of opposing religious denominations and people seeking the agent's job often filed complaints about McLaughlin and his family. None were ever proven and it is clear that some were frivolous. Sitting Bull's death, however, provided an opportunity to remove McLaughlin. Disgruntled reservation residents and politicians used McLaughlin's part in the affair—he ordered the Indian police to arrest Sitting Bull—to force his removal as agent. He accepted a position as Special Agent for the Bureau of Indian Affairs.

While her husband travelled, Louise stayed on the reservation and, around 1902, began a career as a Field Matron (Pfaller 1978:193), a position in which she instructed Indian women on cooking, cleaning, and other home management issues.

During these years she also provided help to visiting anthropologists and corresponded with educators at Hampton Boarding School and carried out similar public relations duties. Gilbert Wilson and his entourage visited Standing Rock in 1905 and found Mrs. McLaughlin very helpful. When Frances Densmore arrived at Standing Rock in 1911 to record Lakota songs, Marie Louise McLaughlin acted as interpreter and also provided information to the recorder (Densmore 1918:v; Densmore 1948:182,186). Some of the objects collected by Ms. Densmore were given to her by Mrs. McLaughlin, who had a deep interest in traditional Indian culture. At this time, Marie Louise began to prepare Dakota and Lakota stories for a book. The book, *Myths and Legends of the Sioux*, published in 1913, was illustrated with drawings by local Indian artists.

At the end of her life, Mrs. McLaughlin spent some time at the family home in McLaughlin, South Dakota, and also moved around, living with various family members. She frequently traveled to St. Paul to visit her brother and his family. While James McLaughlin traveled on Indian affairs business, she traveled for pleasure or stayed with one of her sons. McLaughlin regularly sent money to his son Charles to help cover the cost of Louise's stays.

James McLaughlin died in 1923 and Louise McLaughlin in 1924. Although she had not been born on a reservation, she spent most of her life among Indian people and always tried to help them. Both she and her husband were strong advocates of education for Indians and they encouraged many young people to attend eastern schools and then helped them find work on the reservation. Mrs. McLaughlin also spent much time visiting the ill. During one of the times that James McLaughlin's abilities were being questioned, the protestant missionary Mary C. Collins wrote that the agent "and his wife were wearing themselves out working for the Indians" (Pfaller 1978:174). Today, the descendants of James and Marie Louise McLaughlin continue the family tradition of education and public service.

Chapter 10

Changing Trends in Indian Population and Demography

The national census of 1970 counted 792,730 Americans of Native ancestry. While this figure was probably low, it represented the largest Native American population since aboriginal times and, with a growth of 51 percent since the 1960 census, established American Indians as the fastest growing ethnic group in the United States. By 1980 the Indian population had grown to almost one and a half million and by 1990 it was just a few people short of 2 million. Every state, even Hawaii, has a resident Indian population (Table 10.1), although there is no state in which Indians are more than a small percent of the total population. Five states, Oklahoma, Arizona, California, New Mexico and North Carolina account for 50 percent of the total Indian population while twenty-two states account for 85 percent of the Indian population. The Indian populations in the remaining twenty-eight states range from almost 20,000 in Missouri to 1,696 in Vermont. The people described by these figures are a diverse group, representing a wide variety of environments and tribal backgrounds, as well as great differences in current situations.

Less than half the contemporary tribal population lives on reservations or on other Indian-owned lands. The Federal government recognizes over 300 reservations, federal, state, and individually owned. While not all states have reservations, some states have more than others. California has the most reservations, numbering as many as eighty, but some of these reservations, like Alturas Rancheria, encompass less than 50 acres and have less than twenty residents. Most of California's Indian population, however, lives in Los Angeles, San Francisco and other urban areas. One of the California urban areas, Palm Springs, has a reservation, Agua Calienta. New York state has more state-owned reservations than it does federally-owned. Alaska, however, is divided into native villages rather than reservations. Oklahoma, a state with a large Indian population, has no reservations (U.S. Department of Commerce 1971). The Osage tribe maintains a semi-reservation status with the Federal government because of unresolved legal issues, but the other tribes in Oklahoma live on individually owned land. The Navajo Reservation, in the Four Corners area of Arizona, New Mexico, Colorado and Utah, has more than 200,000 people.

Reservations cannot be equated with tribes. While some reservations are the home of a single tribal group, many reservations are held jointly by different tribal groups. Fort Berthold Reservation in North Dakota is held by the Arikara, Hidatsa, and Mandan tribes. In many cases, tribes have been dispersed to different reservations so that Lakota live on many different reservations in the Dakotas. Other tribes, even though large in numbers, do not have reservations because the land was allotted or because the Federal relationship was terminated. On the basis of self-identification the 1990 census counted more than 500 tribes. These tribes are the ones which were named by the respondents and do

Table 10.1. Indian Populations by State

State	1980	1990	State	1980	1990
California	198,155	242,164	Alabama	7,502	16,506
Oklahoma	169,292	252,420	Massachusetts	7,483	12,241
Arizona	152,498	203,527	Georgia	7,442	13,348
New Mexico	105,976	134,355	Wyoming	7,057	9,479
North Carolina	64,536	80,155	Mississippi	6,131	8,525
Alaska	21,869 Ind	85,698	South Carolina	5,665	8,246
	34,144 Esk		Iowa	5,369	7,349
	8,090 Aleuts		Tennessee	5,013	10,039
Washington	58,186	81,483	Connecticut	4,431	6,654
South Dakota	44,948	50,575	Maine	4,057	5,998
Texas	39,375	65,877	Kentucky	3,518	5,769
New York	38,967	62,651	Hawaii	2,655	5,099
Michigan	37,714	55,638	West Virginia	1,555	2,458
Montana	37,153	47,679	Rhode Island	1,365	4,071
Minnesota	34,831	49,909	Delaware	1,307	2,019
Wisconsin	29,320	39,387	New Hampshire	1,297	2,134
Oregon	26,591	38,496	D.C.	996	1,466
North Dakota	20,120	25,917	Vermont	986	1,696
Utah	19,158	24,283			
Florida	18,922	36,335	TOTAL 1980	1,364,033	
Colorado	17,734	27,776	1990	1,959,234	
Illinois	15,846	21,836			
Kansas	15,256	21,865			
Nevada	13,205	19,637			
Missouri	12,129	19,835			
Ohio	11,985	20,358			
Louisiana	11,951	18,541			
Idaho	10,418	13,780			
Pennsylvania	9,179	14,733			
Arkansas	9,364	12,773			
Virginia	9,211	15,282			
Nebraska	9,145	12,410			
New Jersey	8,175	14,970			
Maryland	7,823	12,292			
Indiana	7,782	12,720			

Source: 1980 Census: General Population: U.S. Summary (Pc80-1-B1), Table 62.
1990 Census: General Population: U.S. Summary (CP-1-1A).

not necessarily represent tribes which are recognized by the Federal government or a complete count of Indian tribes in the United States. The United States government recognizes some 317 tribes and bands and 226 Native Alaskan villages. In addition to the Navajo, other large tribes identified in recent censuses are the Sioux, the Cherokee, and the Chippewa. These and six other large tribes, Pueblo, Lumbee, Choctaw, Apache, Iroquois and Creek, make up more than half of the Indian population. The remainder is divided into many other tribal groups.

For the first time, the 1990 census included tribal identity, although proof of tribal membership was not required. People identified themselves as members of 542 different tribes (Anderson 1992). Some of these tribes were very small and others were not federally recognized. Using this method, the census arrived at a figure of 308,132 members for the Cherokee. The Cherokee Nation of Oklahoma has a tribal enrollment of 145,000 and the Eastern Band of Cherokee had 5,287 Indians living on the reservation in 1990. Others claiming Cherokee identity may not be enrolled and, therefore, are not legally considered to be Indian.

Urban-living Indians make up more than half the total Indian population. More Indians live in the large cities than on most reservations. Sioux, Cherokee and Chippewa live in almost every state and in the larger urban areas. Urban Indian populations in the larger cities like Los Angeles, San Francisco, and Chicago continue to grow, but there is also growth in the urban populations near the reservations. Rapid City, Sioux Falls, Bismarck and other cities located in areas of Indian concentration attract a large number of Indian people. Some of this growth can be attributed to increased job opportunities for Indians and to the impact of Federal employment programs which provide assistance for Indians to leave the reservations. Some of this growth, however, must also be due to Indian exposure to modern American culture through TV, movies, and education which make such moves more comfortable. Transportation makes it possible for Tribal People to leave and return to reservations while greater sophistication in the ways of non-Indians makes it possible for Indians to succeed in the city. Indians in the urban areas also provide information and guidance to newcomers in making the change from reservation to city ways.

No matter where Tribal People live, however, they are always in a minority position. The Native American population makes up around 4 percent of the total national population. As a minority, Tribal People have little political power and have found themselves relegated to third or fourth class status when political favors are given out. Few legislators are willing to speak out for tribal programs, and few Indians are able to attract the kind of attention that leads to political power. Statistics, then, are useful in demonstrating some of the factors in modern tribal life. As one of the nation's smaller minority groups, Indians have been ignored, and they have found themselves without advocacy powers. On some reservations Indians may represent a majority of the population, but voting districts are usually organized in such a way as to prevent Indians from obtaining representation and so they remain a political minority.

North Dakota Tribal Population and Demographics

North Dakota is a rural state with a total population of less than one million. Between 1980 and 1990, the state's population dropped from 652,717 to 638,800 (U.S. Bureau of the Census 1983, 1991). With an area of 70,665 square miles, this is a population density of less than 10 people per square mile. (Compare this to 367.9 per square mile for New York state.) The largest cities, Fargo and Grand Forks, are located on the eastern border with sister cities in Minnesota. Fargo and Grand Forks increased their populations and maintained their positions as the state's most populous cities, although Bismarck rivalled Grand Forks for second place. About 4 percent of the total North Dakota population is Indian. While the four reservations in the state, Fort Berthold, Fort Totten, Standing Rock and Turtle Mountain, are important reservoirs of tribal tradition and culture, less than half the Indians living in North Dakota actually reside on the reservations. The largest cities and smaller urban areas just off the reservations have Indian populations. The Bismarck-Mandan metropolitan area has the largest Indian population, because it is near two reservations and because, as the Capital, Bismarck houses many offices and services for Indian people. Cities outside North Dakota, such as Minneapolis, St. Paul, Rapid City and Denver, also attract Indians from North Dakota.

In the decade following 1980, North Dakota's Indian population grew 28.6 percent, from 20,120 to 25,917. This increase, accompanied by a decrease in the non-Indian population, makes Indians, at 4.1 percent, the state's largest minority. In comparison, South Dakota's Indian population is 7.3 percent of the total, while Minnesota's is 1.1 percent.

Increasing urbanization, a general trend in North Dakota, has been much more significant for Indian people. The number of Indian people living in the state's largest cities nearly doubled between 1970 and 1980 and nearly doubled again between 1980 and 1990. During these twenty years, the general populations of these cities increased 27 percent, while the overall population decreased. The movement of Indians to the cities is associated with increased levels of education and improved employment opportunities.

Table 10.2. Growth of Indian Populations in North Dakota Cities

	Total Population		Indian Population	
	1980	1990	1980	1990
Fargo	61,383	74,111	499	796
Grand Forks	43,765	49,425	662	1,115
Bismarck	44,485	49,256	648	1,261
Minot	32,843	34,544	439	724
Jamestown	16,280	15,571	107	130
Dickinson	15,924	16,097	22	109
Williston	13,336	13,131	229	517
Devils Lake	7,143	7,782	281	532
TOTALS	235,159	259,917	2,887	5,184

Source: 1980 Census: General Social and Economic Characteristics, North Dakota. Table:182.
1990 Census: General Population Characteristics, North Dakota. Table:64.

Reservation Populations

It is easy to provide exact figures for the number of Indians who reside on or near the reservations in North Dakota since they receive various services from the Bureau of Indian Affairs and the tribe. While Tribal People may apply for many different programs, not all people are eligible for all programs, but the figures are probably fairly accurate. Each year the Aberdeen Area Agency of the Bureau of Indian Affairs compiles statistical data for the North Dakota reservations. Population statistics are also available from the national census and from the tribes.

Three basic statistics describe reservation populations. Although all the figures are different, each one is significant because it describes a different approach to reservation populations. Taken together, the three statistics provide important information about these groups.

One statistic, a general count of Indians living on a particular reservation, is provided by the census. This figure generally does not distinguish between tribal members, so it may include Indians from other tribes who also live on the reservation. This figure typically does not include Tribal People who live outside the reservation boundaries, but near enough to consider themselves part of the reservation population.

Another figure is provided by the Bureau of Indian Affairs. This represents the service population. It includes those Indian people living on and off the reservation who have some relationship with the Brueau of Indian Affairs. Like the census, this count includes members of other tribes.

Each tribe keeps a list of all its tribal members. Called the tribal roll, this list provides an exact count of all the people who legally claim membership in the tribe. It includes members living on and off the reservation and excludes members of other tribes.

According to the North Dakota census, the number of Indian people living on North Dakota reservations increased slightly in some instances and significantly in others. Without additional information, some of which may become available through analysis of census reports, it is difficult to interpret the changes in population size.

One North Dakota reservation that experienced a significant increase in Native American population was the Turtle Mountain Reservation. In 1980 the Turtle Mountain Indian population was 3,955. The 1990 census provides two different statistics depending on how the reservation is defined. When the reservation trust lands used by Turtle Mountain Band of Chippewa in other parts of North Dakota are included, there are 6,772 people. When only the reservation is considered, there are 4,746 people. Other statistics indicate that many more Tribal People lived off the reservation, but near-by. In 1989 the Bureau of Indian Affairs considered the Turtle Mountain service population to be 9,889. The 1990 Indian population of Rolette County, which includes the Turtle Mountain Reservation, was 8,497. Tribal membership in 1991 was 26,500.

Fort Berthold Reservation also showed an increase in its Indian population, but not of the magnitude of Turtle Mountain's. In 1980 the reservation population was 2,651. The 1990 census found a Native American population of 2,999 while the 1989 Bureau of Indian Affairs service population was 2,663. Mountrail and Ward counties, two of six encompassing the Fort Berthold Reservation, have a total Indian population of 2,357. However, the Ward County population is primarily that of Minot, 60 miles from the reservation. Tribal membership in 1991 was 9,100.

Because Standing Rock Reservation stretches into South Dakota, the census figures are divided between the two parts. There are some significant shifts in population between the two states. In 1980 more Standing Rock Sioux, 2,459, lived in South Dakota than North Dakota, 2,341. The 1990 census for the North Dakota portion, 2,836, shows that the northern population has grown, while the southern section population declined to 2,034. The total Standing Rock Sioux population increased slightly from 4,800 in 1980 to 4870 in 1990. The 1989 Bureau of Indian Affairs service population for Standing Rock, North Dakota portion, was 5,051. For the South Dakota side it was 5,257. The tremendous difference between the reservation population and the service population suggests that many people live off the reservation but continue to avail themselves of Bureau of Indian Affairs services. Tribal enrollment in 1991 was 10,736.

Fort Totten Reservation also had a small increase in Indian population from 2,258 in 1980 to 2,676 in 1990. The 1989 Bureau of Indian Affairs service population was 3,780, while Benson County had an Indian population of 2,772. Tribal enrollment in 1991 was 3,900.

Of greater significance, however, is the demographic breakdown (Table 10.3) of these reservation figures because they show a young population. Birthrate among Native Americans, nationally, is high, and this trend can be demonstrated for North Dakota Indians. Of the total reservation service population, 47 percent are under sixteen years old, a slight decrease from 1973 when 51 percent of the population was under sixteen. Examination of the percentages for each reservation shows a slight decline in the under-sixteen population for every reservation except for Standing Rock. This continues the slight decline noted between 1970 and 1980 and substantiates the idea that the birthrate on the reservations is slowly falling. Compared to the United States national average of 28.6 percent under sixteen, 47 percent is high.

Another significant comparative figure is median age. The median is the point which divides a population in half. In North Dakota in 1990 the median age for White people was 33.1. That is, half the population was less than 33.1 years old and half was older. At the same time, the median age for Indian people was 20.7. (U.S. Bureau of the Census 1992, Table 19). In other words, half of the Indian people in North Dakota were under 21 years old.

The number of aged Indian people in North Dakota, that is, people over 65, is relatively small. Approximately 4 percent of the North Dakota Indian population (Table 10.4) is over 65. Groups that have less than 5 percent of their population in the aged category are said to be young populations. By the same measure, populations with more than 40 percent under 15 are young populations (Shyrock, Siegel and Associates 1976:132). Table 10.3 shows that the actual number of people over age 65 decreased slightly on two reservations and increased on two others. When these figures are converted to percentages of the total population, however, only Turtle Mountain had an increase in the aged population, from 5 percent to 6 percent. The others remained the same from 1980 to 1990. Taking into consideration the fact that the general population is aging, the lack of change in the tribal population is a sign of the depressed conditions on reservations.

Culturally, the older Tribal People are the ones who are responsible for the maintenance and transmission of traditions and are the ones who are responsible for training the younger people in the Indian way. The frequent lament that the elderly are dying and no one is around to carry on the traditions is supported by the statistics. Additionally, the lack of increase in the aged population in a country in which the aged group is increasing, suggests the health problems that still exist on reservations in North Dakota. While we are able to preserve the life and extend the lifespan of non-Indians, we are unable to do so to the same extent for Indians.

The demographics of tribal populations suggest several considerations. First, they show a population with a high "dependency" ratio which occurs when more than half the population is either too old or too young to work and is, therefore, dependent on others. These populations are consumers, not producers. The highest dependency ratios generally occur in developing countries with high birthrates and death rates.

In terms of reservation development, these figures suggest a greater need for day care and for schools rather than for retirement homes and extended care nursing facilities; a greater need for playgrounds and sports facilities than for theaters and shops, and a greater need for maternity services, pediatricians and child health clinics than for gerontological services, but there is an obvious need for preventive medicine for older people. One serious health problem among older Indians is diabetes. Other health problems, such as loss of limbs, loss of eyesight and diminished organ functioning are directly attributable to diabetes. Numerous organizations are seeking a cause and a cure for this dis-

Table 10.3. North Dakota Reservation Populations by Age

	Under 5	5-17	18-64	65+	Median age
Devils Lake					
1980	379	806	967	109	17
1990	413	913	1256	94	18.2
Fort Berthold					
1980	338	889	1293	128	19.3
1990	403	902	1502	141	21.9
Standing Rock					
1980	716	1585	2287	212	18.8
1990	711	1617	2289	195	18.9
Turtle Mountain					
1980	555	1389	1852	225	18.7
1990	596	1422	2501	289	22.3

Source: 1980 Census, North Dakota, General Social and Economic Characteristics.
1990 Census, North Dakota, General Population Characteristics.

Table 10.4. Percent of North Dakota Populations by Age

	Under 5	5-17	18-64	65+
North Dakota All	7.5	20.0	58.3	14.3
White	7.2	19.4	58.5	14.9
Indian	13.6	31.3	51.0	4.2

Source: 1990 Census, North Dakota, General Population Characteristics.

ease, but in the meantime better follow-up care and home-health training for the reservation residents who suffer from this disease are urgently needed.

Populations with high dependency ratios must also be considered from the economic standpoint. The reservation picture is one of large families of young children being supported by a small population of working-age people. The family income is stretched to provide for these children. On reservations where family income is low, many families have difficulty providing for their families.

One other demographic factor, population density, has a bearing on economic and social issues. We have already noted a population density for North Dakota of slightly less than 10 people per square mile. Indian reservations vary tremendously in population density. In 1990 the census bureau collected data to allow for the determination of population density and included this information in its Summary Population and Housing Characteristics report (U.S. Bureau of the Census 1992, Tables:197-211). The four North Dakota reservations have the following densities:

Standing Rock - 3.43 people per square mile

Fort Berthold - 4.09 people per square mile

Devils Lake - 9.15 people per square mile

Turtle Mountain - 71.34 people per square mile

These figures do not represent population density for Indians, because other people also live on the reservations, but they do give an idea of the kinds of interactions possible on the reservations and the kinds of economic problems that we may expect to find. Turtle Mountain is considered a very crowded reservation. Many of the enrolled members of the Turtle Mountain Band of Chippewa cannot live on the reservation because of the crowded conditions. It should be pointed out that crowding is defined differently by different cultures so that a population density which would not necessarily be considered crowded by a New York City resident may be thought so by a Turtle Mountain resident.

Small populations, widely spread over a rural area, find it difficult to attract business, to obtain sewer, electricity, telephone and other services. Noting the population densities, it is not surprising that Turtle Mountain and Devils Lake have been more successful in attracting business than have Standing Rock and Fort Berthold. Standing Rock and Fort Berthold, however, have large land bases which are used for farming and stock ranching, primarily by Euro-Americans. Population density is also reflected in the types of communities and the size of communities which exist on the reservations.

Urban Indian Communities

American Indians became familiar with European-style cities at an early date. John Rolfe married Pocahontas and took her to London in 1614. She died there in 1616. Later, tribal leaders from many tribes went to Washington, D.C. to meet with government officials. These meetings were aimed at convincing tribal leaders of the number and power of White men and served to introduce Indians to the luxuries and other inducements to be found in the urban areas. Tribal youth were taken to boarding schools in the east and introduced to urban life in an attempt to "civilize" them. The men and women educated in these schools often became representatives of their people and traveled throughout the country addressing groups about Indian policy and Indian needs. Many Tribal People traveled throughout North America and Europe as members of Wild West Shows or touring dance groups. Indians also played important roles in the world exhibitions, such as the World Exposition at Omaha and the World's Fairs held in Chicago and St. Louis. During the first and second World Wars and the Korean Conflict, Indian men and women and their families chose to leave the reservation and live in urban environments. Sometimes these families were encouraged to do this by the lack of employment or educational opportunities on the reservation. Sometimes an individual would leave the reservation, marry and settle in a non-Indian community. Other individuals would leave for a while and eventually return to take up life in the more familiar reservation environment. These comings and goings were most often a matter of individual choice.

In 1954 the Federal government adopted the policy of Relocation, aimed at encouraging people to leave the reservation. The goal was to help Indian families move from the reservation to urban areas where there would be better opportunities for employment and better living conditions. Under Relocation, thousands of Indian families left the reservation communities and moved to Chicago, Los Angeles, San Francisco and other large urban areas. In 1962 a survey (U.S. Dept. of Interior 1964) at Standing Rock disclosed that 1094 families lived off the reservation. These families were located in thirty-seven states. The largest number of families were living off the reservation in North and South

Dakota, but other large concentrations were in Los Angeles, Chicago, San Francisco, Denver, Minneapolis and Seattle.

Relocation provided assistance in moving, finding a place to live and aid in finding a job. Many of the families who moved from the reservations were unprepared for life in the city. Initial screening programs broke down under the demand of people to relocate, and many people who were moved to cities were unable to find permanent employment because they lacked training or had family needs. Indians were placed as far from their own reservations as possible, thus accounting for the large Indian populations in the east and west coast cities, and were located in neighborhoods where there were no other Indian families for companionship. The unstated objective of Relocation was to eliminate the need for reservations by urbanizing reservation populations. It was assumed that urbanization would occur quicker if Indians were forced to associate with non-Indians and to live in non-Indian communities. The outcome of Relocation, however, was to move many Indian families to the urban areas and then have them return to the reservation. Although it is impossible to get accurate figures, estimates have been given that as many as 60% of the relocatees returned to the reservation during the first few years of Relocation (Tyler 1973:159). Relocation also caused concern among Tribal Peoples who feared that the program was a prelude to terminating the reservations.

In 1962 Relocation became Employment Assistance with an emphasis on providing training to those in need of employable skills in conjunction with a move to an urban area. The program also permitted Indian families greater choice in a new location, and many Indians now move to urban areas in the Dakotas and Minnesota rather than to more distant cities. Indian populations in Bismarck, Grand Forks, Fargo, Minot (Table 10.2) have been steadily increasing. These areas provide better job opportunities than the reservations; yet they permit constant ties with the reservation community. Minneapolis-St. Paul and Denver also have large tribal populations and attract Native Peoples from North Dakota.

The off-reservation Indian population in North Dakota has increased steadily since 1900 when only eighteen counties reported any Indian residents. By 1960 "forty-three of the state's 53 counties reported Indians among their legal residents" (Wills 1963:119). In 1970 fifty counties in North Dakota reported Indians among their residents. In 1980 only one county in North Dakota reported no Indians living there. Some of these populations were very small, less than 5 people, but the figures do point out the increasing contact between Indians and non-Indians in North Dakota.

Bismarck, the state capital, claimed the largest Indian population of any North Dakota city in 1970. By 1980, however, Grand Forks had an Indian population as large as Bismarck's. The city of Bismarck, population 49,256 in 1990, is situated on bluffs overlooking the Missouri River. Across the river is Mandan, a small city, which also has Indian residents. In 1872, Camp Hancock, formerly called Camp Greeley, was established in what later became Bismarck. Camp Hancock was built to protect the men building the railroad. When the railroad reached Camp Hancock, a city was established and named Bismarck. The headquarter's building was located at Main and First Streets, giving an indication of the importance of the camp in Bismarck's later development. The older section of Bismarck remains today in the modern business district. Some of the older buildings remain, but most of the oldest section of the city has been urban-renewed and a shopping center, civic center, hospital and motel complex have been built. Some of the older homes remain in the residential district between the downtown area and the Capitol which sits on a hill overlooking the city. Newer residential areas have been built south of the downtown area and are now expanding north, east and west of the Capitol district.

In 1980 the Indian population numbered 648. By 1990 it had reached 1,261 (U.S. Bureau of the Census 1992). Attracted by job opportunities, the United Tribes Technical Educational Center, University of Mary, Bismarck State College and other educational and health facilities, Indians continue to move into the city. The Indian population is scattered throughout the city, but in the late 60's a corporation was established to provide housing for low-income families and a number of Native families now live in this development. In other parts of the city where rents are modest, Indian families may form small communities or family units. In addition to United Tribes, which provides a wide range of educational opportunities and work experiences, an Indian Center provides recreational opportunities. The city hosts three powwows a year. One is held in September at the United Tribes' facility south of the city, one is held in the spring at University of Mary and a third spring powwow is held at United Tribes. United Tribes Technical and Educational Center (UTEC) was founded in 1969 to provide vocational and semi-professional training for Indian people. The program has grown and has been involved in curriculum development for North Dakota schools and has assumed a leadership role in Indian education and Indian issues in the state. The presence of the Indian Affairs Commission Office in Bismarck has assisted the growth of United Tribes, as well as encouraged the settlement of tribal people in the city. This trend will undoubtedly continue.

Fargo is the largest city in North Dakota, with a population of 74,111 in 1990. Across the Red River from Fargo is the city of Moorhead, Minnesota. Together these two cities had sufficient population to be treated as a standard metropolitan statistical area in the 1980 census. The Indian population in Fargo-Moorhead was 1,265 in 1990. Fargo, alone, had 796 Indians, one of the four largest urban Indian populations in the state.

Fargo is both an industrial and cultural center. Located at the junction of Interstate 29 and Interstate 94, the city has become a shipping center for the region. Goods are delivered to Fargo and then shipped to other cities in the state. North Dakota State University is located in Fargo; it is a smaller institution than the University of North Dakota but attracts its share of Indian students. Moorhead State University and Concordia College in Moorhead add substantially to the cultural and educational system of the city. As a city, Fargo is spread out along the Red River. Older areas are nearer the river, and newer residential areas are spreading west and south. The downtown area, like others in North Dakota, has been urban-renewed, with sections of smaller, less expensive homes and apartments. The University is located away from the downtown area so that it exists as a community within the community. Between the University and the downtown area are blocks of homes and intermingled community services, such as small grocery stores. On the west side of the city is a large shopping center, the oldest of its size in the state. Along with the shopping center, the whole area along the interstate has been taken over by stores and by an industrial park, motels, restaurants and gas stations.

The Indian community in Fargo is less obvious than it is in other North Dakota cities probably because it is a smaller minority. There is an Indian association, and a powwow is usually held once a year, either at the University or at some other location in the Fargo-Moorhead area.

Grand Forks, population 49,425 in 1990, attracts a large Indian student population because the University of North Dakota offers many special services for Indian students and a program of Indian Studies. Native People find it easier to move to a community where there are other Natives, and as a result, the population of Indian students and their families has grown over the past decade. In 1980 the census estimated 662 Indians living in Grand Forks. By 1990 there were 1,115. The University of North Dakota has an estimated enrollment of over 250 Indian students, suggesting the magnitude of the Indian population in Grand Forks.

Grand Forks is primarily a residential city, with many people working for the University or engaged in providing services to the University community. Grand Forks is presently being developed as a regional service center with medical and commercial services. Industrial development is limited but sugar beet processing plants and potato processing plants are located either in Grand Forks or East Grand Forks, Minnesota. The lack of industry means a small proportion of blue collar jobs, although job vacancies are often listed in the *Grand Forks Herald*. Tourism during the summer provides work for some individuals, but with the increased use of mechanical equipment, the need for migrant farm workers declines every year. During the late 50's the use of Indian labor was replaced by Mexican-American labor, and so Indians will feel the effect of mechanization less than they did in the 50's and 60's.

Grand Forks is divided into older areas on the north and west near the University and the business district, and new areas to the south and west. The older areas provide slightly cheaper housing, although most of the older houses have been urban-renewed. The University area probably has the single largest concentration of Indians because the University provides family housing for many students. The University has attempted not to divide the Indian families too much but to group them so that they can provide support and companionship for each other. Single University students, especially women, may live in dormitories at the University or a group of students may rent an apartment or house together. Away from the University there is no single area of Indian concentration. People live where there is suitable housing, either in their own homes or in rentals.

The tribal community in Grand Forks is active, although most of the activity centers around the students at the University. The University of North Dakota Indian students have their own cultural center and association which sponsors a number of cultural events, including Time Out and a powwow, as well as sporting events throughout the school year.

Minot, population 34,544 in 1990, is the largest city in the northwestern quarter of the state. The older section of the city is built in the flood plain of the Mouse (Souris) River. As the city has spread out from the center, houses and commercial areas have covered the hills edging the Mouse. U.S. Highways 2, 52, and 83 intersect at Minot, making it a commercial center for a large section of North Dakota. Minot is not an industrial city but depends upon farmers from the region, Minot State University and the U.S. Air Force Base for its support. The growth of western North Dakota because of oil and other resource development has had an impact upon Minot and other cities in the region.

The Indian community in Minot is comparatively large, 724 in 1990, and active. Minot is the city closest to the northern part of the Fort Berthold Reservation and provides many shopping, medical and other services for reservation residents who find it natural to move to Minot to live. Minot State University has actively encouraged Indian students to attend and provides services for those students.

Many other cities in North Dakota have Indian populations, but only Trenton and Williston populations are active as Indian communities. Neither Jamestown nor Dickinson has an Indian center nor do these communities sponsor powwows or other Indian cultural events, although organizations in both cities do host small powwows and other cultural events. Jamestown is a small city, population 15,571 in 1990, located in the southeast corner of the state. Its location on the James River is attracting some interest as a tourist area. Much of Jamestown's prosperity comes from the farmers in the region and the payroll for employees of the State Hospital. The city listed 130 Indians in 1990.

Dickinson is one of the fastest growing cities in the state. Its population of 16,097 in 1990 has increased considerably because of the impact of coal and oil development in the region. Dickinson is on the edge of the North Dakota Badlands - Little Missouri National Grasslands area, which makes it a tourist stop. Dickinson is located on the Heart River and is one of the younger cities in the state that is laid out in an orderly fashion. The river forms the south boundary of the city, and Interstate 94 forms its northern boundary. State Highway 22 runs north and south through the city. In addition to tourism and energy development, Dickinson State University serves to attract people to the area. In 1990 the Indian population was 109.

Williston, the most western city in North Dakota, is also one of the fastest growing. Energy development, particularly the oil reserves of the Williston Basin, has turned the city into a boom town. The population of 13,131 represents a dramatic increase over the 1970 population, but a small decline over the 1980 figure. Williston is part of an historical region which draws tourists to the area. The famous Missouri forts of Buford and Union are located just up-river from the town. With the establishment of Lake Sakakawea, Williston is becoming a tourist resort area, as well as a regional live-stock-farming-commercial center for western North Dakota and eastern Montana. Just outside Williston is the small town of Trenton, the focal point for settlement of members of the Turtle Mountain Band of Chippewa who were unable to obtain land on Turtle Mountain Reservation. In 1972, James Howard (Howard 1972:9) estimated that there were four hundred Chippewa in Trenton. The 1990 census identified 525 Indians living in Trenton, 517 in Williston and 1010 in Williams County. Most of the Indians in Williams County probably live around Trenton. Both Trenton and Williston have active tribal organizations. Williston has the All Tribes Center and once had a branch office of the Dakota Association for Native Americans. Trenton has the Trenton Indian Service Area Corporation and a small Bureau of Indian Affairs office.

The cities of Wahpeton and Devils Lake also have tribal populations. The population of 388 Indians living in Wahpeton is associated with the Indian school, and the Sisseton-Wahpeton Reservation. The Indian population of Devils Lake is associated with the Fort Totten Reservation.

One of the similarities between all the North Dakota cities is the lack of an urban ghetto. The truth of a common North Dakota saying, "The cold keeps the riffraff out," can be illustrated by studying the cities in North Dakota. It is necessary to have a certain level of income in order to survive a North Dakota winter. Reservation populations have adapted to the lack of income in a number of ways, but the person who moves to the city gives up these other advantages and must be able to maintain a certain standard of living. For example, reservation residents may be able to supplement their heating by cutting wood or collecting coal. Federal programs to help pay winter heating costs for low income populations help a great deal, but the home-owner or renter must still pay some of the cost. North Dakota cities do not have sections of run-down housing that is available for rent inexpensively nor is there the absentee landlord problem that occurs in larger cities. On the other hand, low income housing has developed slowly. Current procedures are to supplement individual housing costs rather than to build low-rent housing. When Tribal People move to a North Dakota city, then, they find housing wherever they can. North Dakota cities do not have the ethnic enclaves that are found in Rapid City, Minneapolis or in other large cities. Indians moving to cities in North Dakota tend to be those whose education or experience makes it possible for them to find employment that will enable them to live in the available housing and they tend to merge with the other city residents. Consequently, the tribal community presents itself in a cultural sense through organizations and activities, rather than through a geographical unity.

Most of the cities in North Dakota have attracted Indian people because of the educational and employment opportunities they offer. Even though jobs may be limited in these cities because of lack of industrialization, they are much more plentiful than jobs on the reservation. Jobs in service occupations, waiters and waitresses, gas station attendants, and clerks in stores are open to unskilled people and are more available in the larger cities than in the towns near the reservations. In towns near the reservations, prejudice may make it difficult for Indians to get jobs even when there are openings, and so the larger towns have attracted more Indian people. Familiarity with a city often makes it possible to attract friends and relatives to share the opportunities. Larger cities may offer more convenient methods of transportation to the reservation than the towns just off the reservations although the distances may be farther. Larger urban areas outside North Dakota have attracted their share of Indian people, too. Rapid City and Sioux Falls in South Dakota, Denver and Minneapolis have large Indian populations. These populations tend to be more mixed; that is, there are Indians from many different tribes and from many different states. With six reservations in the state, South Dakota's Indian population is almost twice as large as North Dakota's. Populations in the urban areas are, therefore, larger than North Dakota's.

Rapid City, South Dakota, has become a tribal center for much of the population in North and South Dakota. In 1990 the total population of Rapid City was 54,523. The Indian population was 4,891 or 8%, a larger percentage than in any of the North Dakota cities. Robert A. White (1970) has discussed the development of the Indian sector in Rapid City. He points out that some families prefer to live in low-income housing which has been built for them on the north side of the city. This "Sioux Addition" and the related "Lakota Homes" allow people to live in an area where other families and many relatives come from similar backgrounds and have similar interests. These families maintain close ties to the reservation and make frequent trips back and forth between reservation and Rapid City. Other families live in areas equivalent to their income, that is some families are successfully moving into the middle class. Most of these are people with college educations or some business training or experience that enables them to obtain white-collar jobs. They maintain their Indian ethnic identity but are less tied to the reservation and the tribal community.

The issues surrounding the formation and adaptability of enclaves (minority culture groups living as an entity within a larger group) are pertinent to contemporary tribal life. Enclaving is a natural process which occurs when groups of similar ethnic backgrounds live near each other. These enclaves provide companions who speak the same language, share similar culture and values, can help find jobs, housing and make the adjustment to the city easier. Enclaves thus provide a useful service to people. However, the identification of an area as an enclave, Indian, Black, Chicano, or other cultural identity can lead to its exclusion from city processes and to discrimination against its residents. Enclaves often develop in urban areas of low-income housing. An individual resident of such an enclave may find himself the brunt of public hostility. White (1970:183) has pointed out that it was public outcry about the Indian "camp" that brought about the building of "Sioux Addition" originally outside the Rapid City city limits. In other words, public opinion was such that the Indians were moved "out of town." Times have changed and the development has since been incorporated into the city. The impact of such attitudes and treatment of Indian people should be fairly obvious. Police attention is often focused upon such areas and in sections of towns known to have large Indian (or other ethnic minority) populations. Prejudice develops particularly in those areas where the population is readily visible or identifiable, thus the formation of enclaves or ghettos may be a disservice to the minority population. North Dakota cities have avoided this issue by not building low-income housing and by the slow absorption of Indian families into the community. Should the growth patterns of North Dakota cities change, then enclaving might become an issue.

Minneapolis-St. Paul has the largest Indian population of any city in the northern plains area and probably attracts more Indians from North Dakota than Denver simply because of its proximity to the North Dakota reservations. Bismarck to Minneapolis is 420 miles. Bismarck to Denver is 670 miles. South Dakotans, including those who live on the South Dakota side of Standing Rock find it just as convenient to go to Denver. The greater Minneapolis-St. Paul area had a total population of 21,786 Indians in 1990. Many of these, over half, are from the reservations in Minnesota, and the rest are from reservations outside Minnesota.

The 1980 census by tract (Phc80-2-244) for Minneapolis-St. Paul gives the population of Indians in the various units or tracts used in the census. An analysis of these figures shows that Indians live in all areas of the Twin Cities but some tracts have a higher concentration of Indian population than others. A recent survey of an area south of Minneapolis showed 4500 Indians living in an area about 1 1/2 miles square (*Minneapolis Tribune* 1979:38). This concentration of Indians is larger than most of the reservation populations in North Dakota. One area of tribal concentration in Minneapolis is found in the neighborhood along East Franklin Avenue. Another area, known as the near North Side, is also recognized as a community with a high concentration of Indian people. Many Indian families live in other parts of the Twin Cities including expensive suburban areas and in a housing development on the south side built in 1973 for low income families. This development is run by the American Indian Movement (AIM) and an all-Indian staff (*Minneapolis Tribune* 1979:47).

The range of the Indian community in Minneapolis is demonstrated by the number of organizations and centers which are available to Indian people. These organizations and centers are similar to those found in other large cities across the country. The Bureau of Indian Affairs has an area office in Minneapolis, one of its 11 area offices. An area office not only provides services to Indians in the area but acts as an administrative unit and also employs many Indians. Indian centers are located in both Minneapolis and St. Paul. The Minneapolis Regional Native American Center is a new building with exhibit space and meeting rooms. This center provides a variety of cultural and educational services to Indians in the Minneapolis area. The Upper Midwest American Indian Center is more oriented to providing services to Indians moving into the city. The American Indian Movement (AIM) has its headquarters in St. Paul. AIM began as an attempt to police the Indian area of St. Paul in order to provide assistance to Indians. Since then, the movement has gained national and international attention through its advocacy and militant stance on Indian issues.

Other Indian organizations are located in the Twin Cities. The National Indian Education Association headquarters are in Minneapolis. The University of Minnesota-Minneapolis and many other schools in the area offer special programs of support for Indian students. Several Indian culture schools for elementary and high school students are located in Minneapolis-St. Paul. These schools aim to develop positive Indian self-identity while they teach the skills necessary for college and employment. A weekly television program is devoted to Indian issues and Indian culture. The program also carries announcements of events of interest to the watchers.

Native Communities in Other Areas

Because this text focuses on North Dakota Native peoples, the material has dealt at great length with the most frequent locations of North Dakota Tribal Peoples today. However, North Dakota Indian people may be found in many other communities within the United States and Canada. Montana and Canada have Sioux reservations whose people are closely related either to the Devils Lake Sioux or to the Standing Rock people. These reservations were established during the Indian wars when many Indians fled to Canada to avoid the conflict. Although some of the Indians later returned to the United States, many accepted reservation lands in Canada. The Indians in Canada and their relatives in North Dakota constantly communicate. Visiting takes place during powwows on both sides of the border and North Dakotans often go to Canada for Indian healing treatments and other services. The Indian reserves in Canada are smaller in land and population than the reservations in the United States and are much more conservative because of the Canadian government policy of *laissez faire*, and so their population has served as a cultural reservoir for North Dakota Indian populations.

When Europeans first contacted Native Americans they found significant populations spread across the continent. Following the introduction of European diseases and other problems of the contact situation, such as warfare and displacement, the Indian populations declined to the point that some scholars wondered if any would survive. Not only did some survive, but today Native Americans are the fastest growing ethnic group. The census and other records document this growth and other trends, especially urbanization.

LOUISE ERDRICH

Karen Louise Erdrich was born in 1954 in Little Falls, Minnesota, the daughter of Ralph and Rita Erdrich (May 1985:146). She grew up in Wahpeton, North Dakota, where her parents taught at Wahpeton Indian School. Rita Erdrich, the daughter of Patrick and Mary Gourneau, was born and raised on the Turtle Mountain Indian Reservation. Louise is one of seven brothers and sisters (Dorris 1989:124). Although she has not lived on the reservation and does not identify herself as an enrolled member of the Turtle Mountain Band of Chippewa, Louise maintains close ties with family members who live on the reservation and its history figures prominently in her writing.

Louise told *Contemporary Authors* (May 1985:146-147) that both parents influenced her to read and write. Her father encouraged her writing by paying her a nickel for every story and her mother made book covers for her stories. "So at an early age I felt myself to be a published author earning substantial royalties."

In 1972 Louise matriculated at Dartmouth College, Hanover, New Hampshire where she majored in English and Creative Writing (Dorris 1989:116; Wong 1987:196). After graduation she returned to North Dakota and spent a year as a touring poetry teacher in a program sponsored by the North Dakota Council for the Humanities. She visited rural schools, teaching children how to write poetry. From North Dakota she entered Johns Hopkins University, graduating with an MA in 1977 (May 1985:146).

In 1981 Louise married Michael Dorris, professor of Anthropology and Native American Studies at Dartmouth College. He had adopted three children, one of whom, Abel, was the subject of *The Broken Cord* (Dorris 1989), a book on fetal alcohol syndrome. Louise adopted Michael's three children. Later, the couple had three of their own, Persia, Pallas and Aza (Dorris 1989:vii). Abel died in 1992 after being hit by a car as he walked home from work.

Michael Dorris and Louise Erdrich are unusual writers in that they collaborate extensively on each other's work. Since their marriage this collaboration has resulted in numerous well-received books for both of them. She published a book of poetry, *Jacklight* in 1984, the same time her novel *Love Medicine* was released. Both were critical successes, but *Love Medicine* attracted public attention. It also won the 1984 National Book Critics Circle Award and the 1985 Los Angeles Times award for best novel. *Beet Queen*, the second novel set in North Dakota, appeared in 1985 and *Tracks*, which precedes the other two in time, in 1988. The last of the four related books, *Bingo Palace*, appeared in 1994. Between *Tracks* and *Bingo Palace*, Louise and Michael collaborated on a novel, *The Crown of Columbus*, in recognition of the Columbus Quincentennial.

The family continues to live and work in Cornish, New Hampshire, a small New England town not far from Dartmouth College.

Chapter 11

The Economics of Employment

Economic issues play an enormous role in modern tribal life because contemporary Indians are tied, however distantly, to the national economy. A major difference between modern tribal life and the life of the average North Dakotan is due to economic differences. An Indian who chooses to leave the reservation may be able to obtain better housing, a job, and better educational opportunities for his or her children. In some instances, they will be able to live more comfortably and with less prejudice than those who remain on the reservation (Hendrickson 1981:53-54). Those Indians who choose to remain on the reservation will often find themselves without jobs or with low paying jobs or with jobs that are due to Federal programs which may be terminated at any moment. Like North Dakota, reservations are economically disadvantaged for many reasons. Both the state and its reservations are located in areas which are removed from the mainstream. It is ironic that reservations were located in areas which lacked mineral resources or were not suitable for farming or ranching; in other words, these lands were viewed as not suitable for habitation by non-Indians, and now the non-Indians complain because Tribal People are unable to earn a living off this land. In North Dakota some of the reservations have mineral resources, but the tribal leaders are reluctant to be pressured into developing these because in other areas the eventual result has been the despoliation and alienation of tribal land.

Traditionally, Indian subsistence was based on hunting and farming. Some groups, such as the Lakota, placed more emphasis on hunting than on farming while others were known to prefer farming. In both cases, the people were able to provide for themselves through their own skills. They were dependent upon nature, but with large amounts of land and their own knowledge of the land and its resources, they were able to adapt to economic emergencies. The basis for tribal survival was self-sufficiency and sharing. Those who were able to obtain food and other necessities, shared willingly with those who were less fortunate. The villages were small and everyone knew whose food supply had been washed away by the spring floods or whose hunting had been unsuccessful. Since these situations could happen to anyone at any time, no one felt shame to be in need, and people were willing to share what they had, knowing that they could be in a similar situation. A tribal attitude developed that it was not the fault of the individual that these things happened and laying blame or scolding would not improve the situation. A person who always had to be helped and was unable to return the help might feel ashamed at not being able to help those who had helped her or him, but this shame was never expressed by the ones who gave. These attitudes are important to understand because they have a direct bearing upon the understanding of modern Indian economics.

The impact of national economics has been felt by the Plains Indians ever since the Federal government destroyed the buffalo to force the Indians to settle on the reservations. The idea of using food as a weapon was totally alien to the tribal way of thinking. What kind of people would take away a person's means of living? Of course, once the buffalo were gone and the traditional way of life had ended, the Indians had to be provided food. The government gave this food in the form of rations. Food was allotted to each family, according to the number of people in the family. Rations were distributed according to schedules, and ration day became a day of socializing and fun. But rations were also used to force the Indians to submit to the administration's decisions. An Indian who did not send his children to the mission school would receive no rations while a family who sent its children would receive extra rations. Indians who refused to give up wearing Indian clothes were given fewer rations than those who gave up their more obvious Indian attributes.

What happened is obvious. Economics became politics as some people who were willing to give up their tribal ways received more of the resources and were rewarded, first by food and later by jobs. This econo-political base created a new social organization on the reservation. In essence, those who were most reluctant to change their Indian ways were doomed to poverty. Those individuals or families who agreed to exchange their traditions for food and jobs became a new elite—an acculturated elite—favored by the Bureau of Indian Affairs, officials and representatives of church groups. These acculturated people were not necessarily highly regarded by those Indians who did not give up their traditions. Thus today's reservation is where the most traditional and often most economically disadvantaged Indians live. De Mallie (1978:255) has pointed out that the attitude represented by the Oglala leader, Red Cloud, is still current on some reservations today.

> Father, the Great Spirit did not make us to work. He made us to hunt and fish. He gave us the great prairies and hills and covered them with buffalo, deer and antelope. He filled the rivers and streams with fish.
>
> The white man can work if he wants to, but the Great Spirit did not make us to work. The White man owes us a living for the lands he has taken from us (McGillycuddy 1941:103).

Some traditional Indians still believe that having an income from working is equated with being non-Indian, and it follows that being poor becomes equated with being Indian. While poverty is thus partially institutionalized in Indian culture, Whites take the position that Indians are poor because they are dumb or lazy. The economy, then, is part of the complex relationship between Indians and Whites, between conquered and conqueror, and between tradition-oriented and contemporary-oriented Indians.

Income

There are a number of erroneous ideas about the Native American economic situation. Perhaps the most common mistake is the assumption that Indian people receive monthly checks from the Federal government for "being Indian." That is, people believe that Native Americans get payments that other Americans do not. This belief obviously comes from the days when treaties provided annuities, rations and other compensations for the land, but most of these provisions were either limited in date or ended when the treaties were abrogated. Today, tribal people receive government checks for the same reasons non-Indians do; they work for the government or receive social security or have federal pensions.

Because people believe that Indians receive special compensation, they do not understand why Indians often live in poverty. Journalists often focus on the poor conditions found on some of the reservations, but this is a one-sided picture that does not adequately describe the situation.

Reservation economics are extremely complex with inadequate statistics available. Different Federal agencies keep statistics differently and even the national censuses change their accounting methods from one census to the next. The United States Censuses of 1970, 1980, and 1990 provide comparative data for Indians in North Dakota as a whole and for certain aspects of reservation life in particular. Of course, changes have occurred since 1970, but the figures suggest that most of the changes are not in the overall pattern but in basic figures. Indian incomes have increased since 1970, but inflation has increased all incomes so that the proportion of Indians living in poverty remains much the same. Reservation economies are depressing and descriptions of reservation economics made during the 1930's and 1940's are essentially true today. Such descriptions include lack of jobs, poor land for agricultural development, poor training for business and agricultural development, and misunderstandings between Indians and Whites over money. As one reservation resident pointed out, even when Native People achieve a stable income, they still must deal with non-Indian banks and other financial institutions that discriminate against people of color. Poverty has been a way of life for many Indians for several generations. Many of the traditions which helped Tribal People adapt to variations in pre-reservation economics have also helped them to adapt to contemporary economic situations. Sharing, the Give-Away, home crafts, hunting and fishing have helped to maintain Indian life during periods of extreme deprivation. Some people have commented that because of their adaptation to a lower standard of living than White people, Indians will survive the economic crisis of energy depletion while Whites will not.

One unhappy change documented by the 1990 census was a small decrease in the median household income for Indians in the United States. While the median household incomes of all other major ethnic minorities increased, that of Native Americans fell from $20,541 in 1980 to $20,025 in 1990 (Anquoe 1992). This decline indicates the continuing economic difficulties faced by Indian people.

No doubt, average Indian incomes, whether one looks at per capita or household, fall well below the poverty level. The Federal census for 1990 (Table 11.1) indicates that the per capita yearly income of North Dakota Indians averaged $4,755. This is one third of the general North Dakota per capita income. Per capita incomes on the reservations (Table 11.1) ranged from $3,421 at Standing Rock to $5,138 at Turtle Mountain. Indian people living off the reservation in the larger urban areas, Bismarck, Grand Forks, and Fargo, do a little better, but the difference is minor.

The same census clarifies some of the other significant discrepancies between the incomes of non-Indians and Indians. In North Dakota, Indian household incomes (Table 11.2) averaged $17,094 while the average income for White households was more than ten thousand dollars higher, $28,990. The breakdown of household income shows the origin of this difference and that the difference is pervasive. For the reservations as well as North Dakota as a whole, a larger percentage of Indians, in some cases three times as high, falls into the $5000 or less income bracket and there are many fewer Indians in the highest income bracket. Generally, the highest percentage of Whites is in the $15,000 - $24,999 bracket, but for Indians the highest percentage is in the $5,000 - $9,999 group.

The reservations show additional differences between Indian and White household incomes. The percentages of White tend to be spread more evenly through all the income brackets, while Indians lump in the lower income brackets. Converting the percentages to graphs would show bell-shaped curves for Whites and downward sloping lines for Indians.

The statistics (Table 11.3) show two other characteristics of Indian family income: 1. that more members of an Indian family must work in order to obtain that income; for example, in North Dakota two workers are required to make an Indian family income that is almost the equivalent of what one non-Indian earns, and 2. that Indian families are larger than non-Indian families so that the income must go farther.

Table 11.1. Per Capita Income by Race

Place	White	Black	Indian	Asian/Pcf. Is.	Other
North Dakota	11,359	7,875	4,755	9,281	5,356
Devils Lake	8,882	0	3,940	0	12,778
Fort Berthold	10,908	0	4,849	18,000	1,857
Standing Rock	9,515	0	3,421	16,030	3,000
Turtle Mountain	16,056	0	5,138	0	0
Bismarck	13,521	6,473	5,258	19,124	4,237
Grand Forks	12,096	10,578	6,096	9,944	5,528
Minnesota					
Minneapolis	16,936	7,771	5,609	6,072	8,577

Another difference between Indian and non-Indian income is found by looking at the source of income (Table 11.4). Most people derive their income from wages or salaries. The fact that the general North Dakota and the reservation percentages are similar indicates that Indians and non-Indians are working. The difficulty is low income, not laziness on the part of Indian people. Because income is low, a high percentage of Indian people receive some income from public assistance or public welfare programs. Remember that over half of the reservation population is either too young or too old to work, and the need for public assistance becomes more understandable.

Most Indian families in North Dakota have wage or salary income. This point is important because many non-Indians believe that Indians do not work or are too lazy to work. With 34 percent of these families more than one person is working. These figures demonstrate very clearly the problems of Indian employment. While many people work, incomes are low which means more people in a family must work to produce the same level of income as is found in non-Indian families. Indian people have, until recently, not received adequate education or training for the higher paying jobs. Job opportunities on the reservations are limited, and even available work, such as farm labor or construction work, is seasonal. In North Dakota, seasonal jobs last for only a short time since the seasons are short. Public assistance is necessary to make up the difference between earned income and the amount needed to live.

Other sources of income are royalties from mineral leases, rent from land leases, and money paid to individuals as Indian claims are settled. Many non-Indians think that Indians receive a regular income from the Federal government, because they have mistaken the money paid out in claims to be a per-petual grant. However, unearned income benefits less than 15% of the North Dakota Indian families. Money paid out in claims for land taken by the Federal government is paid only once, or at best only occasionally, and while the amounts, $500 to $2,500 per person, may appear to be large, they are minuscule in comparison to Indian needs. It does not take long to spend $2,000 when one has almost nothing. Once the money is gone, nothing else from that source comes in, and so this form of unearned income does not make much impact on Indian life. Money paid out on mineral leases, especially for oil at Fort Berthold, has gone directly to those individuals who own the land, and most Indians have not benefited from these. To assume that all Indians receive money from oil leases is like assuming that all

Table 11.2. Indian Household Income

	North Dakota Whites	%	North Dakota Indians	%	Devils Lake Whites	%	Devils Lake Indians	%	Fort Berthold Whites	%	Fort Berthold Indians	%	Standing Rock Whites	%	Standing Rock Indians	%	Turtle Mountain Whites	%	Turtle Mountain Indians	%
Total Households	237,582	%	6,809	%	324	%	629	%	904	%	801	%	1,160	%	1,178	%	110	%	1,423	%
Income																				
0–5,000	15,985	.06	1,308	.19	30	.09	122	.19	56	.06	144	.09	126	.10	345	.29	2	.01	322	.23
5,000–9,999	27,147	.11	1,694	.24	40	.12	144	.22	120	.13	209	.12	167	.14	263	.22	11	.10	353	.24
10,000–14,999	27,233	.11	948	.13	55	.16	75	.11	133	.14	128	.16	163	.14	132	.11	7	.06	164	.11
15,000–24,999	52,073	.21	1,231	.18	77	.23	149	.23	203	.22	100	.23	214	.18	220	.18	27	.24	191	.13
25,000–34,999	40,963	.17	735	.10	42	.12	59	.09	191	.21	89	.12	231	.19	138	.11	32	.29	182	.12
35,000–49,999	38,319	.16	645	.09	51	.15	68	.10	127	.14	74	.15	130	.11	54	.04	21	.19	139	.09
50,000–74,999	22,446	.09	201	.02	16	.04	12	.01	49	.05	51	.04	95	.08	26	.02	10	.09	53	.03
75,000–99,999	4,656	.01	33	.00	7	.02	0	.00	16	.01	6	.02	25	.02	0		0		19	.01
100,000+	3,760	.01	14	.00	6	.01	0	.00	9	.001	0	.01	9	.001	0		0		3	.001
Median household income	23,123				15,394				16,786				14,541				12,020			
Mean household income	28,990		17,094																	

Table 11.3. Average Family Income by Number of Workers Per Family

	North Dakota	Devils Lake	Fort Berthold	Standing Rock	Turtle Mountain
No. workers	$17,506	$ 6,462	$ 9,226	$ 8,541	$ 5,561
1 Worker	27,936	13,815	18,436	18,145	14,097
2 Workers	36,545	28,358	30,396	26,796	28,627
3 or more	45,815	38,429	43,130	38,535	42,918
Persons/family Family size	3.3	4.40	3.88	4.43	3.68
Household	2.55	4.29	3.48	4.13	3.26

Table 11.4. Number and Percent of Households with Income from Various Sources

	North Dakota		Devils Lake		Fort Berthold		Standing Rock		Turtle Mountain	
	No.	%	No.	%	No.	%	No.	%	No.	%
Total No. of households	241,802	100	955	100	1,720	100	2,345	100	1,536	100
Households with earnings	201,787	.83	722	.75	1,379	.80	1,802	.76	1,048	.68
Wage or salary income	182,738	.75	683	.71	1,183	.68	1,550	.66	1,030	.67
Non-farm self employment	36,021	.14	71	.07	222	.12	234	.09	89	.05
Farm self employment	36,700	.15	116	.12	325	.18	495	.21	34	.02
Interest dividend rental	109,331	.45	174	.18	512	.29	733	.31	172	.11
Social Security	69,359	.28	212	.22	515	.29	526	.22	320	.20
Public assistance	15,105	.06	271	.28	373	.21	635	.27	737	.47
Retirement	22,954	.09	77	.08	148	.08	158	.06	115	.07
Other	24,748	.10	100	.10	209	.12	329	.14	176	.11

Texans receive money from oil leases. A few become wealthy, but the rest do not receive any direct benefits. Land rentals, usually to White farmers, are often small, and if the land is owned by many people, the total income may be only a few dollars a year.

Unfortunately, recent censuses do not report individual incomes and so it is not possible to determine differences in individual incomes. Individual incomes should increase as more educated Indians obtain jobs on the reservations, but it is likely that the same general pattern of a few people having high paying jobs while many have low incomes will continue as long as job opportunities remain limited. The low per capita incomes (Table 11.1) suggest little or no change in reservation employment in the decade since the 1980 census.

Employment

Modern economists give great attention to unemployment statistics as indicators of economic strength or weakness, but such statistics do not always provide an accurate figure. The Bureau of Labor Statistics provides national data on unemployment by counting the number of people actively seeking work who are able to find work. Some observers have pointed out that calculating unemployment rates on the basis of those looking for work may provide a figure that is too low because it does not consider people who are discouraged and no longer looking for work.

The Bureau of Indian Affairs is also concerned with unemployment. The calculation employed by the BIA includes all Indians over age 16 who do not attend school or stay home to care for children. This statistic does not consider whether the person wants a job or would take a job if one were available. Using this method, the Bureau of Indian Affairs arrives at figures ranging from 30 percent to 90 percent unemployed. Levitan and Miller (1993:15) report the average unemployment rate, using the BIA method, to be 45 percent.

The U.S. Census Bureau uses a third method to calculate unemployment rates. This figure compares the number of people who want to work with the number of people who have jobs. The unemployment rate is composed of people who want to work, but do not have jobs. The rates for various North Dakota populations are shown in Table 11.5. In June 1993, the national unemployment rate was 6.9 percent, down from an "eight-year high of 7.7 percent in June 1992" (Crutsinger 1993).

No matter how one calculates the unemployment rate, it is clear that Native Americans have much higher rates than the general population. This is true for North Dakota as a whole as well as for those people living on the reservations in the state. It is also interesting to note that Indian men have a much higher rate than Indian women. In contrast to the general North Dakota population, numerically more Indian women than Indian men are employed and this difference shows up in unemployment rates. An analysis of the work opportunities would show that women have greater possibilities, although wages for women's work tend to be lower.

The 1990 United States census provides some data on the various ways in which North Dakotans gain a living. There are three different calculations: occupation, industry, and class of worker. Occupation and industry are similar, but industry provides more details. Class of worker distinguishes between those who work in the private sector from those in government. Information on industry is presented in Table 11.6 and class of worker is shown in Table 11.7.

The Bureau of the Census actually collects much more detailed data on the industries, but has found it possible to group the information in 17 general categories. Comparing the general North Dakota situation to the reservation situation clearly illustrates the employment situation on the reservation. Agriculture plays an important role in North Dakota's economy, second only to the retail trade as an

Table 11.5. Civilian Employment by Race and Sex

	North Dakota		Devils Lake		Fort Berthold		Standing Rock		Turtle Mountain	
	White	Indian	White	Indian	White	Indian	White	Indian	White	Indian
Male										
Labor force	159,715	4,237	267	433	574	538	806	762	81	824
employed	151,512	2,966	259	290	537	370	778	488	81	486
unemployed	8,203	1,271	8	143	37	168	28	274	0	338
unemployment rate	.05	.29	.02	.33	.06	.31	.03	.35	0	.41
Female										
Labor force	132,824	4,084	165	322	479	521	604	611	74	744
employed	127,325	3,315	155	276	465	408	569	430	74	551
unemployed	5,499	771	10	46	14	113	35	181	0	193
unemployment rate	.04	.18	.06	.14	.02	.21	.05	.29	0	.25

employer. Agriculture is also a significant employer at Fort Berthold and Standing Rock Reservations, but not at Devils Lake Sioux or Turtle Mountain Reservations. The difference is due to the larger size of the western reservations and reflects their more rural nature. Since this category also includes fishing, some people may be engaged in the fishing industry on either Lake Sakakawea or Lake Oahe.

The impact of Devils Lake Sioux Manufacturing shows up clearly in the manufacturing, nondurable goods category. The presence of this major employer makes the Devils Lake Sioux Reservation very different from the others in North Dakota. Whereas educational services is the major employer on the other reservations, this is not true for Devils Lake.

Fort Berthold and Turtle Mountain illustrate the presence of regional shopping centers in the relatively large number of people employed in the retail trade. New Town is the commercial center for the Fort Berthold Reservation and the largest town in a 60 mile radius. Belcourt, at Turtle Mountain, is also a major retail center for the region.

For three reservations, education is a major source of employment. For all four reservations, public administration is a much more important source of employment than it is for North Dakota as a whole. This category is shown more clearly in Table 11.7, Class of Worker.

Job opportunities on or near reservations are limited by the rural, dispersed nature of the population. Those employees who work steadily are usually employed by either Federal or tribal government or through Federally-funded programs (Table 11.7). Because North Dakota generally lacks industrial

Table 11.6. Industry

	North Dakota		Devils Lake		Fort Berthold		Standing Rock		Turtle Mountain	
	No.	%	No.	%	No.	%	No.	%	No.	%
Total employed	287,558		985		1,795		2,269		1,192	
Agriculture, Forestry, Fishing	33,691	.11	116	.11	233	.12	657	.28	35	.02
Mining	4,490	.01	2	.00	75	.04	0	.00	0	.00
Construction	14,886	.05	55	.05	118	.06	86	.03	89	.07
Manufacturing, non-durable goods	8,696	.03	162	.16	27	.01	25	.01	38	.03
Manufacture, durable	9,357	.03	53	.05	92	.05	8	.00	113	.09
Transportation	12,012	.04	21	.02	33	.01	91	.04	58	.04
Communication, public utilities	7,834	.02	14	.01	78	.04	25	.01	8	.00
Wholesale Trade	12,380	.04	8	.00	23	.01	29	.01	6	.00
Retail Trade	53,309	.18	95	.09	216	.12	204	.08	147	.12
Finance, insurance, and real estate	15,471	.05	29	.02	63	.03	49	.02	39	.03
Business and repair	9,494	.03	25	.02	29	.01	33	.01	8	.00
Personal Services	8,842	.03	5	.00	37	.02	25	.01	11	.00
Entertainment and recreation	3,055	.01	21	.02	2	.00	16	.00	16	.01
Health Services	29,907	.10	54	.05	195	.10	127	.05	107	.08
Educational Services	30,632	.10	105	.10	308	.17	384	.16	346	.29
Other professional	19,184	.06	69	.07	108	.06	111	.04	45	.03
Public administration	14,318	.04	151	.15	158	.08	399	.17	126	.10

employment, a relatively high percentage of people are public employees, 18 percent. This percentage did not change between 1980 and 1990. On the reservations, however, government continues to be the most important source of work. The percentages range from 33 percent at Fort Berthold to 55 percent at Turtle Mountain. Very few of these employees are state government workers. The majority are either tribal or federal.

Claims that the Federal government has neglected Indians cannot be substantiated in face of the number of people who directly benefit from the presence of the government. The number of programs financed through direct funding, through grants and through a wide variety of special programs are indeterminable. An estimate has been made that over 1000 federally-funded programs are offered by

Table 11.7. Class of Worker — Employed Person Over 16

	North Dakota		Devils Lake		Fort Berthold		Standing Rock		Turtle Mountain	
	No.	%	No.	%	No.	%	No.	%	No.	%
Private for profit, wage and salary workers	188,613	.65	369	.37	682	.37	534	.23	386	.32
Private not for profit			42	.04	182	.10	109	.04	85	.07
Local gov't workers	21,669	.07	292	.29	225	.12	354	.15	312	.26
State gov't workers	19,062	.06	46	.04	106	.05	144	.06	35	.02
Fed. gov't workers	12,635	.04	105	.10	268	.14	493	.21	314	.26
Self-employed workers	42,769	.14	116	.11	302	.16	570	.25	60	.05
Unpaid family workers	2,810	.00	15	.01	30	.01	65	.02	0	.00
Totals	287,558		985		1,795		2,269		1,192	

fifty-five agencies. While not all tribes are eligible for all these programs, government has a vast impact or possible impact upon Indian life. Those programs of which the greatest use is made involve business assistance, housing, health, education and welfare. Within these divisions are the Indian Health Service, the Indian Land Acquisition Loan Programs, Food Stamp Program, Indian Man Power Programs and Community Action Program, to name a few. In addition to these programs which operate independently of the Bureau of Indian Affairs, there is the Bureau of Indian Affairs itself.

The Bureau of Indian Affairs is a highly complex administrative unit of the Federal government. Currently the Bureau has two main offices, twelve area offices and eighty-two field (agency) offices. The area office covering Nebraska, South Dakota and North Dakota is located in Aberdeen, South Dakota. Each reservation has a field or agency office which represents the Bureau to its local clientele. These agency offices are staffed by both Indians and non-Indians, although an attempt is being made to replace all non-Indians with Indians. The local agencies offer employment through the wide number of programs administered by the Bureau of Indian Affairs.

Tribal government is also a source of employment. Under Self-Determination, tribal governments are encouraged to contract for programs previously handled by other agencies. This decision has promoted the growth of tribal government. Most of the positions in tribal government are salaried, but tribal government employees are not protected from changes in the tribal government, so salaries are not paid to the same person forever. Other jobs, however, can be maintained as long as funds hold out. Most of the North Dakota tribes do not have incomes large enough to support the tribal officials, clerical help and needed programs, and so those funds come from the overheads on grant administration, Federal sources, and economic development programs. While these programs provide employment of varying stability and different kinds, the programs are so diverse and uncoordinated that it is difficult to find out who has authority over specific needs or what a program is designed to accomplish. In former times, Tribal Peoples accomplished necessary duties by doing a task without much coordination or discussion. A person who noticed that something needed to be done would eventually do it. If others chose to help, so much the better; if not, then the doer was showing a sensitivity to community needs to get the job done. The current spider web of programs on Indian reservations very much resembles the traditional style of getting things done. Those individuals who see that something needs doing get a grant or obtain funds to do the task. An overlap of provision of services, of work that is being done and competition between programs is apparent but in view of the effect of these programs on tribal life, it is difficult to recommend that more cohesion be sought. The programs themselves apparently have little long-term impact because funds do not last forever, but they do provide employment in an area in which jobs are scarce. The value of jobs must be weighed against the apparent waste of time and funds involved in the sponsorship of so many programs.

Closely associated with the myth that Indian people get regular checks from the Federal government is the erroneous idea that Indian people get special assistance and programs that are not available to non-Indians. Like the check-myth, this one probably stems from early reservation days when Indians were given many different kinds of assistance in order to help them adjust to reservation life. These kinds of programs no longer exist and Tribal People receive aid on the same basis and under the same programs that non-Indians do, because they are poor. In many instances, reservations qualify for the same economic programs that inner-cities do, and for the same reasons: low income, inadequate housing, health problems and lack of employment opportunities.

Other sources of income are available to Indians living on reservations. While salaries are low, adjustments to income can help to make the salaries or transfer payments go a bit farther. People who choose to live on the reservation often live rent-free in their own house on their own land. Not only do they pay no taxes on the house, but they pay no mortgage. Older homes or replacement homes were originally built at no cost to the Indian owner. Tribal building programs have attempted to have new home builders or new home users rent the houses or pay small amounts to the tribe for the original funding. These amounts are based upon annual income and are graduated according to what the individual or family can afford. Indians who live on the reservation receive free health care. Although many Indians will point out that they would be willing to pay a little in order to get better medical care, they are able to get all of their health needs, including preventive care, pharmaceuticals, optical, dental as well as clinic and hospital care from the Indian Health Service. Some tax relief is also available to Indians who live on the reservation. Those whose incomes are large enough are required to pay Federal income taxes but do not have to pay state income tax, as long as they reside on the reservation. (North Dakota's relatively low income tax means that this is not a great saving for Indian workers, but every little bit helps.) Many Indians do not earn enough to worry about either Federal or state taxes. These adjustments to Indian income may add about 10 percent to the overall income.

One of the reasons that Indians are moving to urban areas in large numbers is the greater availability of jobs. Those Indians who move to urban areas in North Dakota go into private wage and salary work, about 62 percent of the total. Only 32 percent are government workers, and a minor percent are self-employed. The differences in job opportunities are reflected in the variation in income (Table 11.1) that is found among urban Indians. Per capita income increases, but the number of people required to earn more than $20,000 does not change. It is difficult to explain why North Dakota Indians living in rural, reservation, areas have higher incomes than those who live in urban areas. One explanation is that the Federal government, the greatest source of employment for rural Indian people, pays higher salaries than are paid to private wage and salaried workers.

Public Assistance

Those North Dakota Indian families with incomes below poverty level receive assistance from a number of different sources. Both the Bureau of Indian Affairs, State and Federal agencies provide public assistance. Since 1974, the Federal government has administered Old Age Assistance, Aid to the Blind and Aid to the Permanently and Totally Disabled. Tribal People are eligible for assistance under these programs, as long as they meet the same qualifications as other Americans.

Aid to Families with Dependent Children (AFDC) is administered by the State Social Service Agency, which also requires that Indians meet the same criteria as other applicants. Problems continue with state AFDC programs because so few Indians pay state taxes that states do not feel that they should have to provide these funds to Indians. Additionally, Standing Rock with part of the reservation located in South Dakota but considered a North Dakota reservation provides a special problem of jurisdiction. Both states prefer to let the other state assume the burden. Recently, South Dakota, North Dakota, the Bureau of Indian Affairs and Indian representatives met to discuss the situation. The result has been an improvement in services to the Indian population. Those Indians who qualify for public assistance are eligible for food stamps and for direct payments.

Tribal families who do not qualify for North Dakota public assistance programs are aided by the Bureau of Indian Affairs assistance programs. Of the entire Indian budget 60 percent is used for these programs. Direct payments have, in the past, been slightly higher than AFDC payments but not enough to make people choose one over the other. Job programs pay heads of household to do a variety of work on the reservations. These jobs pay a minimum wage which may not go very far if the family is large. Other sources of income are Social Security payments, Veterans' benefits and unemployment benefits. Indian men and women who have served in the Armed Forces are eligible for a variety of Veterans' benefits, including hospitalization. Social Security and unemployment depend upon the individual's having worked a certain length of time before applying for the benefits. In the past few Indians were eligible for these programs, but in 1990 (Table 11.4) 14 percent of Indian households had income from Social Security. Some urban dwellers will work for enough weeks to qualify for unemployment benefits and then return to their reservation to live until the benefits run out.

One controversial form of assistance is the provision of foster homes for tribal children. While it is true that some parents are unable to care for their children, traditional tribal culture had provided for relatives to care for children. To non-Indians, Indian homes and home life are not suitable to the proper rearing of children, but Indians view their way of life as the best way to raise children. Consequently, authorities often remove children and place them in foster homes while Indians believe that they are being cared for properly by relatives. What appears to authorities as improper care and facilities, as disorganization and lack of concern, is the traditional Indian way of socializing the child through the extended family. The result has been that a large proportion of tribal children have been placed in foster homes against the family's will. These foster homes have, up until recently, been non-Indian homes. The effects of these placements have been traumatic for both Indian children who are expected to "act white" and for their parents who have been told they are unfit parents. Today tribes are operating group homes administered by Indian families and are requiring that Indian children be placed in Indian foster homes. The Indian Child Welfare Act of 1978 awarded tribes complete jurisdiction over Indian children on or off the reservation. These foster homes and Bureau of Indian Affairs boarding schools provide assistance to families by caring for the children until the family can be reunited. One hope for the future is that the need for these services will gradually diminish as families are better able to support themselves.

In summary, the current economic situation of American Indians includes elements of traditional culture as well as aspects of modern non-Indian ways. Some Indians have, through education, improved their economic status significantly, but for most the situation remains dire.

GEORGE BALDEAGLE

George Baldeagle was born in 1951 on Standing Rock Reservation, the second child of Dave and Rena Baldeagle. Soon after his birth the family moved to Los Angeles as part of Relocation, a government sponsored plan to find off-reservation work for Native Americans. For many Lakota, life in the city was so different from what they knew that it was very difficult to adjust. Separated from the extended family and close friends that composed the reservation communities, they eased their loneliness with alcohol. Dave, for one, began drinking heavily. Like so many other relocatees, the family soon returned to Standing Rock, finding a home along the Grand River in the southern part of the reservation.

Back home, the family seemed to do better. In the 1950's and early 60's the small reservation communities were composed of relatives, usually descendants of one of the historic Lakota divisions. Blackfeet and Hunkpapa lived along the Grand River on the South Dakota side of the reservation. Descendants of the Yanktonai settled around Cannonball, north of Fort Yates. Relatives took care of each other and the land provided the basics of life. On the bottomlands near the Missouri River they cut wood for fuel, gathered berries and plants for food, and pastured their cattle.

This way of life ended when the closing of Oahe Dam flooded bottomlands along the Missouri. More than 800 families were forced to move from their traditional communities to new locations. George and his family moved to Wakpala, where George started school. By this time his mother had remarried. School did not hold his attention, but he liked sports and became a basketball player. Like other teenagers in his community, he also became involved in drinking..."just like everybody else that grew up there. I thought I was a bigshot or something" (Montaigne 1989:27).

George graduated from high school, but found himself without much chance of a job on the reservation. One of the difficulties of modern reservation life is a lack of jobs. Especially lacking are work opportunities for untrained individuals. After he married and had two small children, he moved his family to Aberdeen, South Dakota, where he found a job in a 3-M plant. His job was routine, but it paid well and his wife worked, too, so the family was financially stable. George took some courses at Northern State College, hoping to become a counselor. Just as it seemed things were going well, George began drinking. Just as had happened with his father, the alcohol took control. Rosemary gave up and returned to Standing Rock, where she divorced him and got custody of the children. He began to wander around South Dakota, working when he could, drinking when he could.

Eventually, with no place to go, George, too, returned to Standing Rock, settling again at Wakpala. He, too, married, a woman, Rosella Bird Horse, with a young son whom George adopted. The little family added four more children. George did not drink and spent a lot of time with his children. At first there was no work, but then George got a job as an assistant to the Community Health Worker. He studied to be an emergency medical technician (Montaigne 1989:27).

It was hard, though, to find housing and support a family on $350 a month. Any available housing at Wakpala did not have running water or electricity. They finally moved into a two-room house with a woodburning stove, but no other amenities. The adults slept in one room and the children slept by the stove in the front room. Getting wood and water was an everyday chore. Driving to town to get food was more time-consuming. They had to go to Mobridge, 10 miles away, the nearest town with stores, to shop.

The hardships began to weigh on George and drink called him. One day in 1987 his half-brother arrived with a bottle of vodka which he encouraged George to share. At first George refused, but the alcohol won and the two men got drunk. George's wife became angry and walked out, leaving him with the children. Some time during the night, George stoked the fire and then went to his sister-in-law's house where he passed out. A fire started from spilled ashes and the five children died.

George Baldeagle served a six year sentence in the Federal Correction Center in Milan, Michigan, for negligence resulting in the death of his children (Montaigne 1989:25,27).

Chapter 12

Reservation Resources and Environmental Issues

The high unemployment and low income rates of reservation residents naturally lead to the question of why the situation exists and how it can be ameliorated. A number of issues must be considered. The natural resources on each reservation vary considerably as does the availability of an infrastructure, that is a network of facilities like communication, transportation and sanitation that is necessary to attract business. The possibilities for economic development on the reservations remain as ambiguous as the attitudes concerning the desirability of development. Some reservations have desirable natural resources; others do not. On some reservations the cost of development and the cost to the environment make developing the resources a questionable issue. All the reservations share similar problems in terms of land, credit, and the support facilities for industrial development.

One of the basic issues is the problem of land use. Before the 1970's the government maintained tight control over tribal land, not only determining how the land was to be used, but also deciding how any income should be used (Levitan and Miller 1993:18-19). Tribal interests, particularly concerns about environmental changes and destruction, were not listened to. Tribal leadership was by-passed and people came to believe they had no control over reservation resources and development. Successful challenges to Federal control over Indian land and resources brought about a change in the system, but conflict between tribal interests and government attitudes continues.

In the Great Plains, agriculture has been the major focus for economic development. While the North Dakota reservations are more or less suited for agriculture, the land ownership problems effectively prohibit the successful development of agriculture.

In the late 1800's the Dawes Act allotted land to Indian individuals. The goal of the act was to provide enough land for each adult to farm effectively. The rest of the land was sold to non-Indians, and the funds were placed in a treasury for the tribe. As a result of the allotment of Indian lands, most of the land on reservations is not owned by Indians. Indian families live next to non-Indian families, even though the reservation is considered to be Indian land. Following allotment, Indians who could not make their land productive ended up selling the land or losing it through bank takeovers. Many Indians tried very hard to make a success of farming, but the size of the allotments was simply not sufficient, in the Northern Plains, to support a family. Non-Indians own most of the land on North Dakota reservations (American Indian Policy Review Commission 1976a:95).

> Ft. Berthold Reservation - 58% non-Indian owned
> Standing Rock Reservation - 64% non-Indian owned
> Devils Lake Reservation - 79-80% non-Indian owned
> Turtle Mountain Reservation - 93% non-Indian owned

The lower percentages on Standing Rock and Fort Berthold reservations are the result of land acquisition for reservoir construction. In fact, one of the points made in favor of reservoir construction was that it would permit the consolidation of land holdings on these two reservations.

In addition to the Dawes Act placing large amounts of reservation land in the hands of non-Indians, the heirship laws further diminished the productive possibilities of Indian land by dividing family plots into smaller and smaller pieces. The original allotments were 160 acres and were subsequently raised to 360 acres for grazing land. Unless the allottee left a will designating how the land should be inherited, the law stated that the lands were to be inherited equally by the descendants of the original owners (assuming that the lands had not been sold or otherwise passed out of Indian ownership). Because of this law, most allotments now have hundreds of heirs. The designers of the Allotment Act did not take into consideration the rapid growth of Indian families or that within three generations the claimants to a single allotment would be numerous. Today there may be many more inheritors than there are acres in the allotment. At the present time an individual may own bits and pieces of land all over the home reservation and on other reservations. None of the pieces are large enough to build on, if a specific piece could be identified as being owned by a specific individual, much less large enough to farm productively. Standing Rock and Fort Berthold land is most suitable for ranching, but an efficient ranch in the Dakotas may require 2,500-3,000 acres (American Indian Policy Review Commission 1976b:25). A single Indian family finds it very difficult to acquire that much land and so even ranching is not too successful for Indians. At Fort Berthold an open range policy has helped to solve this problem, but other reservations do not have this option.

One alternative to the fractionated heirship issue is to sell the land to the tribe or to one tribal member. If the land is to be purchased by the tribe, as is desired by most tribes, then all the heirs must be located, and they must agree to sell the land. Finding several hundred people is not easy nor is it easy to convince the heirs that selling is the best policy. If the individual is currently residing away from the reservation and if the land inherited is large enough to provide a building lot, the individual may prefer to keep the land with the idea of building a rent-free, property-tax free home on it. Indian attachment to land is deep-seated and having land on the reservation assures an individual a basic, fundamental tie with the reservation. Most tribes have land acquisition programs through which they attempt to buy land from the heirs in order to consolidate land into units large enough to farm or ranch. However, tribes actually have very little money at their disposal so that land acquisition is proceeding slowly. Often inheritors do not want to sell their portion of their inheritance, but when they do want to sell, the tribe may not have the money to buy the land. Some non-Indians may offer their land to the tribe at excessive rates, knowing that the tribe cannot afford to buy the land and that this will allow the non-Indian to sell to another non-Indian, or in anticipation of a larger-than-expected gain.

More recently tribes have established programs in which tribal members put their individually owned land in a tribal trust. This removes the land from taxable status and returns it to tribal control, yet allows the owner to use the land as he or she wishes. Such programs help to solve the problem of heirs not wanting to give up their inheritance, while making it more useful to the tribe and other heirs.

Another way around the land fractionation problem is to lease the land. Each tribe and the Bureau of Indian Affairs cooperate in handling land leases for heirs. Rents from land leases provide some income for most tribal members, but these incomes are usually small because of the numerous heirs. Most of the land is leased to non-Indians. Leases are often made for long-terms at rents that, in view of inflation, are now too modest. Tribes are trying to renegotiate these leases and raise fees. Higher fees, however, will discourage Native ranchers and farmers. Tribal People receive preference in land leases and rent at a lower cost than non-Indians, but these enticements have not been sufficient to attract large numbers of Indian land users. Non-Indians living on the reservation often find it convenient to lease the land next to theirs. Such transactions increase the land that can be efficiently worked and increases the chance of profit for the leasor. Table 12.1 shows the distribution of land usage on North Dakota reservations and who makes greatest use of these lands. At Fort Berthold most of the land is open grazing land, and farm lands are mainly used by non-Indians. A similar pattern holds for Standing Rock. The similarities between Fort Berthold and Standing Rock land use patterns are based on their location in the western part of the state. Fort Totten and Turtle Mountain are similar in that the greatest portion of usable land is agricultural, but at Fort Totten the non-Indians have taken up agriculture whereas the Indians at Turtle Mountain are employed in agriculture. Turtle Mountain Reservation, which has the largest Indian population in the state, illustrates the problem of not having enough land to support both population needs and agricultural uses.

Table 12.1. Land Use on Reservations, 1972

	Total Acres	Grazing	Comm. Timber	Non-Comm. Timber	Dry Farm	Irr.	Wild Land
Fort Berthold							
Total	452,430	379,939		10,830	61,455	42	
Used by Indians	337,278	307,426		10,830	18,980	42	
Used by non-Ind.	114,988	72,513			42,475		
Idle (unused)	164						
Fort Totten							
Total	50,725	19,434		7,250	20,810		2,298
Used by Indians	11,276	2,332		7,250	1,164		10
Used by non-Ind.	30,006	14,994			14,849		0
Idle (unused)	9,443	2,108			4,797		2,288
Standing Rock							
Total	845,336	765,074	2,155	10,735	57,650	300	
S. Dak. Total	546,806	497,535	2,155	6,466	36,248		
Used by Indians	299,588	278,440	2,155	6,466	8,955		
Used by non-Ind.	246,995	218,912			27,253		
Idle (unused)	223	183			40		
N. Dak. Total	298,530	267,539		4,269	21,402	300	
Used by Indians	142,003	130,605		4,269	3,629	300	
Used by non-Ind.	155,127	135,564			17,743		
Idle (unused)	1,400	1,370			30		
Turtle Mountain							
Total	69,587	11,887		40,350	13,830		1,906
Used by Indians	63,304	8,454		40,350	12,030		1,240
Used by non-Ind.	4,939	2,755			1,800		
Idle (unused)	1,344	688					666

Bureau of Indian Affairs 1973.

Indians have not gone into agriculture in large numbers. Some tribes have a cultural tradition that does not include farming. The Lakota and Dakota people were primarily hunters who felt that growing foods was most suitably done by women or other tribes. As a result, the Indian men did not take readily to agriculture when it was suggested as a means of subsistence. The men have expressed their tradition in terms of not wanting to cut into mother earth. The development of farm machinery makes agriculture more appealing, but a lack of capital to acquire farm machinery, some of which may cost $50,000 to $100,000 is a deterrent. Indians who want to farm need to be able to obtain the credit to buy seed, gas, machinery, make machine repairs and furnish family subsistence until the crop is sold. Because of their unfortunate image, Indians have trouble in obtaining the kind of credit necessary to go into agriculture in a way that will pay off financially. In addition, banks are often reluctant to lend money to Indians because of Federal claims on the land and legal difficulties in collecting on the reservation. Even non-Indians are finding it difficult to make a living at farming, and the risk may not be worth the energy.

In addition to the need for capital, Indians need in-depth technical assistance. Most non-Indian farmers today have either grown up on farms or have been to agriculture school so that they have a basic knowledge of farming methods. Most Tribal People do not have this kind of background and need a tremendous amount of technical assistance to get into agriculture. The United States Department of Agriculture will provide help to farmers and sponsor specific programs to help Indian farmers, but the funds are insufficient to provide enough agents to get the help to all the Indians who need it.

The Devils Lake Sioux tribe is attempting to solve some of the problems by operating a tribal farm in the Warwick area (E'yanpaha May 1979 vol.4, no.4). The original purchase of 1,000 acres was added to the tribe's holdings. A subsequent purchase of 2,000 acres has also been converted into trust status. A grant from the Economic Development Administration allowed for the purchase of tractors and irrigation equipment for the farm. The tribe is hoping to operate the farm on a sharecropping basis that would benefit both the tribal and the individual farmer-share coffers.

Although the larger reservations have substantial amounts of land suitable for grazing and most of this land is used by Indians, many grazing operations are too small to support the family. A rancher needs 200 cows to support a family of five. General figures show that 86% of the Indian operators have less than 150 cows. At Standing Rock, 60% have less than 150 cows (American Indian Policy Review Commission 1976:42). Fort Berthold has established an open range that permits cows and horses to roam at will on the reservation. While an open range makes for efficient use of the land, caution is required when people drive through the reservation, and instances of rustling on the range have been reported. A more important problem is range management. The American Indian Policy Review Commission quotes a 1975 report by the Government Accounting Office that describes the problem:

> An estimated 13 million acres, or 30 percent of Indian range land are not being properly managed and are in poor condition because (1) the range has been overgrazed, (2) range improvements have not been effectively used or maintained, and (3) limited use has been made of training and education programs (United States Government Accounting Office 1975, pt. 1:31).

The problem of overgrazing is of less concern in North Dakota than in other, more arid, states. The Navajo Reservation in the Four Corners area of New Mexico and Arizona is a classic case of overgrazing, and the hardships brought about by the subsequent reduction of sheep herds have not been forgotten by the Navajo. The adequate supply of rain during the summer months has made overgrazing less of a problem in North Dakota, but a drought still must be kept in mind as a possible source of trouble.

The result of these problems surrounding agriculture and ranching is that fewer and fewer Indians are engaging in these enterprises. Levitan and Miller report that in 1992 more than one million acres of reservation land were not used. Other figures indicate that "two-thirds of Indian owned farmland and 15 percent of grazing land is operated by non-Indians" (Levitan and Miller 1993:23-24).

Timber resources are not present in North Dakota. Turtle Mountain has sizable timbered lands, but most of the trees are suitable only for fence posts and other less important uses. Commercial cutting of timber has never been developed although, with an emphasis on renewable resources, timber may become a more suitable venture in the future.

Mineral development is controversial in North Dakota. Some North Dakota reservations have important minerals in significant amounts. Some of these minerals, coal, oil, sand, gravel, gas and phosphate, are in demand and the reservations are being pressured to develop their resources. All four reservations have sand and gravel, but these resources have not been commercially exploited. Developing a sand and gravel industry has been suggested as a means of improving tribal employment, since the development requires less capitalization and less overhead than other extractive industries. Sand and gravel are needed in construction and this material would be constantly needed. In North Dakota, however, the sand and gravel industry may be seasonal and thus not contribute substantially to the reservation employment situation. Of greatest potential development is the lignite reserve on Fort Berthold and the gas and oil at Fort Berthold. Standing Rock has lignite seams, but they are not suitable for mining. Fort Berthold has an estimated 14.9 billion tons which could be strip mined. Strip mining has received considerable negative press in North Dakota, particularly because of the results of the Four Corners Project and Cheyenne Project. Because of these projects, Three Affiliated Tribespeople are unwilling to discuss the exploitation of this resource. However, it is likely that the Three Affiliated Tribes will be forced into a discussion of the mining by the Bureau of Indian Affairs. Undoubtedly, pressure will be applied to the Bureau of Indian Affairs by coal companies and by energy industries as the supply of coal in other areas becomes scarcer.

Oil and gas have been partially developed at Fort Berthold for a number of years. Profits from this development have been to individuals and not to the tribe as a whole. Recently large sections of the land have been leased for oil exploration, and more people have had a chance to share in the profits. The first producing oil well on the reservation was brought in 1953. As many as 500,000 - 750,000 barrels of oil are pumped on the reservation each year (U.S. Department of Interior 1971:129).

Tribes have recently won the right to tax non-Indian companies that exploit the natural resources found on a reservations. In two cases, *Merrion v. Jicarilla Apache* and *Kerr-McGee Corp v. Navajo Tribe*, heard in the United States Supreme Court, tribes gained important economic opportunities. The Jicarilla Apache wanted the companies that cut their timber to pay the tribe a severance tax, that is, companies would pay a set sum for every foot of lumber they took off the reservation. The Navajo wanted Kerr-McGee and other companies to pay taxes on coal, oil and other minerals (Levitan and Miller 1993:62). In addition the Navajo asked the corporations to pay property and other taxes. State governments commonly levy such taxes on companies that exploit their resources. North Dakota, for example, has severance taxes on coal and oil, so that the state receives an income from the resource. States also tax businesses that do business in the state. For tribes that have an economically valuable natural resource, the right to receive an income when the resource is exploited means that those tribes can use the money to fund tribal programs and to invest in other enterprises. A steady source of income can be an important factor in arranging loans and other financial opportunities. Needless to say, not all tribes have valuable resources and not all tribes are willing to levy taxes, because they see taxes as something that non-Indians do. Other forms of development are still necessary.

Recently, the Federal government has supported the idea that reservations should become repositories for storage of nuclear waste or develop facilities for waste disposal (Levitan and Miller 1993:26-27; Specktor 1993:7). In general, tribes have not been included in Federal regulations concerning hazardous waste because these regulations could violate tribal sovereignty status. Theoretically, tribes have the right to develop their land according to their own best interests. In practice, however, this has sometimes resulted in environmental disasters such as water pollution by mineral or radioactive waste going uncorrected.

The creation of landfill areas to accept waste from off-reservation communities has generated controversy on many reservations. In the Dakotas, Rosebud and Standing Rock had heated discussions over the issue. Such facilities provide income to the tribe as the users must pay for the right to dump the waste in the landfill, but opponents argue that the income does not justify the risk of incurring land, water or air pollution.

Tribes appear to have greater consensus in their opposition to nuclear waste storage. The Energy Department is providing funds to a number of tribes to explore the feasibility of developing such facilities, but some tribes have returned the funds. Others that once seemed in favor of the idea are now rejecting it (Specktor 1993:7). The Prairie Island Dakota of Minnesota have gone one step further in rejecting nuclear waste by protesting the erection of a storage facility just outside the reservation boundaries. Northern States Power has a nuclear energy generating plant near Prairie Island and the company began building a storage facility to house its nuclear waste, but the Prairie Island Dakota have successfully fought in court to prevent completion of the structure.

Water resources are important to all the tribes in North Dakota. Fort Totten has Devils Lake and the Sheyenne River as potential water resources. Fort Berthold has Lake Sakakawea, and Standing Rock has Lake Oahe as developable water resources. Turtle Mountain's many small lakes may be potential water sources. Each reservation has approached the water situation differently. Historically, tribes have had to fight for their right to use or to reserve water for their use. In 1908, the Supreme Court, in the case of *Winter vs. United States* (207 U.S. 564 (1907)), recognized the rights of Indians to all "water resources which arise upon, border, traverse, or underlie a reservation in the amount necessary to satisfy the present as well as future needs of the Indians" (American Indian Policy Review Commission 1977:329). One of the concerns of the Supreme Court was that water be available for irrigation. The Court recognized that, because many of the reservations were located in arid areas, irrigation would be necessary to make the reservations habitable. The Court also recognized that this irrigation might take many years to develop, and therefore, these rights must be reserved for future use of the Indians. As in other decisions relevant to tribal development, interpretation of the Winter's Doctrine has been a continuing problem. Present concern is whether the Doctrine applies to water needed for energy development or only to water needed for irrigation. Standing Rock and Fort Berthold are part of a large number of tribes whose water resources were changed by the construction of dams. Now the water impounded by the dams is needed for energy development, hydro-electric power and coal gasification.

A recent proposal by the Bureau of Reclamation's Industrial Water Marketing Program would make 1 million acre-feet of water from the Missouri River reservoirs available for industrial use. The program would allow the states to market the water as long as a $20 per acre-foot fee is paid to the Federal government. The Indians have formed the Missouri River Basin Tribal Rights Coalition to protest this policy under the Winter's Doctrine, saying that the water belongs to Indians and not to the Federal government (Tucker 1979:80). If the water is sold, then the proceeds should go to the tribes and not to the Federal government. One of the issues is that subsequent usage may be based on present usage. That is, when Indians needed water, in places where Indians have not made use of the water but non-Indians have used it, it was determined that the Indians had abrogated some of the rights to the water. Finally, the major question is whether industrial development is the same as irrigation and whether Indians have any claims under the Winter's Doctrine. In some western states, non-Indians have formed groups to work actively against tribal water rights. There has been little controversy in North Dakota over water rights, because there has been a sufficient supply to meet all needs. With the Federal government attempting to set water policy, however, Indians are becoming more aware of the need to fight to retain their rights, and the issue could surface.

The Devils Lake Sioux Tribe is becoming more concerned about its water resources as the Garrison Diversion nears completion. As originally designed, the Garrison Diversion would carry water intended for irrigation from Lake Sakakawea to the Sheyenne River and thence into Devils Lake. Modifications in the diversion proposal may change this.

Water resources provide another possibility for income, fishing licenses. Tribes have the right to manage hunting and fishing on the reservation and some tribes are starting to assert these rights by requiring non-Indians to buy licenses in order to hunt on reservation land or fish in reservation lakes. There has been some question concerning the extent to which tribes may prosecute non-Indian offenders of tribal hunting and fishing codes, so many tribes make the licenses very inexpensive and treat offenders very courteously, offering them the opportunity to buy the license or escorting them off the water. The Standing Rock Sioux Tribe charges $1.00 for a one day permit to fish in the reservation portion of Lake Oahe. Just as the state uses income from hunting and fishing licenses to improve fishing and to protect game, the tribe uses its income in the same way.

The greatest asset tribes have is land and the various resources found on the land. Since the passage of the Native American Self-Determination Act in 1975, tribes have been gaining more and more control over this asset, but there is often no agreement over how control should be asserted or how the resource should be used. Some people blame tribal leaders for their inability to wrest control from Federal agencies and then, when control is achieved, complain that tribal leaders are misusing the income. Some believe that Federal agencies are more capable of managing the resources for the good of all and that Federal control prevents mismanagement and other costly mistakes. The availability of sufficient funding to develop the resources also remains problematic.

How the resources are to be developed remains a major source of controversy among tribal members. Some of the more tradition oriented people believe that any form of economic development that places land at risk should be avoided, even if this means giving up income and jobs. Others see some use of resources as necessary to the future of the tribe. Others look to other forms of economic development that will provide jobs without exploiting or injuring the reservations' natural resources.

Chapter 13

Reservation Economic Development

Encouraging industrial development on reservations has long been a Federal policy. Even before large scale attempts at industrial development, programs were aimed at providing cash incomes to reservation residents. Many of these programs established under missionary and other societal auspices focused on using traditional skills or teaching new skills to be used in cottage industries. These skills were often associated with crafts to be sold to tourists or to commercial outlets in the larger cities. In 1935 the Department of the Interior established the Indian Arts and Crafts Board. Regional craft outlets were established to encourage the production of arts and crafts. The Sioux Indian Museum and Tipi Shop at Rapid City, South Dakota, serves as an outlet for North and South Dakota Indian crafts, although its impact on North Dakota is considerably less than that on South Dakota. Figures for the amount of income to be derived from such production are not available, but the work certainly provides an important source of income, especially for people who are needed at home. More recently, a number of programs have been designed to attract industries to the reservations.

Beginning in 1955, in addition to Relocation to ease unemployment, the Bureau of Indian Affairs also began a program of attracting industry to the reservations. Today, the Bureau of Indian Affairs is the primary provider of funds for development. In 1992, the Bureau of Indian Affairs spent 24.2 million dollars on economic development (Levitan and Miller 1993:35). Among other things, the BIA offers direct loans and loan guarantees to tribes and individuals who can demonstrate that they have been unable to secure funding from other sources. The direct loans go back to the Indian Reorganization Act and are part of a revolving fund. The loan guarantee program covers up to 90 percent of loans made by lenders.

The BIA industrial development program was designed to minimize costs to the industry and to make such locations profitable, despite the long distance from home plant to reservation and the distances over which products must be transported. The industry was to provide management and capital while the reservation would provide funds to train reservation residents, thus cutting the cost to the company. The promotional literature also pointed out that the large supply of unskilled labor would make it possible to pay lower wages and that there would be tax benefits by building on tribally owned land. The lack of investment capital has been a major cause of the slow economic development on reservations. An industry must have sufficient capital to start and to carry the enterprise along until it is self-supporting. In 1968, Sorkin (1971:118) evaluated the situation of industries located on Indian reservations and found that of 137 enterprises 27 had closed down. The major reasons for closing these industries were insufficient capital and inexperienced management. In their study, Levitan and Miller (1993:36) found that BIA loan opportunities had also suffered defaults, another indication of the problems of developing reservations. Other difficulties have been in establishing markets and in transporting the finished products to the markets. These difficulties continue to plague industries on reservations, despite improved communication and transportation facilities.

Since 1966, the Economic Development Agency has also had a major responsibility for development on reservations and in other depressed areas. In the decade between 1966 and 1976 the Economic Development Agency spent $231 million on Indian programs (American Indian Policy Review Commission 1977:365). In the first ten months of 1992, 5.6 million dollars were spent by the Economic Development Administration on reservations (Levitan and Miller 1993:35). Funds were distributed between industrial parks, other public works, business loans, planning grants and technical assistance. These wide ranging programs cover most of the needs of reservations and have been much more useful than the more narrowly focused programs of the Bureau of Indian Affairs, the Small Business Administration, the Office of Minority Business Administration and other organizations.

In the late 60's the Bureau of Indian Affairs and the Economic Development Agency became interested in the possibility of tourism as an enterprise. At that time the forecast was that the work-week would become shorter and that people would be more interested in travel and recreation. The country as a whole believed that there was a need for tremendous expansions of tourist and recreation facilities to accommodate the expected demand. Tourism was thought to be valuable for reservations because it is labor intensive, that is it employs many relatively unskilled people for little capital outlay. Since Lake Oahe and Lake Sakakawea could provide water sports and other attractions, Standing Rock and Fort Berthold Reservations were identified as ideal locations for tourist-recreation areas. Outside Mobridge, South Dakota, on the Standing Rock Reservation and at Four Bears, outside New Town, North Dakota, on the Fort Berthold Reservation, tourist facilities were built. The Chief Gall Resort complex included a motel, marina, museum and other facilities to attract tourists. Four Bears Resort had similar attractions: motel, marina, campground and museum. Although the Economic Development Agency was careful to point out that these resorts would not be self-sustaining for a number of years and would require considerable advertising effort on the part of the state and local tourist agencies to make the resorts successful, both resorts suffered tremendous financial losses and eventually closed. Other reservation resorts faced similar problems as reported in "Scalping at Crow Creek" (*Reader's Digest* October 1979). Tourists have not flocked to reservations, partially because the reservations are located in areas away from the usual tourist routes and attractions. Both the Chief Gall Resort and Four Bears were located off the popular tourist routes and required detours or specific intentions to stay at the facilities rather than attracting the casual passer-by. Optimistic reports suggesting that the northern plains would attract people from Minnesota and Nebraska did not come true. Present energy shortages suggest that these reports may never be borne out. The resorts have suffered, too, from the lack of trained management and from tribal interference in the operation of the facilities. Motel/resort management requires training in business, personnel, public relations and in the minutiae of such things as food portions, kitchen and room supplies, cleaning techniques and many things the average person is unaware of. Without such knowledge, small things become large problems and costs soar. Tribal councils which had supplied part of the funds for the resorts naturally wanted to see the resorts succeed, but at the same time, be operated by Indians. When problems developed, the councils attempted to solve the problems by changing managers, cutting back on services and in other ways interfering in the running of the complexes. The end result has been the failure of most of the Indian resorts. Chief Gall has not been open as a tourist facility for several years and is now being remodeled into a treatment center for young people. Four Bears operated on reduced services and managed to stay open until 1991. In 1993, the Three Affiliated Tribes remodeled the Four Bears Resort into a combination gambling casino and resort and there is optimism for the success of this enterprise.

Figure 13.1. Devils Lake Sioux Manufacturing Company is owned and operated by the Devils Lake Sioux tribe. (Fred Schneider Photo).

Many of the industries that opened on reservations in the 1970's have closed. One of the few success stories is the Devils Lake Sioux Manufacturing Company. Originally a subsidiary of Brunswick Manufacturing Company, the company is now tribally owned and operated. The company was established in 1973 to manufacture camouflage nets for the United States military. One of the points in establishing the company on a reservation was that the government guaranteed contracts for the first few years in order to get the plant established. With such a base, the plant was unlikely to fail, and it has not. Since its establishment, the company has begun to diversify and enter the competition for contracts to manufacture other products, such as crash helmets. The company employs from 200 to 250 people, over half of them Indians, although not only Devils Lake Sioux, making it the largest employer of Indians in the area (Scaletta 1979:4; Bonham 1992). In 1992 Dakota Tribal Industries acquired three military contracts totalling more than 10 million dollars. Two of these contracts were for making tents and the third was for camouflage (Bonham 1992:5D).

Turtle Mountain residents have greater access to industrial opportunities than do the residents of the other reservations in the state. The fact that there are more people in the area and that the towns in which these industries are located are more attractive to non-Indians has encouraged the development of industry in the area. In addition to the shopping mall, a number of other stores in Belcourt are owned and operated by Turtle Mountain Chippewa. Larger industrial opportunities are presented by the William Langer Jewel Bearing Plant which opened in 1952 in Rolla and by the MDS-Atron Plant in Belcourt in 1971. These plants employ around 200 Indians, a much larger number than is employed by industries on either Standing Rock or Fort Berthold Reservations. The Turtle Mountain Band of Chippewa operate three tribal enterprises: Turtle Mountain Manufacturing makes small trailers for government use while Turtle Mountain Corporation and Uniban make computer components.

Industrialization of reservations has potential for helping to alleviate some of the chronic unemployment on reservations. Before economic development becomes a reality, one problem to be dealt with is that the kind of industry attracted to the reservation must fit into the cultural patterns of tribal life, that is the industry must neither violate the norms of tribal culture nor require the adoption of new values. Indian attitudes toward the land and the environment necessitate that the industry be a clean industry which does not pollute the air or water or other parts of the environment. Electronics and computer parts are relatively clean industries by comparison to sugar beet and potato processing plants.

Indian values toward sharing and helping each other make it more difficult for the kind of plant that operates on a piece-work basis, where criteria for performance are highly regulated, to succeed. To keep increasing the output of an individual, in competition with other people, is exactly the opposite of traditional values. Although few factories in this country have tried the system of assigning a group to a task, as has been tried in Scandinavia, this kind of approach would undoubtedly be more suitable for the reservation than is the competitive approach. Management should understand that some tradition-oriented people do not want to work for more money than they need to live comfortably. The aim of obtaining as much money as possible in order to buy bigger and better things is less important to Indians who espouse more traditional values of generosity and sharing. While some Indians have adopted the get-ahead ethic of the non-Indian, many of the Indians who continue to live on reservations have rejected such an approach. If they have tried and have found that stress is involved, they may prefer not to work because of their need to share the earnings with family and friends. Some Indians also dislike being put in the position of being experts. As a result, they are less interested in becoming managers and foremen than are non-Indians who regard these positions as steps to more money and more prestige. Prestige in traditional reservation culture is not measured by expertise nor by money but by less tangible values. *American Indian Economic Development* (Stanley 1978) clearly shows that the industries which have been most successful have been those which have grown out of the tribal community's identification of needs and development of appropriate industry. This attitude demonstrates even more clearly the need for Indian Self-Determination and the opportunity for Tribal People to be able to control their own lives, to determine their own values and the way in which they want to meet their needs and maintain these values.

The main factor prohibiting industrial development on reservations is the lack of capital. Despite the millions of dollars which have been set aside for Indian needs, tribes have little or no funds to invest in industrial development. Because of the way in which reservation resources have been handled by the BIA, tribes have not been able to use the income for reservation development. The major source of funding for tribal programs was from grants and claims cases. The grants provided funds for specific projects and did not make large amounts of money available for tribal investment. Large sums of money were paid to tribes as the result of land claims cases against the Federal government, but these sums were often controlled by the government and were not available to the tribes. Money other than economic development money which the Bureau of Indian Affairs spends on tribal needs are used to provide health, education and welfare needs for the people. As little as $2,000 a year may be allotted to an Indian tribe for investment and capital needs. While this sum will purchase a few head of cattle for a cattle project, the money will hardly suffice to establish an industry. Thus tribes have been stymied in their attempts to control their own industrial development and have been dependent on finding industries that are willing to provide the capital for locating on the reservation.

One of the greatest deterrents to reservation development is the lack of physical resources. Roads and other transportation facilities, power to operate plants, water and sanitation capabilities for industries are inadequate on most reservations. Industries are unlikely to locate in areas water and sewage are lacking. Small industries which will not tax the system are too small to benefit the reservation economically. Another problem for industries contemplating location on reservations is the quality of life for non-Indian personnel. The lack of adequate housing is a problem for Indians and is even more of a problem for non-Indians who are not eligible for tribal building programs. Adjusting to a rural area may be difficult for non-Indians who move from urban areas.

Despite the problems, tribes are creating their own sources of income. One recent development that meets the criteria of Indian values, yet requires little capital investment, is bingo and casino gaming. All over the country, Indian tribes are building enormous bingo parlors that offer high-stakes bingo games and opening luxurious casinos with slot machines, blackjack tables, baccarat and other high stakes gambling games. This boom began in the 1980's when several tribes learned that they did not have to meet state limitations on high stakes bingo games. The Seminole of Florida were one of the first tribes to generate large amounts of money through the operation of bingo games. One source estimates that in 1985 bingo generated 45 million dollars for the tribe. The result was that "the percentage of the tribal budget received from the federal government fell from 60 percent to 20 percent..." (Cordeiro 1992:207). Quickly recognizing the possibilities, other tribes opened high stakes bingo facilities and by 1987 113 tribes had bingo operations (Cordeiro 1992:207). The financial impact of these games, particularly those located in areas with large populations, was immediate and significant. In 1984 the Shakopee Sioux of Minnesota bingo operation paid off its 1 million dollar debt in less than a year (Cordeiro 1993:207). In 1990, the Shakopee Sioux grossed about $30 million. After all costs, this meant a profit of $4.5 million to the tribe. This money was used to provide payments to tribal members so that no one needed welfare; to support local and national charities; to pay health insurance for all tribal members and cover the cost of college educations for tribal members (Mandan, Hidatsa, Arikara Times, 1990:3). Other tribes made much less money, but still found the income to be a boon to their struggling economies. Between July 1986 and June 1987, the Turtle Mountain Band of Chippewa realized $60,000 in bingo revenue. Still, this represented money the tribe controlled and could determine how to spend.

Bingo has been, and remains, a popular form of economic development for several reasons. It requires little capital to establish a bingo operation. Tribes do not have to borrow large sums of money to start a bingo operation. Many tribes found that vacant buildings could be put to good use as bingo parlors. Offering high-stakes games sets the tribes apart from other, usually charitable, operations. Most states limit the amount a person can win and the number of times an organization can hold bingo games, but tribes do not have to follow these regulations so they can offer large prizes and operate continuously. Some tribes offer prizes as high as a million dollars and such jackpots naturally attract a large number of players. Bingo has been popular with Native Americans for many years, because it is a social event. Reservation churches and other groups held bingo games to raise funds for their activities and these were important social events. For the same reason, Indian people living in Grand Forks and other urban areas often go to bingo games to meet their friends and share information.

The success of bingo encouraged the tribes to move into other forms of gaming. Once a few tribes began the move, others soon followed and states became concerned over the possible problems that could develop. California took a case, *State of California v. Cabazon*, to the United States Supreme Court, which ruled in 1987 that as long as gaming was legal in the state, tribes could offer the game without state interference. Still unhappy with their inability to control gambling on reservations, the states approached Congress and in 1988, Congress passed the Indian Gaming Regulatory Act (IGRA) to provide some state supervision over tribal gaming operations. Basically the Act says that states must negotiate agreements with tribes that want to operate games that are not legal under state law. Despite numerous difficulties with the IGRA, many tribes have opened casinos and are beginning to generate significant amounts of money for tribal uses. One estimate is that Indian casinos generate $6 billion a year (Levitan and Miller 1993:40-41). No wonder tribes are entering into this activity with so much enthusiasm.

Casino gaming presents problems that do not exist with bingo operations. The cost of building a casino can run into millions, depending on the facilities, and this money must be raised by the tribe. Tribes often enter into contracts with gaming organizations who agree to build the casino and manage the operation for a share of the profits. In 1992 the Standing Rock Sioux tribe negotiated the first gaming contract with the state of North Dakota and another with the state of South Dakota. The tribe then signed an agreement with Indian Gaming Management Systems that would have given the company 40 percent of the profits. Indian Gaming Management Systems, in turn, brought in Seven Circle Resorts, a company from Denver, to manage the casino. All this occurred before a site was selected for the casino (Salter 1992:8A,9A). Tribal members opposed paying 40 percent to the management company and in November 1992 the tribal council voted to break the contract (Grand Forks Herald 1992:4C.) Bureau of Indian Affairs regulations state that tribes must receive at least 70 percent of the profits. Since then, development of the casino has been slowed by many other issues, including continued opposition from elders who fear that gambling contributes to other social problems. After having worked out these issues, the Standing Rock Sioux moved ahead quickly and opened the Prairie Knights Casino in December 1993.

In the meantime, the other tribes in North Dakota negotiated their compacts with the state and opened their casinos. Most of these casinos have been basic operations, that is, they offer a variety of gambling opportunities, but little in the way of food, entertainment, and other attractions. The Devils Lake Sioux have two casinos, one at St. Michael and one at Tokio. The Dakotah Sioux Casino at Tokio has "250 slot machines, six blackjack tables," and a poker table (Lone Fight 1993,2B). The Turtle Mountain Chippewa also opened a basic operation. In July 1993, the Three Affiliated Tribes opened a casino in the renovated Four Bears motel. Three months later the tribe announced it had received $700,000 in profits from the combined casino/motel operation (Grand Forks Herald, September 1993b:6A).

The Chippewa and Dakota tribes of Minnesota have been in the gambling business longer than many other tribes and an examination of their operations indicates the opportunities that such development can create. Jackpot Junction, run by the Lower Sioux, has about 1000 employees, 80 percent of whom are Indian. The payroll comes to more than $13 million. The operation brings 30,000 or more people a week to Redwood Falls, a small off-reservation community and this supports local restaurants, motels, stores, and other businesses. The Redwood Falls businessmen now routinely include Indian businessmen in their decision making. The tribe has contributed money to many charitable organizations and, like other tribes, uses some of the income to support tribal members (LeMay 1992:2-3). Among the Lower Sioux, welfare cases dropped by twenty people and AFDC cases went from 18 to three (Levitan and Miller 1993:42). Stories like these contribute to tribes' willingness to enter into gambling as an economic enterprise.

Not everyone is entirely happy with this form of development. States express concern that gambling can attract organized crime and are seeking more stringent rules covering casino operations. Some people believe that the easy availability of gambling increases social problems. They worry that parents will neglect children in order to spend money at the casino or that some people will become addicted to gambling and spend more than they should. In negotiating its compacts with the tribes, the state of North Dakota required that a percentage of all the profits be spent on programs designed to prevent and treat gambling problems.

The development of bingo and other gaming facilities has certainly been the most dramatic economic change for tribes, but some tribes have found other sources of income. One of the major changes in tribal thinking is that not all economic development must provide jobs for tribal members; sufficient income for tribal needs can replace jobs. With this idea in mind, some tribes have acquired businesses that are operated and staffed by non-Indians but provide income to the tribe. The nature of the operation varies.

One of the first tribes to attempt this kind of development was the Passamaquoddy of Maine. The tribe received a multi-million dollar settlement from the Federal government in compensation for treaty violations. The tribe used some of this money to purchase a cement plant. They later sold the plant for three times the price they paid for it. This income was then invested in other enterprises, including loans to other tribes who wanted to buy profitable businesses.

Money from casinos has recently been a source of investment funds for tribes. The Sault Ste Marie Tribe of Chippewa owns a number of businesses in the Upper Peninsula of Michigan. These businesses include a janitorial service, a construction firm, a convenience store, an art shop, an accounting service, a motel, a day care center, a newspaper, an office supply store and housing projects in six cities. The tribe has also established Four Winds Consulting to advise other tribes on investment opportunities. Some of the businesses are Indian owned and operated and some are not. Some employ Indians and some do not. The major concern is that the tribe make a profit from the enterprise (Mandan, Hidatsa, Arikara Times, January 1990:7).

In North Dakota, the Standing Rock Sioux recently bought the Food Services Division of Cloverdale Foods and will expand the business by building a buffalo slaughterhouse. The Food Services Division distributes food, paper goods and other products to schools, hotels, hospitals and other organizations in six states. There are branches in Mandan, N.D., Rapid City, S.D., and Wichita, Kansas. The purchase price of around $11 million will be paid over a number of years (Grand Forks Herald, September 2, 1993a:8C).

The Picuris Indians of New Mexico received a government loan to become part owners of a hotel located about an hour away from the reservation. Most of the employees and the hotel management are not Indian. Whether the hotel will generate sufficient income for the tribe to repay the loan and still leave some profit is a matter of concern to some people. Success in this enterprise, however, will lead others to move in similar directions.

As tribes move into more and more off-reservation enterprises, they find themselves in the middle of a legal dispute concerning taxes. The general rule of thumb is that Indians who operate businesses off the reservation pay the same kind of taxes in the same proportions as anyone else. Taxes may be in the form of licenses, property taxes, income taxes, etc. A question develops when the business is owned by a tribe, usually a tax-exempt organization with rights similar to those held by states. If states do not pay taxes on businesses they own, should tribes have to pay taxes on the businesses they own? Tribes usually argue that they do not, while state and local governments argue that they do. Cases such as these usually end up in court and tribes often lose on this issue.

The Fond du Lac Chippewa Band of Wisconsin attempted to solve this problem by having the land they bought for a casino in downtown Duluth declared part of the reservation by the Bureau of Indian Affairs. Although Duluth city officials were supportive of the casino the tribe wished to build, they were reluctant to see the property removed from taxable status. The tribe, the city and the Federal government worked out a deal whereby the tribe received 25.5 percent of the profits, the city got 24.5, and a joint development commission got the rest (Grand Forks Herald, September 29, 1993c:7A). The agreement was reached in 1986, before the Native American Gaming Act established 70 percent as the minimum tribes should receive. The tribe and the city are now locked in a legal battle over the money which the city says the tribe has not paid.

While tribes may argue that they should not owe taxes on off-reservation property or business, they, like other governing bodies, have the right to levy taxes on businesses on the reservation. Tribes have been reluctant to get into taxing, but a few tribes have begun to realize that taxes can help support tribal needs. A Supreme Court Decision in 1982, *Merrion v. Jicarilla Apache*, reiterated that tribes have the right to tax non-Indians doing business on the reservation. In the original case, the tax was a severance tax imposed on resources being taken from the reservation, but later cases have been more broad-based. In the early 1990's a number of tribes imposed taxes on reservation stores, especially liquor stores or bars, owned by non-Indians. Instead of taxes, some tribes asked that owners buy tribal licenses, just as off-reservation communities may require owners to purchase business licenses. The non-Indian owners were not always happy about the additional cost of doing business on the reservation and some refused to pay, turning to state courts for relief. In view of the United States Supreme Court decisions, local courts viewed the matter as one of tribal sovereignty and tribes handled the matter in their own fashion. The Cheyenne River Sioux sent tribal police to close down a number of businesses that refused to buy licenses and after a few days, most businesses complied.

Another source of income to tribes is selling automobile license plates to tribal members. Tribes in other states began this practice and it was adopted by some North Dakota tribes. At first, the state of North Dakota was reluctant to permit tribes to have their own license plates because it would cause a drop in state income, but this is a right that tribes have had for some time. Now the Devils Lake Sioux and the Turtle Mountain Band of Chippewa have their own license plates which tribal members living on the reservation may buy instead of the state plates. This provides a small, but reliable source of income to the tribe.

It often seems to tribal members that, whenever a tribe tries to improve its economic situation, the state or Federal government tries to interfere. When tribes began to build gaming operations, states first challenged them in court and then successfully lobbied Congress to pass legislation giving states a say in the conduct of the gaming. Perceptions such as these make tribal officials wary and significant success in different economic development situations will be necessary to encourage tribes to consider other possibilities.

Individually Owned Business

Not all economic development takes place at the Federal or tribal level. Some Indians have gone into business for themselves and operate their own businesses. Most of these businesses are construction companies, but gas stations, stores and other individually owned enterprises are found throughout North Dakota.

One kind of Indian operated business is Indian Arts and Crafts. The larger craft shops are tribally operated, but most reservations have individuals who run shops where arts and crafts are sold. At St. Michael's on the Fort Totten Reservation there is a grocery store-post office-craft shop-museum combination. The owners sell supplies for Indian crafts, as well as the finished products. Some of the Indian crafts are made on the Fort Totten reservation, and some are made elsewhere on the northern plains. Other individuals do not own shops but work out of their homes. These people sell Indian crafts or are practicing artists who have studios in their homes.

Indian owned construction companies are located in Belcourt, Williston, Dunseith and St. John. The Northwest Piping Company in Grand Forks is an Indian owned business, as is Jeanottes Welding in Williston.

A painting and decorating store, a bakery, a dress shop and grocery stores are examples of stores owned by Indians. Such stores are sometimes located on reservations and sometimes in more urban areas.

Beauty and barber shops are also Indian owned and operated businesses. Many of the programs aimed at educating men and women used to teach hair cutting and hair dressing skills since it was believed these would be employable skills. Some Indian people have used this knowledge to open and operate their own businesses.

Economic development of the reservations is a desirable goal if the tribes are involved in defining and selecting the industry or other resource to be exploited. People living on the reservations are willing to work and would like to see more jobs available, but they do not want any industry that will be detrimental to their environment or culture. If the tribes can gain control over some funds to encourage economic development, then the future may be brighter.

Chapter 14

Education

Modern Americans face many debates and dilemmas surrounding the structure and content of education. Is age the best criteria for grouping children in classrooms? Should schools provide culturally-based education or is there a basic "American" content that must be taught to all children? Do non-English speaking children learn quicker if taught in their native language or should English be the only language of instruction? These and similar issues affect all parents, but they are particularly significant to Native American and other culturally different parents.

Indian education in North Dakota reflects the general pattern of Indian education in the United States. At the age of five or six, the Indian child, like his non-Indian counterpart, starts school. On or near the reservations a variety of schools are maintained, but Indians have a long history of dissatisfaction with schools and curricula. North Dakota reservations have schools operated by the Bureau of Indian Affairs, and rural community, consolidated schools operated by a school district and attended by tribal and non-Indian children, and church schools operated by various denominations. Each of these schools must meet state requirements for teachers and curriculum. Each of these schools has its own goals and attitudes regarding its work. Providing for the education of Indian children was significant almost from the beginning of the colonization of our country. Many of the colonists were pious readers of the Bible who believed that only by teaching the Indians to read the Bible could their souls be saved from eternal damnation. Education would also provide a means of "civilizing" the Indians. Right from the start, the Indians objected to the provision of education for their youth. When invited to send their young men to the College of William and Mary, members of the Six Nations replied that they appreciated the opportunity but found that, when the men returned, they were not trained in the ways of Indians and "were, therefore, neither fit for Hunters, Warriors nor Counsellors" (McLuhan 1972:57). Ever generous and obliging, the Six Nations offered to educate non-Indian boys.

Most of the Federal treaties and some Acts included provisions for educational facilities. In 1819 Congress moved away from dealing with tribes separately by passing the Civilization Fund Bill which was to provide support to religious groups to set up schools among Indian tribes. Instead of dealing with each tribe on a separate basis, Congress now agreed to provide education for all tribes whether or not it had been agreed upon in a treaty. The bill was called the Civilization Fund because its goal was to teach reading, especially the Bible, and farming so that tribal people would become settled farmers, that is, "civilized." For more than a century, these twin goals of teaching the fundamentals, along with vocational training, directed Indian education.

Following the passage of the Civilization Fund Bill, vocational schools were set up east of the Mississippi, and Indian students were subsidized to attend schools of higher education, all operated and staffed by religious groups. The first real change from this approach to Indian education occurred in the late 1800's during the Allotment period, when off-reservation boarding schools were established. Up until Allotment, the attitude had been that educated students could serve as examples to their parents and that this would help to make changes in Indian culture. During the Allotment period, the idea grew that only by getting children away from the influence of their parents could changes be made. In North Dakota boarding schools were built at Wahpeton and Bismarck. No consideration of the idea that change was not desired by the Indian parents and that the government was following an unpopular policy was taken. The issues developed during these early years, education at home, education away from home and family, or education according to Indian interests and desires, continue to the present day.

Indian Education in North Dakota

At the time most of the North Dakota reservations were established, the Board of Commissioners of Indian Affairs was in charge of the selection of men to serve as agents on the reservations. In 1872, the Board also assigned the reservations to various religious denominations for education and conversion

Figure 14.1. Bismarck Boarding School once educated many North Dakota Indian children. Photo by Frank B. Fiske. (Courtesy State Historical Society of North Dakota).

of the Indians. The government provided partial funding for the schools conducted by the missionaries, although it was also expected that the parent organizations would support the activities of their missionaries.

Devils Lake Sioux

Fort Totten Reservation was assigned to the Catholics. This commitment continued a tradition of education by Catholic missions which had existed before the reservation was established. In 1874, the Gray Nuns, Sisters of Charity, opened a school at Fort Totten. The school was a two story brick structure, open to girls of all ages and boys under 12 (Meyer 1967:228). The school taught the basics of reading, writing and arithmetic and offered training in manual labor for the boys and domestic arts for the girls (Peterson 1985:19-20). In order to encourage attendance at the school, the agent allowed double rations to be issued. Children received their rations at school and no ration deduction was made from the parents whose children were at the school. Under such inducement, the school was soon filled. The Office of Indian Affairs, however, ordered that the double ration system cease and informed the sisters that they had to buy their own food, instead of being supported by the Agency (Meyer

Figure 14.2. Four Winds School at Fort Totten incorporates Indian symbols in its architecture. (Fred Schneider Photo).

1967:233). McLaughlin, the agent, was able to solve the problem by increasing the sisters' pay while he deducted the cost of the rations (Peterson 1985:21). In 1879 a manual labor school for older boys was opened under the direction of the Benedictine Brothers.

In 1880 the military post, Fort Totten, was abandoned, and the buildings were taken over by the Indian Bureau to be used as a school. The school continued to be staffed by the Gray Nuns, who were now considered to be government employees. Under the new system enrollment declined rapidly. Most of the students were Turtle Mountain Chippewa and the Devils Lake Sioux complained that their children were mistreated and refused to send them to school (Meyer 1967:240).

About 1920 the government stopped supporting the Gray Nuns and hired regular teachers to staff the BIA school. The Gray Nuns were supported entirely by the Catholic Church, and when their school burned, they rebuilt it as the Mission School of the Little Flower at St. Michaels, just south of the agency town of Fort Totten. In 1937 two day schools were established in areas away from the agency, but attendance did not increase. In 1972 a new elementary school building was opened at Fort Totten. This is a public school with an Indian controlled school board. High school students were bussed to schools off the reservation.

Four Winds, a new school at Fort Totten, housing grades kindergarten through twelve, opened in 1984. This facility was designed to bring together all the Indian students for an Indian-designed and taught curriculum. Parents have a choice between sending their children to non-Indian public schools on or off the reservation or to a school with a majority of Indian students and an Indian-oriented administration. The present reservation school system includes state supported schools and tribally run schools. State supported schools are at Warwick, Sheyenne, Oberon and Minnewaukan. High school students may also go to school in Devils Lake. St. Michaels School, formerly the Catholic Mission school, is now operated by the tribe with contract funds from the Bureau of Indian Affairs (Neumann 1981).

Fort Berthold

Fort Berthold was first assigned by the Board of Commissioners of Indian Affairs to the Episcopalians and then to the Congregationalists. A short-lived government day school was established in 1870. The first permanent school was opened in 1876 by Rev. C.L. Hall who built a combination house, school and church at Like-A-Fishhook Village. This school took over the efforts of the government day school. In this early school, Arikara were taught in one room and Mandan and Hidatsa children in another room. Between 1876 and 1885 the school was only moderately successful because of the considerable opposition among the Indians. Crow-Flies-High was outspoken in his attempt to avoid sending his children to school. One of his reasons for leaving the reservation was to avoid submitting his children to White education. After 1885, however, the school became more successful in attracting Indian students. The original school was enlarged, and a government boarding school was established at Fort Stevenson. This school was the focus of considerable protest by both Indians and non-Indians because of the horrible conditions. In 1889, Wolf Chief wrote to the Indian commissioner and asked for a new school to be built on the reservation because of the terrible conditions at the old fort (Meyer 1977:144). When the buildings burned, the school was not reopened. The Congregational school continued, although attendance remained small. In 1898 a Catholic school, St. Edward's, was established at Elbowwoods. Although St. Edward's was slow in opening, a significant number of students was soon enrolled.

In the late 1890's, day schools were built at various points on the reservation. Schools were opened at Armstrong for Arikara children, a second at Independence for Mandan-Hidatsa children living in that area, another at the agency and a fourth at Shell Creek. At the turn of the century, Fort Berthold had two mission schools, a government boarding school and three day schools on the reservation. By this time some of the teachers were Indians who had gone to Carlisle and other schools for higher education. The schools now began to conduct classes in English, under a directive from the Federal government that prohibited use of native languages in the classroom. The government schools came under constant criticism from Indian and non-Indian residents in the area. In 1910, the Catholics took over the running of the government boarding school, a move much opposed by Rev. C.L. Hall, the Protestant missionary in the area. The enrollment at the day schools was low, and eventually some of them were closed. In the 1930's, most reservation children were being educated in off-reservation boarding schools.

In 1934, the Indian Reorganization Act brought a complete change in governmental ideas about Indian education. John Collier, Commissioner of Indian Affairs and author of the Indian Reorganization Act, was against boarding schools and disagreed with the idea that Indian children should be educated to become White. Collier ordered that Indian languages and culture should be taught in the schools and that children should not be forced to speak English. He also tried to reorganize the reservation school systems by making schools more community-oriented. On the Navajo reservation, day schools were established with the concept that they should provide a service to local residents. Free water, showers, laundry, sewing machines and meeting rooms were made available to local residents (Parman 1976:196). At Fort Berthold, four day schools were built in 1937; one at Nishu, one at Beaver Creek, one at Lucky Mound and one at Red Butte. Shell Creek and Independence day schools continued to enroll students. Elbowwoods school was taken over by the BIA and became a full high school. At this time, the mission schools were finally discontinued. Public school districts also began to have more control over the BIA schools. With the building of Garrison Dam, these schools had to be relocated. The BIA wanted Indian students to attend public schools, but the Indians prevailed, and the schools were relocated and re-established.

Today, the BIA operates schools at Mandaree, Twin Buttes and White Shield. Schools at New Town, Parshall, and Roseglen are public schools operated by the district. The schools at Mandaree, New Town, Parshall, Roseglen and White Shield have tribally-controlled school boards.

Standing Rock

The treaties that established Standing Rock Reservation obligated the Federal government to provide educational facilities for the Indians, but the provision of education was delayed by the concerned attitude of the Sioux. In 1872, Agent J.C. O'Conner expressed the prevalent attitude by noting that the primary concern was to keep the Sioux peaceful by providing for their needs and not initiating any extreme changes in their way of life (Iyan Woslate Wo'Oyake 10). Later, the reservation was assigned to Catholic missionaries who established mission schools.

In 1873, the Agency moved from Grand River to Standing Rock. At that time, the agent requested that a school be established. Not until 1876, however, did the possibility of a school become a reality when Father Martin Marty, Father Chrystom Foffa and Brother Giles arrived at Standing Rock to begin a school. In 1877 two boarding schools were opened, one for boys and one for girls. The boys' school was run by Benedictine Brothers under Father Jerome Hunt and the girls' school was directed by Mrs. DeGrey, a part-Indian, assisted by The Benedictine Sisters. These schools enrolled about sixty children. The girls' school consisted of one building which served as dormitory, dining hall, kitchen and classroom for pupils and teachers (Duratschek 1947:72-74). The girls studied English, geography, housework, needlework, singing, cooking and mending. The boys' boarding school was small in size but maintained an active schedule of practical and academic instruction. Boys spent half the day in farm work and the other half in academic pursuits. In 1878 an industrial farm, St. Benedict's Agricultural Boarding School for Boys, was built about fifteen miles below Fort Yates. The school was also staffed by Benedictine Brothers. The course of instruction included tailoring, shoe-making, carpentry and farming and dairying, as well as academic instruction in reading, writing, arithmetic and geography. Agent Stephans moved the girls' school to the Agricultural School in 1880 to remove the girls from the attentions of the soldiers at the fort. The girls then received instructions in dairying, baking, gardening, in addition to their other subjects.

The opening of the reservation to other denominations brought about the establishment of several more schools. In 1883, Rev. T.L. Riggs built a day school at Antelope on the Grand River. By 1884, reservation schools enrolled a total of 266 Standing Rock children. The Agricultural School had 68 students. The Boarding School had 131 registered pupils and the Riggs School had 67 enrolled. In 1886 the school system of Standing Rock showed the following number of students (Fletcher 1888:265).

Figure 14.3. Schoolroom at Fort Yates Boarding School, ca. 1900. Photo by Frank B. Fiske. (Courtesy of State Historical Society of North Dakota).

Agency boarding 116

Boys' boarding 48

No. 1 day 21

No. 2 day 21

No. 3 day 14

Cannon Ball day 61

Grand River day 50

Attendance rates were low, however, and the above enrollments are only a small proportion of the school-age children living on the reservation (Iyan Woslate Wo'Oyake:32). In 1890 an Episcopal school, St. Elizabeth's, was established at Wakpala (Chapman 1965:38). By 1900 the Federal government had begun to move away from supporting church operated schools. In 1901 the Federal government announced that children attending mission schools would no longer receive rations. The lack of Federal support caused many mission schools to close their doors. Some tribes took over the support of the mission schools and some schools continued under reduced enrollments.

Today, the schools at Standing Rock are supported by three different sources: the Bureau of Indian Affairs, state public education and churches. The Bureau of Indian Affairs supports tribally operated elementary schools at Bullhead and Little Eagle and a complete educational program at Fort Yates. Fort Yates also has a public school for students from the Fort Yates district. A new high school was built at Fort Yates in 1979. State supported public schools are found throughout the reservation. At Solen, Selfridge, McIntosh, McLaughlin and Wakpala are public schools for grades kindergarten through twelve. The public schools accept Indian students who live in their districts. Johnson-O'Malley funds and Federal Impact Aid help to offset the costs of educating Indian students in public schools. A Catholic elementary school, St. Bernard's, at Fort Yates is supported by the Catholic church.

Turtle Mountain Reservation

The schools at Turtle Mountain Reservation followed the basic pattern established on other reservations, although the events happened in a much shorter time period because the reservation was not established until 1882. The first schools for Indian children were Catholic mission schools. The Chippewa and Metis had been Catholic since the early days of non-Indian settlement. Father Belcourt started a school, managed by Sisters of Mercy, on the reservation in 1885. By 1886 this school, called St. Mary's Boarding School, had an attendance of thirty-eight students, with accommodations for seventy (Fletcher 1888:285). Ten years later the school had enrolled 130 pupils (Commissioner of Indian Affairs Annual Report, 1895, p.11). The original school burned in 1907 and was rebuilt in 1935 by Benedictines and renamed St. Ann's Ojibwa School (American Indian Policy Review Commission 1976d:361). An off-reservation school at St. Johns also served Indian students (Fletcher 1888:177).

After the Federal government stopped supporting mission schools, day schools were built on the reservation. In 1891, the agent reported three government day schools, an Episcopal day school called Bishop Walker, and St. Mary's Boarding School serving the students of Turtle Mountain (Commissioner of Indian Affairs Annual Report, 1891:319). The day schools were administered from Fort Totten. The reporter noted that the attendance at the day schools was irregular and thought that feeding the children a midday meal would encourage more regular attendance. By 1919 five day schools on the reservation were enrolling a total of 273 students (Commissioner of Indian Affairs Annual Report 1919:165). In 1931 the Turtle Mountain Community School incorporated the other day schools and added a high school education. In 1974, St. Ann's School was turned over to the tribe to be operated as a BIA contract school, administered by the tribe. In 1977, the Turtle Mountain Chippewa Tribe assumed control of all the reservation schools, contracting with the BIA for funds to run the system. The tribe is in complete charge of the reservation school system, hires teachers and establishes curricula. The tribally operated school system includes Dunseith Day School, the Turtle Mountain Community School and Ojibway Indian School. Public schools in Dunseith, St. John, Rolla and Rolette also serve Indian Students.

In addition to the elementary and secondary day schools, all four reservations have tribal colleges. Most of these colleges were begun in the early 1970's to serve the adult education needs of the reservations. Today these colleges not only offer programs leading to high school diplomas for adults, but also prepare many students for careers and further education at four-year colleges in North Dakota.

Federal Support for Tribal Education

Because of the treaty agreements and Congressional acts, the Federal government has a continuing responsibility to support tribal education on the reservation. The Federal government interprets this obligation to mean that Native American students who attend schools off the reservation should not receive special financial aid from the Federal government. Native American college students must apply for help from the same sources as non-Indian students; neither the tribe nor the Federal government pays their way.

Today, two Federal agencies have major responsibilities for administering the Federal Indian education programs. The Department of Education, formerly the United States Office of Education, has programs aiding educational activities for which tribes are eligible and has established an Office of Indian Education to serve tribal people. The other major agency involved in tribal education is the Bureau of Indian Affairs which provides funds, either directly or indirectly, for Indian needs.

The United States Department of Education is responsible for administering the various Congressional acts which provide assistance to education, whether for general purposes or specifically for Indians. The major programs that benefit Indians have been described by the American Indian Policy Review Commission task force on education. These acts are (American Indian Policy Review Commission 1976d:93-97):

- The Elementary and Secondary Education Act

- The Indian Education Act

- School Assistance in Federally Affected Areas

- Emergency School Aid

- Education for the Handicapped Act

- Occupational, Vocational and Adult Education Acts

- Higher Education Act

- Library Services and Construction Act

- Tribally Controlled College Act

Many of these acts have different parts or titles which provide various programs and services. Some of the services are quite similar and add to the bureaucratic difficulties. For example, both Title VII of the Elementary and Secondary Education Act and section 708c of the Emergency School Aid Act support bilingual education programs. Each program is designed to meet specific eligibility requirements, and the applicants are responsible for determining which program best meets their needs. Each program has its own administration and management. Similarly, support for higher education for Indian students is provided under a number of programs with the students often being required to apply to a number of agencies before funds are received. The bureaucratic entanglements can cause considerable delay in receiving funds and make accountability difficult. Federal agencies place tight restrictions on the way their funds are spent and maintain close supervision over programs that they fund.

Traditionally, the BIA has been most concerned with Indian education and the largest part of its funds has gone to that purpose. The BIA is concerned with the direct operation of schools for Indians, such as day schools, boarding schools and dormitories for students who live too far away to commute. The BIA also administers Johnson-O'Malley funds, which go to public school districts with more than 10 percent Indian students. These funds are administered by parent boards and are used to assist programs for Indian students. The BIA also provides scholarships and other assistance for higher education and career education. Nationwide, BIA schools enroll about 20 percent of school age Indians. The BIA is currently under mandate from the Federal government to show that its schools are providing quality education for Indian students. If the BIA fails to do this, the educational programs of the BIA will be transferred to the Department of Education.

The state of North Dakota has the major role in Indian education. Of all Indian students, 60 percent attend public elementary and secondary schools. Since Indians on reservations do not pay state property taxes, the funds supporting Indian students in state schools come from Federal sources. Direct tuition costs are paid by the BIA, sometimes in the form of partial support of the school. Schools enrolling more than 10 percent Indian students are eligible for Johnson-O'Malley funds. Federal Impact Area Aid is also available to help offset the costs of the reservation students who attend public schools. Of the 336 operating school systems in North Dakota, however, less than 5 percent have Indian student populations amounting to more than 10 percent of the student body, and so Federal aid is not extensive.

Issues and Indian Education

The Indian Self-Determination Act made possible a new kind of school system, the tribally controlled school. Formerly, schools operated by the BIA received little input from Indian parents or teachers. The original goal of the schools was to "civilize" the Indians through the children, but in recent years, this goal has begun to change. Civilizing the Indian meant obliterating all traces of Native language and tradition. Children were punished for speaking their language even when it was the only language they knew. English was taught by force, if necessary. Teachers hired to teach in BIA schools were hired more for their willingness to teach in the remote schools than for their interest in or knowledge of Indian culture. Changes are taking place under the Self-Determination Act because tribes are taking over the operation of their schools. Tribal administration of the schools means that the BIA provides the money, and the tribe hires the personnel, establishes curricula and supervises general operations. Along with the Indian-controlled schools is the increasing availability of Indian teachers. The tribes now have Indians with teaching certificates who can teach in the tribally controlled schools.

The parents feel more in control of the education their children are receiving, because the parents also elect the school boards that supervise these tribally controlled schools.

Other schools, while maintained and operated by the BIA, have parent-controlled school boards. More parents are expressing concern about the education of their children and are becoming active in selecting teachers, in developing curriculum, in orienting the schools to better meet the needs of the students.

All the Indian schools in North Dakota have some Indian teachers and Indian resource people and make some effort to teach Indian culture and history, although there are still many non-Indians teaching in these schools. One concern expressed by tribal leaders is that many non-Indian teachers do not live in the community in which they teach. Tribal leaders see this as demonstrating a lack of support for tribal interests and they wish some way of solving the problem could be found.

Students who attend public schools often find themselves in a minority situation, and they suffer from feelings of discrimination and cultural differences. Since less interest in Indian culture is shown in schools in which Indian students are in the minority, even though they may represent a large number of students, the Indian students who attend these schools are either very much oriented toward White culture or find themselves isolated. The assumptions on which these schools are based are often not the same assumptions as Indians make. Competition is often stressed, especially for grades. The cultural values of achievement, amassing material goods, having nice homes and good jobs are often not relevant to Indian students, who have been taught to share or who have seen how difficult it is to get a good job on the reservation. The state of North Dakota now requires that teachers who are planning to teach in North Dakota have courses in Indian Studies and in cross-cultural awareness so that they can better relate to Indian students.

The major issue in Indian education is how much the education should reflect tribal traditions and values. Some parents want their children to be taught their native language, to be brought up in a system which emphasizes learning by doing and respect for elders, that stresses the traditional values of sharing, generosity and hospitality and kinship with all living things. Other parents want their children to receive the kind of education that will help them compete successfully with non-Indians for jobs. These parents believe that until Indians have the same skills as non-Indians, they will not have complete control of the reservations or be free to make choices. The attitudes of the parents naturally influence the children. Alternative schools that stress Indian language, values and traditions have developed in some locations. There are no alternative Indian schools in North Dakota. Alternative schools attempt to teach children in the traditional way, involving elders in the school. Parents who have questioned the kind of education their children receive in the reservation schools often choose to send their children to Catholic schools or will move to urban areas where they feel their children will receive an education that will equip them for the future.

Indian drop-out rates are high in secondary school and higher in college. Only a small percentage of Indian students who enter college as freshmen go on to graduate. A number of reasons account for the high drop-out rates. One reason is the conflict between reservation life and school demands. Indian children are given much responsibility and often find they cannot handle their home responsibilities and their school work. Tradition-oriented families stress participation in Indian events and activities which may conflict with attendance at school. This conflict apparently affects students most in their change from elementary to middle school. Some psychologists see this time as a basic identity crisis where the child must choose between the traditional Indian way and the non-traditional, White-oriented way. Pressure from parents and peers is greatest at this point. High school drop-out may also stem from family pressure or from general disinterest in education. The drop-out rate may also reflect the fact that tribes still have little ability to offer a tribally-based education. Tribes must follow state laws concerning curriculum and teacher education requirements and these prevent tribes from making changes which could make the educational experience more positive for Native students.

In college, dropping out may be related to financial troubles, poor grades and lack of interest in college courses. Most Indian students receive some financial support, but many do not receive enough to meet their basic needs. These students often change to a tribal community college in order to better their financial situation. Culture shock is another problem for Indian students going to college. Moving away from the reservation, from family and friends for the first time can be a great personal loss, and some students are unable to adjust to the separation. One of the ways of counteracting this shock is for students to attend a tribal college or a college where other students from home are found. Lack of cultural awareness on the part of teachers also continues to affect Indian students in college. Many college courses do not take into account Indian values. Biology, for example, may require students to dissect animals which is in direct opposition to Indian beliefs about the kinship of humans and animals and respect for all things. Support programs, Indian Studies courses and the presence of more Indian students on campus help students to deal with the problems they meet.

College is attracting more Indian people. The change is made clear by the different rates reported in the 1980 and 1990 Federal censuses. In 1980, 4.9 percent had completed four years of college. In 1990, the figures ranged from 4.4 percent with four or more years of college at Devils Lake to 8.3 percent at Fort Berthold. Many of the college students are women and many have families. Indian women are finding it easier to get jobs and to become the main family support. Most of the students at the University of North Dakota are majoring in education, following the nationwide trend (American Indian Policy Review Commission 1976d:277). Many jobs on the reservation are in the schools, and college graduates are getting positions in these school systems.

Many non-Indians believe that Indian students in higher education receive complete support from the Federal government, but this is not true. The attendance of Indian students at college is supported by BIA education assistance, tribal education assistance, the North Dakota Indian Scholarship Program and by basic education grants available to all Indian or non-Indian students. A Native American student applies first to the same programs that fund non-Indians. Other sources may help to make up the difference between student needs and support received from normal sources. The Indian Scholarship Service, the Association on American Indian Affairs and churches provide private scholarships for Indian students. Many of these are based on need and grade points and so are not open to all Indian students. The programs provide tuition, books and, sometimes, basic support costs, but the actual amount varies according to the student. A decade ago, Indian students who attended college received substantial support for living allowances, but the increased number of students has reduced the money available for each student. There are strict grade requirements for continued support. The BIA and tribal education officers keep close watch over the students who receive support from them and identify courses and programs which they feel are appropriate or inappropriate for students.

The North Dakota Post-Secondary Education Commission gave the following figures for Indian students enrolled in higher education in North Dakota in 1990 (*Statistical Abstract of North Dakota* 1991).

University of North Dakota	218
North Dakota State University	47
Minot State University	106
Dickinson State University	16
Valley City State University	10
Mayville State University	7
North Dakota State University—Bottineau	24
North Dakota State School of Science—Wahpeton	37
Bismarck State College	45
Lake Region Community College	17
University of North Dakota—Williston	29
Jamestown College	10
University of Mary	53
TOTAL	617

Tribal colleges are also meeting the need for higher education. Each reservation in North Dakota has a tribal community college which provides programs from basic education skills to vocational to college level credit courses that may be transferred to four-year institutions. These colleges are funded by the Federal government, by the tribes and through grants from Federal agencies. In North Dakota, the tribal colleges are affiliated with other colleges and can draw on programs and staff of the larger schools. The University of North Dakota and other state colleges offer extension courses at the tribal colleges, helping to meet the needs of people in the local communities. The tribal colleges serve important needs of the Indian community by providing education that is more accessible than that in other parts of the state. People can take courses at the tribal colleges without leaving their families or jobs. The tribal colleges are in tune with local needs and are responsive to community needs and interest. Many students begin their higher education at a tribal college and then transfer to one of the other state institutions.

The number of college graduates and the availability of special programs is increasing the number of Indian students interested in post-baccalaureate education. More Indians are now going on to law school, to medical school, and to other graduate programs in education and business administration. Until recently, funds for these students were very limited. The BIA believed that an Indian student accepted into a graduate program should be funded by the program through teaching assistantships, scholarships and any other means open to all graduate students. Such programs are limited, however, and the BIA now makes available a limited number of scholarships for graduate students. The North Dakota Indian Scholarship Board recently set aside funds to be used to support graduate students. The Indians into Medicine (INMED) Program provides some support for medical school students.

In general, Indian education today is in a growth period. On the reservations, parent advisory boards, Indian controlled school boards and tribally operated schools are changing the views of Indians about education. The Federal government is still vitally involved in Indian education and provides funds for most Indian education programs, tribal and individual, but the impact of the Federal government is mediated by the Indians themselves and gives the Indians a sense of Indian control. As more Indian people receive degrees from colleges and professional schools, more Indians will be working in education and the sense of Indian involvement and control will increase.

VINE V. DELORIA, SR.

Vine Deloria, Sr. was born in 1901, near Wakpala, on Standing Rock Reservation. Vine considers himself a member of the Hunkpapa band of Lakota, although his grandfathers and grandmothers were not from that division. The Deloria family is better known among the Yanktons in South Dakota because the original Deloria, Philippe des Lauriers, married a Yankton woman and his son, Vine's grandfather Francis, had over 20 children, many of whom lived at Yankton.

Despite having a French father, Francis Deloria was raised as a traditional Yankton and grew up to become a well known healer and tribal leader. He was called Saswe by the Yanktons. Following the Indian way, he married three women (Murray 1974:26). One wife, Sihasapewin, was a member of the Blackfoot division of the Lakota. The other two wives were from Crow Creek and Rosebud Reservations in South Dakota. His three wives provided Francis with many children and all were happy together. Vine Deloria, Sr. recalled his father, Phillip, taking him to the family homestead and pointing out the log houses where each wife lived. Francis lived by himself in another large house and the wives took turns cooking for him (Deloria 1987:100). In the late 1860's Francis became interested in Christianity, but refused to become a Christian because he would have to give up two of his wives. Finally, after the death of one of the wives he made the choice and sent the other wife back to her people. On December 25, 1871 he was baptized as an Episcopalian and remained a devout Christian to the end of his life. His wife also became a Christian and this established a trend followed by their descendants.

Vine's father, Philip Deloria, (Tipi Sapa) was born (1854) near Mobridge, South Dakota (Olden 1918:1) and raised on the Yankton Reservation. Because of his father's interest in education and Christianity, Philip was sent to day school on the reservation (Deloria 1987:105) and later attended Nebraska College and Shattuck School in Faribault, Minnesota (Olden 1918:13). In 1874 Phillip Deloria was made a deacon in the Episcopal Church and also assumed the post of tribal leader. In 1890 or 91 he was sent to Standing Rock to establish a mission. Soon after the move he was ordained as an Episcopal priest (Olden 1918:14).

At the time of Vine's birth his father was an Episcopalian minister assigned to Standing Rock Reservation. Three much older sisters, Lyma, Ella and Susie, took great care of their little brother. Soon after Vine's birth, three year old Phillip Deloria died. His parents were so grief-stricken and were so worried that Vine might die, too, that they neglected him. The head of St. Elizabeth's School, where Ella was a student, suggested that Ella bring him to the school and everyone would look after him (Murray 1974:85). Ella later became an anthropologist. She was known for language studies and her collections of stories from elders. Vine's mother died when he was fourteen. Both Ella and Susie had received educations in schools away from the reservation and, following his mother's death, Vine was sent to a military boarding school.

Vine spent his first fifteen years on the reservation, attending St. Elizabeth's School. At age 15 he entered Kearney Military Academy in Kearney, Nebraska, but returned every summer until he was 22 (Deloria 1971:173). In a 1974 interview, Vine described school life to Janette Murray (Murray 1974:85).

> There was always a lot of activity at the school. The older children went to school in the afternoon and the younger ones in the morning. All morning the older children worked. The boys cared for the cows, pigs, chickens, and horses. They cut the hay and stacked it. They had an ice house, a carpenter shop, a coal house, a blacksmith

shop. These big boys would set up the heavy logs on saw horses and mark them off at certain distances. Then the little boys would cut them with the saws.

The Deloria family lived in a white house convenient to both St. Elizabeth's School and the Church of St. Elizabeth's Mission (Olden 1918:xvi). The family always spoke Lakota/Dakota at home and Vine recalled (Murray 1974:91) that Ella tried to help him with his English studies, but he found the language difficult. He later achieved acclaim for his skill as a speaker in both Dakota/Lakota and English.

He and his friends enjoyed themselves as country boys do. At age 12, later than most of his friends, he finally got a saddle horse of his own. One of his reminiscences concerned riding young calves, a sport not approved by the owners of the herd, but much enjoyed by the riders. The boys also went to dances, helped fight prairie fires and did odd jobs. These were farm boys and they all had chores to do: care for the cattle or horses, hauling water, helping with haying, burning trash and harvesting. When he was fourteen and fifteen, Vine worked for his brother-in-law, Fred Lane, an Englishman, buying horses. Vine's job was to act as interpreter and, when the herd was large enough, drive it back to the ranch (Deloria 1971:186-191).

In 1916, Vine left the reservation to attend school (Cash and Hoover 1971:108) and did not return until the late 20's or early 30's (Murray 1974:106; Cash and Hoover 1971:109). He followed in his father's footsteps and became an Episcopalian minister. He first attended Bard college, studying "history, biography, poetry, social problems, economic problems, morality" (Demallie and Parks 1987:109) in order to obtain a BA. He then studied at General Theological Seminary, obtaining a Bachelor of Divinity degree and being ordained a deacon in the church in the same year. The following year he received his priesthood (1960:61). At first he served, like his father, in the Indian mission field, but he eventually left that calling and served as rector and vicar for various dioceses in the Midwest and Plains (Gridley 1960:62). He rose in the church hierarchy, becoming Arch-Deacon of the Episcopal Church of South Dakota (Murray 1974:255). Following his retirement he continued to be active in church and Native American functions. Two sons, Vine Deloria, Jr. and Phillip, are well-known educators and writers.

Chapter 15

Indian Health

The health and wellness of Indian people is of great concern to both Indian and non-Indian people. Non-Indian attention to Indian health began very early in Indian-European contact when tribal people succumbed to diseases introduced by Europeans. Present day statistics show that tribal health is still not as good as that of non-Indians. Indian health has been one aspect of the relationship between the Federal government and tribes because medical care, usually with the provision of a doctor and medical facilities for the tribe, was included in many treaties. Other aspects of the health issue include the nature of the illnesses which afflict Tribal People, the quality and nature of health care services, the need for education to improve healthful living, and the cultural behaviors which may contribute to or prevent healthy living.

The Federal government has an interest in tribal health, because it must provide services for Tribal People. Economic factors are clearly related to health, because one must have sufficient income to afford a healthy environment and diet. Geographic factors are related to Indian health because some areas are more prone to certain kinds of diseases than others. In addition, the distance from health care services may be directly related to the death rate or to the ability to utilize the services. Ideas about the nature of illness and attitudes towards medical treatment and doctors may also influence the way in which tribal people utilize the services which are available to them. Some tribes have specific dietary preferences which may lead to poor nutritional practices. The stress of being poor or the inability to find a good job may lead to mental health problems, such as suicide and alcoholism.

People have a number of conflicting ideas about Indian health in the "good old days," before European contact. One idea is that Indians, and other ancient people, lived very short lives before the advent of modern medicine. Others say, however, that Tribal People lived much longer lives before the Europeans introduced new diseases. In fact, each of these points contains some truth and some error. Pre-contact Indian health was too complicated to be summarized in a single phrase.

The evidence for the pre-contact health position of Tribal People comes primarily from skeletal remains, but the comments of early explorers and the winter counts also provide pertinent information. Skeletal remains provide some of the only evidence for death rates and general population figures. An obstacle in using skeletal material arises because some bones, particularly those of infants and children, are less likely to be preserved and may lead to skewed figures for death rates. Another limitation is that many health problems afflicting human beings do not leave their marks upon human bone, and so the cause of death can rarely be established solely upon the basis of skeletal evidence. The nature of burial practices in the northern plains where Indians practiced scaffold burial, exposing the bodies on platforms raised in the air rather than burying them in the ground, often left little trace of their population. Sometimes the bones were gathered up and reburied but not always. Cemeteries may have been used for so many years that the remains do not represent the population at a specific time. Despite these problems, however, skeletal remains are the only solid evidence available from which to reconstruct general patterns of tribal health before it was disrupted by European diseases and alcohol.

Skeletal remains from three burial mound sites in South Dakota (Bass and Phenice 1975) show a high mortality rate and a large number of individuals with varieties of arthritis and periostitis (inflammation of the fibrous membrane that covers all bones). These mounds are about 1,500 years old, but the health problems of the individuals represented in the mounds appear to be fairly similar to the health problems of later peoples. A high infant mortality rate, from 40-50 percent of the children dying before the age of two, is seen in these mound burials. This high rate is common throughout North America and is not really different from that found in other parts of the world before the development of modern natal care. Skeletal remains of individuals between the ages of three and sixteen showed few signs of ill health. Malnutrition is one of the signs of poor health that leaves permanent marks on bone, but no such indications were found on the remains from these mounds. Four youngsters suffered from otitis media, an infection of the middle ear that still plagues Native children. After the age of twenty, most of the individuals showed some signs of periostitis and arthritis. Osteoarthritis, the form of arthritis most often found in prehistoric populations, was common throughout North America. The older individuals also showed considerable tooth loss due to infection and chipping. Few caries were found in any of the individuals from any of the mound sites, suggesting that the diet of the people was not conducive to tooth decay but that the tooth loss was due to the use of the teeth.

Lewis and Clark spent a winter among the Mandans and had an opportunity to treat some people for health problems. One of the common complaints during that winter was frost bite. On January 10, 1805, the Lewis and Clark journal records that an Indian boy about thirteen had spent the night in extreme cold with only his moccasins, leggings and a buffalo robe to protect him. His feet were badly frostbitten, and later the boy (Sunday, January 27th) had some of his toes amputated (Reid 1947-48:134). After spending more than a month at Ft. Clark, the young man returned to his people. Other cases of frostbite are also mentioned in the journals. One of the interesting events in the Lewis and Clark journals is the birth of a child to one of the wives of Charbonneau. Most scholars assume this wife to be Sakajawea. The difficult childbirth contradicts the common belief that Indian women had easy childbirths. The mother was given medicine composed of two rings of rattlesnake rattle crumbled in water. Shortly after being given this dose, the baby was born with no further complications (Reid 1947-48:146).

There are many sources of information concerning the state of health in aboriginal America. Contemporary health professionals are interested in this aspect of healing, because it may help them to develop health systems that are more relevant to modern tribal needs. One element that needs to be considered are Native American beliefs about the causes and treatment of ill health.

Ideas About Illness and Treatment

Throughout North America, Native ideas about the causes of disease were closely associated with religious beliefs and practices. Most tribes recognized that accidents happened but questioned why a particular accident should happen to a particular person. To most human beings many illnesses and their ultimate resolution appear to be mysterious. The same symptom can end in different ways. A stomach ache can be a simple reaction to the wrong kind of food and a person will recover completely in a relatively short time or it can be appendicitis which, without proper treatment, may worsen and result in death, or it can indicate a slowly degenerating illness such as ulcer or cancer. Many illnesses will, over time, appear to heal themselves. Successful treatment of health problems involves recognizing or identifying the cause of the problem and specifying the treatment that fits the cause. Even today physicians are aware that patients feel better once the cause of the problem is diagnosed and treatment can begin. Most tribes recognized several major causes of accidents and illnesses, but all involved a belief in the supernatural or sacred powers held by humans, plants, animals or other phenomena and the capacity of these powers to do good or evil. It is likely that health problems with obvious natural causes, such as fractures, wounds, animal and insect bites, or skin irritations were attributed neither to supernatural causes nor treated by specialists. If the apparently simple mishap became complex, or mysterious, however, then the unnatural causes would be involved in the diagnosis and treatment.

Unnatural causes of illness could be sorcery (often called witchcraft), spirit intrusion, soul loss, disease-object intrusion and violation of sacred rules. These basic causes had selective manifestations and attributes varied from tribe to tribe, but some general similarities, particularly among the Northern Plains tribes, may be noted. Sorcery was performed by one person against another. The sorcerer may have had special powers which enabled the harm to be done, although in some tribes, any person who could obtain the necessary materials could use those materials against another person. Sorcery often involved one of the other causes of ill health mentioned above. Sorcerers sometimes sent objects, such as sticks, bones, pebbles, and small pieces of hide into a person's body to cause disease. Among the Plains Cree, jealousy was a common reason for an evil person to send a foreign object into another person's body by simply ordering his spirit helper to take it to the victim (Mandelbaum 1940:163). Only a healer with stronger powers could remove the object and save the sufferer's life. When such curing took place, the evildoer would die instead of the patient. Another kind of sorcery consisted of a person making a little figure that represented the recipient of the malevolence and putting the foreign object into the figure or wiping the figure with the medicine that caused ill health (Mandelbaum 1940:164).

Frequent causes of disease were evil spirits, who often mimicked good spirits in order to confuse humans. The Lakota had a number of evil spirits, including *Iyo, Gnaskinya* (Crazy Buffalo), *Anog Ite* (Double Face), *Canoti* (Tree Dwellers), Goblins and Dwarfs. The most feared of these was Crazy Buffalo, because he often appeared like Tatanka, the good buffalo, and fooled people into doing wrong. Crazy Buffalo was also thought to send insanity or paralysis (Walker 1980:94; Hassrick 1964:215). The Mandan believed that the Old Woman Above's daughter was an evil spirit and that the sun had evil attributes which caused insanity, drought and other misfortune. The sacred bundle associated with these spirits was so sensitive that neighbors would blame the bundle keeper for any kind of accident (Bowers 1950:297). Evil spirits could also send objects into a person (Hassrick 1964:249). The only way to avoid illness caused by evil spirits was to hold ceremonies regularly and seek strong spiritual protection.

Violating sacred instructions was certain to bring on accidents or illnesses. A young Hidatsa man who dreamed of the Horse ceremony never obeyed the dream until one day a horse kicked him and severely injured him. The investigation into the event concluded that the kicking was caused by the supernatural in an effort to get the man to follow the vision instructions (Bowers 1965:283). A person who consistently had bad luck would be thought to have somehow violated one of the supernatural rules in caring for the sacred bundles. The Mandan told about a man who used his mother's brother's mink hide without permission and suffered a fall from a horse as a punishment for taking the sacred bundle. Since there were many rules and regulations involving the sacred, people found it easy to transgress and to suffer the ill effects. Major sanctions prevented the use of sacred objects or symbols without permission, either from the owner or the supernatural. A Plains Cree man who painted a sacred symbol on his tipi without being given permission in a vision would bring about his own or a relative's death (Mandelbaum 1940:123).

The treatment was directly related to the cause of the problem, but many ceremonies were designed as preventive medicines. Keeping a healthy mind and body, following the tribal and sacred laws and practicing ceremonies faithfully would help people to ward off evil. Seeking and finding a strong spirit protector was so important that everyone was assumed to have some kind of spiritual power in order to survive at all. The healthiest individuals were those whose spirit powers were the strongest.

The ceremony with the greatest power to ward off evil and illness was the sweatlodge, a small dome shaped shelter made of willow and covered with hides, where people sat in steam made by water sprinkled over hot rocks. A priest led the participants in prayers, and the steam purified the body while it carried the prayers to heaven. The prayers involved all the sacred beings in a ceremony of purification. By removing the evil and contamination of daily life, the participants were strengthened in their power to resist illness and misfortune. A person emerging from the sweat lodge felt as though he was reborn.

Another method of preventing serious illness was to acquire a spirit protector and have that Being give the person a sacred protective object or bundle of objects. The Plains Cree wore or carried amulets, sacred objects carried in a beaded bag, to protect themselves from evil. These objects were given in a vision and could be bones, stones, roots or any other item that was imbued by the supernatural protector with power to protect. Children were often given amulets by the elder who gave them their name (Mandelbaum 1940:165). At birth, each Lakota child was given two beaded turtle or lizard-shaped amulets: one contained the umbilical cord, and the other was a decoy. Both were used until the child was old enough to seek his or her own protection (Hassrick 270-271). The objects that protected a warrior were called *wotawe* by the Lakota. Some of these were worn at all times while others were used during the ceremonies held by the men before going on raids or into battle (Walker 1980:264-265).

When all efforts failed, however, and a person succumbed to bad luck or ill health, he/she had many treatments available. Accidental injuries and ill health which seemed to have natural causes were treated by people who were knowledgeable about setting bones and herbal remedies. These people had learned their craft from others with similar skills, and through years of studying these people became quite skillful in the treatment of most of the common health problems which Native Peoples faced. Gilmore (1919) and Rogers (1980) identify many of the plants used as medicines by the Plains Indians. Some of these include: a tea from the roots of the western ragweed used as a laxative (Rogers 1980:35); pulverized dotted gayfeather roots used to improve one's appetite; skeleton plant tea used to stop diarrhea in children (Rogers 1980:38); powdered hairy puccoon root for chest wounds (Roger 1980:40) and roots of the Canadian milk-vetch used for chest pains and coughing (Roger 1980:45).

The Lakota called the men who were familiar with the treatment of common problems *pejuta wicasa* and the women *pejuta winyan*, medicine man and medicine woman. Fine-Day, a Plains Cree man, described setting broken legs which he learned how to do when his own leg was broken. He noted that the only requirement to do such work was knowing how to do it and being brave enough to try (Mandelbaum 1940:169). The Hidatsa acquired the right to practice medicine by purchasing a sacred bundle that included the curing of certain diseases. Sacred bundles dedicated to Grizzly Bear, either hereditary or personally acquired through a vision, included the right to doctor (Bowers 1965:357) as did the Big Bird (Bowers 1965:364), Missouri River (Bowers 1965:372), Creek (Bowers 1965:382-389), and other bundles. Probably a member of every family would have some kind of medicine powers, and so doctoring was most often done within the family.

Uncommon problems and illnesses which did not respond to the common remedies required the services of a specialist who had supernatural powers to cure. Just as today we distinguish between specialists and family practitioners, the sacred specialists should be distinguished from the medicine men because they were recognized by the Indians as different. English speakers do not often recognize or understand the differences and call all Indian healers medicine men.

The Lakota words for these specialists were *wicasa wakan* and *winyan wakan*, "sacred man" and "sacred woman", and even within these general categories there were more specific terms for those who specialized in curing. In English, people who have supernatural powers to cure or to contact the gods are sometimes called "shamans," but this word applies to the sacred men of some Asian tribes and most Native Americans do not accept it. When it was considered necessary to obtain the services of a specialist, gifts would be sent to the person selected to perform the curing ceremony. If the sacred man or woman accepted the gifts, he or she indicated his or her willingness to attempt the cure. Wolf-Chief, a Hidatsa man, described his mother's assistance in the case of the daughter of Bear-Looks-Out, whose illness had not been cured by others. Strikes-Many-Women was successful, which meant that she received much acclaim for the power of her curing. In general, however, Strikes-Many-Women was reluctant to cure others, because it could mean that her power would be too weak to aid her own family if it were needed (Bowers 1965:385-389).

The Lakota man or woman who aspired to become a sacred person underwent a long period of training. Black Elk (Black Elk 1932) clearly exemplifies the process. Often the potential sacred person received hints about the possibility long before he or she was able to understand the meaning of the hints. The primary step to obtaining sacred power was to undergo the vision-seeking process. If the vision suggested that the person should become a sacred person, then that person needed to spend many years in apprenticeship to other sacred men, learning all the attributes of sacredness, praying, and assisting in performing ceremonies. Gradually, the apprentice took more and more initiative in the ceremonies, until he or she was accepted as able to work without direction from another (Powers 1977:60-62). Sword, one of the Lakota sacred men who trained James Walker, listed three ways of treating the sick. The medicine man gave medicines which had to be swallowed or smoked or steamed. A magician caused or cured illness, but no one knew how this was done. The holy man treated the sick by a ceremony that included his sacred symbols and objects (Walker 1980:92-93).

Curing rituals included songs, prayers, medicines and activities designed to attract the help of the supernaturals. Sometimes the shaman was able to remove objects which were causing the problem. In the case of Bear-Looks-Out's daughter mentioned above, Strikes-Many-Women asked her husband Small Ankle to begin the cure with the skills he had received in a vision. He began by reciting his dream and directions for curing. Small Ankle made a mash of chokecherries, burned cedar incense and prayed. After eating the chokecherries, the girl began to feel better. Strikes-Many-Women then continued the cure with her prayers, songs and medicines, particularly peppermint and buffalo heart grease, which she rubbed on the girl. When the girl seemed much better, Strikes-Many-Women used a turtle shell from her sacred bundle to learn whether the girl would live or die (Bowers 1965:386-387).

Another way to seek a cure from the supernatural was to vow to sponsor a sacred ceremony. A man with a sick wife or child could vow to dance the Sun Dance or similar ceremony if the patient recovered. Sometimes it was only necessary for the man to vow to sponsor the dance and then find a sacred person to conduct it. At other times the man actually participated in the dance. Other kinds of ceremonies, such as the Midewiwin, Yuwipi and Holy Dance were held as curing ceremonies, too.

The Impact of European Settlement on Native Health

The general health of the Indians of the Northern Plains appears to have been satisfactory before the advent of the Europeans. The early visitors report that the Indians were vigorous, sturdy people.

The high infant mortality rate was offset by the birthrate, and the populations were generally stable. New diseases introduced by Europeans, however, had a devastating impact upon the tribal population. Whooping cough, influenza, diptheria, measles, chickenpox and cholera were dangerous to Europeans, but Indians had little or no immunity to these diseases, and so the impact was deadly. The traditional beliefs about the causes of disease could neither explain the new diseases nor why the Europeans were less affected by them, and so the physical affects were exacerbated by psychological problems. Other health hazards, in the form of alcohol and dietary changes, were also created by European-Americans.

Smallpox has been considered the greatest scourge of Tribal People, but other contagious diseases, like measles, chickenpox and whooping cough were very serious, too. Lehmer and Jones (1968:90-91) discuss the impact of European diseases, particularly smallpox, on the Arikara. Citing a study by Stearn and Stearn (1945), Lehmer and Jones identify four major outbreaks of smallpox on the Upper Missouri: 1780-1781 (or 1781-1782), 1801-1802, 1837-38 and 1856. These smallpox epidemics are documented in the literature, but earlier outbreaks are suggested by the winter counts, which mention epidemics in 1714, 1722, 1746 and 1762 (Howard 1976). Recognition and identification of smallpox epidemics in the winter counts is difficult, because the Indians did not call the disease smallpox. Undoubtedly, smallpox and other contagious diseases reached the plains long before the first White traders entered the area, because the diseases were transmitted from one tribe to another.

The impact of smallpox on native populations is clearly demonstrated by the reports of fur traders and other visitors. The smallpox epidemic of 1780 may have killed 75% of the Arikara. Truteau (Nasatir 1952,II:299), who visited the Arikara in 1795, says that the total effect of three outbreaks was to reduce the number of Arikara villages from thirty-two to two and the population of 4,000 warriors to about 500 men. Lewis and Clark (Reid 1947-48:60) reported a reduction from ten villages to three villages and noted that the Mandan had been reduced from thirteen villages to two. Detailed information on the impact of the smallpox epidemic of 1837 is available through Chardon, who was stationed at Fort Clark, and described the misery of the Indians. Chardon recorded in his journal the number of deaths and the way in which the people reacted to the deaths of their loved ones.

The smallpox virus was carried to Fort Clark by the steamboat St. Peter's which docked July 19, 1837. Although it was known that there were people on board who had smallpox, the captain considered it more important to continue the trip up the river than to return to St. Louis. The manner in which the disease moved from the boat to the Indian community is important, because a rumor arose that the United States government or Army gave blankets infected with smallpox virus to the Indians in order to cause their deaths. We have no evidence that such action ever occurred on the Upper Missouri, but a blanket, taken from a man ill with the disease, apparently started the smallpox epidemic among the Indians. However, three Indian women on the boat might have transmitted the disease to other members of the three tribes. Chardon's record indicates that those who did not die from the disease often committed suicide rather than live without their families. A number of ceremonial dances were held in vain attempts to ward off smallpox. People have also noted that the traditional tribal treatment for illness, the sweatlodge, would have been detrimental in the case of a disease like smallpox which included a high fever. The course of the disease reduced the Mandan to a population of around 150. A higher percentage of the Hidatsa and Arikara survived. Another consequence of the epidemic was to make the three tribes more vulnerable to attacks from the Lakota, some of whom had been vaccinated and so were less affected by the smallpox.

Before the Europeans, the tribes of the Upper Missouri and most parts of North America had no alcoholic beverages nor addictive drugs. Consequently, the introduction of liquor and the subsequent problems which alcohol caused must be directly attributed to non-Indians, who soon learned that

Indians could be made to hunt and trap furs in exchange for liquor. Charles Jean Baptiste Chaboillez, a fur trader whose post at Pembina attracted the Chippewa into the Red River Valley, kept a journal in which he noted the goods taken in and given out in trade. Daily entries indicated that anyone arriving at the post was given something to drink. In addition, Indians who brought furs and meat to trade were paid with rum and other goods. Gallons of rum were sent to the Indian camps in order to persuade the Indians to do what the fur trader wanted. The journal also recorded the frequent result of the exchange of rum for goods—lengthy drinking bouts, some of which required the intervention of the fur trader (Hickerson 1959). The pattern of drinking as a group activity during which all available liquor was consumed was established during the fur trade and continues today.

The disastrous effects of the presence of alcohol were so obvious that some tribes attempted to avoid its introduction to them and the Federal government prohibited the sale of alcoholic beverages to Indians in the Trade and Intercourse Act of 1802 (Prucha 1975:21). Despite these efforts, unscrupulous individuals continued to make liquor available to those Indians who wanted it, and Indians and non-Indians continued to appeal to the Federal government to enforce the laws against selling alcohol to Indians.

Changes in diet brought about by the introduction of foods new to Indians and the destruction of traditional sources of food, especially the buffalo, also adversely affected tribal health. Two major additions to the Native diet were salt and sugar. Salt had been available only in small amounts, and so most traditional recipes were made with little or no salt. Sugar, like salt, was available in limited amounts, either as sugar made from box elder or maple tree sap or as honey, and so while most Indians had a fondness for sugar, they were not often able to satisfy it. Traders made salt, sugar, coffee, wheat flour and many other goods available to Indian cooks. We have not isolated the changes in health that may have occurred because of the introduction of new foodstuffs, but some nutritionists believe that the high incidence of diabetes among contemporary Indian populations is due to these changes.

The other major change in diet was brought about by the destruction of the buffalo, the primary source of food for Plains Indians. It seems impossible that the millions of buffalo that roamed the plains could have been reduced to so few that there was fear for their extinction, but it happened. Farmers who fenced the plains, railroad builders, sportsmen hunters, buffalo hide hunters and the army had a hand in diminishing the size of the herds. In 1882, toward the end of commercial buffalo hunting, 200,000 hides were shipped east (Dary 1975:120). Certainly the army also recognized that the lack of buffalo would mean that Indians would have no reason to leave the reservations and that this would encourage them to adopt non-Indian ways, but the effect was much greater. The buffalo was not only a source of food and other necessities but a great symbol of strength to the Indian people. The failure of the buffalo herds to return not only resulted in starvation but also culminated in attempts like the Ghost Dance to encourage the buffalo to come back. Indians equated the loss of buffalo with the loss of supernatural power to combat illness and other problems.

Health During the Early Reservation Period

The interface between traditional tribal medicine and modern health systems began with the establishment of reservations. The treaties which reserved the land for Indian use also included provisions for doctors to be assigned to the reservations. The treaty makers recognized that tribal health had suffered from new diseases and that the changes in life style required by settlement on the reservation would cause additional problems. Thus, the provision for medical care was an important item in most treaties. Along with minimal health care, the treaties guaranteed food and agricultural assistance to help replace the wild plant foods and the buffalo that had been the mainstay of most Indian diets. Some treaties defined the amounts and kinds of foodstuffs while others were more general. All of the treaty provisions, however, were closely tied to the belief that Tribal People must adopt Euro-American ways and that food and medicine could be used to force the change. Many of the changes which the Federal government, agents, missionaries and other non-Indians thought were essential appeared less than sensible to the Indians. A group of Yanktonai who had established successful farms on the east bank of the Missouri were forced to move to the reservation and take up lands that were not so suitable for farming. Indians were told that they could hold social dances but no religious ceremonies, an indication of lack of understanding of the nature of Indian dances, all of which had religious significance. The most drastic influences on Indian health, however, were the changes in diet, the modifications in living conditions, the presence of chronic diseases and the introduction of new concepts of illness and its appropriate treatment.

Perhaps the greatest influence on tribal health was brought about by the changes in diet that occurred with reservation life. Not only were new foods made the dietary staples, but frequently an insufficient food supply provided neither a balanced diet nor an adequate intake of calories. The food and clothing promised to Indians by treaties were called "rations" and "annuities." Rations were distributed regularly while the annuities were distributed annually. Rations usually consisted of meat, either low grade beef or salted pork, flour, sugar, coffee, candles and soap. Because the authorities hoped that Tribal People would be forced to turn to agriculture for a living, the rations were always viewed as supplements to agricultural products and never as substitutes. Although many tribes had faced periods of starvation when they were dependent upon hunting and wild plant foods, the possibility of eventual relief through their own efforts remained. The new system provided little opportunity for relief and constant deprivation became the way of life for many Indians.

Successful farming was extremely difficult and there were only a few years when the produce from Indian agriculture was sufficient to carry a group through the winter. The agents at Fort Berthold frequently reported that the crops had failed and advised that stock ranching would be more suitable to the land and climate than agriculture. Dr. Washington Matthews, a surgeon with the United States Army at Ft. Berthold, spent a great deal of time learning Hidatsa culture which he reported on in a monograph published by the United States Geological Survey in 1887. Matthews described some of the effects of the change in the Indian diet:

> ...When subsisting for the most part on fresh meat, these Indians had the soundest gums and teeth; and no flesh when wounded healed more rapidly than theirs. Lately, however, since the increase in the consumption of bacon and flour among them, and the destruction of their game, there have been many cases of scurvy, a disease which was particularly fatal to them in the winter of 1868-96; and a tendency to abscesses, to suppurative terminations of diseases, and to a sluggish condition of wounds, manifests itself (Matthews 1877:25).

Matthews goes on to note that in the past ten years many Hidatsa, Mandan and Arikara had died of hunger or diseases brought on by starvation (Matthews 1877:32).

Living conditions may also have contributed to ill health. Most tribes, even those who occupied the earthlodge villages, spent part of the year away from the villages. Leaving the villages allowed the refuse that had accumulated during their occupation to deteriorate and any vermin to die. Settlement of the reservations meant that people were forced to live year round in one place and without modern sanitation facilities, dirt and waste became problems. Reports of the final years of Like-A-Fishhook Village suggest the extent of the problems. Conditions were somewhat different at other reservations, because the tribes were used to living in tipis rather than in permanent houses, and so for these people the change to a settled way of life brought the need to adapt to a totally different life style as well as the problems of adequate housing and sanitation.

Most of the diseases that afflicted Tribal People during the early reservation period were chronic diseases like tuberculosis which are attributable to poor living conditions and insufficient diet. The contagious diseases like smallpox had done their work, and the physicians were able to provide vaccines for those who were not made immune by exposure to the disease. Measles and chickenpox continued to break out from time to time.

The health problems of Indians continued to be graver than those of non-Indians until quite recent times. The Meriam Report (Meriam 1928) concluded that Indians suffered from high death rates, high tuberculosis rates, high incidence of trachoma, inadequate health facilities, improperly qualified personnel, deficient diets, poor preventive medicine programs, and substandard living conditions. In 1955 another study of Indian health cited tuberculosis, pneumonia and other respiratory diseases, diarrhea and other enteric diseases, accidents, eye and ear diseases and defects, dental disease and mental illness as the urgent health problems of Indians (American Indian Policy Review Commission Task Force 1976e:39). Since 1955, when the Public Health Services assumed control of Indian health services, some striking changes in Indian health have occurred in the reduction in death rates, particularly those from chronic diseases, and in increased availability of medicine to reservation populations, although new anxieties about diabetes and alcoholism have risen.

Present-Day Health Issues

Indian health problems, despite gains made since 1955, continue to be greater than those of non-Indians. The overall death rate is higher than for the general population, and the average age of death is younger for Indians. Some diseases, especially diabetes, occur in much greater frequency, and some communicable diseases which are so rare in the average population that they are no longer included in statistical reporting, still afflict Indian people in significant numbers. A number of programs aimed at improving all aspects of Indian health, including the training of Indian personnel to staff clinics and hospitals, specific research focused upon diseases which particularly impact Tribal People, and increased funding for nutrition and preventive programs have been developed to eliminate the disparities between Indian and non-Indian well-being.

Extreme caution should be used in evaluating the statistical evidence for Indian health because the figures are not actually comparable. The calculations for the national health picture are based on the population as a whole and are often adjusted to take into account specific age differences in health status. Today's figures for the Indian population represent only those people who are served by the Indian Health Service, which is about half the total Indian population, and the rate is based on figures from the census or vital statistics bureau. The statistics for Indian health are not usually adjusted for age differences, and the population is so small that figures are often calculated for three year groups instead of for a single year.

Communicable diseases, particularly those associated with poverty or substandard living conditions, continue to cause problems for a certain segment of the tribal population. Although statistics indicating the rate of many communicable diseases are no longer kept for the general population, the few that are available for comparison indicate the extent of the disparity between Indians and non-Indians. Table 15.1 compares rate per 100,000 for Indians and all others in the United States for diseases which have comparable figures. The rate per 100,000 or 1,000 is calculated from the actual number of cases in a given population and is used so that populations of varying sizes may be compared. The figures given here are for only Indians living on or near reservations or served by urban Indian clinics. The high incidence of contagious diseases like chickenpox, measles, mumps and whooping cough can be attributed in part to those Indians who live in rural areas and do not get the immunizations required in more urban areas. Tuberculosis, rheumatic fever, trachoma and other diseases are correlated with living conditions and nutrition. Other diseases that affect Indian people in significant numbers are no longer considered serious in the general population and records of their incidence are no longer kept. One such illness, otitis media, an acute inflammation of the middle ear affecting children and resulting in hearing problems, is the health problem most frequently treated by the Indian Health Service. Some of the health problems can be traced to cultural variations in response to illness, some to living conditions, some to the availability of preventive medicine and early medical treatment and others to low income impact on nutrition.

An even more drastic change in Indian health status is reflected in the decline in neonatal mortality, which now approaches that of the country as a whole (Table 15.2). The infant mortality rate for Indian children remains almost twice as high as for Whites, but the breakdown into neonatal and post-neonatal deaths shows that the cause for the high rate is death between one month and one year, not related to the birth itself. The deaths of children in infancy can be related to the continued presence of communicable diseases and poor living conditions. The Federally funded program Women, Infants and Children (WIC) which provides nutrition supplements to pregnant and lactating low income women and to their children under five years of age is probably most responsible for the decline in infant mortality. Not only does the program provide an adequate diet for women during their pregnancy, but pregnant women get regular checkups that can prevent the development of life-threatening or fetal endangering situations. Youngsters also receive regular checkups while on the WIC Program, and this program has been helpful in treating childhood illnesses in their early stages.

Table 15.1. Rates of Reported New Cases of Notifiable Diseases, 1978 (Rate per 100,000 population)

	Indians and Alaska Natives	U.S. All Races
Chickenpox	547.6	80.4
Gonococcal Infections	1219.9	468.3
Hepatitis, infectious	361.0	13.5
Measles (rubeola)	40.7	12.3
Meningitis, aseptic	13.2	3.0
Mumps	94.4	7.8
Rheumatic fever	66.8	0.6
Rubella (german measles)	23.4	8.4
Salmonellosis	13.4	13.5
Syphilis, all forms	88.9	30.0
Tuberculosis, new active	66.0	13.1
Typhoid fever	0.1	0.2
Whooping cough	4.0	1.0

Taken from U.S. Public Health Reports, Indian Health Service, 1979.

Table 15.2. Infant mortality rates, by race, 1986.

Category	Neonatal	Postneonatal	Infant
White	5.8	3.1	8.9
Native American	5.0	5.3	10.3
Black	11.7	6.3	18.0
Japanese	2.5	5.3	4.0
Other	4.0	1.6	5.9

Rates per 1000 live births.
Neonatal is 0-28 days,
Postneonatal is 28 days to 1 year.
Infant mortality is 0-1 year.

Source: *Health Status of the Disadvantaged: Chartbook 1990.* U.S. Department of Health and Human Services. Tables 23, 24, 25.

Death rates and causes of death (Tables 15.3, 15.4) clearly indicate that Indian health problems are different from those of the rest of the population, although this record is changing rapidly. The death rate for Indians, despite improvements in Indian health, continues to be greater than the death rate for non-Indians. The causes of death vary greatly, not only between non-Indians and Indians, but from reservation to reservation. A leading cause of death for Indians is accidents, particularly motor vehicle accidents. The reason for these accidents may be that reservations are in rural areas necessitating driving great distances over roads that may not be well-surfaced. Because of ill-operating automobiles, the high accident rate may be charged to the nature of the vehicles, as well as to the kinds of driving situations. Cancer and heart disease, the leading causes of death among the national population as a whole, are not so important to Indians. On the other hand, cirrhosis, most often resulting from heavy drinking, is a much greater worry for Indians, and adult onset diabetes affects twice as many Indians as non-Indians.

The impact of diabetes is great, not only as a cause of death, but because the quality of life is reduced and the disease contributes to other causes of death. Adult onset diabetes occurring in people, usually women, over the age of thirty-five, is often treatable through diet and supplementary insulin. For Tribal People, however, the changes in diet can be unmanageable because of low-income or food preferences that are not permitted to the diabetic person. In recent years attempts have been made to evaluate the impact of diabetes on the whole family and to focus upon helping all of the family to deal with the diabetic person. Uncontrolled diabetes can result in loss of limbs due to poor blood circulation, blindness, kidney and other organ failure. An increasing number of elderly Indian people are having their legs amputated because of the side-effects of diabetes. Other health matters may not lead directly to death, but like diabetes, they affect the quality of life for the individual and the people around them. One such problem is alcohol abuse which most Indians feel is the leading health problem. There are a number of characteristics of drinking that make it difficult to judge the extent of the problem. Obtaining adequate statistics on alcohol use by different populations is impossible. Lacking statistical evidence, we are forced to rely on cultural explanations for differences between Indian and non-Indian drinking.

Table 15.3. Leading Causes of Death, Age-Adjusted Rate Per 100,000 Population, 1986-1988.

	U.S. All Races	Indian and Alaska Natives	Aberdeen Area
All Causes	541.7	551.4	1067.5
Major Cardiovascular Disease	216.8	166.9	
Diseases of the Heart	175.0	135.4	288.5
Cerebrovascular Diseases	31.0	24.1	47.8
Atherosclerosis	3.7	3.5	4.5
Hypertension	5.0	1.7	1.9
Malignant Neoplasms	133.2	83.4	151.1
Accidents	35.2	83.2	135.5
Motor Vehicle	19.4	47.7	72.6
All Other	15.7	35.5	62.9
Chronic Liver and Cirrhosis	9.2	26.4	63.9
Diabetes Mellitus	9.6	20.6	35.4
Pneumonia and Influenza	13.5	15.2	37.9
Homicide	9.0	16.3	25.4
Suicide	11.9	15.0	25.2
Chronic Obstructive pulmonary diseases and allied conditions	18.8	9.6	30.4
Tuberculosis	0.5	2.1	7.3

Source: *Health Status of Minorities and Low-Income Groups.* 1991. U.S. Department of Health and Human Services. Table 15.

Because many reservations are dry, the person who wishes to drink must drive to bars off the reservation. The result is a public perception that many Indians are drinkers and have more frequent contact with the law. Continuing a pattern established during the fur trade, Indians are more likely to drink as part of a group and are likely to remain with the group until the supply is gone. "Binge drinking" calls attention to the group whereas the non-Indian pattern of drinking at home or at small parties does not. A number of studies have documented the different patterns of drinking behavior between Indians and non-Indians (Kline and Roberts 1972, Levy and Kunitz 1975, Task Force on Indian Alcoholism 1969). Not only is drinking a form of social behavior, but this behavior is much more common among young men. Differences between tribes appear to be related to whether the traditional tribal culture permitted people to behave uncontrollably or whether a person was expected to maintain self-control at all times. The problem drinker seems to develop earlier among Indian people than among non-Indians and Native People have more serious consequences from drinking than do other populations.

Explanations for Indian drinking behavior are varied. Some researchers have suggested that drinking functions to relieve tensions by making aggressive or immoderate behavior more acceptable. Drinkers are allowed to get away with saying things or doing things that would not be acceptable if they were sober. Since drinking is a group activity , drinking may also promote group solidarity, and in urban

Table 15.4. Leading Causes of Death, North Dakota Reservations, Age-Adjusted Rate Per 100,000 Population, 1986-1988.

	Fort Berthold	Fort Totten	Standing Rock	Turtle Mountain
All Causes	759.2	851.3	1295.8	993.0
Diseases of the Heart	211.9	164.3	315.8	353.3
Cerebrovascular Diseases	25.4	66.8	54.6	62.7
Atherosclerosis	0.0	0.0	0.0	21.4
Hypertension	0.0	0.0	0.0	0.0
Malignant Neoplasms	115.2	61.7	208.2	174.8
Accidents	120.8	232.4	216.4	83.1
Motor Vehicle	53.0	75.6	77.7	61.4
All Other	67.9	156.8	138.8	21.8
Chronic Liver and Cirrhosis	38.4	59.3	55	53.5
Diabetes Mellitus	60.5	16.8	60.2	11.4
Pneumonia and Influenza	35.1	7.5	57.9	40.8
Homicide	23.9	27.4	46.0	6.9
Suicide	20.5	33.8	22.4	11
Chronic Obstructive pulmonary diseases and allied conditions	23.6	20.5	23.0	42.8
Tuberculosis	0.0	0.0	0.0	12.1

Source: *Aberdeen Area Profile*. Indian Health Service, 1993.

areas, drinking often provides the only way for people to socialize. Studies have also shown that many Indians are non-drinkers and that in Indian society much more positive support is given to a person to stop drinking than in non-Indian society. Once an Indian person has made a general announcement that he/she intends to stop drinking, other Indians give that person a lot of attention and encouragement. Older Indians are likely to refer to their years of sobriety as a proud accomplishment. People who fail to achieve their objective are not regarded as failures but are given credit for trying.

The negative aspects of alcohol abuse are obvious. The individual who drinks to excess not only endangers his or her own health but also contributes to the problems of others. Indian people have greater rates of cirrhosis than the general population. The damage done by alcohol abuse can be partially alleviated through proper nutrition and the high rate of alcohol-associated health problems probably reflects the state of Indian nutrition as much as it does the extent of the problem. Alcohol abuse also results in the individual coming into contact with law enforcement officials, either because the individual is driving while under the influence or because of crimes which he has committed while he was drinking. In addition, alcohol abuse can result in child neglect and child abuse, spouse abuse, family disintegration and other social problems. Fetal alcohol syndrome which can occur in children born to mothers who drink more than an extremely small quantity is a recently recognized problem (Dorris 1989). These additional aspects of drinking have made Indian people perceive alcohol as their greatest health problem.

The concern about alcohol-associated problems has resulted in many attempts to solve or ease the problem. Religions, such as the Native American Church, the Church of Latter Day Saints, and Pentecostals, which expressly prohibit drinking alcoholic beverages have increased their attendance in recent years. Alcoholics Anonymous groups familiar with Indian culture have been started on reservations. Programs such as the Red Road have been designed especially to work with Native alcohol problems. The success of the Alkali Lake Band of British Columbia in combating alcohol abuse has encouraged many tribes to take positive steps toward dealing with the problem. In North Dakota a program funded by the state legislature and administered through the North Dakota Indian Affairs Commission has started an education program on reservations. This program is designed to make school age children aware of the dangers of alcohol and other drugs. Half-way houses and other institutions have also been established on the reservations.

While alcohol is considered the major health problem, alcohol is also related to a series of other Indian health issues which have received less attention. Recent studies (Oetting and Beauvais 1982) have indicated an increase in the use of drugs by young Indians, and others have expressed concern that little attention is given to mental health issues affecting Indian people. Some studies have attempted to relate alcohol and drug abuse to psychological issues, particularly self-perception of one's place in either Indian or non-Indian society, but the results are not of high enough quality to allow judgements to be made.

Many researchers have proposed answers to the question of why Indians have high rates of alcohol abuse. Some researchers are investigating the possibility of a genetic difference that makes it more difficult for Indian people to drink safely. Some have suggested that alcoholism simply represents the extension of the pattern begun with the introduction of alcohol and that more experience will enable Indians to gain better control over their use of the product. Others have argued that the alcohol and drug usage reflects the serious psychological situation of life on the reservation. Taking away their culture and livelihood has left Tribal Peoples with a poor self-image and nothing to do except drink. One point made by some researchers is that reservations, because of their isolation, provide few opportunities for people to get together and drinking serves as a means of socializing. The answers are probably much more complicated and involve a multitude of cultural, physical, economic and psychological factors.

Provision of Health Services for Tribal Peoples

Health services are made available to Indian people under several different programs. All Indians are eligible for Federal programs which serve low-income segments of the population, such as Medicare and Medicaid, WIC, Food Stamps, and nutrition programs. Some of these programs require adjustment to Indian cultural values and so have not been utilized as much as they could be. The major provider of health care for Tribal People is the Indian Health Service (IHS).

The Indian Health Service grew out of the demands by physicians for better facilities for their patients. By 1900 several hospitals had been built on the larger Indian reservations, and attempts were made to get more health officials to the reservations. Service to Indians, however, continued to be minimal, and Indian health continued to be much worse than the national picture. In 1928 the Meriam Report concluded that Indian health was a major concern. Continuing complaints from both Indians and health officials resulted in shifting the department of Indian health from the aegis of the Bureau of Indian Affairs to the Public Health Service in 1955. Since 1950, the change in Indian health, as demonstrated by the statistical decline in infant mortality and communicable diseases and the increase in longevity, has indicated that this shift was successful. Problems remain, particularly those associated with providing adequate care to culturally different Tribal Peoples, many of whom live in remote areas, but the success has been marked.

Kane and Kane (1972:xi) have pointed out that the Indian Health Service is unique in its goal to provide comprehensive health care to a culturally diverse population. Other Federally funded health-care programs are aimed at specific populations or limited kinds of services. Such a general orientation naturally leads to problems. The Indian Health Service is the source of medical care, inpatient/outpatient treatment, emergency, pharmacy, optometry, dental, field health, preventive medicine, school health and environmental health for all Indians living on or near Federally recognized reservations and in some urban areas. In North Dakota the Indian Health Service operates, administers and staffs hospitals, clinics, and other programs. There are IHS hospitals at Belcourt and Fort Yates. Fort Berthold has the Minnetohe Health Center, located outside New Town, and smaller clinics at major population centers. Standing Rock Reservation also has clinics. Reservations like Fort Berthold and Fort Totten which do not have hospitals utilize the facilities of nearby hospitals through a contract arrangement with the Indian Health Service. The local health service agencies, or units, are linked into a bureaucratic structure that includes area offices, such as the one for the northern plains located in Aberdeen, South Dakota, and the head office in Rockville, Maryland. The area offices maintain records pertaining to Indian health, coordinate programs and serve as liaisons between the head office and the local service units.

One major problem centers around providing complete medical care to populations that are often scattered over large areas. In the late 1800's physicians who went to the reservations discovered that they would have to travel many miles in order to reach a patient. Although automobiles have made reaching remote areas quicker and easier, delivering health care in distant areas remains uncertain. In North Dakota a person may have to travel sixty miles or more to get to a hospital or to find special treatment. In such circumstances the patient may delay treatment until a condition becomes acute and is harder to treat. Diabetes is a disease that requires frequent monitoring, but since patients do not always feel ill, they may not make the effort to get the care they need. Serious side-effects can result. Other obstacles in the way of effective health include getting reservation residents to bring their children into the clinic for immunizations, getting women to seek early pre-natal care, and getting the elderly to accept the health care they may need. Some of the larger reservations have instituted mobile health units which can visit remote areas and provide regular health services, but most reservations rely on the patients to travel to the clinic or hospital.

Major criticisms of the Indian Health Service have been directed to the cultural differences between doctors and patients. Until recently few of the IHS staff were Indian, and the non-Indians were often neither familiar with the demands of rural health care nor with the particular needs of American Indians. One area of conflict has been between traditional healers and modern physicians. Indians commonly seek treatment by Indian traditional methods for diseases which are considered Indian. In many ways this approach to medicine is common to all people. In contemporary American culture, people seek professional treatment only when the situation does not react to self-treatment. Health professionals do not usually approve of patients treating themselves and so when Indian people prefer Indian medicine, the non-Indian physicians often become upset. Early physicians rejected tribal medical practices outright and spent considerable time trying to convince Indian people that non-Indian medical treatment was better. J.R. Walker's attempts to train Lakota healers in non-Indian ways were reciprocated, and the Lakota holy men taught him about their beliefs and practices.

More recently, some doctors and nurses have recognized that Indian medicine can help patients psychologically, and in some instances, physically. If a person feels better because a holy man has been involved in the cure, then the person will get better quicker. Colleges of nursing are giving great attention to cultural concerns of their patients, and this information is sure to benefit all people. Other cultural differences have to do with relationships between men and women, with different attitudes toward questions, differing perspectives on how people should behave and with different ideas about health in general. Indian men may not be comfortable with female health personnel and Indian women may not want to be treated by non-Indian men. Indian people find that answering personal questions required by the Indian Health Service is embarrassing for them. Such values may prevent people, particularly the elderly, from obtaining the services they need. Indian people sometimes complain that not enough attention is given to them, that the clinics and other services are too rushed and that medical decisions are made too quickly. All of these attitudes and values contrast with the way in which the traditional holy person acts, and so Indian people still prefer to find medical assistance that more nearly meets their expectations and beliefs.

Soon physicians who are more familiar with Indian culture will be available to practice on the reservations. Up until now the few Indians who have obtained medical degrees have been employed by the Federal government or by institutions who need minority representation, and few of these Indian people have ever practiced on the reservation or been involved in direct treatment of Indians. But this situation should change within the next few years as the students currently in medical school finish their training. The Indians Into Medicine (INMED) program at the University of North Dakota and similar Federally funded programs across the country are recruiting young Indians into medicine and providing support systems and financial aid for those who want to attend medical school. The results of these programs have been doctors, dentists, nurses and laboratory technicians who are able to take jobs on reservations.

Indian health is of great consequence to Indian and non-Indian people, because health relates to many other aspects of life. A person in good health is more able to deal with the stress of modern living while poor health increases stress. The major Indian health issues today are diabetes and alcohol abuse, not only because of the many people afflicted with these problems but because these diseases reach out to involve other members of the family, tribe and state. States and the Federal government have established numerous programs to deal with these and other health problems, but cultural factors have hindered the acceptance of such programs. Today, Indian people are receiving training in all health disciplines so that they may be able to integrate modern medicine with the many cultural factors that are involved in the acceptance of contemporary medical practices. These doctors, nurses, dentists and laboratory technicians will take positions on the reservations and be the transition between the old and the new in health care for all reservation residents.

Health has been, and remains, a matter of great concern for Indian people. Some health issues symbolize the conflict between Indian and European ways that began at contact. Other issues reflect the current economic situation or the continuation of traditional ideas about disease and curing. For most Indian people, however, poor health becomes a very personal issue when family members suffer more often and die younger than other Americans.

Chapter 16

A Glimpse Into the Future

What does the future hold for Tribal People? One hundred years ago the answer was thought to be assimilation and the eventual disappearance of tribal culture. Educational philosophies and Federal policies were aimed at hastening the expected disappearance. As recently as two decades ago, people still anticipated the absorption of Indians, first into a generalized "pan-Indian" culture, and then into the national population. Today we are less certain that assimilation will occur and we are no longer so positive that assimilation should occur. Four hundred years of contact have changed Indian culture without diminishing Indian tribal identities. An Indian "heart" persists even when dressed in cowboy boots and jeans. It lives in a suburban split level as easily as in a one room log cabin; in a motor home as often as in a tipi; in an M.D. as well as in a medicine man.

Those who prophesied the disappearance of American Indians based their forecasts on ethnocentric assumptions and failed to understand the difference between culture change and extinction. Societies may adopt some characteristics of other cultures without giving up their own culture. This ability to integrate new customs and ideas indicates a strong, healthy, growing society.

People and societies, like all living organisms, must grow and growth is change. From this point of view culture change is a sign of life, not death; of growth not decay. American Indian societies have adapted to new ideas and new ways; an indication of their strength not their failure. We may view American Indian change as bad or unhealthy because we have romantic notions about the "good old days" or because we see the problems caused by conflicts between tribal and modern life styles. Perhaps the rapidity with which modern life changes also causes us stress, yet few people who long for the "good old days," would want to return to washing clothes by hand or using a horse and buggy for transportation.

Recent research suggests that Tribal People are adapting to cultural changes in different ways. Indian populations are diversifying into traditional, transitional, marginal and bicultural orientations (Corfman 1979). These four groups are distinguished by their attitudes toward Indian and non-Indian cultures. The traditional people prefer to speak their native language and place great emphasis on maintaining as many Indian ways as possible. Non-Indian ways are not highly valued by the traditional Indian people. Transitional Indian people are oriented toward White culture. They do not speak their native language and are trying to teach their children to live in the same way as the non-Indians around them. Transitional people do not place much positive value on Indian ways or being Indian because they believe that Indian ways cannot survive in modern America. The bicultural people are at home in both traditional and non-Indian cultures and have positive attitudes toward both ways of life. Although the children of bicultural parents may have been raised in urban environments, they study their native language, attend powwows and spend time on the reservation with their more traditional relatives. The marginal people are those who have no positive feelings for either Indian or non-Indian culture. Marginal people are not comfortable with themselves as Indian but they do not want to be non-Indian. The members of this last group are often in the lowest socioeconomic class and have the least education and the most social/psychological difficulties. Although the research that defined these four different attitudes was concentrated on people living in an urban area, similar groups appear to exist on the reservations as well. Oetting and Beauvais (1982) found that their reservation-based elementary and high school students could also be grouped into these four categories on the basis of their answers to questions concerning attitudes toward Indian and non-Indian life styles. One major difference between the studies is in the relative sizes of the four groups. The urban study (Corfman) found that 23 percent of the families could be classed as bicultural; 22 percent as traditional; 47 percent were transitional and only 16 percent were considered to fall into the marginal category. The study of school-age reservation children found more than 50% of the children could be placed into the marginal category. The reservations, then, are not only the home of traditional tribal people, but may also be the location of those individuals who are having the greatest difficulty in adapting to the presence of non-Indians and contemporary American life.

Because the members of the traditional, transitional and bicultural groups have strong positive value orientations, these people seem to be better adjusted and more accepting of themselves and others than the marginal people are. The traditional Indians may also be found in the lowest socioeconomic levels but they may be less stressed by their position than the marginals, since not working is related to their identity as traditional Indians. On the other hand, the marginal population may have a wide variety of social and psychological problems. Oetting and Beauvais found that the marginal school children were more likely to be drug and alcohol users than the children of bicultural or traditional orientations.

These findings enable us to suggest what the future may hold for different Indian people. Tradition-oriented people will continue to be a reservoir of native language and customs for their families and for others. For tradition-oriented people the preservation of Indian ways will be a priority. Transitional Indian people may find themselves in a difficult position if their attempts to move into non-Indian cultures are prohibited by lack of education or employment opportunities. Successful transitional people will be assimilated into the general population, while unsuccessful people may find themselves moving into a marginal position. The bicultural group is likely to grow, particularly in urban settings. Education will benefit this group the most as they learn to feel more comfortable with their dual identities. The marginal people will continue to have difficulties of many different kinds. Programs designed especially for marginal people may help them or their children move into a category more psychologically satisfying than the marginal one, but prognosis is not good.

We should be aware that all four of these categories present Tribal People with enormous personal difficulties. Traditional-oriented people must find great internal strengths to support their ideas and values against societal pressures to change. Bicultural people always have a sense of schizophrenia or, as Indian people say, "living in two worlds." In addition, they may face pressures from both tribal and non-Indian societies to be role-models. Indian people attempting to make the transition from Indian to White ways risk being rejected by their culture of birth as well as their culture of choice. The problems of marginal people are well documented in numerous studies of reservation life. Indian writers have also used these people as protagonists in their novels.

How can we encourage the development of the bicultural approach toward both Indian and non-Indian cultures that seems to be the most satisfying and successful mode of adaptation? Education is one key. The move away from assimilationist thought of the past centuries may be partially responsible for the increased bicultural adaptation of younger Indians. Now that Indian identity and culture is being given a positive orientation in schools, children no longer have to choose one way over the other.

In off-reservation schools, Indian culture programs are important builders of confidence and a positive self-image for Indian children. If television, movies and textbooks provide children with some positive role models, Indian self-images and self-esteem might be further enhanced.

On the other hand, it may be necessary to devise different educational systems to meet the needs of these different orientations. A responsive educational system will recognize the right of some Indian people to establish schools that teach only Indian culture or, even more unorthodox, the right of some parents not to submit their children to a non-Indian education at all. Indian tribes may be accorded the same rights as the Amish and other conservative religious groups to educate their children in their own way.

The children of transitional and marginal parents may need special programs to help them deal with the stresses of their situation. Transitional children may need to be taught how to live comfortably in non-Indian environments. Marginal children may need programs that will provide them with a strong sense of self-worth and an understanding of the root of their problems.

Education will also precipitate some changes as more Indian people are available to serve Indians. The Bureau of Indian Affairs must eventually yield dominion to Indian people as the incumbents retire and are replaced by qualified Indian people. Indian control of the Bureau of Indian Affairs should result in a shift away from assimilationist policies toward support for Indian rights. Indian people will be designing programs for Indian people. Subtle changes in the attitudes of the administrators may give the Bureau a more "Indian" atmosphere.

Schools on and off the reservation will be staffed and administered by Indian people who will provide positive role-models for the students and more Indian-oriented curriculum. Ultimately we may find textbooks written by Indian educators specifically for Indian students.

One of the most obvious predictions is that the medical problems presently faced by the reservations will be met by Indian doctors, nurses and other health-care professionals. Progress toward this end may appear slow, but we know that it is occurring.

Other Indian people will take up the challenge of creating more responsive tribal governments. Some tribes will undoubtedly adopt a system of checks and balances similar to the Federal government. Other tribes may prefer to return to an older form that encourages consensus. Novel methods of dealing with the contemporary issue of factionalism may be found.

Economic development will arrive more slowly and it is likely that the process of young employables leaving the reservation to work will continue for many years. Hopefully, however, we will no longer regard this urbanization as a step toward assimilation or a sign of poor reservation conditions, but will understand it is merely a way of providing for the reservation inhabitants and maintaining the reservation as a reservoir of traditional culture. Urban Indians will rely on the reservation to provide the positive experience of Indian ways and reservation Indians will rely on urban Indians to assist them when they need what the city has to offer.

Lest this future glimpse appear too rosy, we should note that there will be dark shadows, too. The Federal government's control over Indian lands and policies makes further challenges to Indian sovereignty probable. The twenty year swing of the pendulum away from Self-determination toward Termination is due within the next decade and only extreme vigilance will prevent another disaster.

If 50 percent is an accurate estimate of the number of reservation inhabitants falling into the marginal category, then alcohol abuse, child abuse, suicide and related problems will not be successfully curbed without extensive cultural enhancement, economic, social, and medical programs. Alcoholism, child abuse and other socially-based problems tend to become permanent when children grow up in homes with such problems. An abused child all too often grows up to become an abusive parent.

Because Indian people have larger than average families we can predict that, without intervention programs, the problems will increase dramatically.

The Federal government and the state of North Dakota have established policies and proposals to deal with some of the reservation problems, but the expectation for continued support for such programs is grim. Much more probable are increased cuts in Federal and state programs. The impact of Federal funding cuts on tribal programs will be severe. Those who depend upon Federal grants or programs for their jobs will become unemployed. Unemployment means that people will have to move to urban areas, stressful for those educationally and psychologically unprepared for such a move, or face drastic changes in living conditions. Unemployment stress appears to correlate with increased alcohol abuse and the concomitant family problems. Programs for marginal people will be cut and these people will suffer additional losses in self-esteem.

Henrietta V. Whitemen, a Cheyenne educator, has thought about the future of Indian people and visualizes the ideal Indian person of the future as a combination of warrior, scholar and community activist (1976). "The warrior I envision is none other than an individual equipped with special, strategic skills to assume the fight for American Indian survival in a non-Indian-dominated world." The scholar will fill professional positions that deal with Indian people and the activist will work to create positive community-oriented programs. Whitemen closes her remarks with a popular quote from Sitting Bull that expresses Indian hopes for the future.

> Take the best of the white man's road, pick it up and take it with
> you. That which is bad leave alone, cast it away. Take the best of
> the old Indian ways—always keep them. They have been proven
> for thousands of years. Do not let them die.

References

Abel, Annie Heloise, editor
  1932   *Chardon's Journal at Fort Clark, 1834-1839.* Pierre: South Dakota State
          Department of History.
  1939   *Tabeau's Narrative of Loisel's Expedition to the Upper Missouri.* Norman:
          University of Oklahoma Press.

Ahler, Stanley A., Thiessen, Thomas D. Trimble, Michael K.
  1991   *People of the Willows: The Prehistory and Early History of the Hidatsa Indians.*
          Grand Forks: University of North Dakota Press.

Albers, Patricia
  1974   *The Regional System of the Devils Lake Sioux: Its Structure, Composition,
          Development and Functions.* Dissertation, Department of Anthropology,
          University of Wisconsin-Madison.

American Indian Policy Review Commission
  1976a   *Report on Tribal Government.* Washington, D.C.: U.S. Government Printing
          Office.
  1976b   *Report on Federal Administration and Structure of Indian Affairs.* Washington,
          D.C.: U.S. Government Printing Office.
  1976c   *Report on Federal, State, and Tribal Jurisdiction.* Washington, D.C.: U.S.
          Government Printing Office.
  1976d   *Report on Indian Education.* Washington, D.C.: U.S. Government Printing Office.
  1976e   *Report on Indian Health.* Washington, D.C.: U.S. Government Printing Office.
  1976f   *Report on Urban and Rural Non-Reservation Indians.* Washington, D.C.: U.S.
          Government Printing Office.
  1977   *Final Report of the American Indian Policy Review Commission, Volume I.*
          Washington, D.C.: U.S.Government Printing Office.

Anderson, Mary
  1992   "Census figures misleading." *Indian Country Today*, December 3, 1992.

Anquoe, Bunty
  1992   "Indians fall in poverty stats." *Lakota Times*, November 5, 1992.

Axtell, James
  1992   *Beyond 1492.* New York: Oxford University Press.

Bad Gun
  1908   Bad Gun (Rushing-After-The-Eagle). *Collections of the Historical Society of
          North Dakota* 2:465-470.

Bailey, R.
  1993   "Another delay in treaty payments." *Turtle Mountain Star.* December 20, 1993:1.

Bass, William and Terrell W. Phenice
    1975   Prehistoric Skeletal Material from Three Sites in North and South Dakota. In *The Sonota Complex and Associated Sites on the Northern Great Plains* by Robert W. Neuman. Nebraska State Historical Society Publications in Anthropology Number 6. Lincoln: Nebraska State Historical Society.

Berkhofer, Robert
    1978   *The White Man's Indian: Images of the American Indian from Columbus to the Present.* New York: Alfred A. Knopf.

Bismarck Tribune
    1981   *North Dakota Indians: A Time of Transition.* October 23, 1981.

Black Elk
    1953   *The Sacred Pipe.* Norman: University of Oklahoma. (Reprint Penguin Books 1971.)

Blakeslee, Donald J.
    1993   Modeling the Abandonment of the Central Plains: Radio carbon Dates and the Origin of the Initial Coalescent. In Prehistory and Human Ecology of the Western Prairies and Northern Plains, edited by Joseph A. Tiffany. *Plains Anthropologist Memoir 27.*

Bloomfield, Leonard
    1933   *Language.* New York: Holt, Rinehart and Winston.

Boller, Henry A.
    1868   *Among the Indians: Four Years on the Upper Missouri, 1858-1862.* Philadelphia. (Reprint Lakeside Classics; Bison Books 1972).

Bonham, Kevin
    1992   "Dakota Tribal Industries gets 3 military contracts." *Grand Forks Herald,* November 6, 1992.

Bowers, Alfred W.
    1950   *Mandan Social and Ceremonial Organization.* Chicago: University of Chicago Press. (Reprint Midway Reprints 1973).

    1965   Hidatsa Social and Ceremonial Organization. *Bureau of American Ethnology Bulletin* 194. Washington, D.C.: Smithsonian Institution and U.S. Government Printing Office.

Brackenridge, Henry M.
    1906   Journal of a Voyage up the River Missouri Performed in Eighteen Hundred and Eleven. In *Early Western Travels* edited by R. Thwaites, vol.6.

Bradbury, John
    1904   Travels in the Interior of America in the Years 1809, 1810, and 1811. In *Early Western Travels,* edited by R. Thwaites, vol.5.

Brakel, Samuel
    1978   *American Indian Tribal Courts: The Cost of Separate Justice*. Chicago: The
            American Bar Association.

Brasser, Ted. J.
    1975   Metis Artisans. *The Beaver*. Autumn: 52-57.
    1976   *"Bou'jou, Neejee!"*. Ottawa: National Museum of Man.

Bray, Edmund and Martha Coleman Bray
    1976   *Joseph N. Nicollet on the Plains and Prairies*. St. Paul: Minnesota Historical
            Society.

Brown, Donald E.
    1991   *Human Universals*. Philadelphia: Temple University Press.

Brown, Stuart E., Jr., editor
    1976   Letters from Dakota; or Life and Scenes among the Indians: Fort Berthold
            Agency, 1889-1890. *North Dakota History* 43:5-31.

Bureau of Indian Affairs.
    1973   *Aberdeen Area Statistical Data*. Aberdeen, South Dakota: Bureau of Indian
            Affairs, Aberdeen Area Office.
    1979   *Aberdeen Area Statistical Data*. Aberdeen, South Dakota: Bureau of Indian
            Affairs, Aberdeen Area Office.

Butler, William B.
    1976   Context. In Fay Tolton and the Initial Middle Missouri Variant, edited by W.
            Raymond Wood. *Missouri Archaeological Society Research Series No. 13*.

Carroll, John
    1986   *The Arrest and Killing of Sitting Bull*. The Arthur H. Clark Company.

Case, Rev. Harold
    1977   *100 Years at Fort Berthold*. Bismarck: Bismarck Tribune.

Cash, Joseph H. and Hebert T. Hoover
    1971   *To Be An Indian* New York: Holt, Rinehart & Winston.

Catlin, George
    1844   *Letters and Notes on the Manners, Customs and Condition of the North American
            Indians*. Philadelphia. (Reprint Dover Books 1973).

Cavalli-Sforza, Luigi Luca
    1991   Genes, Peoples and Languages. *Scientific American*, November, 104-110.

Chafe, Wallace L.
    1968   Language and Linguistics. In *An Introduction to Cultural Anthropology* edited by
            James A. Clifton. Boston: Houghton Mifflin Co.

Chapman, William
    1965   *Remember the Wind: A Prairie Memoir*. New York: J.B. Lippincott Company.

Clifton, James A.
    1989   *Being and Becoming Indian*. Chicago: The Dorsey Press.

Colson, Elizabeth
    1971   *Indian Reservations and the American Social System*. Paper read at 67th Annual Meeting of the American Anthropological Association, Seattle, Washington.

Cordeiro, Eduardo E.
    1992   The Economics of Bingo: Factors Influencing the Success of Bingo Operations on American Indian Reservations. In *What Can Tribes Do?* edited by Stephen Cornell and Joseph P. Kalt. Los Angeles: American Indian Studies Center, University of California.

Corfman, Eunice, editor
    1979   Families Today: A Research Sampler on Families and Children. Vol. 1. *Science Monographs* No. 1. Washington, D.C.: U.S. Department of Health, Education and Welfare; Public Health Service, Alcohol, Drug Abuse, Mental Health Administration.

Costo, Rupert and Jeannette Henry
    1977   *Indian Treaties: Two Centuries of Dishonor*. San Francisco: American Indian Historical Society.
    1980   Who is an Indian. *Wassaja/The Indian Historian* 13,15-18.

Coues, Elliot editor
    1897   *New Light on the Early History of the Greater Northwest: Manuscript Journals of Alexander Henry and David Thompson, 1799-1814*. (Reprint Ross and Haines 1965).

Cramer, Joseph L.
    1974   Drifting Down the Yellowstone River with Captain William Clark, 1806: A Pictographic Record of the Lewis and Clark Expedition. *Archaeology in Montana* 15:11-21.

Crawford, John
    1976   Michif: A New Language. *North Dakota English*, vol.1, no.4:3-10.

Crutsinger, Martin
    1993   "Unemployment improves slightly to 6.9 percent." In *Grand Forks Herald*, June 5, 1993.

Curtis, Edward S.
    1908   *North American Indians*. Vol.3, The Yanktonai, The Teton Dakota. Cambridge: The University Press.
    1909   *North American Indians*. Vol.5, The Mandan, The Hidatsa,The Arikara. Cambridge: The University Press.

Dary, David A.
    1975   *The Buffalo Book*. New York: Avon Books.

Deloria, Ella
    1944   *Speaking of Indians*. New York: Friendship Press.
    1967   Some Notes on the Yankton. *Museum News*, vol.28, nos.3-4:1-30.

Deloria, Vine, Jr.
    1970   *We Talk, You Listen: New Tribes, New Turf*. New York: Dell Publishing Company. (Reprint Delta Books 1972).
    1974a   *Behind the Trail of Broken Treaties: An Indian Declaration of Independence*. New York: Dell Publishing Company. (Reprint Delta Books 1974).
    1974b   *God is Red*. New York: Dell Publishing Company. (Reprint Delta Books).

Deloria, Vine, Sr.
    1971   Interview in *American Indian II* edited by John R. Milton. Vermillion, S.D.: University of South Dakota.
    1987   The Establishment of Christianity among the Sioux. In *Sioux Indian Religion* edited by Raymond DeMallie and Douglas Parks. Norman: University of Oklahoma Press.

Delorme, David P.
    1955   History of the Turtle Mountain Chippewa Band of Indians. *North Dakota History* 22,no.3:121-134.

DeMallie, Raymond
    1978   Pine Ridge Economy: Cultural and Historical Perspectives. In *American Indian Economic Development* edited by Sam Stanley. The Hague: Mouton Publishers.
    1982   Introduction to reprint edition of Lowie, *Indians of the Plains*.

DeMallie, Raymond and Douglas R. Parks.
    1987   The Establishment of Christianity among the Sioux. In *Sioux Indian Religion* edited by Raymond DeMallie and Douglas Parks. Norman: University of Oklahoma Press.

Denig, Edwin T.
    1961   *Five Indian Tribes of the Upper Missouri: Sioux, Arikaras, Assiniboines, Crees and Crows*. Edited by John C. Ewers. Norman: University of Oklahoma Press.

De Trobriand, Phillippe Regis
    1951   *Army Life in Dakota*. Edited by Lucille M. Kane. St. Paul,Minnesota: Alvord Commission.

Dewdney, Selwyn
    1975   *The Sacred Scrolls of the Southern Ojibway*. Toronto: University of Toronto Press. (Reprint 1977).

Dorris, Michael
    1989   *The Broken Cord*. New York:Harper & Row.

Dorsey, George
    1904   Traditions of the Arikara. *Carnegie Institution of Washington Publication* 17. Washington, D.C.: Carnegie Institution.

Dorsey, James O.
    1894   A Study of Siouan Cults. *Bureau of American Ethnology Annual Report* 11:156-200; 351-544. Washington, D.C.: U.S. Government Printing Office.
    1897   Siouan Sociology: A Posthumous Paper. *Bureau of American Ethnology Annual Report* 15:218-222. Washington, D.C.: U.S. Government Printing Office.

Dorsher, Mike
    1989   Last Stand on the Reservation. *Bismarck Tribune*, December 31, 1989.

Drumm, Stella
    1964   *Journal of a Fur-Trading Expedition on the Upper Missouri, 1812-1813.* New York: Argosy- Antiquarian.

Duratschek, Sister Claudia
    1947   *Crusading Along Sioux Trails.* St. Meinrads, Indiana: Abbey Press.

Eastman, Mary
    1849   *Dahcotah: or, Life and Legends of the Sioux Around Ft. Snelling.* New York: John Wiley.

Ewers, John C.
    1963/64 The Emergence of the Plains Indian as the Symbol of the North American Indian. *Annual Report of the Board of Regents of the Smithsonian Institution*: 531-544.
    1986   *Plains Indian Sculpture: A Traditional Art from America's Heartland.* Washington, D.C.: Smithsonian Institution Press.

E'Yanpaha
    1979   Tribe Operating Farm in the Warwick Area. May 1979, vol.4, no.4:1.

Fagan, Brian M.
    1991   *Ancient North America: The Archaeology of a Continent.* New York: Thames and Hudson.

Fletcher, Alice C.
    1888   *Indian Education and Civilization.* Bureau of Education Special Report to the Senate. Washington, D.C.:U.S. Government Printing Office.

Frison, George C.
    1965   Spring Creek Cave, Wyoming. *American Antiquity*, vol.31, no.1, 81-94.
    1968   Daugherty Cave, Wyoming. *Plains Anthropologist*, vol.13, no.2, 253-295.
    1978   *Prehistoric Hunters of the High Plains.* New York: Academic Press, Inc.

Getches, David, Daniel M. Rosenfeldt and Charles Wilkinson
    1979   *Cases and Materials on Federal Indian Law.* St. Paul, Minnesota: West Publishing Company.

Giago, Tim
    1992   Winners write history unless the winners are Indians. *Grand Forks Herald*, September 7.

Gillette, John M.
    1906   The Medicine Society of the Dakota Indians. *Collections of the State Historical Society of North Dakota* 1,no.5:459-474.

Gilman, Carolyn and Mary Jane Schneider
    1987   *The Way to Independence*. St. Paul: Minnesota Historical Society Press.

Gilmore, Melvin
    1919   Uses of Plants by the Indians of the Missouri River Region. *Bureau of American Ethnology Annual Report* 33:43-154. (Reprint University of Nebraska Press 1977).
    1927a   Arikara Tribal Organization. *Indian Notes* 4:322-350.
    1927b   Origins of the Arikara Silverberry Drink. *Indian Notes* 4:125-127.
    1928a   The Cattail Game of Arikara Children. *Indian Notes* 5:316-318.
    1928b   The Making of A New Head Chief by the Arikara. *Indian Notes* 5:411-418.
    1930a   The Arikara Book of Genesis. *Michigan Academy of Science, Arts and Letters, Papers* 12:95-120.
    1930b   Notes on gynecology and obstetrics of the Arikara Tribe. *Michigan Academy of Science, Arts and Letters, Papers* 14:71-81.

Goddard, Ives
    1978a   Eastern Algonquian Languages. In *Handbook of American Indians* vol.15 edited by Bruce Trigger. Washington, D.C.: Smithsonian Institution Press.
    1978b   Central Algonquian Languages. In *Handbook of American Indians* vol. 15 edited by Bruce Trigger. Washington, D.C.: Smithsonian Institution Press.

Gourneau, Charles
    1988   *Old Wild Rice*. Belcourt, North Dakota.

Gourneau, Patrick (Aun nish e nau bay)
    1971   *History of the Turtle Mountain Band of Chippewa Indians*. Belcourt, North Dakota.

Grand Forks Herald
    1980a   Reservation Natives Pose Officials Extradition Woes. June 30, 1980.
    1980b   N.D. Won't Rule on Tribal Judgements. July 14,1980: 10B.
    1992   Standing Rock cancels contract with gaming company. November 7,1992.
    1993a   Sioux tribe buys food distributor. September 2, 1993.
    1993b   Three Affiliated Tribes get $700,000 in profits. September 28, 1993.
    1993c   Duluth, tribe battle over casino profits. September 19, 1993.

Greenberg, Joseph H., Turner, Christy G., and Stephen L. Zegura
    1986   The Settlement of the Americas: A Comparison of the Linguistic, Dental and Genetic Evidence. *Current Anthropology*, vol.27, no.5:477-497.

Gregg, Michael L.
1985   An Overview of the Prehistory of Western and Central North Dakota. *Cultural Resources Series, Number 1*. Billings, Montana: Bureau of Land Management.

Gridley, Marion
1960   *Indians of Today*. Chicago: Indian Council Fire.

Grimm, Thaddeus C.
1985   Time-Depth Analysis of Fifteen Siouan Languages. *Siouan and Caddoan Linguistics*, June, 1985.

Grinnell, George Bird
1923   *The Cheyenne Indians: Their History and Ways of Life*. New Haven: Yale University Press.

Gudschinsky, Sarah C.
1956   The ABC's of Lexicostatistics (Glottochronology). *Word* 12:175-210.

Gun that Guards the House
1908   Story of a Medal, Related by its Owner, Gun-That-Guards a House. *Collections of the State Historical Society of North Dakota* 2:470-473.

Haberman, Thomas W.
1978   *Archaeological Test Excavations at Lake Tewaukon* (32SA211): A Protohistoric occupation Site in *Southeastern North Dakota*. Grand Forks: University of North Dakota Department of Anthropology and Archaeology.

Hagan, William T.
1961   *American Indians*. Chicago: University of Chicago Press.
1966   *Indian Police and Judges*. New Haven: Yale University Press.

Hanson, Marshall
1962   *Plains Indian and Urbanization*. Dissertation, Department of Anthropology, Stanford University.

Hassrick, Royal
1964   *The Sioux: Life and Customs of a Warrior Society*. Norman: University of Oklahoma Press.

Hendrickson, Lucille
1981   North Dakota Indians: A Time of Transition. In *Bismarck Tribune*, October 1981.

Hesketh, John
1923   History of the Turtle Mountain Chippewa. *Collections of the State Historical Society of North Dakota* 5:85-154.

Hickerson, Harold
    1956   The Genesis of a Trading Post Band: The Pembina Chippewa. *Ethnohistory*
               3:289-345.
    1959   The Journal of Charles Jean Baptiste Chaboillez, 1797-1798. *Ethnohistory* 6:265-
               316; 363-427.

Hilger, Sister M. Inez
    1959   Some Customs of the Chippewa on the Turtle Mountain Reservation of North
               Dakota. *North Dakota History* 26, no.3:123-125.

Hodge, Frederick W.
    1907   *Spanish Explorers in the Southern United States: 1528-1543.* New York: Charles
               Scribner's Sons.

Hodge, William
    1981   *The First Americans: Then and Now.* New York: Rinehart and Winston.

Hoffman, Walter
    1884   The Mide'wiwin or "Grand Medicine Society" of the Ojibwa. *Seventh Annual
               Report of the Bureau of American Ethnology.*

Hoover, Herbert T.
    1980   Sitting Bull. In *American Indian Leaders: Studies in Diversity* edited by David R.
               Edmunds. Lincoln: University of Nebraska Press.

Horan, James
    1986   *The McKenney-Hall Portrait Gallery of American Indians.* New York: Bramhall
               House.

Howard, James H.
    1952b   A Yanktonai Dakota Mide Bundle. *North Dakota History* 19, no.2:133-139.
    1953   Notes on Two Dakota Holy Dance Medicines and Their Uses. *American
               Anthropologist* 55, no.4:608-609.
    1955a   The Tree Dweller Cult of the Dakota. *Journal of American Folklore* 68:462-472.
    1955b   Two Dakota Winter Count Texts. *Plains Anthropologist* 5:13-30.
    1966a   *The Dakota or Sioux Indians: A Study in Human Ecology.*Dakota Museum:
               University of South Dakota, Vermillion. (Reprint J. & L. Reprint Co. 1980).
    1966b   *The Plains Ojibwa or Bungi.* Dakota Museum: University of South Dakota,
               Vermillion. (Reprint J. & L. Reprint Co. 1977).
    1972   Notes on the Ethnogeography of the Yankton Dakota. *Plains Anthroplogist*
               17:281-307.
    1976   The John K. Bear Winter Count. *Plains Anthropologist Memoir* 11.
    1984   *The Canadian Sioux.* Lincoln: University of Nebraska Press.

Howard, James and Wesley Hurt
    1952   A Dakota Conjuring Ceremony. *Southwestern Journal of Anthropology*, vol.8,
               no.3:286-296.

House Executive Documents, 2nd Session, 48th Congress, 1884-1885.

House Executive Documents, 2nd Session, 52nd Congress, 1892.

Huddleston, Lee Eldridge
    1967   *Origins of the American Indians*. Austin: University of Texas Press.

Hunt,David and Marsha Gallagher
    1984   *Karl Bodmer's America*. Lincoln: University of Nebraska Press.

Hurt, Wesley R.
    1969   Seasonal Economic and Settlement Pattern of the Arikara. *Plains Anthropologist*,
            14:32-37.

Hurt, Wesley and James H. Howard
    1950   Two Newly-Recorded Dakota House Types. *Southwestern Journal of
            Anthropology* 6, no.4:423-427.

Iyan Woslate Wo-Oyake (Standing Rock History) n.d. Fort Yates, N.D.: Standing Rock Sioux Tribe.

Jacobson, Clair
    1980   A History of the Yanktonai and Hunkpatina Sioux. *North Dakota History* 47, no.
            1:4-24.

James, Edwin
    1956   *Narrative of the Captivity and Adventures of John Tanner*. Minneapolis:Ross and
            Haines, Inc.

Jenks, Albert E.
    1898   The Wild Rice Gatherers of the Upper Great Lakes. *Bureau of American
            Ethnology Annual Report* 19:1013-1137. Washington, D.C.: U.S. Government
            Printing Office. (Reprint J. & L. Reprint 1977).

Joyes, Dennis C. and Tom Jerde
    1970   Northeastern Montana Archaeology. *Archaeology in Montana*, 11 (4):1-14.

Kane, Robert L. And Rosalie A. Kane
    1972   *Federal Health Care (With Reservations!)*. New York: Springer Publishing Co.

Kappler, Charles J.
    1904   *Indian Affairs, Laws and Treaties*. Washington, D.C.: U.S. Government Printing
            Office.

Keating, William H.
    1824   *Narrative of an Expedition to the Source of St. Peter's River, Lake Winnipeek,
            Lake of the Woods, etc. Performed in the Year 1823*. (Reprint Ross & Haines
            1959).

Kingman, A. Gay
 1991 The Duro Decision: Criminal Misdemeanor Jurisdiction in Indian Country. Hearing before the Committee on Interior and Insular Affairs, House of Representatives. Serial No.102-4.

Kline, James H. and Arthur C. Roberts
 1972 A Residential Alcoholism Treatment Program for American Indians. *Quarterly Journal of Studies on Alcohol* 34.

Kofski, Jim
 1979 Tribal Judge: Ouster Risks Court's Future. *Grand Forks Herald*, May 18, 1979:3A.

Lake Mohonk Conference Proceedings
 1885 *Annual Address to the Public*. Philadelphia: Indian Rights Association.

Lame Deer, John (Fire) and Richard Erdoes
 1972 *Lame Deer: Seeker of Visions: The Life of a Sioux Medicine Man*. New York: Simon and Schuster.

Landes, Ruth
 1968a *Ojibwa Religion and the Midewiwin*. Madison: University of Wisconsin Press.
 1968b *The Mystic Lake Sioux: Sociology of the Mdewakantonwan Santee*. Madison: University of Wisconsin Press.

Laubin, Reginald and Gladys
 1957 *The Indian Tipi*. (Reprint Ballantine Books 1965).

La Verendrye, Pierre Gaultier de Varennes Sieur de
 1927 *Journals and Letters of Pierre Gaultier de Varennes Sieur de la Verendrye and his Sons*. Edited by Lawrence J. Burpee. Toronto: The Champlain Society.

Law, Laura
 1953 *History of Rolette County, North Dakota and Yarns of the Pioneers*. Minneapolis: Lund Press.

Lawson, Richard
 1982 *Dammed Indians*. Norman: University of Oklahoma Press.

Law Week
 Oliphant and Belgarde v. Suquamish Tribe. 46:4292-4306.

Leakey, Richard and Levin, Roger
 1977 *Origins*. New York: E. P. Dutton Co.

Lehmer, Donald J.
 1971 Introduction to Middle Missouri Archaeology. *National Park Service Anthropological Papers* 1. Washington, D.C.: U.S. Department of the Interior.

Lehmer, Donald J. and David T. Jones
    1968   Arikara Archaeology: The Bad River Phase. *Smithsonian Institution River Basin Surveys Publications in Salvage Archaeology*, No. 7. Lincoln, Nebraska.

LeMay, Konnie
    1992   Non-Indian communities win too with gaming. *Winners Circle* (Indian Country Today Special Edition) November 5, 1992.

Levitan, Sar and Elizabeth I. Miller
    1993   *The Equivocal Prospects for Indian Reservations*. Washington, D.C.: The George Washington University, Center for Social Policy Studies.

Levy, Jerrold E. and Stephen J. Kunitz
    1975   *Indian Drinking: Navajo Practices and Anglo-American Theories*. New York: McGraw-Hill.

Lincoln, Kenneth
    1993   Ind'n Humor. New York: Oxford University Press, Inc.

Lone Fight, Tony
    1993   DL SIOUX will open new casino in Tokio. *Grand Forks Herald,* July 2, 1993.

Lowie, Robert H.
    1913   Dance Associations of the Eastern Dakota. *Anthropological Papers of the American Museum of Natural History* 11:102-142.
    1913   Societies of the Hidatsa and Mandan. *Anthropological Papers of the American Museum of Natural History* 11:294-358.
    1915   Societies of the Arikara Indians. *Anthropological Papers of the American Museum of Natural History* 11:645-678.
    1917   Social Life of the Mandan. *Anthropological Papers of the American Museum of Natural History* 21:7-16.
    1919   The Hidatsa Sun Dance. *Anthropological Papers of the American Museum of Natural History* 16:411-431.
    1954   *Indians of the Plains*. New York: American Museum of Natural History. (Reprint with new introduction University of Nebraska Press 1982.)
    1956   *The Crow Indians*. New York: Holt, Rinehart and Winston. [Originally published 1935].

MacGregor, Gordon
    1948   Attitudes of the Fort Berthold Indians Regarding Removal from the Garrison Reservoir Site and Future Administration of their Reservation. *Missouri River Basin Investigation Report* 49, Billings, Montana.

Mallery, Garrick
    1893   Picture Writing of the American Indians. *Bureau of American Ethnology Annual Report* 4. Washington, D.C.: U.S. Government Printing Office.

Mandan, Hidatsa, Arikara Times
    1990   Shakopee Sioux Enjoy Proceeds from Bingo. January 11, 1990.

Mandelbaum, David
    1940   The Plains Cree. *Anthropological Papers of the American Museum of Natural History* 37:155-317. (New and revised edition Canadian Plains Research Center Saskatchewan 1979).

Matthews, Washington
    1873   *Grammar and Dictionary of the Language of the Hidatsa.* New York: Cramoisy Press. (Reprint AMS Press, Inc.)
    1877   Ethnography and Philology of the Hidatsa Indians. *U.S. Geological and Geographical Survey, Miscellaneous Publications* 7. (Reprint Plains Anthropologist 1969:14-45).

Mattison, Ray H.
    1954   The Army Post of the Northern Plains, 1865-1885 *Nebraska History* 35:17-43.
    1955   The Indian Reservation System on the Upper Missouri, 1865-1890. *Nebraska History* 36:141-172.

May, Hal, editor
    1985   Louise Erdrich. *Contemporary Authors.* Detroit, Michigan: Gale Research Company, Book Tower.

Maximilian, Prince Alexander Philip, of Wied-Neuwied,
    1906   Travels in the Interior of North America, 1832-1834. In *Early Western Travels,* vols. 22-25, ed. by R. Thwaites.

McCone, R. Clyde
    1966   Cultural Factors in Crime among the Dakota Indians. *Plains Anthropologist* 11:144-151.

McGee, W. J.
    1894   The Siouan Indians. *Bureau of American Ethnology Annual Report* 15:151-204. Washington, D.C.: U.S. Government Printing Office.

McGhee, Robert
    1984   Contact Between Native North Americans and the Medieval Norse: A Review of the Evidence. *American Antiquity*, vol.49, no.1, 4-26.

McGillicuddy, Julia
    1941   *McGillicuddy: Agent.* Stanford: Stanford University Press.

McLaughlin, James
    1910   *My Friend the Indian.* Boston: Houghton Mifflin Co.

McLuhan, T.C.
    1972   *Touch the Earth.* New York: Pocket Books.

McNickle, D'Arcy
    1978   *Wind from an Enemy Sky.* San Francisco: Harper and Row.

Meriam, Lewis et.al.
    1928   *The Problem of Indian Administration*. Baltimore: Johns Hopkins Press.

Meyer, Roy
    1967   *History of the Santee Sioux*. Lincoln: University of Nebraska Press.
    1977   *The Village Indians of the Upper Missouri*. Lincoln: University of Nebraska Press.

Minneapolis Tribune
    1979   *Picture Magazine*. November 18, 1979:1-58.

Montaigne, Fen
    1989   Standing Rock. *Philadelphia Inquirer*, February 26.

Morgan, Lewis Henry
    1871   Systems of Consanguinity and Affinity. *Smithsonian Contributions to Knowledge* 17. Washington, D.C.: Smithsonian Institution.

Moulton, Gary
    1983   *Atlas of the Lewis and Clark Expedition*. Lincoln: University of Nebraska Press.
    1987   *Journal of the Lewis and Clark Expedition*. Vol. 3. Lincoln: University of Nebraska Press.
    1993   *Journal of the Lewis and Clark Expedition*. Vol. 8. Lincoln: University of Nebraska Press.

Murray, Janice
    1974   Ella Deloria. PhD. Dissertation University of North Dakota.

Murray, Stanley N.
    1985   The Turtle Mountain Chippewa, 1882-1905. *North Dakota History*, 51 (1):14-37.

Nasatir, A. P.
    1952   *Before Lewis and Clark*. St. Louis: St. Louis Historical Documents Foundation.

Native American Justice Issues in North Dakota
    1978   Washington: U.S. Government Printing Office.

Neuman, Robert W.
    1975   The Sonota Complex and Associated Sites on the Northern Great Plains. *Publications in Anthropology* 6. Lincoln: Nebraska State Historical Society.

Neumann, Jim
    1981   Fort Totten School Construction Finally Becomes Reality. *The Fargo Forum*, July 27, 1981:9.

North Dakota Indian Affairs Commission
    1985   *Fact Sheet: Fort Totten, Fort Berthold, Standing Rock, Turtle Mountain*. Bismarck: North Dakota Indian Affairs Commission Office.

North Dakota Legal Services, Inc.
    1980   *Newsletter*. Vol. 1, no.2:1-8.

Oetting, E. R. and Fred Beauvais
    1982   *Drug Use among Native American Youth: Summary of Findings (1975-1981).* Western Behavioral Studies. Ft. Collins, Colorado: Colorado State University.

Olson, James A.
    1962   *Red Cloud and the Sioux Problem.* Lincoln: University of Nebraska Press.

Olden, Sarah Emilia
    1918   *The People of Tipi Sapa.* Milwaukee, Wis.:Morehouse Publishing Co.

Ortiz, Roxanne Dunbar
    1978   *The Great Sioux Nation: Sitting in Judgement on America.* San Francisco: Moon Books.

Oyaka Newsletter 1979

Parks, Douglas R.
    1979   Bands and Villages of the Arikara and Pawnee. *Nebraska History* 60:214-239.

Parman, Donald L.
    1976   *The Navajos and the New Deal.* New Haven: Yale University Press.

Pecore, Ed
    1987   *National Review*, May 8.

Peterson, Susan
    1985   Doing "Women's Work": The Grey Nuns at Fort Totten Indian Reservation, 1874-1900. *North Dakota History* 52 (2):18-25.

Pettipas, Leo
    1969   Early Man in the Swan River Valley, Manitoba. *Manitoba Archaeological Society Newsletter* 6(3):3-22.

Pfaller, Louis
    1978   *James McLaughlin: The Man With An Indian Heart.* New York: Vantage press.

Pond, Samuel W.
    1908   The Dakotas or Sioux in Minnesota as they were in 1834. *Minnesota Historical Collections* 12:319-501. (Reprint Minnesota Historical Society 1986.)

Powers, William K.
    1977   *Oglala Religion.* Lincoln: University of Nebraska Press.
    1982   *Yuwipi: Vision and Experience in Oglala Ritual.* Lincoln:University of Nebraska Press.

Provinse, John H.
    1937   The Underlying Sanctions of Plains Indian Culture. In *Social Anthropology of North American Indians*. Edited by Fred Eggan. Chicago: University of Chicago Press.

Price, John
    1979   *Native Studies: American and Canadian Indians*. New York: McGraw-Hill.

Prucha, Francis
    1971   *Indian Peace Medals*. Madison: Wisconsin State Historical Society.
    1973   *Americanizing the American Indians*. Cambridge, Massachusetts: Harvard University Press.
    1975   *Documents of United States Indian Policy*. Lincoln University of Nebraska Press.

Rahill, Peter J.
    1953   *The Catholic Indian Missions and Grant's Peace Policy, 1870-1884*. Washington, D.C.: The Catholic University of America Press.

Reader's Digest
    1979   Scalping at Crow Creek.

Reid, Russell
    1930   The Earthlodge. *North Dakota Historical Quarterly*, 4:174-185.

Reid, Russell, editor
    1947-48 *The Journals of Lewis and Clark in North Dakota*. Bismarck: North Dakota State Historical Society.

Riggs, Stephen
    1852   *Grammar and Dictionary of the Dakota Language*. Washington, D.C.: Smithsonian Institution.
    1890   A Dakota-English Dictionary. *Contributions of American Ethnology* 7. Washington, D.C.: U.S. Government Printing Office.
    1893   Dakota Grammar, Texts and Ethnography. *Contributions of American Ethnology* 11. Washington, D.C.: Department of the Interior.

Roberts, Ricky L.
    1977   Population Estimates. In The Talking Crow Site, edited by Carlyle Shreeve Smith. *University of Kansas Publications in Anthropology*, 9.

Robinson, Doane
    1904   History of Dakota or Sioux Indians. *Collections of the South Dakota State Historical Society* 2. (Reprint Ross and Haines 1956).

Robinson, Elwyn B.
    1966   *History of North Dakota*. Lincoln: University of Nebraska Press.

Rogers, Dilwyn J.
1980   *Lakota Names and Traditional Uses of Native Plants by* Sicangu (Brule) People in the Rosebud Area, South *Dakota.* St. Francis, South Dakota: The Rosebud Educational Society, Inc.

Ronda, James P.
1984   *Lewis and Clark among the Indians.* Lincoln:University of Nebraska Press.

Ross, Rupert
1992   *Dancing with a Ghost.* Markham, Ontario: Octopus Publishing Group.

Salter, Peter
1992   Cannon Ball's big boom. *Bismarck Tribune* October 4, 1992.

Sauer, Carl O.
1971   *Sixteenth Century North America.* Berkeley: University of California Press.

Scaletta, Sue Ellyn
1979   DLSMC Made Money from Day One. *Grand Forks Herald*, June 23,1979:4.

Schmidt, Steve
1994   A Future, without bars. *Grand Forks Herald* February 6, p.1.

Schneider, Fred
1975   *The Results of Archaeological Investigations at the Moe Site (32MN101), North Dakota.* Grand Forks, North Dakota: University of North Dakota Department of Anthropology and Archaeology.

Seymour, Flora Warren
1941   *Indian Agents of the Old Frontier.* New York: Appleton Century.

Sherzer, Joel
1976   An Areal-Typological Study of North American Indian Languages North of Mexico. *North-Holland Linguistic Series* 20. New York: Elsevier Publishing Company, Inc.

Shryock, Henry S., Jacon S. Siegel and Associates
1976   *The Methods and Materials of Demography.* Condensed edition by Edward G. Stockwell. New York: Academic Press.

Siebert, Frank Jr.
1967   The Original Home of the Proto-Algonquian People. In *Contributions to Anthropology. Linguistics* I. Ottawa: National Museum of Canada Bulletin 214.

Skinner, Alanson
    1914a   The Cultural Position of the Plains Ojibway. *American Anthropologist* 16:314-318.
    1914b   Notes on the Plains Cree. *American Anthropologist* 16:68-87.
    1914c   Political Organization, Cults and Ceremonies of the Plains Cree. *Anthropological Papers of the American Museum of Natural History* 11.
    1914d   Political and Ceremonial Organizations of the Plains Ojibway. *Anthropological Papers of the American Museum of Natural History*, 11.
    1919a   The Sun Dance of the Plains Ojibway. *Anthropological Papers of the American Museum of Natural History* 16:311-315.
    1919b   The Sun Dance of the Plains Cree. *Anthropological Papers of the American Museum of Natural History* 16:283-292.
    1919c   A Sketch of Eastern Dakota Ethnology. *American Anthropologist* 21:164-174.
    1919d   Notes on the Sun Dance of the Sisseton Dakota. *Anthropological Papers of the American Museum of Natural History* 16:381-385.
    1920   Medicine Ceremony of the Menomini, Iowa, and Wahpeton Dakota. *Indian Notes* 4:262-302.
    1925   Tree-Dweller Bundles of the Wahpeton Dakota. *Indian Notes* 2:66-73.

Smith, G. Hubert
    1972   Like-a-Fishhook Village and Fort Berthold, Garrison Reservoir, North Dakota. *Anthropological Papers* 2, National Park Service. Washington, D.C.: U.S. Department of Interior.

Sneve, Virginia Driving Hawk
    1973   *The Dakota's Heritage*. Sioux Falls, S. Dakota: Brevet Press.

Snipp, C. Matthew
    1989   *American Indians: The First of This Land*. New York: Russell Sage Foundation.

Sockbeson, Henry
    1990   Repatriation Act Protects Native Burial Remains and Artifacts. *NARF Legal Review*, Vol. 16, no.1:1-4.

Sorkin, Alan L.
    1971   *American Indians and Federal Aid*. Washington, D.C.: Brookings Institution.

Specktor, Mordecai
    1993   Court of Appeals Deals Setback to NSP's Nuclear Waste Dump at Prairie Island. *The Circle*, July, p.7.

Spencer, Robert, Jesse Jennings et al.
    1977   *The Native Americans*. New York: Harper and Row.

Stanley, Sam
    1978   *American Indian Economic Development*. The Hague: Mouton Publishers.

Statistical Abstract of North Dakota
　　　　1979
　　　　1991

Stearn, E. Wagner and Allen E.
　　　　1945　　*The Effect of Smallpox on the Destiny of the Amerindian*. Boston: Bruce
　　　　　　　　Humphries Inc.

Stewart, Frank H.
　　　　1974　　Mandan and Hidatsa Villages in the Eighteenth and Nineteenth Centuries. *Plains
　　　　　　　　Anthropologist* 19:287-302.

Stipe, Claude E.
　　　　1971　　Eastern Dakota Clans: The Solution of a Problem. *American Anthropologist* 73
　　　　　　　　(5):1031-1035.

Sturtevant, William and Sam Stanley
　　　　1978　　Indian Communities in the Eastern States. *The Indian Historian*, 1 (3):15-19.

Syms, E. Leigh
　　　　1970　　The McKean Complex in Manitoba. In *Ten Thousand Years: Archaeology in
　　　　　　　　Manitoba* edited by Walter Hlady. Winnipeg: Manitoba Archaeological Society.
　　　　　　　　123-139.

Taylor, Graham D.
　　　　1980　　*The New Deal and American Indian Tribalism*. Lincoln: University of Nebraska
　　　　　　　　Press.

Taylor, Joseph Henry
　　　　1932　　*Frontier and Indian Life and Kaleidoscopic Lives*. Washburn, North Dakota:
　　　　　　　　Washburn's Fiftieth Anniversary Committee.

Taylor, Robert B.
　　　　1973　　*Introduction to Cultural Anthropology*. Boston: Allyn and Bacon, Inc.

Theisz, Ronnie
　　　　1975　　*Buckskin Tokens: Contemporary Oral Narratives of the Lakota*. Aberdeen, South
　　　　　　　　Dakota: North Plains Press.

Thomas, Davis and Karin Ronnefeldt, editors
　　　　1976　　*People of the First Man: Life among the Plains Indians in their Final Days of
　　　　　　　　Glory: The Firsthand Account of Prince Maximilian's Expedition up the Missouri
　　　　　　　　River, 1833-1834*. New York: E. P. Dutton.

Thompson, David
　　　　1962　　*David Thompson's Narrative: 1784-1812*. Edited by Richard Glover. Toronto: The
　　　　　　　　Champlain Society.

Thwaites, Reuben Gold, editor

    1904-05 *Original Journals of the Lewis and Clark Expedition, 1804-1808.* New York: Dodd, Mead and Company.

    1906   *Travels in the Interior of North America, 1832-1834.* Vols.22-24 of Early Western Travels. Cleveland: Arthur H. CLark Co.

    1906   *Journal of a Voyage up the Missouri River; Performed in 1811 by Henry M. Brackenridge.* Early Western Travels vol.6.

Tucker, Bob

    1979   Indian Water Rights Issue Eventually May Erupt in N.D. *Grand Forks Herald,* May 20, 1979:8C.

Turner, Christy G.

    1989   Teeth and Prehistory in Asia. *Scientific American,* February, 88-96.

Turosak, Greg

    1981   North Dakota Indians: A Time of Transition. *Bismarck Tribune,* October 23.

Tyler, S. Lyman

    1973   *A History of Indian Policy.* Washington, D.C.: U.S. Department of the Interior, Bureau of Indian Affairs.

U.S. Bureau of the Census

    1973   *1970 Census of the Population, American Indians,* PC(2)1F. Washington, D.C.: U.S. Government Printing Office.

    1973   *1970 Census of the Population, Characteristics of the Population: North Dakota.* Washington,D.C.: U.S. Government Printing Office.

    1973   *1970 Census of the Population: U.S. Summary* PC(1)C1. Washington, D.C.: U.S. Government Printing Office.

    1983   *1980 Census of the Population, Characteristics of the Population: South Dakota.* Washington, D.C.: U.S. Government Printing Office.

    1983   *1980 Census of the Population, Characteristics of the Population: North Dakota, General Social and Economic Characteristics.* Washington, D.C.: U.S. Government Printing Office.

    1983   *1980 Census of the Population, Characteristics of the Population: Minnesota.* Washington, D.C.: U.S. Government Printing Office.

    1985   *1980 Census of the Population. U.S. Summary: American Indians.* Washington, D.C.: U.S. Government Printing Office.

    1991   *1990 Census of the Population, Summary Population and Housing Characteristics, North Dakota.* 1990 CPH-1-36.

    1993   *1990 Census of the Population, Social and Economic Characteristics, North Dakota.* 1990 CP-2-36.

U.S. Department of Commerce

    1971   *Federal and State Indian Reservations.* Washington, D.C.: U.S. Government Printing Office.

    1972   *Indian Economic Development: An Evaluation of EDA's Selected Indian Reservation Programs.* Washington, D.C.:U.S. Government Printing Office.

U.S. Department of Interior
    1964   Family Plan and Rehabilitation Programs, Standing Rock Reservation. *Missouri River Basin Investigations Project Report* No. 177. Billings, Montana.
    1971   The Fort Berthold Reservation Area: Its Resources and Development Potential. *Missouri River Basin Investigations Project* No.196. Billings, Montana.
    1973   Standing Rock Reservation: Its Resources and Development Potential. *Missouri River Basin Investigations* No. 206. Billings, Montana.
    1976   The Fort Totten Reservation: Its Resources and Development Potential. *Planning Support Group Report* No. 239. Billings, Montana.

United States Government Accounting Office
    1975   *Report to the Committee on Interior and Insular Affairs, U.S. Senate: Indian Natural Resources—Opportunities for Improved Management and Increased Productivity.* Washington, D.C.: U.S. Government Printing Office.

Valentine, Anne
    1979   Tribal Court Control is Challenged. *Grand Forks Herald*, June 13, 1979:1D.

Vecsey, Christopher
    1993   *Handbook of American Indian Religious Freedom.* New York: Crossroad.

Vestal, Stanley
    1932   *Sitting Bull.* New York: Doubleday and Co.

Vogel, Virgil
    1972   *This Country Was Ours.* New York: Harper & Row.

Waldman, Carl
    1988   *Encyclopedia of Native American Tribes.* New York: Facts on File Publications.

Walker, James R.
    1980   *Lakota Belief and Ritual.* Edited by Raymond J. DeMallie and Elaine A. Jahner. Lincoln: University of Nebraska Press.
    1982   *Lakota Society.* Edited by Raymond J. DeMallie. Lincoln: University of Nebraska Press.
    1983   *Lakota Myth.* Edited by Elaine A. Jahner. Lincoln: University of Nebraska Press.

Wallis, Wilson
    1921   The Sun Dance of the Canadian Dakota. *Anthropological Papers of the American Museum of Natural History*, 16:317-380.

    1977   The Canadian Dakota. *Anthropological Papers of the American Museum of Natural History* 41.

Warren, William
    1885   *History of the Ojibways.* St. Paul: Minnesota Historical Society. (Reprint Ross & Hains 1974).

Washburn, Wilcomb E. Editor
    1973   *The American Indian and the United States:A Documentrary History*. 4 volumes. New York: Random House.
    1976   The Historical Context of American Indian Legal Problems. In *American Indians and the Law* edited by Lawrence Rosen. Durham, North Carolina: Duke University Press.

Wedel, Waldo R.
    1981   Towards a History of Plains Archaeology. *Great Plains Quarterly*, vol.1, no.1.

Weibel-Orlando, Joan
    1991   *Indian Country, L.A*. Urbana: University of Illinois Press.

Weitzner, Bella
    1979   Notes on the Hidatsa Indians based on data recorded by the Late Gilbert L. Wilson. *Anthropological Papers of the American Museum of Natural History* 56,2:183-322.

Wheat, Joe Ben
    1978   Olsen-Chubbuck and Jurgens Sites: Four Aspects of Paleo-Indian Economy. In Bison Procurement and Utilization: A Symposium, edited by Leslie B. Davis and Michael Wilson. *Plains Anthropologist Memoir 14*.

White, Robert A.
    1970   The Lower Class "Culture of Excitement" Among the Contemporary Sioux. In *The Modern Sioux*. Edited by Ethel Nurge. Lincoln: University of Nebraska Press.

Whiteman, Henrietta V.
    1976   Spiritual Roots of Indian Success. In *Contemporary Native American Address*. Edited by John R. Maestas. Salt Lake City: Brigham Young University.

Wied-Neuwied, Prince Alexander Philip Maximilian of
    1843   *Travels in the Interior of North America*, 1832-1834. In Early Western Travels, vols. 22-24, Edited by Reuben Gold Thwaites.

Will, George F.
    1934   Notes on the Arikara Indians and their Ceremonies. *Old West Series*, 3:5-48.

Willey, P. and Thomas E. Emerson
    1993   The Osteology and Archaeology of the Crow Creek Massacre. In Prehistory and Human Ecology of the Western Prairies and Northern Plains, edited by Joseph A. Tiffany. *Plains Anthropologist Memoir* 27.

Wills, Bernt Lloyd
    1963   *North Dakota: The Northern Prairie State*. Ann Arbor, Michigan: Edwards Brothers, Inc.

Wilson, Gilbert L.

    1914   *Goodbird the Indian*. New York: Ravell Press. (Reprint Minnesota Historical Society 1985).

    1917   Agriculture of the Hidatsa Indians: An Indian Interpretation. *Bulletin of the University of Minnesota. Studies in Social Sciences* No.9. Minneapolis: University of Minnesota. (Reprint J. & L. Reprints 1977).

    1921   *Waheenee*. St. Paul: Webb Publishing Co. (Reprint North Dakota Historical Society 1971; University of Nebraska Press 1982).

    1924   The Horse and the Dog in Hidatsa Culture. *Anthropological Papers of the American Museum of Natural History* 15:127-311. (Reprint J & L Reprint, 1978).

    1934   The Hidatsa Earthlodge. *Anthropological Papers of the American Museum of Natural History* 33:341-420. (Reprint J & L Reprint 1978).

Wissler, Clark

    1914   *The Influence of the Horse in the Development of Plains Culture*. American Anthropologist, n.s. 16:1-25.

    1938   *The American Indian*. New York: Oxford University Press.

Wood, W. Raymond

    1971   Biesterfeldt: A Post-Contact Coalescent Site on the Northeastern Plains. *Smithsonian Contributions to Anthropology* No. 15. Washington, D.C.: Smithsonian Institution Press.

    1976   Summary and Conclusions. In Fay Tolton and the Initial Middle Missouri Variant, edited by W. Raymond Wood. *Missouri Archaeological Society Research Series No. 13*.

    1986   *The Origins of the Hidatsa Indians: A Review of Ethnohistorical and Traditional Data*. Lincoln: J & L Reprint Company.

Wood, Raymond and Tom Thiessen

    1985   *Early Fur Trade on the Northern Plains*. Norman: University of Oklahoma Press.

Woods, Samuel

    1850   Pembina Settlement. House of Representatives, 31st Congress, 1st Session, Ex.Doc.No.51.

Yuen Ren Chao

    1968   *Language and Symbolic Systems*. New York: Cambridge University Press.

Zimmerman, Larry J. and Lawrence E. Bradley

    1993   The Crow Creek Massacre: Initial Coalescent Warfare and Speculations about the Genesis of Extended Coalescent. In Prehistory and Human Ecology of the Western Prairies and Northern Plains, edited by Joseph A. Tiffany. *Plains Anthropologist Memoir 27*.

Index